STRIKING
FIRST

**Preemptive and Preventive Attack
in U.S. National Security Policy**

KARL P. MUELLER

JASEN J. CASTILLO

FORREST E. MORGAN

NEGEEN PEGAHI

BRIAN ROSEN

Prepared for the United States Air Force

Approved for public release; distribution unlimited

PROJECT AIR FORCE

The research described in this report was sponsored by the United States Air Force under Contract F49642-01-C-0003. Further information may be obtained from the Strategic Planning Division, Directorate of Plans, Hq USAF.

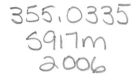

Library of Congress Cataloging-in-Publication Data

Striking first : preemptive and preventive attack in U.S. national security policy / Karl P. Mueller ... [et al.].
    p. cm.
    Includes bibliographical references.
    ISBN 0-8330-3881-8 (pbk. : alk. paper)
    1. National security—United States. 2. Preemtive attack (Military science)
  3. United States—Military policy. 4. United States—Defenses. I. Mueller, Karl P.

UA23.S835 2006
355'.033573—dc22

2006016181

The RAND Corporation is a nonprofit research organization providing objective analysis and effective solutions that address the challenges facing the public and private sectors around the world. RAND's publications do not necessarily reflect the opinions of its research clients and sponsors.

RAND® is a registered trademark.

Cover design by Pete Soriano

Published 2006 by the RAND Corporation
1776 Main Street, P.O. Box 2138, Santa Monica, CA 90407-2138
1200 South Hayes Street, Arlington, VA 22202-5050
4570 Fifth Avenue, Suite 600, Pittsburgh, PA 15213
RAND URL: http://www.rand.org/
To order RAND documents or to obtain additional information, contact
Distribution Services: Telephone: (310) 451-7002;
Fax: (310) 451-6915; Email: order@rand.org

Preface

Following the terrorist attacks against the United States on September 11, 2001, preemptive and preventive attack became the subjects of extensive policy attention and debate as the nation embarked on a global campaign against al Qaeda, associated terrorist groups, and their sponsors and supporters. U.S. leaders recast the national security strategy to place greater emphasis on the threats posed by violent nonstate actors and by states from which they might acquire nuclear, biological, or chemical weapons, and promised that the United States would take advantage of opportunities to strike at potential adversaries before they attacked.

In response to this shift in policy emphasis, RAND Project AIR FORCE conducted a study, titled "Preemptive and Preventive Military Strategies in U.S. National Security Policy," to examine the nature and implications of this doctrine of preemption. This study focused on addressing three central questions: First, under what conditions is preemptive or preventive attack worth considering or pursuing as a response to perceived security threats? Second, what role should such "first-strike" strategies be expected to play in future U.S. national security policy? Finally, what implications do these conclusions have for planners and policymakers in the U.S. Air Force (USAF) and the other armed services as they design military capabilities and strategies to support national policy and deal with emerging security threats in the next decade?

The research reported here was sponsored by the Director of Operational Planning, Headquarters, U.S. Air Force, and conducted within the Strategy and Doctrine Program of RAND Project AIR FORCE.

RAND Project AIR FORCE

RAND Project AIR FORCE (PAF), a division of the RAND Corporation, is the U.S. Air Force's federally funded research and development center for studies and analyses. PAF provides the Air Force with independent analyses of policy alternatives affecting the development, employment, combat readiness, and support of current and future aerospace forces. Research is conducted in four programs: Aerospace Force Development; Manpower, Personnel, and Training; Resource Management; and Strategy and Doctrine.

Additional information about PAF is available on our Web site at http://www.rand.org/paf.

Contents

Figures and Table

Summary

As the United States recast its national security policy following the September 11, 2001, terrorist attacks, President Bush and administration officials announced that under some circumstances in the future the United States would strike enemies before they attack, because deterrence and defense provide insufficient protection against threats from fanatical terrorists or reckless rogue states armed with weapons of mass destruction (WMD). The 2002 National Security Strategy (NSS) codified this doctrine, declaring that in the future, "preemptive" attack would be an important U.S. tool for dealing with anticipated threats from terrorists and from rogue states developing nuclear, biological, or chemical weapons. The NSS did not suggest that the United States would always strike first against such threats, but declared that the United States would not necessarily wait until an enemy attack was imminent to strike first.

Preemption, Prevention, and Anticipatory Attack

Although the NSS and other U.S. policy statements use the term "preemption" to refer to striking first against perceived security threats under a variety of circumstances, generations of scholars and policymakers have defined preemption more restrictively, distinguishing it from preventive attack.

Preemptive attacks are based on the belief that the adversary is about to attack, and that striking first will be better than allowing the enemy to do so. Preemption may be attractive because it promises to make the difference between victory and defeat, or merely because it will make the ensuing conflict less damaging than it would be if the enemy struck first. Preemptive attacks are quite rare, though the possibility of preemption was a central concern of nuclear strategists during the Cold War; the archetypical example is Israel's attack against Egypt in 1967 that began the Six-Day War.

Preventive attacks are launched in response to less immediate threats. Preventive attack is motivated not by the desire to strike first rather than second, but by the desire to fight sooner rather than later. Usually this is because the balance of military capabilities is expected to shift in the enemy's favor, due to differential rates of growth or armament, or the prospect that the opponent will acquire or develop a powerful new offensive or defensive capability. Israel's 1981 raid on the Osirak nuclear facility was a classic preventive attack, as was Operation Iraqi Freedom, the U.S.-led invasion of Iraq in 2003.

Preemptive and preventive attacks have important differences; in addition to those already noted, international law holds that truly preemptive attacks are an acceptable use of force in self-defense, while preventive attacks usually are not. However, they are driven by similar logic, and since it is often useful to talk about both at the same time, the authors use the term *anticipatory attack* to refer to the broader category that includes both types of strategies. Anticipatory attack can be viewed as a continuum ranging from purely preemptive to purely preventive actions: All of them are offensive strategies carried out for defensive reasons, based on the belief that otherwise an enemy attack is (or may be) inevitable, and it would be better to fight on one's own terms.

Preemptive and preventive attacks are distinct from "operational preemption," taking military actions within an ongoing conflict that are intended to reduce the enemy's capabilities or to achieve other effects by acting before the enemy launches an attack or takes some other undesirable action, such as deploying or dispersing its forces. Anticipatory attacks often involve operational preemption, but need not do so, and operational preemption may occur in any sort of conflict.

Costs, Benefits, and Risks of Striking First

Strategists and policymakers who are contemplating preemptive or preventive attacks should take a host of military and political considerations into account. Together these determine two fundamental strategic variables: the degree of *certainty* that the adversary will strike if the anticipatory attack is not launched, and the *first-strike advantage* expected from carrying out the anticipatory attack compared to allowing the opponent to attack on its own terms. The more certain the enemy threat is, and the greater the advantage offered by striking first appears, the more attractive anticipatory attack will be.

The Advantage of Striking First

How much better off the state expects to be if it carries out the anticipatory attack than if the adversary attacks at the time and in the way of its choice is in large part a military question. If attacking promises great success while defense is unpromising, the first-strike advantage will be large. When considering preempting an imminent threat, it is the benefits and costs of literally striking first, and of being struck, that matter. For preventive attacks, the consequences of expected changes in the combatants' strengths and vulnerabilities between the time when a first strike would be launched and the time when the enemy would choose to attack are what count.

However, examining the military component of the first-strike advantage can be no more than a first step in understanding its role in national security policy. Anticipatory attacks usually entail significant political costs in the international arena, especially when the threat that prompts them does not appear dire to others; these can outweigh even considerable military advantages to striking first, as they did in Israel's decision not to launch a preemptive attack against Egypt in October 1973. Concern for national or personal reputations can press either for or against striking first. There are also domestic political costs and benefits to take into account, and considerations of law and morality are often intertwined with these political concerns.

The Certainty of the Threat

If there is a first-strike advantage, the second major factor in deciding whether to launch an anticipatory attack comes into play: The degree of certainty that the enemy attack that it is intended to avert is otherwise inevitable. If it were absolutely certain that the enemy were going to attack and that no deterrent measures could prevent this, anticipatory attack would automatically be the best policy to choose if it appeared better than being attacked. However, the future is rarely this certain, and the possibility that the enemy attack is not in fact inevitable must be considered. The less certain it is that the enemy will attack if given the opportunity, in spite of any deterrent measures or exogenous events in the meantime, the less weight should be given to the first-strike advantage. There are two principal sources of uncertainty in assessing the likelihood of an enemy attack. One is imperfect intelligence, being less than certain about the adversary's plans, intentions, or motivations because insufficient information about them is available. The other is not being confident about what the future holds because this is genuinely uncertain. The first tends to dominate in cases of imminent threats, while in seeking to prevent longer-term actions, existential uncertainties become more powerful.

Weighing the Pros and Cons of Anticipatory Attack

If striking first appears highly advantageous against a seemingly certain threat, anticipatory attack becomes a relatively easy choice, as it was for Israel in 1967. However, such situations are extremely rare in international politics. Conversely, and much more commonly, if a threat is fairly uncertain and anticipatory attack appears only marginally better than the alternative, leaders readily turn to other strategies, particularly deterrent ones, as the United States did when the Soviet Union was first developing nuclear weapons.[1]

Two types of situations present far more difficult decisions. The first occurs when the enemy is expected to attack, but the advantage of striking first does not appear large enough to make anticipatory attack

---

[1]   See the appendixes to this volume for descriptions of these and other preemptive and preventive attack cases.

a simple choice. If striking first appears far worse than the status quo, even slight uncertainty about the inevitability of the enemy attack may be enough to make attempting to avoid the conflict appear better than initiating it; for the United States, the Cuban missile crisis was such a case.

The second class of difficult cases arises when states possess large first-strike advantages, but are significantly uncertain about when, or even whether, they will be attacked. This type of situation looms large in the current security environment, particularly when threats of potential nuclear attack or the possibility of nuclear or particularly dangerous biological weapons being acquired by terrorists is involved. In such cases, the costs of not acting to prevent the threat from materializing have the potential to be extremely high. However, the costs of striking unnecessarily may also be considerable, and rallying international and domestic approval for anticipatory attacks to prevent threats that are not certain tends to be difficult.

Legality and Legitimacy of Anticipatory Attack

Whether an anticipatory attack would be permissible under international law is an important consideration for decisionmakers, if not always in its own right, then because legality affects perceptions of the legitimacy of the attack, and thus its political costs and benefits. The establishment of the International Criminal Court also raises the possibility that judgments could be rendered and enforced against U.S. officials and military personnel involved in planning, ordering, or participating in an attack that is deemed to be illegal.

In general, the use of force is legal in international politics only when it is necessary for national or collective self-defense, or is authorized by the United Nations Security Council. Because the latter is highly unlikely in cases of preemptive or preventive attack, for such attacks to be legal they must meet the requirements for "anticipatory self-defense." Based on the principle that armed force must be used only as a last resort, the criteria for anticipatory self-defense have traditionally held that the attacker must have certain or nearly certain knowledge that an attack by its adversary is imminent.

This "restrictionist" standard prohibits preventive attacks, as well as preemption against uncertain or ambiguous threats. In response to the emergence of threats such as nuclear weapons that can be employed with little warning, legal scholars (whose arguments carry great weight in adjudging international law) have proposed some changes to these criteria, though none has yet gained widespread acceptance. One is that anticipatory attack should be permissible if the attacker is about to lose the ability to forestall the threat (as in the case of the Osirak raid), even if the enemy attack itself is not yet imminent. Another proposal is that terrorists should be considered always to pose an imminent threat due to the nature of their attacks.

A further-reaching possibility, consistent with current U.S. policy statements, is that attackers should be permitted greater latitude to strike first against more severe threats (such as possible nuclear attack) than against milder threats, such as being allowed to strike based on less certain information. However, this has not yet been proffered to any significant degree by legal scholars, most of whom hold that the degree of potential harm from a security threat does not affect the legality of striking first against it. In general, a trend may be developing toward setting more permissive conditions under which first strikes would be legal, allowing action further in advance of enemy attack and perhaps against threats that are less certain, but it is too early to draw such a conclusion with certainty.

Legitimacy is a broader, more flexible, and more ambiguous concept, informed by perceptions of legality but affected by many other factors as well. If a military action is clearly legal, this generally confers considerable legitimacy upon it. However, an action may also be considered legitimate if it is perceived to be undertaken for a moral purpose, even if it does not strictly accord with the law. Judgments of an attack's legitimacy (unlike its legality) may also change over time, and vary among different audiences.

Striking First in Future U.S. National Security Policy

The post-2001 U.S. doctrine of anticipatory attack is cast in deliberately ambiguous terms, and the National Security Strategy does not even raise the possibility of striking first against targets other than terrorists or hard-to-deter states possessing or pursuing weapons of mass destruction. Yet these are categories that encompass the most serious threats likely to face the United States during the near to medium term, so to entertain the possibility of carrying out preventive as well as preemptive attacks against them is very significant: Past U.S. leaders have also occasionally considered but almost never launched anticipatory attacks in response to perceived security threats, and situations in which such actions have appeared even moderately attractive have been relatively few and far between.

However, both changing international conditions and the distinctive attitudes and beliefs of the current administration make the United States more likely to carry out anticipatory attacks than it has been in previous decades. First, the sorts of threats against which deterrence and defense provide the least reliable protection now loom larger than they did in past decades. The perceived inadequacy of deterrence relates primarily to extremist adversaries whose behavior the United States has little ability to influence; reduced confidence in the adequacy of defensive measures is due mainly to the rise of highly destructive terrorist threats, especially the possibility of nuclear attacks. Second, the unprecedented military preeminence of the United States expands the range of possible uses of military force that American leaders can reasonably consider, including conducting anticipatory attacks. Finally, current U.S. leaders have made clear that they are less concerned by the possibility of diplomatic fallout from their actions than other recent administrations have been, reducing the weight of one often prominent cost of striking first. (See pp. 93–94.)

Nevertheless, most of the considerations that have caused anticipatory attacks to be infrequent in the past continue to apply today, so it is very unlikely that large-scale anticipatory attacks will become commonplace in U.S. security policy. Many threats cannot be usefully addressed by anticipatory attack because they are not recognized early enough to be averted, and although intelligence may be improved and military responsiveness increased, some threats are intrinsically difficult to anticipate. Moreover, even when such opportunities do exist, they are often militarily unattractive or the military advantages they offer appear meager compared to their potential political costs. (Ironically, this is particularly true for the United States, because the military power that gives it unrivaled ability to launch anticipatory attacks also reduces the need for them: The more powerful a state is, the more likely it is to be able to deal effectively with most of the threats it faces through deterrence or defense.) Major preventive attacks in particular often promise less than decisive results unless the attacker is willing to conquer, occupy, and remake the target state, as the United States is now seeking to do in Iraq. (See pp. 94–96.)

The 2003 invasion of Iraq has further reduced the probability of major anticipatory attacks by the United States in the near future. The occupation of Iraq will continue to require large numbers of American troops for some years to come, reducing the number of U.S. ground forces available for similar operations elsewhere. Mustering either domestic or international political support for another operation like Operation Iraqi Freedom (OIF) and motivated by similar concerns would be extremely difficult following the discovery that Iraq did not in fact possess a large arsenal of biological and chemical weapons or a substantial nuclear weapons development program. The credibility both of intelligence assessments of WMD threats and of U.S. policymakers advocating anticipatory attacks will be dramatically weaker in the wake of OIF. The postwar costs of the Iraqi (and Afghan) occupations may further reduce the palatability of military operations likely to lead to similar occupations. Finally, the likelihood that OIF will be reprised elsewhere may also be reduced by its success, as the rapid defeat of the Iraqi regime by a relatively small invasion force should tend to discourage other states from provoking a U.S. invasion. However, these factors apply far less powerfully to attacks, such as most counterterrorist operations, that do not involve large-scale, sustained military operations and other OIF-like costs, especially when they can be conducted covertly. (See pp. 96–98.)

Leading Scenarios for U.S. Anticipatory Attack

Traditionally, anticipatory attacks have been contemplated most prominently in nuclear stand-offs, and in rivalries among states seeking to conquer—or to avoid conquest by—their neighbors. For the United States, there are three types of scenarios in which anticipatory attack is likely to be most relevant in the near to medium term.

Preempting cross-border aggression against vulnerable allies, in the form either of invasion or of coercive bombardment, could foil or blunt such attacks, especially by North Korea against South Korea or by China against Taiwan. However, a conventional first strike could not be expected to disarm North Korea effectively, let alone China, so while preemptive attack might limit U.S. and allied damage, it would involve starting a very expensive war, and would probably appear unacceptable unless it seemed very certain that an enemy attack was imminent and could not be averted short of war. (See pp. 99–101.)

Striking first against terrorists is of course attractive; against suicide attackers, there is no other time to do so. Deciding to preempt terrorist attacks at the tactical or operational level—for example, to arrest or kill the members of a terrorist cell before they can mount their intended attack, or before they take some other dangerous action such as gaining control of a nuclear weapon—is generally an easy policy decision, and such preemption is likely when sufficient information about the terrorists' identities, locations, or plans is available. Such attacks are typically carried out by police forces or occasionally by military special operations forces (SOF). Preventive attacks against terrorists—that is, attacking a terrorist group before they initiate hostilities—involve considerations similar to those for preventive attacks against states, and the possibility of starting a conflict that might otherwise have been avoided will loom large in policymakers' thinking if the target group is powerful. (See pp. 101–102.)

Attacking states to prevent the spread of weapons of mass destruction—principally nuclear or sophisticated biological weapons—into terrorist or other unacceptably dangerous hands may be the most important and the most challenging role for anticipatory attack in the current security environment. However, several factors limit how often such operations are likely to be carried out by the United States. First, nuclear proliferation is infrequent—only two states currently in the nuclear club (Pakistan and North Korea) joined it in the past two decades, and only one other country (Iran) appears poised to develop nuclear weapons in the next few years. Although the world may be entering a period of accelerated nuclear proliferation, it is by no means clear that this is the case. Moreover, states that do have serious WMD programs can be expected to take concerted measures to limit their vulnerability to preventive attack, as Iraq did very successfully following the Osirak raid. (See pp. 103–105.)

Political Consequences of Anticipatory Attack

When considering striking first, it is critical to consider potential effects on third parties, particularly in cases of preventive attack as a response to WMD proliferation. It is likely that such attacks, at least if they are effective, will deter some states from pursuing the development of weapons that might bring a similar fate down upon themselves. However, it is also likely that others will conclude that U.S. propensity and capability for preventive attack makes it all the more important to possess nuclear weapons or some other powerful deterrent to American attack, especially if the United States appears unwilling to risk conflict with states that do possess nuclear weapons. As a general tendency, one should expect that weaker states will be relatively susceptible to intimidation, while larger or more powerful ones will be better equipped to develop such weapons in ways that are less vulnerable to attack—it should come as no surprise that Iran has been less inclined to give up its nuclear program since OIF than Libya was. (See pp. 105–106.)

Threatening or launching preventive attacks may also increase the likelihood of other states attacking their enemies preventively. This is not likely to be a matter of countries simply imitating the United States, but rather the result of U.S. policy and actions weakening international norms against such first strikes, making it less politically costly to violate them. This does not mean that there will be an epidemic of preventive attacks in hotspots around the world, but it would be surprising if preventive attacks did not become more common if the United States maintains that they are potentially acceptable. (See pp. 106–107.)

Implications for Future U.S. Defense Planning

The following are the study's principal conclusions regarding the importance of preemptive and preventive attack for the U.S. armed services. In general, planners should not expect preparing for such operations to be a key driver for change in U.S. military capabilities.

Anticipatory attack is a niche contingency. If U.S. anticipatory attacks will be considered more often than in previous decades, but large ones will remain quite infrequent, the armed forces, especially the U.S. Air Force, will need to be prepared to conduct first strikes, but will not be able to optimize for them. Fortunately, anticipatory attacks do not call for a suite of capabilities fundamentally different from those required for other types of operations. In fact, on the whole, they will tend to be *less* demanding than the requirements for defensive warfare, because they will by definition be fought on terms relatively favorable to the United States. (See pp. 107–108.)

Military requirements for anticipatory attack are largely case-specific. At the operational level, requirements for anticipatory attack against a Chinese invasion force assembling near Taiwan, North Korea's nuclear weapons, or a terrorist group preparing to attack the United States will have far less in common with each other than each will have with the requirements for fighting the same adversary in a defensive or retaliatory scenario. (Consider that Operation Iraqi Freedom would have looked essentially the same if Saddam Hussein had been found to have orchestrated the September 11 attacks, in which case it would have been a counteroffensive campaign instead of a preventive one.) What is needed will depend upon the characteristics of the adversary, the details of key target sets, likely contributions of U.S. allies, and so on. Therefore, a general inclination toward or against anticipatory attacks on the part of national leaders will tell military planners relatively little about how to prepare for them. Instead, it is the probability of carrying out particular types of anticipatory attacks against specific adversaries that should be taken into account when investing in military capabilities. (See pp. 108–109.)

Anticipatory attack strategies place high demands on strategic intelligence capabilities. For preemptive strategies, assessing the inevitability and imminence of the enemy attack is enormously important for sound strategic decisionmaking. For preventive attacks, the future capabilities and intentions of the adversary matter most, shifting the intelligence problem to one primarily of prediction. Although any military strategy suffers if intelligence about the enemy is deficient, anticipatory attack is particularly dependent upon understanding the enemy's intentions, which often presents uniquely challenging problems for collectors and analysts of intelligence because of the limited degree to which intentions can be deduced from observing easily visible objects and actions. Even when dealing with threats that require conspicuous preparations by the adversary, determining whether these represent the prelude to an attack or merely feints or defensive measures is likely to depend on collecting closely held information through human or signals intelligence. This does not mean that it is impossible to divine the enemy's intentions or that the United States should not try to improve its ability to do so. However, the intelligence problems involved are intrinsically difficult ones that can be reduced but not eliminated, and expectations about the utility of anticipatory attack should always take this into account. Not only does the U.S. Air Force operate a wide variety of reconnaissance and surveillance systems that are critical for collecting intelligence to assess potential threats from adversaries and to estimate the prospects for dealing with these through anticipatory attack, its traditional focus on strategic attack, manifested most recently in its institutional advocacy of effects-based operations, also should place the service in the forefront of thinking about how to gather and analyze such information. (See pp. 109–112.)

Preempting cross-border aggression requires being able to strike quickly and decisively. If the threat can materialize with little warning, it becomes necessary to position and maintain the appropriate forces in a posture that permits the preemptive attack to be launched on relatively short notice, whether through forward basing, rapid deployment, long-range strikes, or a combination of these. However, the ability to react rapidly also depends upon collecting and processing the necessary intelligence, and on decisionmakers deciding to launch the attack, quickly enough for the armed forces to act. (See p. 112.)

Preventive attacks to eliminate nuclear threats call for extremely effective intelligence and strike capabilities. Permanently removing a state-level nuclear threat by using military force will generally require not only destroying weapons (if they have been built) and production facilities, but replacing the regime that chose to develop them; doing this against any plausible future adversary would be a far more ambitious and costly undertaking than the relatively easy invasion of Iraq. If the goal is merely to degrade an enemy nuclear program temporarily, more limited force may be sufficient, but the attack usually must be powerful and thorough enough to cripple the enemy's efforts for a substantial period, and in the post-Osirak world no state developing such weapons will make this easy to do. Against a target state that already possesses nuclear weapons, the ability to destroy not just some but all of the weapons in a preventive attack is likely to be a minimum strategic requirement under any but the most desperate circumstances. The greatest constraint on doing all of these things will be intelligence regarding the targets, though the ability reliably to destroy the elements of the target sets, which are likely to be limited in number but very well protected, may require powerful defense-suppression capabilities and specialized ordnance for attacking hardened and deeply buried targets, or for destroying targets while minimizing nuclear or other environmental contamination. To the extent that preventive attacks are less likely to be supported by allied and other states than more clearly defensive operations, preparing to carry out such attacks may also call for emphasizing forces that can be employed with relatively little in the way of international cooperation, including basing and overflight permission, such as reconnaissance, surveillance, strike, and support aircraft able to operate at very long ranges or from the sea, and to reach their targets stealthily or by flying above denied airspace. (See pp. 112–113.)

Military requirements for anticipatory attacks against terrorists depend on the frequency of such operations and the balance between attacks against small groups and sustained operations

against insurgencies. Because counterterrorist operations are primarily the domain of police and, to a lesser degree, SOF, conducting such attacks on a limited scale has little effect on military force structure, but doing so intensively over the longer term would require substantial increases to SOF force structure, a path down which the United States has begun to move since September 2001. Preventive attacks against insurgent groups resemble other counterinsurgency warfare, so doing a lot of either one calls for corresponding investment in U.S. and allied SOF and other military and nonmilitary components that are disproportionately required in counterguerrilla, foreign internal defense, and related operations. (See pp. 113–114.)

Reliance on anticipatory attack as a key strategy can be perilous. Anticipatory attack can be very alluring, and there is a danger that both political and military leaders will place too much stock in it, as occurred in Europe before 1914 and in Israel after the success of the Six-Day War. Because anticipatory attack offers certain advantages (such as seizing and retaining the military initiative) that are likely to be particularly resonant for military leaders, while the potential diplomatic or other political costs are outside the narrow focus of military planning, military leaders must be especially wary of overestimating the desirability of striking first. (See pp. 115–116.)

Preemption may be an attractive strategy for U.S. adversaries. This study focuses on anticipatory attack as a strategic tool for the United States. However, states or other actors expecting to be attacked by the United States may perceive powerful incentives to strike first; dangerous though it is to start a war against the world's only superpower, allowing the United States to attack on its own terms is likely to be even worse. It is only when a U.S. attack appears to be inevitable that a state should be willing to start such a war as a defensive measure, but if such a perception exists, striking first may appear to be the only way for a weaker adversary to compensate for its military disadvantage. Chinese military doctrinal writings already raise the possibility of striking first against U.S. forces in the event of a confrontation over Taiwan. The possibility of enemy preemptive attacks has important implications for U.S. military planning. Deterring preemption by threats of escalation or retaliation is unlikely to be effective when facing enemies who expect to suffer regime change or catastrophic losses to an imminent U.S. attack, since they will have little to lose. Thus, discouraging such threats will depend on active and passive defenses, including designing forces, basing architectures, and deployment schemes with the objective of minimizing their vulnerability to preemptive attacks. (See pp. 116–118.)

Anticipatory attacks call for extensive communication between civilian and military leaders. Nowhere is the Clausewitzian dictum that war is an extension of politics truer than in preemptive and preventive attack. In order to provide the necessary capabilities, military planners must know what their political leaders intend with respect to anticipatory attack, with far more specificity than is provided by broad policy statements such as the National Security Strategy. Senior military officers need to keep national decisionmakers familiar with the extent and limits of their capabilities, particularly if preemptive options are going to be considered in conditions where the time available for making strategic choices is limited. Such information should ideally be familiar to political leaders long before a crisis develops, since an understanding of the extent and limits of the possible should be taken into account even during routine peacetime security policymaking. (See pp. 118–119.)

Acknowledgments

The authors wish to thank the following people for their contributions and assistance to this study.

Three project action officers, Lt Col Ronald Sanders, Lt Col Jay Kreighbaum, and Maj Michael Pietrucha, provided indispensable support and advice. We also received helpful feedback from a number of other USAF Air Staff officers and employees, particularly Maj Gen Michael Gould, Dr. Christopher Bowie, Lt Col William DeMaso, and Maj Jonathan Dagle. Faculty members and students of the USAF's School of Advanced Air and Space Studies (SAASS) offered many thoughtful comments, especially Dr. Richard Andres and Col Tom Ehrhard.

Among our RAND colleagues, Lynn Davis, Col Igor Gardner, Ted Harshberger, Stephen Hosmer, Donna Kinlin, Maj Steve Kiser, and Robert Mullins all made important design and research contributions to this project. Nora Bensahel, Natalie Crawford, Roger Cliff, Robert Ellenson, Andrew Hoehn, Judy Larson, Michael Rich, David Shlapak, and Alan Vick provided many insightful comments and ideas as the study and its associated briefings evolved, and Ralda Williams provided valuable administrative support throughout the project. Finally, Adam Grissom, Jonathan Kirshner, and John K. Setear provided extensive and detailed reviews of the draft report, and this final version has benefited enormously from their suggestions and comments.

Glossary

AAIA	Aden-Abyan Islamic Army
ANZUS	Australia, New Zealand, and the United States
AWACS	Airborne Warning and Control System
CIA	Central Intelligence Agency
EBO	effects-based operations
ExComm	Executive Committee of the National Security Council
FBI	Federal Bureau of Investigation
FROG	Free Rocket Over Ground
GCC	Gulf Cooperation Council
GPC	General People's Congress
IAF	Islamic Action Front
ICBM	intercontinental ballistic missile
ICC	International Criminal Court
ICG	International Crisis Group
ICJ	International Court of Justice
IDF	Israeli Defense Force
IDF/AF	Israeli Air Force

IRBM	intermediate-range ballistic missile
IRF	Islamic Revival Foundation
ISA	Islamic Salvation Army
JCS	Joint Chiefs of Staff
KLA	Kosovo Liberation Army
MRBM	medium-range ballistic missile
NATO	North Atlantic Treaty Organization
NEO	noncombatant evacuation operation
NJM	New Jewel Movement
NPT	Treaty on the Non-Proliferation of Nuclear Weapons
NSC	National Security Council
NSS	National Security Strategy
OAS	Organization of American States
OECS	Organization of Eastern Caribbean States
OIC	Organization of the Islamic Conference
OIF	Operation Iraqi Freedom
PAF	Project AIR FORCE
PDRY	People's Democratic Republic of Yemen
PIJ	Palestine Islamic Jihad
PLO	Palestine Liberation Organization
PRC	People's Republic of China
SAASS	School of Advanced Air and Space Studies
SAC	Strategic Air Command
SAM	surface-to-air missile

ShIK	Albania's intelligence service
SOF	special operations forces
SWNCC	State-War-Navy Coordinating Committee
U.N.	United Nations
UNEF	United Nations Emergency Fund
USAF	U.S. Air Force
USAID	U.S. Agency for International Development
USIA	U.S. Information Agency
USSR	Union of Soviet Socialist Republics
WMD	weapons of mass destruction
WSEG	Weapons Systems Evaluation Group
YAR	Yemen Arab Republic
YSP	Yemeni Socialist Party

CHAPTER ONE

Striking First: Preemptive and Preventive Attacks

The best, and in some cases, the only defense, is a good offense.
—Secretary of Defense Donald Rumsfeld[1]

Introduction

In the months following the terrorist attacks against New York and Washington on September 11, 2001, the United States progressively recast its national security policy. Probably the single most prominent feature of this process, and certainly the one that produced the most debate, was the decision to place dramatically greater emphasis on "preemption": defending oneself by attacking an enemy before it strikes, instead of seeking to deter attacks or striking back if deterrence fails.[2]

---

[1] U.S. Department of Defense, "Secretary Rumsfeld Speaks on '21st Century Transformation' of U.S. Armed Forces (Transcript of Remarks and Question and Answer Period): Remarks as Delivered by Secretary of State Donald Rumsfeld, National Defense University, Fort McNair, Washington, D.C., Thursday, January 31, 2002," Washington, D.C., 2002.

[2] Although the preemption doctrine dominated headlines about the evolution of U.S. grand strategy after September 2001, other features were arguably more significant; see John Lewis Gaddis, "A Grand Strategy of Transformation," *Foreign Policy*, Vol. 133, 2002, pp. 50–57.

The United States has considered striking first as a response to security threats in the past,[3] though it has done so quietly and has rarely carried out such attacks.[4] However, the overt emphasis recently placed on preemption in statements by U.S. leaders, which culminated in the 2002 National Security Strategy (NSS)[5] and became known as "the Bush Doctrine," is unprecedented in modern American history. It caused alarm in many quarters, raising fears that the United States would become a more aggressive superpower or that its foreign policy might become recklessly adventurous.[6] Meanwhile, several other states declared that they would also consider striking their potential enemies first under some circumstances; by the end of 2003, these included not only traditionally bellicose military powers such as Israel and North Korea, but also China, Australia, and even Japan.[7]

This study examines preemptive attack and preventive war as strategic options available to states facing apparent threats to their national security, especially the United States—thus it is both more and less than a detailed study of current U.S. national security policy. It focuses on identifying factors and conditions that affect the likelihood of preemptive or preventive attack being useful, both to inform national security decisionmaking and as a basis for anticipating the demands

---

[3] John Lewis Gaddis, *Surprise, Security, and the American Experience*, Cambridge, Mass.: Harvard University Press, 2004.

[4] In the 60 years prior to the invasion of Iraq in 2003, the 1983 invasion of Grenada was the only occasion on which the United States used force on a large scale in order to remove a perceived future security threat prior to being attacked.

[5] George W. Bush, *The National Security Strategy of the United States of America*, Washington, D.C.: Executive Office of the President, 2002a. See also George W. Bush, *National Strategy to Combat Weapons of Mass Destruction*, Washington, D.C.: The White House, 2002b.

[6] See, for example, Thomas E. Ricks, "NATO Allies Trade Barbs Over Iraq," *The Washington Post*, February 9, 2003, p. A1.

[7] Ian Bostock, "Canberra Would Order Pre-Emptive Strikes," *Jane's Defence Weekly*, December 11, 2002, p. 18; "Japan Threatens Force Against N Korea," *BBC News*, February 14, 2003.

that the pursuit of such strategies can be expected to place on armed forces in the future.[8]

The Doctrine of Preemption and the U.S. National Security Strategy

Although deterrence plays an important role in the National Security Strategy promulgated in 2002, the document emphatically calls for the United States to strike first in anticipation of attacks by terrorist groups or "rogue states."[9] This doctrine of "preemption," as the authors label it, is a response to what many see as the leading security challenges currently facing the United States.[10]

---

[8]   This study does not explicitly examine the question of whether the new doctrine of striking first is prudent policy (although many of the issues discussed below do bear on this question), since this has been widely debated in other works, but instead focuses on examining the probable manifestations and implications of the policy. For additional assessments and analyses of the Bush Doctrine and current U.S. grand strategy, see, among many others, Robert Jervis, "Understanding the Bush Doctrine," *Political Science Quarterly*, Vol. 118, No. 3, 2003, pp. 365–388; G. John Ikenberry, ed., *America Unrivaled: The Future of the Balance of Power*, Ithaca, N.Y.: Cornell University Press, 2002; Charles Kupchan, *The End of the American Era: U.S. Foreign Policy and the Geopolitics of the Twenty-First Century*, New York: Vintage Books, 2003; Henry Kissinger, "Preemption and the End of Westphalia," *New Perspectives Quarterly*, Vol. 19, No. 3, 2002, pp. 31–36; Zbigniew Brzezinski, *The Choice: Global Dominance of Global Leadership*, New York: Basic Books, 2004.

[9]   The 2002 NSS's statements regarding striking first are excerpted in their entirety in Appendix D. A revised NSS, released in 2006, discussed striking first less extensively, but states, "The place of preemption in our national security strategy remains the same" (George W. Bush, *The National Security Strategy of the United States of America*, Washington, D.C.: The White House, 2006, p. 33).

[10]   Richard K. Betts, "The Soft Underbelly of American Primacy: Tactical Advantages of Terror," *Political Science Quarterly*, Vol. 117, No. 1, 2002, pp. 19–36; Stephen M. Walt, "Beyond bin Laden: Reshaping U.S. Foreign Policy," *International Security*, Vol. 26, No. 3, 2001/2002, pp. 56–78. The analysis that follows is based on the assumption that the National Security Strategy reflects the intentions of its authors at the time it was written, without attempting to determine whether the administration might have held intentions regarding preemptive attack substantially at odds with those described in its rhetoric and declaratory policies.

Two related categories of security threats stand out in this con-stellation, although whether they are genuinely new or have merely become newly prominent as other types of threats have receded is open to debate. The first is the appearance of terrorist nonstate actors that both have the capability to conduct highly destructive attacks against the United States and desire to do so: Al Qaeda is far more power-ful than the relatively minor terrorist groups that launched attacks against American targets during the Cold War and is more inclined to cause very large numbers of casualties, while its strategy of directly attacking U.S. targets sets it apart from other highly capable terrorist groups such as Hizbollah and the Tamil Tigers.[11] The second source of threat is aggressive "rogue states" that persistently defy the norms of the international system,[12] such as Iran and North Korea, which are dangerous to the United States particularly insofar as they might provide nuclear, biological, or other highly destructive arms to terrorist groups (or might inadvertently allow terrorists to take control of such weapons from them).[13]

---

[11] Daniel Benjamin and Steven Simon, *The Age of Sacred Terror*, New York: Random House, 2002; Ian O. Lesser, Bruce Hoffman, John Arquilla, David F. Ronfeldt, Michele Zanini, and Brian Michael Jenkins, *Countering the New Terrorism*, Santa Monica, Calif.: RAND Corporation, MR-989-AF, 1999. For differing views of the new terrorism and the threat of terrorist attacks using weapons of mass destruction see, respectively, Martha Crenshaw, "Why America: The Globalization of Civil War," *Current History*, Vol. 100, No. 650, 2001, pp. 425–432; John Parachini, "Putting WMD Terrorism into Perspective," *The Washington Quarterly*, Vol. 26, No. 4, 2003, pp. 37–50; and John Mueller, "Six Rather Unusual Proposi-tions About Terrorism," *Terrorism and Political Violence*, Vol. 17, No. 4, 2005, pp. 487–507.

[12] The "rogue state" label has often come under attack for being used as a dramatic but unhelpful label for the principal minor-power enemies of the United States, and for overstat-ing the degree of recklessness or irrationality of such regimes' foreign policies. As a more rig-orous concept, based on state objectives and behavior, it must be extended to include coun-tries such as Stalin's Soviet Union or Mao's China. See John E. Mueller and Karl P. Mueller, "The Methodology of Mass Destruction: Assessing Threats in the New World Order," *Jour-nal of Strategic Studies*, Vol. 23, No. 1, 2000, pp. 163–187, p. 165.

[13] On the potential relationship between terrorists and states with WMD, see Kissinger (2002); on the conditions under which deterrence might fail to prevent the transfer of nuclear weapons from rogue states to terrorists, see Jasen J. Castillo, "Nuclear Terrorism: Why Deterrence Still Matters," *Current History*, Vol. 102, No. 668, 2003, pp. 426–431.

It is against these two categories of threat that the National Security Strategy suggests first strikes will tend to be useful, including ones against threats "before they are fully formed," because deterrence and defense will not provide adequate security: "Traditional concepts of deterrence will not work against a terrorist enemy . . . whose so-called soldiers seek martyrdom in death and whose most potent protection is statelessness."[14] The basis for believing that striking first may be necessary as a counterproliferation measure against rogue states centers on the perceived recklessness of such regimes: "[D]eterrence based only on the threat of retaliation is less likely to work against leaders of rogue states more willing [than Cold War adversaries] to take risks, gambling with the lives of their people, and the wealth of their nations."[15]

The preemption doctrine is presented with a considerable degree of ambiguity, presumably in order to maximize the range of U.S. strategic options. There is no class of threats against which the National Security Strategy indicates the United States would always strike first, and Washington has implemented the doctrine selectively, most notably in pursuing conspicuously different approaches toward the threats of nuclear weapon development by Iraq and North Korea. The NSS also raises the possibility of striking first only in response to threats from terrorists or from states seeking nuclear, biological, or chemical weapons; for example, while it indicates that the United States will maintain armed forces "strong enough to dissuade potential adversaries from pursuing a military build-up in hope of surpassing, or equaling,

---

[14] George W. Bush (2002a, p. 15). See also President Bush's June 1, 2002, commencement speech at the U.S. Military Academy: "Deterrence—the promise of massive retaliation against nations—means nothing against shadowy terrorist networks with no nation or citizens to defend. Containment is not possible when unbalanced dictators with weapons of mass destruction can deliver those weapons on missiles or secretly provide them to terrorist allies" (White House, "President Bush Delivers Graduation Speech at West Point, United States Military Academy, West Point, New York," West Point, N.Y., August 1, 2002a).

[15] George W. Bush (2002a, p. 15). For contrasting views of rogue state risk propensity, see, for example, Mueller and Mueller (2000).

the power of the United States," it does not suggest attacking prospective rivals in order to prevent such challenges.[16]

Preemption and Prevention

Although the National Security Strategy and other recent policy statements use the "preemption" label to refer to a wide range of actions that involve striking the first blow against perceived security threats, generations of historians, social scientists, legal scholars, and policymakers have defined preemption more restrictively, distinguishing preemptive from preventive attack. These traditional definitions are in some respects problematic, as will be discussed below, but understanding the differences between them is essential whether one is approaching this subject as a matter for theoretical analysis or for practical policymaking.

Preemptive Attack

Reduced to its essence, a preemptive attack is one that is launched based on the expectation than the adversary is about to attack, and that striking first will be better than being attacked. The benefit of preempting the enemy attack may be so great that it is expected to make the difference between victory and defeat, or it may be more marginal, merely promising to reduce the amount of damage to be expected from the resulting conflict. In either case, the fundamental consideration driving preemption is the belief that it is preferable to strike the first blow than to allow the enemy to do so.[17]

Many definitions of preemption, including the one officially adopted by the U.S. Department of Defense, are more restrictive, specifying that that state launching a true preemptive attack must be

---

[16] George W. Bush (2002a, p. 30, which assumes that U.S. military preponderance will successfully deter rivalry).

[17] In some cases, preemption may require not merely attacking before the enemy does so, but attacking prior to some other enemy action that will make preemption impossible, such as mobilizing or dispersing forces in preparation for an offensive, or receiving weapons from (or transferring them to) a third party.

certain that the enemy attack is imminent.[18] Such definitions, usually informed by considerations of legal justification for the use of force (discussed in Chapter Three of this monograph), are excessively narrow for most analytical purposes. Whether or not an attack intended to preempt enemy aggression that appears likely but less than certain is legally justifiable, it is in all other respects preemptive in nature. The same is true if the perceived advantage of striking first causes a state to attack an enemy that it believes is irrevocably committed to launching its own attack, even if the enemy action does not appear literally imminent.

However, even if they must be relaxed to some degree in practice, the interconnected principles of certainty and imminent threat remain central to preemption. Preemptive attack is a response to the belief that an enemy attack is inevitable, or at least is likely to be inevitable, regardless of whatever deterrent measures might yet be taken. The more imminent the enemy attack, the less opportunity there will be to deter it; conversely, enemy aggression that is far from imminent is unlikely to be truly inevitable, since much could happen in the intervening time to avert it. Moreover, the more distant the prospect of enemy attack, the weaker preemptive motives become even if deterrence is hopeless, because one can simply choose to preempt later if the situation does not improve. In contrast, when facing an imminent threat of attack against which preemption might be useful, leaders face intense time pressure when making decisions about whether or not to strike first.

One historical example is almost universally cited as the archetype of preemptive attack: the 1967 Six-Day War, which Israel initiated by attacking Egypt and then Syria in order to avert a coordinated assault by its neighbors. The Arab air forces were devastated by the carefully choreographed Israeli surprise attack, and Israel went on to seize the Sinai peninsula, the Golan Heights, and the West Bank in short order. However, what is perhaps most noteworthy about the Six-

---

[18] The Department of Defense defines "preemptive attack" as "[a]n attack initiated on the basis of incontrovertible evidence that an enemy attack is imminent" (Joint Chiefs of Staff, *Department of Defense Dictionary of Military and Associated Terms*, Washington, D.C.: Joint Chiefs of Staff, 2004, p. 415).

Day War for the study of preemption is its near uniqueness: It is arguably the only unambiguously preemptive war in the last century, and is at a minimum the most prominent example of a very small category.[19] Far more common, though still relatively infrequent in the recent historical record, are preventive wars.

Preventive Attack

Preventive attacks have much in common with preemptive ones, but they are launched in response to less immediate threats. Both types of attack are alternatives to waiting for an expected enemy blow to fall, but preventive attack is motivated not by the desire to strike first rather than second, but by the desire to fight sooner rather than later.[20]

There are many conditions under which a state might prefer not to delay fighting an apparently inevitable war, or even one that merely appears likely. The most obvious one is when the balance of military capabilities between the adversaries is shifting, or is expected to shift, in the enemy's favor, because of differential rates of growth, development, or armament; fear that the opponent will acquire or develop nuclear weapons or some other new offensive or defensive capability that will fundamentally alter the correlation of forces is a variation on this theme of particular salience today, as in the U.S.-led preventive attack against Iraq in 2003.[21] Anticipating unfavorable shifts in the allegiance or capabilities of allies can produce similar incentives for preventive war. Fighting sooner rather than later may appear to offer

---

[19] Dan Reiter, "Exploding the Powder Keg Myth: Preemptive Wars Almost Never Happen," *International Security*, Vol. 20, No. 2, 1995, pp. 5–34. The most extensive literature on preemptive attack focuses on preemptive scenarios and incentives for nuclear attack, particularly between the United States and Soviet Union during the Cold War; for further discussion, see Chapter Two.

[20] The Department of Defense officially defines "preventive war" (somewhat awkwardly) as "[a] war initiated in the belief that military conflict, while not imminent, is inevitable, and that to delay would involve greater risks" (Joint Chiefs of Staff, 2004, p. 419). See also Lawrence Freedman, "Prevention, Not Preemption," *The Washington Quarterly*, Vol. 26, No. 2, 2003b, pp. 105–114.

[21] Although Washington and London described the Iraq War as "preemption" in keeping with the newly broadened use of that term, it would have been genuinely preemptive only if Iraq appeared poised to launch an attack that could not have been preempted later.

the prospect of winning instead of losing, or it may serve merely to make fighting less costly or to delay the emergence of a more serious threat.

In 1914, for example, German leaders believed that rapid industrialization would soon make Russia too powerful to defeat,[22] and faced the prospect that their only major ally, Austria-Hungary, would continue to weaken. Because they also believed that a major European war was inevitable, going to war in 1914 appeared to offer better prospects of success than waiting several years and fighting on less favorable terms, which became one of the powerful factors that propelled Europe into the First World War.[23]

In considering either preemptive or preventive attack, leaders must make assessments regarding the adversary's military capabilities and intentions, but these take different forms. When dealing with immediate threats of attack, the relevant military capabilities are ones that already exist, so estimating them is a straightforward problem, although it may be difficult in practice and the necessary intelligence may be far from perfect. Assessing the opponent's intentions tends to be the greater challenge, since preparations for attack, even if they are visible, do not always indicate that the enemy is actually committed to striking.

---

[22] In fact, the Germans (like many others) overestimated the rate of Russian economic development, and were incorrect in making this assessment, especially since German military power was growing substantially more rapidly than that of Russia's key ally, France (see Paul M. Kennedy, "The First World War and the International Power System," *International Security*, Vol. 9, No. 1, 1984, pp. 7–40, pp. 7–34; and William C. Wohlforth, "The Perception of Power: Russia in the Pre-1914 Balance," *World Politics*, Vol. 39, No. 3, 1987, pp. 353–381). However, in decisions about war initiation and deterrence, perceptions are what matter, and objective reality comes into play only insofar as it affects them—and in determining the results of the conflict if and when war breaks out.

[23] Preemptive motivations were also at work in this case: Once the July Crisis began, the widespread belief that armies fighting on the offense would overwhelm those defending against them caused Germany, Russia, and France all to want to strike before their enemies could do so. For an overview of these and other factors contributing to the outbreak of World War I, see James Joll, *The Origins of the First World War*, 2nd ed., New York: Longman, 1992.

When facing longer-term threats that might call for preventive war, the capabilities that matter are those that will exist in the future, and forecasting these naturally tends to involve a great degree of uncertainty. Paradoxically, estimating the opponent's future intentions may be comparatively simple, because it is general rather than specific behavior patterns that will matter. Beliefs that adversaries will inevitably attack in the long run tend to be based not on specific intelligence regarding their long-term plans, but instead on general models that attribute aggression to patterns of power distribution, geopolitics, or particular leaders, ideologies, or regime types—as in the case of German fears of a rising Russia or U.S. concerns about a nuclear-armed Iraq. Moreover, preventive attack may be attractive even in cases where the possibility of enemy attack does not appear to be literally inevitable, but merely too likely to be acceptable given its expected costs. In such cases, for example when a potentially aggressive neighbor is expected to acquire nuclear weapons, it may not be necessary to believe that the opponent *will* attack, but only that it *might* do so.

Anticipatory Attack

As the preceding discussion indicates, preemptive and preventive attack differ in a number of important respects: The utility of preemption is based on the benefits of being the attacker instead of the defender, while preventive war is motivated by the desire to fight sooner rather than later; preemptive attacks are far less common than preventive ones, and so on. Even more important, international law holds that truly preemptive attacks are an acceptable use of force in self-defense, while preventive attacks usually are not, which tends to increase greatly the political costs associated with launching preventive wars.[24]

However, preemptive and preventive attack also have much in common. Because they share a common strategic logic, much that is true about one applies as well to the other, so it is often useful to discuss them together. Moreover, because the inevitability and imminence of an enemy attack, and one's certainty about it, are rarely absolute, borderline cases can emerge that defy easy classification as either preemp-

---

[24] These legal issues are discussed in detail in Chapter Three of this monograph.

tion or prevention, though they clearly involve at least one or the other, and sometimes both motivations.[25] Distinguishing between preemptive and preventive attack can be even more difficult when the variables associated with the two ideal types do not vary together. Although the inevitability, certainty, and imminence of a threat tend to be related, they are not always closely coupled. For example, one may be certain that the adversary will inevitably attack if left to its own devices, but uncertain as to whether or not it will do so imminently. Or, as Israel perceived in deciding whether to attack Iraq's Osirak nuclear facility in 1981, and as U.S. leaders faced during the Cuban Missile Crisis, a long-term threat, typical of preventive attack situations, may be preventable only by striking immediately, due to a closing window of opportunity, a circumstance more commonly associated with preemption. In such ambiguous cases, assigning a preemption or prevention label may not only be difficult, but may not in fact be very important.

Therefore this analysis also employs a broader strategic category that encompasses both preemption and prevention: anticipatory attack.[26] Anticipatory attacks—both preemptive and preventive—are

---

[25] The situation is analogous to the more familiar relationship among deterrence, compellence, and coercion: It is sometimes useful to refer specifically to deterrence or compellence, but since these two policy categories have much in common, and have a significant area of overlap where they meet, it is often preferable to talk about coercion in general. Consequently, scholars who use the "coercion" term in its narrower, colloquial sense to refer to compellence are left with no label for the important broader category. (Compellence involves coercing the target to alter its behavior, while deterrence is coercion to preserve the status quo; compelling an enemy to halt an action once it is underway can equally well be described as deterring it from continuing.) See David E. Johnson, Karl P. Mueller, and William H. Taft V, *Conventional Coercion Across the Spectrum of Operations: The Utility of U.S. Military Forces in the Emerging Security Environment*, Santa Monica, Calif.: RAND Corporation, MR-1494-A, 2002, pp. 7–15; and Thomas C. Schelling, *Arms and Influence*, New Haven: Yale University Press, 1966, pp. 69–78.

[26] Another reason to introduce the "anticipatory attack" supercategory is that recent use of the "preemption" label to refer to what has traditionally been described as preventive war, particularly in governmental rhetoric but also among analysts and pundits who are new to the subject since 2001, has seriously muddied the terminological waters, at least for the near term. While it is appropriate to rail against this obfuscatory development, it is unrealistic to expect policymakers who have become accustomed to thinking in terms of a single category encompassing both preemption and prevention to recant—or to be attentive to critical arguments that appear to be entirely semantic.

offensive strategies carried out for defensive reasons.[27] More specifically, they are based on the expectation that the adversary will—or is unacceptably likely to—commit armed aggression in the future, and are launched in order to reduce or eliminate the threat by initiating the conflict on terms relatively favorable to the attacker. Anticipatory attack is thus an alternative to both defense and deterrence as a strategy to deal with perceived security threats.

The scope of anticipatory attack extends across a continuum ranging from narrowly preemptive attacks, in which the attacker seeks to strike the first blow against an enemy that is itself about to attack, to preventive attacks intended to address less immediate threats before the opportunity to do so deteriorates. Many factors tend to vary across the spectrum, including the nature of the military advantage that the attacker seeks to exploit, the types of intelligence required to inform the decision to attack, the temporal pressures under which it must be made, and the presumptive legality and legitimacy of the action. However, the basic logic of the approach remains the same, and a state considering anticipatory attack must weigh the expected costs and benefits— both military and political—of the strategy against those of being attacked on the enemy's terms, and against whatever possibility exists that the adversary will not in fact strike if the anticipatory attack is not launched. (These factors are the subject of more detailed discussion in the next chapter.) However, while this monograph examines anticipatory attack as a whole, the analysis that follows will refer more specifically to preemptive or preventive attack whenever possible.

The anticipatory attack category does not include opportunistic aggression: attacks whose timing is based on the necessity or advantage of striking at a favorable moment, but for which the underlying motivation is offensive—that is, A attacking B not to forestall B attacking A, but simply because B is especially vulnerable, or in order to prevent B from interfering with A's plans to attack a third party. For example, Germany conducted invasions of Norway in 1940 and of the Balkans

---

[27] Preemptive and preventive attacks can thus be thought of as occupying a middle ground between purely offensive and purely defensive uses of force, with prevention at the more offensive and preemption at the more defensive end of the anticipatory attack spectrum.

in 1941 in order to strengthen its flanks against possible Allied counterattacks during the invasions of France and the Soviet Union, respectively.[28] Similarly, the Japanese attack on Pearl Harbor was motivated by the desire to cripple U.S. military power in the Pacific before it could be used against Japan during the planned conquest of Southeast Asia, an offensive that was in turn driven by the perceived need to secure a source of petroleum before a U.S. oil embargo could bring the Japanese war effort in China to its knees.[29] Such cases have significant parallels with anticipatory attacks, and understanding the latter may shed considerable light upon them, but they fall outside of the domain of this analysis.[30]

Anticipatory attacks are also related to, but distinct from, other types of anticipatory policy actions. When faced with security threats, states often take anticipatory coercive or defensive measures. In the face of an imminent attack, for example, leaders might decide to alert or mobilize their forces rather than launch an assault of their own, particularly if it appears that there is little or nothing to be gained by attacking but that defensive preparations might yet bolster deterrence or at least limit damage from the enemy attack. During crises, states often take diplomatic actions for defensive or deterrent purposes, while a host of peacetime military and nonmilitary actions are con-

---

[28] The invasion of Norway was the more preemptive of the two operations, as the British were already preparing to mine Norwegian waters when the Germans struck, as a prelude to a planned occupation of Norway (Earl F. Ziemke, *The German Northern Theater of Operations, 1940–1945*, Pamphlet No. 20-271, Washington, D.C.: U.S. Government Printing Office, 1959, pp. 10–17).

[29] Scott Douglas Sagan, "From Deterrence to Coercion to War: The Road to Pearl Harbor," in Alexander L. George, William E. Simons, and David Kent Hall, eds., *The Limits of Coercive Diplomacy*, 2nd ed., Boulder, Colo.: Westview Press, 1994a, pp. 57–90.

[30] A more borderline case is presented by the Soviet invasion of Finland in 1939, which was blatantly aggressive but was motivated in large part by Stalin's defensively minded fear that Finland would collude in a future German invasion of Russia. The campaign was a debacle for the Red Army, partly because the Kremlin had optimistically believed assurances from communist Finnish exiles (who had fled to the Union of Soviet Socialist Republics [USSR] in 1918) that the Finnish people would welcome Soviet forces as liberators (Karl P. Mueller, *Strategy, Asymmetric Deterrence, and Accommodation: Middle Powers and Security in Modern Europe*, dissertation, Princeton, N.J.: Princeton, University, 1991, Chapter Five).

ducted in order to prevent, weaken, deter, or divert potential security threats, and many of these are essentially anticipatory in nature, insofar as they must take into account the emergence, timing, and certainty of potential aggression by adversaries.[31] Thus, making decisions about such actions may have much in common with making choices regarding anticipatory attack, although they are alternatives to it.

Anticipatory Attack Versus Operational Preemption

As the term is used here, anticipatory attack is a strategic-level choice; that is, it involves initiating conflict or taking some other action that is effectively an act of war, such as violating the sovereignty of a non-combatant state during an ongoing conflict. Thus, deciding to mount an anticipatory attack is an act of national policy, usually with implications extending beyond the immediate conflict, and is a matter for decision by the national leadership.

An anticipatory attack is typically the opening phase of a war, which may be fought for limited objectives or in which regime or national survival may be at stake for one or both combatants. However, this is not always the case. An especially devastating first strike may leave the target unable or unwilling to fight back, or in a situation of considerable asymmetry of capabilities, the target may simply be unable to retaliate regardless of the attack's effects. Anticipatory attacks may also occur at lower levels of intensity that do not trigger sustained conflict but are still strategic in nature, as in the 1990 assassination of mercenary artillerist Gerald Bull to disrupt the Iraqi program that he was leading to develop a "supergun" capable of striking Israel.[32]

---

[31] A good example of what might be called "preemptive deterrence" was Operation Vigilant Warrior, the rapid deployment of U.S. forces to the Persian Gulf in late 1994 in response to threatening movements of Iraqi forces toward Kuwait. See W. Eric Herr, *Operation Vigilant Warrior: Conventional Deterrence Theory, Doctrine, and Practice*, Maxwell Air Force Base, Ala.: Air University Press, 1996.

[32] James Adams, *Bull's Eye: The Assassination and Life of Supergun Inventor Gerald Bull*, New York: Times Books, 1992. Particularly in such small-scale anticipatory attacks, it is also possible that the identity of the attacker will not be obvious, reducing the likelihood that wider hostilities will ensue.

Anticipatory attack should thus be distinguished from what might be called "operational preemption," taking military actions within the context of an ongoing conflict that are intended to reduce the enemy's capabilities or to have other effects by striking before the enemy launches an attack or takes some other undesirable action.[33] For example, during the 2003 invasion of Iraq, Allied air forces sought to prevent the Iraqi leadership from ordering ballistic missile and chemical weapon attacks against Israel or the Coalition by disabling Iraqi communications nodes. This measure was operationally preemptive in the sense that it sought to eliminate the enemy's capability to carry out an anticipated action, but it was a matter of military campaign strategy. In contrast, Operation Iraqi Freedom as a whole was a preventive attack in that it was intended to eliminate the threat that Iraq would directly or indirectly attack the United States or its allies in the future if it were not attacked first.[34] Conversely, Operation Enduring Freedom, the 2001 invasion of Afghanistan, was neither a preemptive nor a preventive attack, since the adversary had already initiated hostilities against the United States, but was operationally preemptive to the extent that one of its objectives was to eliminate al Qaeda's Afghan base of operations before further terrorist attacks could be mounted from it.

Studying Preemptive and Preventive Attack

This monograph explores the utility and limitations of anticipatory attack as a response to security threats, and in particular as an element of U.S. national security policy, by approaching the subject from several directions. Chapter Two examines the existing historical and social scientific literature regarding the question of when anticipatory attack is a potentially useful strategy, and develops a theoretical framework

---

[33] See Gaddis (2004, p. 54).

[34] At the tactical level, of course, much of combat involves preemptive action, with units or individuals seeking to engage their enemies before they can be attacked. The conditions under which it is permissible to fire upon a target in anticipation of being attacked are a central concern in virtually all rules of engagement.

both to serve as a basis for the rest of the analysis and for policymakers to use when considering such military options. Chapter Three analyzes the international legal dimensions of preemptive and preventive uses of force and their effects on perceptions of legitimacy, factors that almost always loom large and sometimes exert a dominant influence when leaders are considering anticipatory attack as a policy option.

Chapter Four draws conclusions and identifies policy implications about the use of anticipatory attack, drawing on the analyses in the first three chapters and on examinations of a set of 12 historical case studies. These results are presented at two levels of policy: grand strategy, where the focus is on the use of anticipatory attack as an element of U.S. national security strategy, and military strategy and operations, where the goal is to derive, from the higher-level analysis, useful insights and prescriptions for the armed services and joint commands regarding the potential need to prepare to execute anticipatory attacks in the future.

The 12 case studies (listed in Table 1.1) are described in three appendixes at the end of this monograph. They include cases in which anticipatory attacks were launched and others in which such strategies were considered by decisionmakers but were rejected in favor of alternative options. The cases selected for analysis here are all from the post-1945 era, and in all but one the prospective attacker was a liberal democracy, either the United States or Israel. Inevitably, all of them were either overt uses of force or covert operations that failed to remain covert.[35] Each of the attacks that was considered or launched falls into one of three categories that are particularly relevant for contemporary American foreign policy:[36] attacks to eliminate or reduce threats of interstate aggression, attacks against threatening terrorist nonstate actors, or attacks to limit the development or spread of dan-

---

[35] By definition, the authors do not know about covert attacks that have remained so. However, such operations constitute an important subgroup within the population of anticipatory attacks.

[36] The case summaries are divided among the three appendixes differently (U.S. interstate, Israeli interstate, and counterterrorist anticipatory attack cases, respectively, in Appendixes A, B, and C) in order to make them easier to refer to, and so as to group together cases with related historical narratives.

gerous military capabilities.[37] Because the cases were chosen based on their individual significance for policymaking in the near future, rather than selected randomly, conclusions should not be drawn from them regarding the overall likelihood of states to employ anticipatory attack strategies, the rate of success of such actions, or other quantifiable variables along these lines.[38] Instead, their purpose is to provide qualitative illustration and information for the accompanying analysis.[39]

Many additional cases were not included in the set simply because of the project's time and resource limits. However, two that are absent merit specific explanation: U.S. consideration of preventive attack against North Korea in 1994 and subsequently in response to Pyongyang's nuclear weapons program, and the preventive attack by the United States, Great Britain, and Australia against Iraq in 2003. Although these cases are particularly salient to current discussions of anticipatory attack, they were excluded for several reasons, particularly because the classification of U.S. deliberations in the North Korean case and the recentness of the Iraq case at the time this study was conducted meant this it would not have been possible to address these two cases at a satisfactory level of detail and accuracy in an unclassified form. Nevertheless, the recent Iraq war is inevitably a pervasive presence in the discussions that follow, just as it was central to placing anticipatory attack in the forefront of U.S. security policy debates in the first place.

---

[37] These are not the only forms that anticipatory attack might take, merely the ones that appear most salient for the United States in the near future.

[38] A number of works that do attempt to measure such factors are discussed or cited in Chapter Two.

[39] For example, anticipatory attacks against nonstate actors make up only four of the 12 cases in the appendixes, partly because of the rarity of overt first strikes against such adversaries in the past, but this should not be taken to imply that states will be the most prominent class of target for anticipatory attack in the future.

Table 1.1
Preemptive and Preventive Attack Case Studies, 1945–2002

Case	Potential Attacker	Target	Nature of Threat	Attack Launched	Result	Appendix
Soviet Nuclear Prevention (1945–55)	United States	USSR	Nuclear capability	No	Deterrence	A
Sinai Campaign (1956)	Israel	Egypt	Conventional attack	Yes	Israeli victory	B
Cuban Missile Crisis (1962)	United States	USSR/ Cuba	Nearby nuclear basing	No	Missiles withdrawn	A
Chinese Nuclear Prevention (1963–1964)	United States	China	Nuclear capability	No	Deterrence	A
Six-Day War (1967)	Israel	Egypt/ Syria	Conventional Attack	Yes	Major Israeli victory	B
October War (1973)	Israel	Egypt/ Syria	Conventional attack	No	Arab attack checked	B
Osirak Raid (1980–1981)	Israel	Iraq	Nuclear capability/ attack	Yes	Target destroyed	B
Invasion of Grenada (1983)	United States	Grenada	Soviet base; subversion	Yes	Regime change	A
Mishal Assassination (1997)	Israel	Hamas	Terrorism	Yes	Operation failed	C
Tirana Raids (1998)	United States/ Albania	Islamists	Terrorism	Yes	Targets arrested	C
Jordanian Crackdown (2002)	Jordan	Islamists	Unrest/ terrorism	Yes	Target suppressed	C
Yemen Hellfire Attack (2002)	United States	Al Qaeda	Terrorism	Yes	Target killed	C

CHAPTER TWO

The Best Defense?
When and Why States Strike First

Introduction

Although it has always been understood that the United States might strike first in order to blunt or foil an imminent attack, the recently declared American policy of striking first states that U.S. leaders will not necessarily wait until a threat becomes imminent to use force against it. Thus, what is new about the "preemption" doctrine first promulgated in 2001–2002 is not the promise to preempt imminent threats, but the judgment that protecting U.S. national security may require launching preventive attacks. The distinction between preemption and prevention is important, not least—but also not only—because the international community has traditionally considered preemption to be a potentially legitimate form of self-defense while viewing most prevention as illegitimate aggression.[1] However, as the preceding chapter explains, it is sometimes also useful, both for theorists and for policymakers contemplating striking first as a response to security threats, to examine preemption and prevention as parts of a broader category of anticipatory attack.

---

[1] Useful discussions on this point include Freedman (2003b); François Heisbourg, "A Work in Progress: The Bush Doctrine and Its Consequences," *Washington Quarterly*, Vol. 26, No. 2, 2003, pp. 75–88; and Walter B. Slocombe, "Force, Pre-Emption, and Legitimacy," *Survival*, Vol. 45, No. 1, 2003, pp. 117–130. The next chapter of this monograph explores in detail the question of whether and how international law and society might come to regard some preventive attacks as legal or legitimate in the future.

Working from the definitions presented in Chapter One, this chapter develops a framework for analyzing anticipatory attack strategies, proceeding in two steps. First, it reviews existing theories about preemptive and preventive attack, and their origins in analyses of the causes of the First World War and of nuclear strategic stability during the Cold War, in order to describe what historians and social scientists have learned about this subject. Second, it summarizes the considerations that policymakers should weigh when considering possible anticipatory attacks, and organizes these into a scheme that applies to both preventive and preemptive attacks. This framework is intended not only to structure the ensuing discussions in this project, but also to be heuristically useful for practical strategy making.

Prevention and Preemption in International Politics

There is an extensive literature in diplomatic history and international relations that uses the words "preemption" and "prevention" to describe types of wars. A preventive war, in this view, "generally refers to a war fought now in order to avoid the risks of war under worsening circumstances later."[2] Typically, this results when a state that is facing the prospect of a serious decline in its economic or military capabilities relative to those of states it considers to be likely future enemies decides that it is worth fighting a war in order to avoid an unfavorable shift in the actual or perceived balance of power that will increase its vulnerability to coercion, damage, or defeat.[3]

---

[2] Jack S. Levy, "Declining Power and the Preventive Motivation for War," *World Politics*, Vol. 40, No. 1, 1987, pp. 82–107, p. 82.

[3] Michael Eliot Howard, *The Causes of Wars and Other Essays*, Cambridge, Mass.: Harvard University Press, 1983, p. 18. Note that the definition of preventive attack presented in Chapter One and used in this monograph is somewhat narrower, encompassing only cases in which a state attacks in order to avoid being attacked later by an enemy, not merely to stave off relative decline (though some theorists, such as John J. Mearsheimer, *The Tragedy of Great Power Politics*, New York: Norton, 2001, argue that there is no real distinction between defending one's power and one's security).

The history of international politics is replete with countries that gambled on war to improve their long-term security. According to Thucydides, the Peloponnesian War stemmed from "the growth of Athenian power and the fear which this caused in Sparta."[4] Similar fears have also beset more modern great powers, sometimes driving them to war. Since 1792 there have been eight wars among major powers started by one that saw an opportunity to prevent a decline in its relative power: France versus Austria in 1792; Prussia versus Austria in 1866; Prussia versus France in 1870; Japan versus Russia in 1904; Germany versus Russia in 1914; Britain and France versus Germany in 1939; Germany versus the Soviet Union in 1941; and Japan versus the United States in 1941.[5] More recent examples of preventive attacks include Israel's war against Egypt in 1956, the Israeli air strike against the Iraqi nuclear facility at Osirak in 1981, and the U.S.-led invasion of Iraq in 2003.[6]

In contrast, preemptive wars erupt when one state concludes not only that an attack by an adversary is likely but that it is imminent, and that striking first is the best option to deal with this pending aggression. Unlike launching preventive wars, when states choose to attack preemptively they typically must decide and act under severe time constraints. The need to decide quickly whether to attack or absorb a potential blow tends to be a key feature that differentiates preemptive from preventive wars. Preemptive wars are quite rare, partly because leaders who are plotting aggression often try to avoid making this obvi-

---

[4] Thucydides, *History of the Peloponnesian War*, Rex Warner, trans., Baltimore, Md.: Penguin, 1954, p. 49.

[5] Sometimes both great powers saw an opportunity to strike. This list is a consensus among most analysts of major-power preventive wars since 1792. Some lists are longer or shorter, but the crucial point remains that the preventive motive was a key cause of war. For a longer list, see Stephen Van Evera, *Causes of War: Power and the Roots of Conflict*, Ithaca: Cornell University Press, 1999, pp. 76–78; other treatments include Levy (1987, p. 83); Alfred Vagts, *Defense and Diplomacy*, New York: Kings Crown Press, 1956, pp. 263–350; A. J. P. Taylor, *The Struggle for Mastery in Europe, 1848–1918*, Oxford: Clarendon Press, 1954; and Scott Douglas Sagan, "The Origins of the Pacific War," *Journal of Interdisciplinary History*, Vol. 18, No. 4, 1988, pp. 893–922.

[6] These first two of these cases are summarized in Appendix B, as is the Six-Day War.

ous in order to enjoy some measure of surprise when they attack their victims.[7] Classic examples of preemptive wars include the July Crisis of 1914 and the Six-Day War of 1967, in which Israel preemptively attacked Egypt and Syria.

Many scholars contend that the boundary between preemption and prevention is also the threshold separating wars of opportunity from wars of necessity, and therefore legitimate from illegitimate use of force. This is consistent with the dominant tradition in international law, although as the next chapter describes, legal scholars are now debating whether some preventive wars should be considered acceptable as technological and other changes increase the possibility that if preemption is narrowly defined, states will have no opportunity to preempt serious threats to their security, particularly from terrorists armed with weapons of mass destruction. For all of these reasons, it can be useful as well as customary to differentiate preemptive from preventive attacks when considering certain dimensions of this subject, though it is sometimes more helpful to deal with the broader category of anticipatory attack as a whole. Reduced to their fundamentals, preemption involves striking the first blow against an enemy rather than allowing the enemy to strike first, while prevention is motivated by the desire to fight an adversary sooner rather than later.

Preemptive War and First-Strike Advantage

For decades, international relations scholars have examined the conditions under which states tend to decide in favor of preemptive or preventive war. While historians have focused on why policymakers of the past might have concluded that war was necessary, international relations theorists have explored the recurring factors that drive states to use force first. They first examined how crises might become unstable, prompting decisionmakers to undertake preemptive strikes or start preemptive wars in order to avoid suffering the effects of an enemy first strike. They have also explored how fluctuations in relative economic and military capabilities create windows of opportunity that give states incentives to launch preventive wars prior to anticipated unfavorable

---

[7]   Reiter (1995).

shifts in the balance of power. This line of research sprang primarily from concerns about nuclear deterrence during the Cold War.

The nuclear arms race between the superpowers during the Cold War was accompanied by the birth and evolution of modern deterrence theory. One of the key insights derived from deterrence theory was that some nuclear force postures might give an adversary an incentive to strike first during a crisis. Security analysts, especially those at the RAND Corporation, sought to understand what kinds of nuclear forces and postures would make deterrence more or less robust.[8] In the 1950s, concern over the vulnerability of American bombers, then the sole arm of the U.S. nuclear deterrent, led Albert Wohlstetter to write about the importance of secure second-strike capabilities.

Wohlstetter warned that during a potential confrontation between the superpowers, American bombers deployed close to the Soviet Union could prove an irresistibly tempting target for preemption. Rather than wait for the United States to mount an attack, the Soviets might try to limit the damage from an American nuclear strike by attacking first. Because of this temptation, deterrence theorists argued, credible nuclear deterrence threats required that the United States possess sufficient retaliatory capability to survive an enemy first strike so as to make an enemy preemptive attack appear pointless. Vulnerable nuclear forces would be threatening, but not necessarily deterrent, while survivable forces would maintain what Wohlstetter described as the "Delicate

---

8   Fred M. Kaplan, *The Wizards of Armageddon*, New York: Simon and Schuster, 1983.

Balance of Terror."[9] Eventually, both superpowers developed nuclear arsenals with secure second-strike forces.[10]

Throughout the Cold War, as new nuclear weapons, delivery systems, strategies, and targeting doctrines were developed or proposed, one of the key criteria against which each was judged—and about which strategic theorists argued—was the effect it could be expected to have upon crisis stability. Would it increase or decrease the incentives for one side to strike first, especially in the context of a crisis in which it might expect to be attacked, even at the risk of starting a war neither side might want?[11] Whether particular developments such as ballistic missile defenses, multiple or highly accurate missile warheads, leadership targeting, and limited nuclear options appeared to be stabilizing or destabilizing were often the subject of intense debate, since the answers depended on factors such as whether the Soviets were cautious or risk-acceptant and the relative importance that the Kremlin attached to its population, industry, and armed forces, all of which fed back into assessments of their likely effect on perception of first-strike advantage. The larger the apparent advantage of striking first, the

---

[9]   Albert J. Wohlstetter, *The Delicate Balance of Terror*, Santa Monica, Calif.: RAND Corporation, P-1472, 1958; and the more widely cited Albert J. Wohlstetter, "The Delicate Balance of Terror," *Foreign Affairs*, Vol. 37, No. 2, 1959, pp. 211–234.

[10] Many approaches were used to reduce the vulnerability of nuclear forces, most prominently the deployment of land-based missiles in hardened underground silos or on mobile launchers and the deployment of submarine-launched ballistic missiles. For summaries of the nuclear era, see Lawrence Freedman, *The Evolution of Nuclear Strategy*, 3rd ed., New York: Palgrave Macmillan, 2003a; Karl P. Mueller, "Strategic Airpower and Nuclear Strategy: New Theory for a Not-Quite-So-New Apocalypse," in Phillip S. Meilinger, ed., *The Paths of Heaven: The Evolution of Airpower Theory*, Maxwell Air Force Base, Ala.: Air University Press, 1997, pp. 279–320; and David Alan Rosenberg, "The Origins of Overkill: Nuclear Weapons and American Strategy, 1945–1960," *International Security*, Vol. 7, No. 4, 1983, pp. 3–71.

[11] Classic works on the subject include Wohlstetter (1958, 1959); Glenn Herald Snyder, *Deterrence and Defense: Toward a Theory of National Security*, Princeton, N.J.: Princeton University Press, 1961; and Schelling (1966). A more recent framework for assessing crisis stability is developed in Glenn A. Kent and David E. Thaler, *First-Strike Stability: A Methodology for Evaluating Strategic Forces*, Santa Monica, Calif.: RAND Corporation, R-3765-AF, 1989.

greater the likelihood of a superpower crisis escalating to nuclear war would presumably be.

For example, the central strategic problem facing the United States was extending the American nuclear umbrella to deter an invasion of Western Europe by the Warsaw Pact.[12] To credibly extend deterrence to its NATO allies, U.S. planners concluded that they needed to be able to use nuclear weapons first. However, threatening a massive nuclear strike against Russia in response to a Soviet invasion of Germany seemed unlikely to be credible, since it would invite a massive retaliatory strike against the American homeland. In the familiar question of the era, "Would the U.S. trade Boston for Bonn?" American strategists tried to resolve this problem by giving themselves a wider variety of military options for responding to Soviet aggression in Europe. These measures included bolstering North Atlantic Treaty Organization (NATO) conventional forces, introducing tactical and theater nuclear forces to Western Europe, and developing strategic counterforce capabilities that would allow the United States to strike Soviet nuclear forces rather than cities.

Proponents of counterforce capabilities argued that these weapons would not only make American deterrent threats more believable, by allowing attacks that might not trigger all-out retaliation against U.S. cities, but would also provide the ability to limit the damage done to the United States, should a nuclear war begin, by weakening the Soviet nuclear arsenal. They also feared that the Soviets might be willing to accept enormous casualties in a nuclear war if they expected to fare better in it than the United States, and therefore argued that deter-

---

[12] This problem and strategies for resolving it are described in Freedman (2003a); Earl C. Ravenal, "Counterforce and Alliance: The Ultimate Connection," *International Security*, Vol. 6, No. 4, 1982, pp. 26–43; and Janne E. Nolan, *Guardians of the Arsenal: The Politics of Nuclear Strategy*, New York: Basic Books, 1989.

rence depended on threatening to disarm and to defeat, and not merely devastate, the Soviet Union in a nuclear exchange.[13]

The problem with counterforce capabilities, however, is that they threaten to make crises more dangerous. Armed with counterforce weapons, decisionmakers on one side might be tempted to strike first, in the belief that such an attack could cripple the enemy's nuclear arsenal. This possibility also increases the enemy's incentives to preempt by creating a "use them or lose them" situation. In short, counterforce capabilities, especially if they are vulnerable to enemy attack, can create incentives for striking first for largely defensive reasons.[14] Fortunately, deterrence proved more robust than many expected during the Cold War, as the superpowers proved to be hugely reluctant to risk nuclear or even major conventional war with each other.

Students of international relations built upon these insights about crisis stability between nuclear powers to examine the effects of incentives for preemption in the conventional arena as well.[15] Through extensive examination of the causes of World War I and the events of

---

[13] Although this summary lumps them together, there are a variety of arguments made in favor of counterforce capabilities. A representative sample of these views comes from Colin S. Gray and Keith Payne, "Under the Nuclear Gun: Victory Is Possible," *Foreign Policy*, No. 39, 1980, pp. 14–27; Colin S. Gray, "Nuclear Strategy: The Case for a Theory of Victory," *International Security*, Vol. 4, No. 1, 1979, pp. 54–87; and Victor Utgoff, "In Defense of Counterforce," *International Security*, Vol. 6, No. 4, 1982, pp. 44–60. For a balanced argument in favor of second-strike counterforce, see Scott Douglas Sagan, *Moving Targets: Nuclear Strategy and National Security*, Princeton, N.J.: Princeton University Press, 1989.

[14] Charles L. Glaser, *Analyzing Strategic Nuclear Policy*, Princeton, N.J.: Princeton University Press, 1990; Robert Jervis, *The Illogic of American Nuclear Strategy*, Ithaca, N.Y.: Cornell University Press, 1984; Robert Jervis, *The Meaning of the Nuclear Revolution: Statecraft and the Prospect of Armageddon*, Ithaca, N.Y.: Cornell University Press, 1989; and the offense-defense theory references cited below. For arguments that dismiss this line of logic, see Stephen Peter Rosen, "Nuclear Arms and Strategic Defense," *Washington Quarterly*, 1981, pp. 82–99; and Richard K. Betts, "Surprise Attack and Preemption," in Graham T. Allison, Albert Carnesale, and Joseph S. Nye, eds., *Hawks, Doves, and Owls: An Agenda for Avoiding Nuclear War*, New York: Norton, 1985, pp. 54–79.

[15] The foundations of offense-defense theory were first outlined in George H. Quester, *Offense and Defense in the International System*, New York: Wiley, 1977; and Robert Jervis, "Cooperation Under the Security Dilemma," *World Politics*, Vol. 30, No. 2, 1978, pp. 167–214.

the July Crisis of 1914, scholars have suggested a causal relationship between beliefs about military technology and perceived incentives to strike first in a crisis. Specifically, they argue that preemptive motives for war can emerge when military planners believe that prevailing conditions, particularly the state of military technology, on balance favors conquest or the seizing of territory, a condition referred to as offense dominance. When offense is dominant, decisionmakers will tend to see advantages to striking before an opponent does. Alternatively, when conditions make holding territory easier than seizing it, defense is dominant and crises tend to be stable because no advantage appears to result from striking first.[16]

The July Crisis of 1914 that preceded the First World War has become the signature example of how such conditions can drive states to attack preemptively. The assassination of the Hapsburg heir, Archduke Franz Ferdinand, in Sarajevo was the catalyst for a confrontation between two blocs of great powers. On one side, the Austro-Hungarian Empire, encouraged by Germany, used the assassination as a rationale for declaring war on Serbia, a Balkan power that threatened Vienna's influence in the region. Germany stood poised to defend Austria-Hungary, its only reliable continental ally. On the other side, Russia decided to stand firmly behind its Serbian ally, fearful of backing down once more in a diplomatic crisis over the Balkans. France and an ever-cautious British Empire threatened war to prevent any German effort to change the territorial status quo in Europe.[17]

Although many of the great powers in the crisis faced pressures to mount preemptive attacks, analysts tend to focus on German decision-

---

[16] The key recent works on offense-defense theory include Van Evera (1999); Charles L. Glaser and Chaim Kaufmann, "What Is the Offense-Defense Balance and Can We Measure It?" *International Security*, Vol. 22, No. 4, 1998, pp. 44–82; and Sean M. Lynn-Jones, "Offense-Defense Theory and Its Critics," *Security Studies*, Vol. 4, No. 4, 1995, pp. 660–691; for criticism of these arguments, see Reiter (1995); Keir A. Lieber, "Grasping the Technological Peace: The Offense-Defense Balance and International Security," *International Security*, Vol. 25, No. 1, 2000, pp. 71–104; and Richard K. Betts, "Must War Find a Way? A Review Essay," *International Security*, Vol. 24, No. 2, 1999, pp. 166–198.

[17] On the July Crisis, see Jack S. Levy, "Preferences, Constraints, and Choices in July 1914," *International Security*, Vol. 15, No. 3, 1990, pp. 151–186.

making as the epicenter of the crisis.[18] The German General Staff had long worried about the prospect of fighting a two-front war. Cursed with unfortunate geography, the German Empire had to contend with France to its west and Russia to the east, each a powerful state in its own right. German planners concluded they could defeat either France or Russia alone, but that they would have trouble fighting both at the same time. In their view, once the crisis erupted and it looked like war could result, Germany would have a window of opportunity for victory that depended on its ability to mobilize more quickly than Russia. Once mobilized, the German Army would strike west to knock out France quickly and then redeploy to the east to defeat Russia. The prevailing belief in the power of the offense and the ease of conquest not only put great pressure on German military leaders to mobilize and attack rapidly in order to defeat the French before Russia was fully prepared to fight, but also made their ambitiously offensive war plans appear feasible.

It is important to note that the offense-defense balance argument depends not on the objective state of military technology, but instead on whether decisionmakers perceive an offense- or defense-dominant environment. In the case of pre-1914 Europe, the military organizations of the day exhibited an almost universal belief in the superiority of the offense. These beliefs not only ignored the lessons of recent conflicts, like the American Civil War and the Boer War, but also misjudged the implications of existing military technology, such as barbed wire and machine guns.[19] As it turned out, World War I proved that defense dominated the battlefield, and the July Crisis loomed large for

---

[18] On the importance of mobilization and war, see Barbara Wertheim Tuchman, *The Guns of August*, New York: Macmillan, 1962; and Marc Trachtenberg, "The Meaning of Mobilization in 1914," *International Security*, Vol. 15, No. 3, 1990, pp. 120–150.

[19] Some contend a lack of civilian oversight of military planning as well as the pervasiveness of Social Darwinist thinking among political and military leaders contributed to this belief in offense dominance. See Jack Snyder, "Civil-Military Relations and the Cult of the Offensive, 1914 and 1984," *International Security*, Vol. 9, No. 1, 1984a, pp. 108–146; and Stephen Van Evera, "The Cult of the Offensive and the Origins of the First World War," *International Security*, Vol. 9, No. 1, 1984, pp. 58–107. For analyses of other cases of misperception of offense dominance, see John R. Carter, Jr., *Airpower and the Cult of the Offensive*, Maxwell Air Force Base, Ala.: Air University Press, 1998.

Cold War scholars as a precedent that might be repeated in a superpower nuclear confrontation, if the opposing leaders or militaries came to believe that their security would be improved by striking first.[20]

In reexamining these arguments about preemptive incentives, Dan Reiter has found that as an empirical matter, preemptive wars happen less often than we might expect.[21] Specifically, he finds that since 1815 there have been only three genuinely preemptive wars: the 1967 Arab-Israeli War, the Chinese Attack on United Nations Forces during the Korean War, and the July Crisis of 1914.[22] In Reiter's view, policymakers are aware that preemptive pressure might exist in a crisis. With this knowledge, political leaders and military planners of states involved in a confrontation will use diplomacy to avoid wars they would rather not fight in the first place. Nonetheless, analysts such as Stephen Van Evera contend that while the sample size of preemptive wars is small—but not as limited as Reiter claims—the preemptive wars that have happened were devastating and might well be replicated in the future.[23]

Preventive War and the Balance of Power

Arguments about the offense-defense balance are also used to explain preventive motives for war, when conditions prompt states to start a war rather than waiting to fight later under potentially unfavorable circumstances. When combined with shifts in relative military power, advances in offensive weaponry can motivate a state to make use of its advantages quickly before they disappear. How rapid power shifts cause war is a familiar story: When a state's relative economic and military capabilities begin to decline, a window of opportunity may appear

---

[20] On the conduct of World War I, helpful reviews include Basil Henry Liddell Hart, *The Real War, 1914–1918*, Boston: Little, Brown, 1964; and John Keegan, *The First World War*, New York: A. Knopf, 1999.

[21] Reiter (1995); Van Evera (1999).

[22] Some have argued that this set of cases is actually even smaller, on the grounds that the July Crisis had less to do with preemptive pressures than with the great powers keeping their alliance commitments. See Scott Douglas Sagan, "1914 Revisited: Allies, Offense, and Instability," *International Security*, Vol. 11, No. 2, 1986, pp. 151–176.

[23] Van Evera (1984, especially footnote 19).

to open for it to defeat potential opponents before it becomes too weak to do so.[24] When the offense-defense balance favors the offense, states' motivations to jump through such windows and go to war sooner rather than later should be increased because victories should be faster, less expensive, and more decisive.[25]

The years before World War I have also served as an important example of the pressures that can drive states to launch preventive as well as preemptive wars. Before the war, German military planners and political leaders believed that their relative power position vis-à-vis Russia would erode over time. Not only could Russia draw on its vast population to field a large army, but it would be an increasingly modern one as the once-primitive empire industrialized. Economic modernization also allowed Russia to improve its railroads, enhancing its ability to mobilize and deploy its forces. Meanwhile, Germany's only major ally, Austria-Hungary, was a state in apparently terminal decline. Such an unfavorable balance of power appeared particularly dangerous for Germany because of its geographic position between France and Russia. Moreover, the German military, like the military organizations of most European great powers, believed that technology favored the offensive, facilitating the easy conquest of territory by an aggressor. In combination, all of these factors prompted Germany to use the July Crisis as pretext to fight what it saw as the inevitable war against Russia, as German decisionmakers concluded that it would be better to fight Russia in 1914 before the balance of power tipped decisively against it.[26]

One interesting finding of the preventive war literature, however, is the extent to which states often fail to jump through strategic windows of opportunity when they appear to open. Decisionmakers may

---

[24] Dale C. Copeland, *The Origins of Major War*, Ithaca: Cornell University Press, 2000; Jack S. Levy, "The Causes of War and the Conditions of Peace," *Annual Review of Political Science*, Vol. 1, 1998, pp. 139–165; Hans Joachim Morgenthau, *Politics Among Nations: The Struggle for Power and Peace*, 4th ed., New York: Knopf, 1967.

[25] Van Evera (1984, pp. 73–104).

[26] Those making the same or similar interpretations include Fritz Fischer, *War of Illusions: German Policies from 1911 to 1914*, Marian Jackson, trans., New York: Norton, 1975; Mearsheimer (2001, pp. 213–216); and Copeland (2000, Chapter Four).

prefer to fight today rather than tomorrow, but both international and domestic constraints keep this from happening as frequently as one might expect, especially if the effects of the offense-defense balance are powerful. As reflected in international law, there are international norms against wars of aggression, so states attacking first even for defensive reasons risk acquiring a reputation for reckless and aggressive behavior, at best hampering their ability to form alliances and at worst triggering the formation of countercoalitions or even the launching of preventive wars against themselves. Many countries, therefore, prefer to play the role of victim rather than that of attacker, forgoing opportunities to strike first.

Among domestic constraints, Randall Schweller has found that democracies rarely launch preventive wars, attributing their reluctance to both domestic norms against starting wars and the difficulties governments might have in rallying their populations for war.[27] Schweller's argument appears increasingly dubious given new research[28] and the recent U.S.-led preventive war against Iraq. However, Richard Ned Lebow contends that such incentives against preventive war are not unique to democracies. He finds evidence that German decisionmakers should have gone to war against Russia much earlier than 1914, but domestic pressures and worries about their international reputation made launching a war difficult.[29]

Understanding the conditions under which states tend to have preemptive or preventive incentives for war provides useful advice about matters such as how to configure nuclear arsenals and other military forces to increase stability and why leaders should beware of appearing too aggressive or being overconfident during a crisis. However, because most of this research does not weigh the costs and benefits of prevention or preemption as instruments to improve a state's

---

[27] Randall L. Schweller, "Domestic Structure and Preventive War: Are Democracies More Pacific?" *World Politics*, Vol. 44, No. 2, 1992, pp. 235–269.

[28] Jack S. Levy and Joseph R. Gochal, "Democracy and Preventive War: Israel and the 1956 Sinai War," *Security Studies*, Vol. 11, No. 2, 2001, pp. 1–49.

[29] Richard Ned Lebow, "Windows of Opportunity: Do States Jump Through Them?" *International Security*, Vol. 9, No. 1, 1984, pp. 147–184.

security, it provides relatively little guidance to decisionmakers about whether and how they should consider striking first in particular situations. Therefore, the next section of this chapter presents a framework for examining the costs and benefits of particular anticipatory attacks, in order to identify conditions under which policymakers might want to strike first.

The Costs, Benefits, and Risks of Anticipatory Attack

Strategists and policymakers who are contemplating preemptive or preventive attacks must, or at least should, take a wide variety of military and political considerations into account when making their decisions. However, it is often useful to combine these myriad concerns into two larger sets of variables that provide a first-order summary of the incentives for and against striking a potential enemy first: the degree of certainty that the adversary will strike if the anticipatory attack is not launched, and the net benefit expected from carrying out the anticipatory attack compared to the results that are expected if the adversary is allowed to attack on its terms, to which the authors refer somewhat loosely as the *first-strike advantage*.[30] The following sections address each of these in some detail.[31] Broadly speaking, the more certain the enemy threat is, and the greater the advantage striking first appears to offer, the more attractive anticipatory attack will be (see Figure 2.1).[32]

---

[30] The latter term is something of a misnomer; in preventive war cases what matters is the advantage expected from fighting sooner rather than later, not the advantage expected from striking first per se. However, this label can serve comfortably under both preemptive and preventive circumstances as long as its true meaning is borne in mind.

[31] Although the focus here is on the use of military instruments, there are a variety of non-military instruments available to policymakers that also play important strategic roles. For a discussion, see Richard Haass and Meghan L. O'Sullivan, *Honey and Vinegar: Incentives, Sanctions, and Foreign Policy*, Washington, D.C.: Brookings Institution Press, 2000.

[32] Figure 2.1 represents only cases in which there exists some first-strike advantage. The y-axis could be extended below the origin in order to encompass the many cases in which anticipatory attack is simply less advantageous than being attacked by the adversary, but in these cases there is no incentive to strike first.

Figure 2.1
Anticipatory Attack as a Policy Option

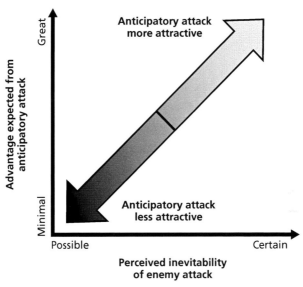

This framework applies across the spectrum of anticipatory attacks, and the fact that it does so serves to illustrate the argument presented in Chapter One that preemption and prevention are closely related strategic categories in spite of their significant differences. These differences certainly matter: Whether or not a threat is imminent, and whether it is the timing of the conflict or which side is the attacker that is at issue, have important implications for many of the factors that influence the choice of strategy. However, the shape of the problem and the logical framework required to address it are essentially the same. Moreover, if preemption and prevention are recognized to be variations on a single theme, then ambiguous situations that involve elements of each, or that do not fall neatly into one category for another reason, become less troublesome to analyze.

The Advantage of Striking First

When states are contemplating the use of force as an anticipatory response to an expected attack, they calculate whether there is an advantage to striking the opponent first. That is, how much better off does the state expect to be if it carries out the anticipatory attack than if it refrains from striking and the adversary instead attacks at the time and in the way of its choice?[33]

This is in large part a military question. Launching an anticipatory attack may be powerfully attractive because striking the first blow (in preemption) or fighting sooner rather than later (for preventive attacks) is likely to make the difference between winning and losing the conflict. The first-strike advantage might also be great because, while the basic outcome of the war appears likely to be the same either way, launching the anticipatory attack will dramatically reduce the expected costs of the war. If offense is dominant in the relationship—if attacking promises great success while defense is unpromising—the first-strike advantage will tend to be large, but in each case the two sides' specific military capabilities and vulnerabilities, and their menus of strategic choices, must be assessed. For example, other things being equal, Israel can be expected to be more inclined than the United States toward launching anticipatory attacks in response to major security threats because of the relative fragility of being a small state with little strategic depth.[34]

The substance of this calculus will be different at the preemptive and preventive ends of the anticipatory attack spectrum. When dealing with imminent threats, the benefits and costs of literally striking first are what matter. Against less immediate threats, it is not the effects of striking or receiving the first blow that loom large, but the consequences of expected changes in the combatants' strengths and weaknesses between the time when an anticipatory attack would be launched and the time when the enemy would choose to strike if left to its own devices. Yet the basic issue in both cases is one of assessing

---

[33] In most cases there will be some uncertainty as to whether an anticipatory attack will succeed as intended if it is carried out, so assessing the costs and benefits of striking first also requires considering what the results of success and the results of failure would be, weighting these estimates according to the expected probability of that each outcome will occur.

[34] See the cases in Appendix B.

the difference in value between the results of attacking and of allowing the adversary to do so.

There is more to first-strike advantage than the military dimension, however. Anticipatory attacks usually entail significant political costs in the international arena, especially in cases where the threat that prompts them does not appear dire and imminent to outside observers, and these can outweigh even considerable military advantages to striking first, as was the case in Israel's decision not to launch a preemptive attack against Egypt in October 1973. There are usually also important domestic political costs and benefits to take into account, something of which the Kennedy administration was acutely aware during the Cuban missile crisis. These considerations may argue in favor of or against striking first, depending on the circumstances and the state in question.[35] Such political factors, especially those related to international reaction, are typically shaped in part by expected perceptions of the legality or illegality of the attack, a subject addressed in detail in the next chapter.

Often intertwined with these political concerns is a final set of factors affecting the advantage to be expected from striking first that is internal to the decisionmakers: considerations of morality. These often play a major role in decisions regarding the use of force, but are especially prone to do so in cases of anticipatory attack, since the act of striking first may itself appear to be morally problematic. For example, when U.S. leaders were considering the possibility of preventive war against Stalin's Soviet Union during the first decade of the Cold War, moral and philosophical revulsion at the idea of striking first played a leading role in the Truman and Eisenhower administrations' deci-

---

[35] In the Cuban missile crisis, the Kennedy administration expected the domestic political costs of appearing to take too soft a line with the Soviets to be extremely high in the impending midterm elections, and invading Grenada fit nicely into the Reagan administration's policy of reinvigorating the image of the United States as an assertive superpower. In contrast, one of the factors cited by U.S. leaders in deciding against launching a preventive war against the Soviet Union in the late 1940s was the belief that the American people would reject preventive war out of hand, even against a regime they regarded as profoundly evil. For details of these cases, see Appendix A.

sions not to do so.[36] On the other hand, moral considerations may also encourage leaders to carry out anticipatory attacks in spite of their physical costs or risks. Such concerns can also take the form of policymakers' concern with how their actions will be viewed by history.

It is possible to set political and moral considerations aside and assess first-strike advantage in purely military terms. In fact, this is typically a natural first step in the process, since in most cases an anticipatory attack that does not offer military advantages will not be worth carrying out and thus need not be given further attention. However, in the final analysis, decisions about whether or not to go to war are inherently political, and national leaders must take into account the full range of costs and benefits of launching or refraining from a preemptive or preventive attack. Therefore, assessments of first-strike advantage must incorporate the nonmilitary as well as the military consequences of the decision, and in the end the former may well override the latter.

The Certainty of the Threat

If there is a first-strike advantage, the second major factor in deciding whether to launch an anticipatory attack comes into play: the degree of certainty that the enemy attack that it is intended to avert is otherwise inevitable. If it were absolutely certain that the enemy were going to attack and that no deterrent measures could prevent this, then an assessment of the first-strike advantage would be a sufficient basis for making the choice: In this case, if striking first were better than being attacked, it would automatically be the best policy to choose.

However, in most cases in the real world, the future is less certain than this, and in fact there are three possibilities that must be considered: attacking, being attacked, and the chance that in the absence of the first, the second will not happen. The less certain it is that the enemy will attack if given the opportunity, the more the advantages offered by anticipatory attack must be discounted. By definition, an

---

[36] See Appendix A. Indeed, revulsion at the prospect of preventive war figured more prominently in the statements of many opponents of the idea than did the potentially catastrophic human and material costs of such a conflict.

anticipatory attack is a defensive action, undertaken because doing so appears better than being attacked, not because attacking is preferable to the peaceful status quo. Therefore, if a first-strike advantage exists but there is only a 50-50 chance that the enemy is determined to attack, then launching an anticipatory attack is equally likely to make the situation better or to make it worse.[37]

For the enemy attack to be inevitable, two conditions must be met. The further one's assessment of the threat falls short of one or both of these two conditions, the less certain the threat will be. First, the opponent must be inclined to attack (in the more deterministic theories of international politics,[38] it would be appropriate to say "destined to attack") if left to make policy on its own. Second, there must be no possibility that deterrent actions or exogenous events will divert it from this course of action at some point before the attack occurs. It is primarily the second factor that leads to the widespread (though not universal) assumption that only imminent threats can be certain: The more immediate the danger, the smaller the chance that something can be done or will simply happen beforehand to prevent it.[39]

There are two principal sources of uncertainty in threat assessments regarding the likelihood of an enemy attack. One is imperfect intelligence, simply being less than certain about the adversary's plans,

---

[37] Of course, in any case where the first-strike advantage is greater than zero and the certainty of the threat is less than complete, the decisionmaker will want to know not only how much better it is to attack than to be attacked, but also how much worse attacking will be than the status quo. The latter variable is not included in the summary of this framework presented in Figure 2.1 in order to keep it relatively simple and two-dimensional, a simplification that is acceptable because this diagram is not a complete prescriptive model.

[38] For examples, see Robert Gilpin, *War and Change in World Politics*, Cambridge and New York: Cambridge University Press, 1981; Jacek Kugler and A. F. K. Organski, "The Power Transition: A Retrospective and Prospective Evaluation," in Manus I. Midlarsky, ed., *Handbook of War Studies*, Boston: Unwin Hyman, 1989, pp. 171–194; and A. F. K. Organski and Jacek Kugler, *The War Ledger*, Chicago: University of Chicago Press, 1980. For an example of long cycles of war arguments, see William R. Thompson, *The Emergence of the Global Political Economy*, London and New York: Routledge, 2000.

[39] On the difficulty of making assessments, see Jonathan Kirshner, "Rationalist Explanations for War?" *Security Studies*, Vol. 10, No. 1, 2000, pp. 143–150; and James D. Fearon, "Rationalist Explanations for War," *International Organization*, Vol. 49, No. 3, 1995, pp. 379–414.

intentions, or motivations because insufficient information about them is available; this is, of course, a problem familiar to leaders and strategists when dealing with all manner of decisions about security policy.[40] Acquiring this kind of information might occur through traditional assessments of an adversary's military capabilities, the clandestine acquisition of information, or through the normal course of diplomacy. The other source of uncertainty is independent of intelligence capabilities and cannot be overcome by improving them: being uncertain about what the future holds because it is intrinsically uncertain (including being uncertain about whether military or nonmilitary deterrent measures might yet avert the expected attack before it happens). The first of these tends to be the larger issue in cases of imminent threats, for it will generally be the case that the opponent is either about to attack or is not, and even that particular deterrent measures either will be sufficient to succeed or will not be. In seeking to prevent longer-term actions, however, existential uncertainties can become very powerful. For example, a state that has yet to acquire a dangerous military capability may not yet have decided with any degree of finality whether, how, or against whom to employ it—yet the mere possibility that it will be used against the state considering anticipatory attack may nevertheless be too serious to permit delay in removing the threat.

Weighing the Pros and Cons of Anticipatory Attack

Figure 2.1 illustrates the basic relationship between certainty and first-strike advantage. The more certain a threat is, and the greater the advantage of attacking on relatively favorable terms is over being attacked at the enemy's convenience, the more attractive anticipatory attack becomes. If striking first appears highly advantageous against a highly certain threat—which usually also means an imminent one—anticipatory attack becomes a relatively easy choice, as preemption

---

[40] At a more detailed level, intelligence may also fall short because of imperfect understanding of available information—this works out to the same thing, although the difference is important if one seeks to address the problem, since better data collection cannot entirely compensate for inadequate intelligence analysis, and in some cases will not help at all.

was for Israel in 1967.[41] However, such situations are extremely rare in international politics,[42] not least because states tend to avoid posing clearly dangerous threats against targets that could effectively eliminate them by striking first. Conversely, and observed vastly more frequently, if a threat is fairly uncertain and anticipatory attack looks only marginally better than riding out the enemy attack would be, leaders will readily turn to other strategy options, particularly deterrent ones; in such cases, it is likely that anticipatory attack will not receive serious policy consideration at all. This was essentially the situation faced by U.S. leaders considering preventive war against the Soviet Union and later against China.

Two types of situations present leaders with far more difficult choices. One category is cases in which a state is fairly certain about a security threat, but possesses only a small first-strike advantage. This is a classic problem in preemptive attack (see Figure 2.2): expecting that the enemy will attack, without the advantage of striking first being large enough to make pursuing anticipatory attack a simple choice. If there is some first-strike advantage, but launching an anticipatory attack appears far worse than the status quo—for example, because the ensuing conflict would be risky or highly destructive even if fought under optimal circumstances, or would be politically costly—even a small degree of uncertainty as to whether the enemy attack is really inevitable may be enough to make an attempt to avoid the conflict appear better than striking first, even if it is a long shot. For the United States, the Cuban missile crisis was such a case: The fact that there appeared to be some chance that options short of anticipatory attack would resolve the crisis made pursuing them worthwhile, given the risks of initiating hostilities against Soviet forces in Cuba. This is a fundamental reason why preemptive attacks are generally so uncommon in international politics.

---

[41] This was also true in the case of the U.S.-Albanian raids against Islamist militant groups in Tirana discussed in Appendix C. The idea that anticipatory attack can ever be an easy choice may appear strange, and in practice it rarely if ever appears to be so. However, the factors that make striking first difficult for leaders to embrace, notably fears of political fallout, are incorporated into the first-strike advantage variable as it is used here.

[42] Reiter (1995).

Figure 2.2
Anticipatory Attack Against Relatively Certain
Threats

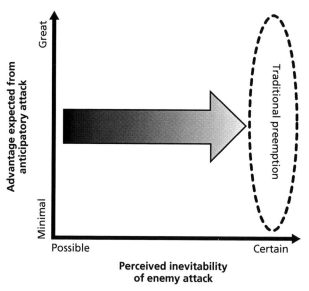

RAND *MG403-2.2*

The second class of difficult cases arises when states possess large first-strike advantages, but are substantially less than certain about when, or even whether, they will be attacked by the threat (Figure 2.3). Such conditions are common when preventive war is under consideration since, as noted above, more distant threats tend to be less certain unless one holds a very deterministic view of the origins and incidence of international conflict. When it is uncertain that an enemy attack is inevitable and the costs of being attacked are limited, foregoing an opportunity for anticipatory attack in order to avoid the risk of starting a war that might have been avoided is commonplace. However, when the first-strike advantage is great, anticipatory attack may become attractive even against a threat that is quite uncertain.

This type of situation looms large in the security environment currently facing the United States, particularly when a threat of nuclear attack or the possibility of nuclear weapons being acquired by terrorists is involved. In such cases, the costs of not acting to prevent the

Figure 2.3
Anticipatory Attack Against Severe but Uncertain Threats

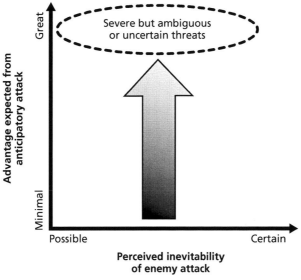

RAND *MG403-2.3*

development or acquisition of nuclear weapons by an adversary that will be difficult to deter may be extremely high, while preventive attack may promise a far better outcome—provided that it can produce decisive results, eliminating (or substantially delaying) the threat rather than merely reducing it. This was essentially the situation that Israel faced with respect to the nascent Iraqi nuclear threat in 1980–1981: Although it was not certain that deterrence would fail to avert an Iraqi nuclear attack, the costs of this occurring would be extremely high, and the Israeli government finally opted for preventive attack. Twenty-four years later, the United States also launched a preventive attack against Iraq; in this case, the probability and severity of the threat were both probably lower (as, it turned out, was the quality of the intelligence that motivated the war), and the United States did not face a closing window of opportunity as the Israelis had, but the attack promised a permanent solution to the problem and the secondary benefits of the invasion initially appeared to be considerable.

In the future, cases of this sort—characterized by considerable first-strike advantage, but also by substantial uncertainty about the inevitability of the threat—will likely continue to dominate the anticipatory attack policy agenda, presenting U.S. leaders with difficult decisions to make. Rallying international and domestic support for preventive attacks to deal with threats that are neither imminent nor certain tends to be intrinsically difficult, and their political costs can be high. (Of course, how serious these challenges are depends on the scale of the first strike, since small-scale operations incite less opposition and require less support than do major wars, and in some cases may be conducted covertly.) This is due in part, but only in part, to the problem of offering justification for preventive attacks that is consistent with international law; the next chapter discusses efforts to modify the relevant legal standards.

CHAPTER THREE

Attacking in Self-Defense: Legality and Legitimacy of Striking First

The United States' View of Anticipatory Attack

In the months following the September 11, 2001, terrorist attacks, U.S. leaders' statements about their inclination to launch anticipatory attacks in response to security threats greatly intensified debates about the legality and legitimacy of using force against adversaries who have not yet initiated hostilities. This chapter examines these issues, not only because of their intrinsic importance, but also to better understand the circumstances under which leaders are more or less likely to opt for preemptive or preventive attack, since the legal and political interpretations of such strategies are an important factor in estimating their costs and benefits.

The United States has not made clear what specific criteria must be met before it will conduct an anticipatory attack, and this ambiguity is no accident. Announcing specific conditions under which a first strike definitely would or would not be carried out would constrain the conduct of policy, and might be exploited by opponents—it is for the latter reason that military rules of engagement are routinely classified. Such deliberate ambiguity about the precise circumstances under which the United States will employ force is consistent with long-held policy, as in President George H. W. Bush's 1993 statement:

> I know that many people would like to find some formula, some easy formula to apply, to tell us with precision when and where to intervene with force. Anyone looking for scientific certitude is in for a disappointment. In the complex new world we are enter-

ing, there can be no single or simple set of fixed rules for using force. . . . To adopt rigid criteria would guarantee mistakes involving American interests and American lives. And it would give would-be troublemakers a blueprint for determining their own actions.[1]

Examining President George W. Bush's speeches after September 11, 2001, and the 2002 National Security Strategy sheds some light on the question of when U.S. leaders expect to engage in an anticipatory attack. In the 2002 State of the Union address, President Bush said,

I will not wait on events, while dangers gather. I will not stand by, as peril draws closer and closer. The United States of America will not permit the world's most dangerous regimes to threaten us with the world's most destructive weapons.[2]

Speaking to the graduating class at West Point the following summer, the President declared that containment and deterrence will not work against "terrorist networks . . . and unbalanced dictators with weapons of mass destruction. . . . If we wait for threats to fully materialize, we will have waited too long."[3] In emphasizing the goal of preventing threats from forming, not merely attacking to stop dangerous capabilities from being used, both of these statements indicate the willingness to conduct preventive as well as preemptive attacks.[4]

The National Security Strategy explains the U.S. justification for striking first, and the circumstances in which it would be appropriate,

---

[1] George H. W. Bush, "Remarks at the United States Military Academy at West Point, New York," West Point, N.Y.: January 5, 1993.

[2] White House, "President Delivers State of the Union Address: The President's State of the Union Address, The United States Capitol, Washington, D.C.," Washington, D.C.: The White House, 2002c.

[3] White House (2002a).

[4] This stands in contrast to the statements of previous generations of U.S. leaders, most notably the framers of NSC-68, who expressed willingness to launch a preemptive attack against the Soviet Union but ruled out preventive war on the grounds that "[i]t goes without saying that the idea of 'preventive' war . . . is generally unacceptable to Americans." See Appendix A.

in slightly greater detail, emphasizing the difficulty of defense against terrorist threats:

> Given the goals of rogue states and terrorists, the United States can no longer solely rely on a reactive posture as we have in the past. The inability to deter a potential attacker, the immediacy of today's threats, and the magnitude of potential harm that could be caused by our adversaries' choice of weapons, do not permit that option. We cannot let our enemies strike first. . . . The greater the threat, the greater is the risk of inaction—and the more compelling the case for taking anticipatory action to defend ourselves, even if uncertainty remains as to the time and place of the enemy's attack. To forestall or prevent such hostile acts by our adversaries, the United States will, if necessary, act preemptively.[5]

Together these statements sharpen the picture of the U.S. conception of anticipatory attack and the circumstances under which it would be appropriate. The list of potential targets, at least in the declaratory policy, is limited to terrorists and to "rogue states," "dangerous regimes," or "unbalanced dictators" who possess or may acquire "weapons of mass destruction." The National Security Strategy draws a positive correlation between the risk of inaction and the willingness to conduct an anticipatory attack. It makes clear that the existence of uncertainty as to the time and place of an attack against the United States will not be a barrier to striking first.

The National Security Strategy recognizes that preemptive attack is firmly grounded in international law. "For centuries, international law recognized that nations need not suffer an attack before they can lawfully take action to defend themselves against forces that present an imminent danger of attack."[6] Commentators on international law typically opined that for such an attack to be legal, there must be an imminent threat, "most often a visible mobilization of armies, navies, and air forces preparing to attack."[7]

---

[5]   George W. Bush (2002a, p. 15).

[6]   George W. Bush (2002a, p. 15).

[7]   George W. Bush (2002a, p. 15).

However, the National Security Strategy argues that these criteria, which are the indicia of an attack by a state using conventional means, are inapplicable to threats that employ methods and weapons that can be "easily concealed, delivered covertly, and used without warning."[8] In arguing for the permissibility of striking first in situations that do not fit the traditional notion of "imminent threat," the National Security Strategy declares, "We must adapt the concept of imminent threat to the capabilities and objectives of today's adversaries."[9] In other words, the United States is claiming that anticipatory attack must now be legal in circumstances that do not literally constitute an imminent threat.

The substance of the argument becomes clearer when viewed in the context of other public pronouncements by administration officials. In speaking about the "emerging consensus" regarding the limits of state sovereignty, Richard Haass, Director of Policy Planning for the Department of State, announced:

> Quite simply, countries have the right to take action to protect their citizens against those states that abet, support, or harbor international terrorists, or are incapable of controlling terrorists operating from their territory. . . . [In addition], states risk forfeiting their sovereignty when they take steps that represent a clear threat to global security. When certain regimes with a history of aggression and support for terrorism pursue weapons of mass destruction, thereby endangering the international community, they jeopardize their sovereign immunity from intervention —including anticipatory action to destroy this developing capability.

> The right to self-defense—including the right to take "pre-emptive" action against a clear and imminent threat—has long been recognized in international law and practice. The challenge today

---

[8]   George W. Bush (2002a, p. 15).

[9]   George W. Bush (2002a, p. 15).

is to adapt the principle of self-defense to the unique dangers posed by the proliferation of weapons of mass destruction.[10]

Haass argues that the issue is not one of changing the concept of imminent threat itself, but adapting the legal principle of self-defense so that it applies to situations that do not involve an imminent threat. The question that follows is whether international law allows adapting the principle of self-defense in such a way that the resulting legal standard would be consistent with the United States' conception of the circumstances under which striking first is appropriate.

A subsidiary question is whether the law even matters. That is, if international law does not allow such an adaptation, will that affect the policy decisions of the United States or otherwise affect the United States negatively? This chapter concludes that, first, international law is sufficiently ambiguous that it may permit the above adaptation of the legal standard of self-defense. Second, even if the law does not permit the degree of adaptation required for a particular action to be considered legal, depending on the nature of the threat and the fealty a particular administration pays to international law, legal considerations may not prevent the United States from striking first. However, the perceived illegality of an action affects perceptions of its legitimacy, and that may affect the success of the action through its influence on other nations either as a help or a hindrance. Moreover, even though the perceived illegality of an action alone may not bar that action, striking first when that attack is believed to be illegitimate will entail costs, even if they are difficult to measure, and this may influence the United States to forego launching such anticipatory attacks.

---

[10] Richard N. Haass, "Sovereignty: Existing Rights, Evolving Responsibilities: Remarks to the School of Foreign Service and the Mortara Center for International Studies, Georgetown University, Washington, D.C., January 14, 2003," Washington, D.C.: U.S. Department of State, 2003.

International Law

International law bears little resemblance to domestic law. There exists "no international legislature to make it, no international executive to enforce, and no effective international judiciary to develop it or resolve disputes about it."[11] International law is instead based on consent. Nations voluntarily subject themselves to the laws under which they live. They do this through two mechanisms: by signing international agreements, and by acting in a manner that becomes custom.[12]

The formation of customary international law requires more than states merely following a certain course of conduct. It also requires that states follow that course of conduct in the belief that such practice is required by law. Thus, customary international law has two distinct elements: (1) the general practice of states and (2) states' acceptance that this general practice is compelled by law.[13] These requirements raise several questions. What constitutes state practice? How much practice is required, and how many states are required to take part in it? Are the practices of every state given the same weight or do they differ in their importance? What type of dissent from the custom is required such that the custom will not bind a dissenting state? While some authoritative writings shed light on these issues,[14] there are few concrete answers. Thus, customary international law is often ambiguous and subject to conflicting interpretations.

In determining whether a principle has become international law, consideration is given to the rulings of international tribunals and to the writings of scholars. The effect of these sources on international law differs from their effect on domestic law. Specifically, the international

---

[11] Louis Henkin, Oscar Schachter, Richard C. Pugh, and Hans Smit, eds., *International Law: Cases and Materials*, 3rd ed., St. Paul, Minn.: West Pub. Co., 1993.

[12] American Law Institute, *Restatement of the Law, the Foreign Relations Law of the United States*, St. Paul, Minn.: American Law Institute Publishers, 1987, section 102.

[13] American Law Institute (1987, section 102).

[14] For example:

> "Practice of states" . . . includes diplomatic acts and instructions as well as public measures and other governmental acts and official statements of policy, whether they are unilateral or undertaken in cooperation with other states. . . . Inaction may constitute

legal system views the rulings of tribunals less authoritatively than does the domestic legal system. The rules and principles espoused by an American court in reaching its decision become binding precedent in its jurisdiction—in short, these rules and principles become the law. In the international legal system, court opinions are viewed as evidence of what the law is, but the rules they state are not themselves the law.[15] Generally, substantial weight is accorded to these opinions, but the specific degree of weight often depends on several factors, including the unanimity of the tribunal and the political contentiousness of the underlying issue.[16] In contrast, adjudging international law relies more heavily on the opinions of scholars as to what the law is than does adjudging domestic law.[17]

---

state practice, as when a state acquiesces in acts of another state that affect its legal rights. The practice necessary to create customary law may be of comparatively short duration, but . . . it must be "general and consistent." A practice can be general even if it is not universally followed; there is no precise formula to indicate how widespread a practice must be, but it should reflect wide acceptance among the states particularly involved in the relevant activity. Failure of a significant number of important states to adopt a practice can prevent a principle from becoming general customary law though it might become "particular customary law" for the participating states. A principle of customary law is not binding on a state that declares its dissent from the principle during its development. (American Law Institute, 1987, section 102, comment b)

See also Michael Byers, "The Shifting Foundations of International Law: A Decade of Forceful Measures Against Iraq," *European Journal of International Law*, Vol. 13, 2002, pp. 21–41; and Anthony D'Amato, "Trashing Customary International Law," *The American Journal of International Law*, Vol. 81, No. 1, 1987, pp. 101–105, explaining the formation of customary international law, particularly how treaties contribute to custom, in critiquing the International Court of Justice's decision in Nicaragua v. United States.

[15] American Law Institute (1987, section 103); Henkin et al. (1993, pp. 119–123).

[16] For example, in commenting on the weight given to decisions of the International Court of Justice, one scholar noted that such decisions are "generally accepted as the 'imprimatur of jural quality' when the Court speaks with one voice or with the support of most judges. However judgments and advisory opinions by a significantly divided court have diminished authority. This is especially true when the issues are perceived as highly political and the judges seem to reflect the positions of the states from which they come" (Henkin et al., 1993, p. 120).

[17] American Law Institute (1987, section 103); Rebecca M. M. Wallace, *International Law: A Student Introduction*, 3rd ed., London: Sweet and Maxwell, 1997, pp. 27–28; Henkin et al. (1993, pp. 123–125).

With the exception of treaties, the sources of international law allow for, and indeed create, considerable uncertainty as to precisely what obligations, rights, and actions international law imposes, permits, and proscribes. This is especially true for issues heavily intertwined with international politics, such as whether and under what circumstances it is legal for a nation to use force without first being attacked. What custom may be gleaned from the practice of states is often unclear. There exist few international tribunal decisions that reflect on the legal use of force.[18] Scholarly writings on the legality of the right to engage in anticipatory attack differ wildly. On highly political matters, it is often difficult to discern advocacy about what the law should be from analysis about what the law is. The result is that while international law is often unclear, it is especially unclear regarding the matter of whether, and under what circumstances, it is proper to engage in an anticipatory attack.

Legal Use of Force

Through the United Nations (U.N.) Charter, international law mandates that states refrain from using or threatening force. According to Article 2(4), "All Members shall refrain in their international relations from the threat or use of force against the territorial integrity or political independence of any state, or in any other manner inconsistent with the Purposes of the United Nations."[19] As a U.N. member state, the United States is bound by this prohibition. In addition, the prohibition likely has become a principle of customary international law, which

---

[18] The tribunal opinion that most directly confronts the propriety of resorting to force without having been attacked is International Court of Justice, *Military and Paramilitary Activities in and Against Nicaragua (Nicaragua v. United States)*, International Court of Justice, 1986. However, Nicaragua v. United States is of questionable authority due to the lack of unanimity among the judges, the forceful dissenting opinions, and the highly political issue involved. See D'Amato (1987).

[19] United Nations, *Charter of the United Nations*, San Francisco: United Nations, 1945, article 2(4).

binds nonmember states as well.[20] Therefore, the legality of any use of force depends on whether exceptions to the prohibition apply. Two such exceptions could potentially permit the United States to launch an anticipatory attack: force authorized by the U.N. Security Council, and use of force in self-defense.[21]

Force Authorized by the Security Council

The United Nations Charter provides a procedure for the Security Council to authorize the use of force. First, the Security Council must determine that there exists a threat to the peace, a breach of the peace, or an act of aggression. Second, the Security Council will recommend or decide what action to take to maintain or restore international peace and security. The Security Council will first consider non-forceful measures, such as sanctions, but if the Security Council determines that such measures have been or will be inadequate to remedy the situation, it may authorize the use of force.[22]

Through this procedure, the U.N. Charter implicitly grants the Security Council the right to authorize an anticipatory attack: It per-

---

[20] International Court of Justice (1986, p. 14, paragraph 188); L. Oppenheim, Robert Y. Jennings, and Arthur Watts, eds., *Oppenheim's International Law*, 9th ed., London: Longmans, 1992, pp. 7–8, citing the International Law Commission in its draft Articles on the Law of Treaties for the principle that the prohibition on the use of force is a rule of ius cogens, which are norms recognized by the international community as peremptory and permit no derogation.

[21] Other doctrines may exist to permit the use force—such as humanitarian intervention—but they are not relevant to the current discussion and their legal standing is uncertain. See, for example, Jianming Shen, "The Non-Intervention Principle and Humanitarian Interventions Under International Law," *International Legal Theory*, Vol. 7, 2001, pp. 1–32 ("the concept of humanitarian intervention has no actual legal basis in international law" and can only be exercised as collective intervention authorized by the Security Council, p. 16); Amy Eckert, "The Non-Intervention Principle and International Humanitarian Interventions," *International Legal Theory*, Vol. 7, 2001, pp. 49–58 (where sufficient cause exists, humanitarian intervention may be exercised by the U.N., regional organizations, ad hoc coalitions of states, and even single states); and Louis Henkin, "Kosovo and the Law of 'Humanitarian Intervention,'" *The American Journal of International Law*, Vol. 93, No. 4, 1999, pp. 824–828 (claiming that unilateral intervention by military force by a state or group of states is unlawful but recognizing the arguments of scholars who feel otherwise).

[22] United Nations (1945, articles 39, 41, and 42).

mits the Security Council to authorize force in response to a threat to the peace where there has not yet been a breach of the peace or an act of aggression. In addition, the Security Council can authorize force to *maintain* peace and security. If peace and security are to be maintained, as opposed to restored, then peace has not yet been breached.

In practice, the Security Council is extremely unlikely ever to authorize an anticipatory attack. Indeed, there have been few cases in which it has approved uses of force on a large scale under any circumstances— the U.N. defense of South Korea in 1950 being a rare exception—not least because doing so requires the consent or at least the acquiescence of the five permanent members of the Council.[23] Assembling the required consensus to approve a preventive war is intrinsically difficult, as the deliberations about attacking Iraq in 2002–2003 illustrated. Additionally, even if the necessary support could be assembled to endorse a preemptive attack, it is difficult to imagine the Security Council acting with the speed that preemption would require.

Self-Defense

A more practically relevant exception to the legal prohibition on the use of force is self-defense. The U.N. Charter allows for self-defense under Article 51, which provides that "[n]othing in the present Charter shall impair the inherent right of individual or collective self-defence if an armed attack occurs against a Member of the United Nations."[24]

Significant debate exists as to whether nations may act in self-defense in anticipation of an attack ("anticipatory self-defense"), or

---

[23] The Security Council authorized states to use force against North Korea in 1950 and Iraq in 1990, and to use force in Somalia in 1992, the former Yugoslavia in 1992 (the Security Council extended its original authorization to Bosnian safe areas in 1993 and Croatia in 1994), Haiti in 1994, Albania in 1997, East Timor in 1999, and Liberia in 2003 (Christine D. Gray, *International Law and the Use of Force*, Oxford and New York: Oxford University Press, 2000; Thomas M. Franck, "When, If Ever, May States Deploy Military Force Without Prior Security Council Authorization?" *Washington University Journal of Law and Policy*, Vol. 5, 2001, pp. 51–68, pp. 53–57). This list does not include U.N. peacekeeping missions the Security Council authorized after a military action had concluded. For example, the Security Council authorized peacekeeping in Kosovo but did not authorize NATO's military action in Kosovo.

[24] United Nations (1945).

whether nations must wait to be attacked before acting.[25] Prior to the implementation of the U.N. Charter, customary international law included a right to anticipatory self-defense; however, Article 51 specifically cites only an "armed attack," not an anticipated attack, as the condition for acting in self-defense. "On one reading this means that self-defense is limited to cases of armed attack. An alternative reading holds that since the article is silent as to the right of self-defense under customary law (which goes beyond cases of armed attack), it should not be construed by implication to eliminate that right."[26] Commentators do not agree even on what the majority view is: Most hold that the customary right to anticipatory self-defense survived the U.N. Charter, while others claim that the majority view is that the U.N. Charter foreclosed the right. In spite of this dispute, it appears that the majority view is that there still exists a right to anticipatory self-defense, and this view is informed by extensive state practice of acting according to such a claimed right.

The criteria for self-defense, anticipatory or otherwise, emanate from the *Caroline* case, which involved the Mackenzie Rebellion against British rule in Canada. The *Caroline* was a small steamer used by insurgents who were operating from U.S. soil. On December 29, 1837, the *Caroline* was moored on the American side of the Niagara River with 33 American citizens aboard. British forces boarded the *Caroline*, attacked the occupants, set the vessel ablaze, and sent it over Niagara Falls. Several of the *Caroline*'s occupants were injured, one was killed on the dock, and only 21 of the 33 were ever accounted for.[27] The United States protested the British action as a violation of its sovereignty and the British claimed that it was a valid exercise of self-defense. In the ensuing exchange of letters between Secretary of State Daniel Webster and British Foreign Minister Lord Ashburton, Webster claimed that, to be just, self-defense should be limited to cases

---

[25] The existence of a legal right to anticipatory self-defense, attacking before being attacked, is critical as it is the legal basis for the doctrine of anticipatory attack.

[26] Oscar Schachter, "The Rights of States to Use Armed Force," *Michigan Law Review*, Vol. 82, 1984, pp. 1620–1646, p. 1633.

[27] Henkin et al. (1993, p. 872).

in which the "necessity of self-defence is instant, overwhelming, and leaving no choice of means, and no moment of deliberation."[28] Webster also argued that any act taken in self-defense must not be "unreasonable or excessive" and must be limited by, and kept within, the necessity that justifies the self-defense.[29]

The criteria Webster stated for the lawful use of self-defense have been reduced to necessity and proportionality, and these have gained almost universal acceptance as customary international law.[30] However, standards regarding these criteria are subject to wildly divergent interpretations.

Proportionality

Assessing proportionality is inconsequential for determining *whether* resorting to force in self-defense is justified.[31] Rather, it is relevant for determining *what* actions may be taken in self-defense (whether anticipatory or not). For an act taken in self-defense to be "proportional," it must be "sufficiently related to the justifiable ends,"[32] which are to defeat an ongoing or future attack or eradicate a threat that has become actionable.[33] This restriction does not limit the magnitude, scope, or

---

[28] Daniel Webster, letter to British Foreign Minister Lord Ashburton, August 6, 1842, in U.S. Department of State, *Digest of International Law*, Washington, D.C.: U.S. Department of State, 1906, p. 412, in Louis Henkin, Oscar Schachter, Richard C. Pugh, and Hans Smit, eds., *International Law: Cases and Materials*, 3rd ed., St. Paul, Minn.: West Pub. Co., 1993, p. 872.

[29] Henkin et al. (1993, p. 872), quoting "Letter from Mr. Webster to Mr. Fox, April 24, 1841," *British and Foreign State Papers*, Vol. 29, 1857, pp. 1129–1139, p. 1138.

[30] See, e.g., Oscar Schachter, "In Defense of International Rules on the Use of Force," *University of Chicago Law Review*, Vol. 53, 1986, pp. 113–146, pp. 131–132. The principles of necessity and proportionality extend beyond self-defense and apply to all international uses of force.

[31] Judith Gail Gardam, "Proportionality and Force in International Law," *American Journal of International Law*, Vol. 87, No. 3, 1993, p. 404 ("at no time has much attention been paid to [the] requirements" of proportionality).

[32] Gardam (1993, p. 404).

[33] Michael N. Schmitt, "Preemptive Strategies in International Law," *Michigan Journal of International Law*, Vol. 24, 2003, pp. 513–548, p. 532.

targets of the action in self-defense to the magnitude of, scope of, or forces used in the attack that brought about the defensive action. For example, the magnitude and scope of Operation Enduring Freedom— involving tens of thousands of troops and the overthrow of a regime— exceeded the magnitude and scope of the attacks al Qaeda perpetrated on September 11, 2001. Nonetheless, the action of the United States was proportional because, to eradicate the threat posed by al Qaeda, which had become actionable, it was necessary to ensure that it would no longer have sanctuary in Afghanistan.

Similarly, the demands of proportionality permit the targets of a defensive action to be those other than the attacking forces. Again the issue is whether striking those targets is sufficiently related to the goal of defeating or deterring an attack or eradicating a threat. The 1991 Gulf War, which was one of collective self-defense, provides a useful example. There, the justifiable goal was, at a minimum, the removal of Iraqi forces from Kuwait.[34] Thus, the permissible targets were not limited to the Iraqi forces in Kuwait, but extended to targets such as infrastructure and other military forces that would bring about the Iraqi withdrawal from Kuwait.[35]

Necessity

The legality of resorting to force in self-defense depends on the criterion of necessity. When an attack is underway, the need to use force in self-defense is readily apparent. However, when an attack has not yet occurred, and a state wishes to act in anticipatory self-defense, necessity is more complicated.

At its simplest, necessity demands that no reasonable alternative to the use of force exists. Possible alternatives would include pursuing

---

[34] It could be argued that an additional justifiable goal was the assurance that Iraq would no longer have the ability to threaten international peace and security. U.N. Security Council Resolution 687 cited "the need to be assured of Iraq's peaceful intentions in light of its unlawful invasion and occupation of Kuwait" and made several disarmament demands to ensure that Iraq was no longer a threat to international peace (United Nations, *Resolution 687 (1991) of 3 April 1991*, S. C. Res. 687, 46th Sess., 1991).

[35] Of course, all targets must also be permissible targets under the law of armed conflict in order for attacking them to be legal.

diplomatic, judicial, economic, or other options short of using force, including referring the matter to the U.N. Security Council. Thus, force may not be used unless these options failed or would have failed to deter the anticipated threat. Another possible alternative to using force is to wait for conditions to change. Thus, there must be a need to use force at the time when force is employed.

Necessity, despite its nearly universal acceptance as a requirement for the use of anticipatory self-defense, is subject to widely diverging interpretations. The restrictionist view holds that the standard announced by Webster in the *Caroline* case applies.[36] There must be a necessity of self-defense that "is instant, overwhelming, and leaving no choice of means, and no moment of deliberation."[37]

This conception of necessity can be broken down into three separate elements. The first is the triggering event that invokes the right to self-defense. The second is the degree of likelihood that the triggering event will occur. The third is the temporal aspect of that triggering event. Most who hold the restrictionist view require all three elements to reach a high threshold in order to be met. The triggering event must be an armed attack. It must be certain that an attack will occur, or as

---

[36] A majority of international scholars who believe that there is a right to anticipatory self-defense adopt this view. See, for example, Oppenheim, Jennings, and Watts (1992, p. 420) ("The basic elements of the right of self-defence were aptly set out in connection with the *Caroline* incident in 1837 . . . "); Clive Parry and John P. Grant, eds., *Parry and Grant Encyclopaedic Dictionary of International Law*, New York: Oceana Publications, 1986, p. 361 ("Under customary international law, it is generally understood that the correspondence between the USA and UK of 24 April 1841, arising out of the *Caroline* Incident . . . expresses the rules on self-defense . . . "). Some commentators dispute the notion that principles of the *Caroline* case should be applied to all acts of self-defense. See Timothy Kearley, "Raising the Caroline," *Wisconsin International Law Journal*, Vol. 17, No. 2, 1999, pp. 325–346, pp. 329–330 (asserting that Webster "had no intention of creating any general rules for the use of force by a state in self-defense," but rather "directed his highly restricted conditions only to uses of force by one state within the territory of another state which had violated no international legal obligations to the first state that might have justified that first state's use of force"). Thus, under Kearley's interpretation, the restrictionist view applies only when the use of force was not precipitated by a breach of an international legal obligation.

[37] Webster (1842).

close to certain as one can be about an event that has not yet occurred. And the attack must be imminent.[38]

This restrictionist approach may have been warranted in 1837 when it was first proffered, and probably for many decades thereafter, but the tools of modern warfare and the nature of the current threat environment suggest that it has become archaic. The destructive power of today's weapons, together with modern means of delivery, make it possible to launch attacks that are debilitating, even decisive, with little or no warning, shortening or even eliminating altogether the time between when it is known that an attack is imminent (thus enabling the right of anticipatory self-defense under the restrictionist view) and when the attack occurs. Not only may missiles be on the way to a target before it is known that the attack is coming, but terrorists operating in secret may carry out attacks causing great destruction without warning, without them ever having become visibly imminent. These and other contemporary threats may be impossible to prevent after it becomes clear that they are imminent.[39]

The purpose of self-defense and anticipatory self-defense is to permit self-help to defeat, stop, or prevent an attack. Implicit in the legality of anticipatory self-defense is the recognition that the international community may not act effectively, if at all, to prevent an attack that has not yet occurred. Yet, modern weapons and methods can make anticipatory self-defense (self-help to prevent an attack) impossible if it must comport with the restrictionist view. To phrase it slightly

---

[38] It is important to note the difference between an action taken as anticipatory self-defense and an action taken in self defense as part of an ongoing conflict. Once a conflict begins, the issue of anticipatory self-defense becomes moot. Counterstrikes are acts of self-defense. In those cases, there is no issue as to whether some triggering event is imminent so that it justifies an attack. The attack will be legal if the conflict is ongoing, provided that it comports with the laws of armed conflict.

[39] Tensions between restrictive rules on the use of force and evolving military techniques and technology that make those rules anachronistic is not new. For example, at the time of World War I, the laws of war governing naval commerce raiding, such as requirements that merchant ships be warned of impending attacks, were incompatible with warfare using submarines that depended upon stealth for their effectiveness and survival. As in that case, when the law evolves too slowly to account for new realities, the law tends to be ignored until it evolves to better reflect reality.

differently, under the restrictionist view of self-defense, it would often be illegal to take any action that would prevent a future attack. For example, consider the September 11 attacks. It was not known with certainty or near certainty that those attacks would occur, let alone that they were imminent, until after they had concluded. Under the restrictionist view, the right of self-defense did not mature until after the attacks had been concluded, and there existed no point at which the purpose of self-defense could have been realized.[40]

Growing recognition of the inconsistency between the purpose of anticipatory self-defense and its legality under the restrictionist standard has led to calls for revising the legal standard for self-defense. For example, Haass notes:

> Traditionally, international lawyers have distinguished between pre-emption against an imminent threat, which they consider legitimate, and "preventive action" taken against a developing capability, which they regard as problematic. This conventional distinction has begun to break down, however. The deception practiced by rogue regimes has made it harder to discern either the capability or imminence of attack. It is also often difficult to interpret the intentions of certain states, forcing us to judge them against a backdrop of past aggressive behavior. Most fundamentally, the rise of catastrophic weapons means that the cost of underestimating these dangers is potentially enormous.[41]

Some international legal scholars, having noticed the inadequacy of the restrictionist view of anticipatory self-defense, have proffered alternative standards;[42] however, none of these has yet emerged as the primary minority view.

---

[40] Al Qaeda had carried out previous attacks against the United States, so that an attack against the group prior to September 11 (like the 1999 U.S. cruise missile attack against al Qaeda bases in Afghanistan) could be interpreted as simple rather than anticipatory self-defense. Note though that in none of the previous attacks—on the USS *Cole* or the U.S. embassies in Kenya and Tanzania—was there warning that an attack was imminent, either.

[41] See Haass (2003). Of course, the deception about which Haass complains is neither a new problem in international security, nor a behavior pattern peculiar to rogue states.

[42] These alternative standards all involve different conceptions of the criterion of necessity. They do not advocate a different standard for proportionality.

Alternative Standards for Anticipatory Self-Defense

To take one illustrative example, Michael Schmitt argues that the right to self-defense to respond to threats cannot be based on a strict application of restrictionist rules requiring certainty of an attack that is imminent. Instead, he argues, different situations should be treated differently and consideration must be given to all factors that affect the ability of a state to achieve the self-help purpose that underlies the right of self-defense.

Such factors include, but are not limited to, the strength of the state that would act in self-defense, the defensive options available, the threatened state's ability to counter an attack, and the attacker's timeline. As defensive options diminish or the likelihood of their success diminishes, the permissibility of anticipatory attack increases. Weak states should be permitted to act before strong ones would be when facing identical threats because weak states tend to have fewer options. Anticipatory attack against terrorists would be permissible before it would be against most states, and longer before any future attack, because the terrorists' tactics may present few defensive opportunities. In short,

> each situation presents a case-specific window of opportunity within which a State can foil an impending attack. Depending on the circumstances, the window may extend for some time, perhaps even to the moment of attack, or be very limited. . . . [T]he correct standard for evaluating a preemptive operation must be whether or not it occurred during the last possible window of opportunity in the face of an attack that was almost certainly going to occur.[43]

The restrictionist view requires certainty or near certainty that an attack will occur, and that this triggering event—the attack—be imminent. Schmitt's standard can be broken into the same three elements. Like the restrictionist view, Schmitt would require certainty or near certainty that an attack will occur and he would require that the triggering event be imminent. The difference lies in the triggering

---

43 Michael N. Schmitt (2003, pp. 534–536).

event itself. Whereas the restrictionist view requires that the anticipated attack itself be imminent, Schmitt believes the triggering event
to be any action or change that constitutes the closing of the "window
of opportunity within which a State can foil an impending attack."[44]
In other words, the triggering event would be the loss of the ability
to forestall a future attack, which might occur long before the attack
itself became imminent. Thus, under Schmitt's more permissive standard, Israel's 1981 preventive attack against the Osirak nuclear reactor
would be legal, assuming that Iraq would have attacked Israel once it
developed nuclear weapons, since the reactor was about to go on line
and the Israelis believed that bombing the facility after this point was
unacceptable due to the radioactive fallout that would be released.[45]

Notwithstanding that this approach is more expansive than the
restrictionist view, the standard Schmitt proffers is too restrictive to fit
the statements of the Bush administration regarding when anticipatory
attack may be appropriate. The differences relate to the two types of
threats that most concern the Bush administration, which are also the
two types of threats that most cause the restrictionist standard to be
insufficient: those posed by terrorism and by weapons of mass destruction (either in the hands of terrorists or rogue regimes).

In requiring certainty or near certainty of an attack and the imminent loss of the ability to forestall a future attack, Schmitt's standard
does not offer a solution to the lack of forewarning that is often charac-
teristic of terrorist attacks. Nor would it offer much advantage over the
restrictionist standard to a state facing the possibility of a catastrophic
surprise attack by nuclear or biological weapons. In both cases, a high
degree of knowledge about the adversary's intentions is required in
order to be nearly certain that the enemy attack will be launched and
to know when the last viable opportunity to prevent it has arrived, and
such precise information is frequently unavailable even to states with
highly sophisticated intelligence capabilities. Thus Schmitt may still
be setting an unrealistically demanding legal standard for anticipatory
attack.

---

[44] Michael N. Schmitt (2003, p. 534).

[45] See Appendix B for details of the Osirak case.

Some scholars argue that what is needed is not a new legal standard, but a different conception of the current restrictionist standard. Greg Travalio and John Altenburg acknowledge the virtual impossibility of locating the point at which a terrorist attack could be said to be imminent, or even of knowing that any particular attack will occur, but they dispute the contention that the restrictionist standard is unworkable with respect to terrorist organizations. Rather, they claim that the standard may be adapted to the nature and *modus operandi* of terrorists.

> [A] state may legitimately act on the assumption that, given the consistently demonstrated unconventional nature and operational methods of certain international terrorist organizations, an attack by such organizations is always "imminent." If a terrorist organization has committed prior attacks, or has explicitly or implicitly announced its intention to do so, then any future attack can be considered imminent for purposes of the [restrictionist] standard.[46]

This suggested adaptation would address the greatest weakness of the restrictionist view as it is currently understood. It would permit anticipatory attack without having to wait until it is known that an attack is imminent. However, this adaptation may be too limited in that it applies only to terrorist organizations, and in fact only to terrorists who have already launched at least one attack or indicated their intention to do so.[47] It could also be applied to rogue states, or any other adversary, that meet these criteria for altering the conception of imminence: (1) the adversary has demonstrated a willingness to use

---

[46] Greg Travalio and John Altenburg, "Terrorism, State Responsibility, and the Use of Military Force," *Chicago Journal of International Law*, Vol. 4, No. 1, 2003, pp. 97–120, p. 116.

[47] The adaptation is also problematic because it would equate to a new doctrine under which it would always be legal to launch anticipatory attacks against terrorists. The adaptation itself does not expressly authorize this, but it creates conditions—the prior commission of terrorist attacks or explicitly or implicitly expressing the intent to do so—that likely will be met by almost every terrorist organization. Such a doctrine of anticipatory counterterrorism may be advisable, but international law evolves slowly and does not typically welcome new legal doctrines that permit the use of force. Thus, Travalio and Altenburg's suggestion may not find much support among other international legal scholars.

unconventional weapons and operational methods, and (2) it has committed prior attacks, or explicitly or implicitly demonstrated an intention to do so.[48]

Most problematic for the Bush administration's conception of preemption is that few legal scholars agree that the weapons a potential adversary possesses or the degree of harm it may inflict is relevant in assessing whether the right to anticipatory self-defense has matured. In its various statements on the topic, administration officials, including the President, have specifically cited potential adversaries who possess or seek weapons of mass destruction as potential targets of anticipatory attack. Yet, few if any scholars have cited weapons of mass destruction or, more generally, the harm that a potential attacker state may inflict as a factor that should be considered in assessing the legality of anticipatory self-defense.[49]

Instead, most international legal scholars hold, although not explicitly, that in assessing whether a state is legally permitted to conduct an anticipatory attack, a situation involving a potential attacker using weapons of mass destruction capable of killing tens or hundreds of thousands of people is legally indistinguishable from a situation that involves a potential attacker who possesses only conventional weapons that would do far less damage. That is, regardless of the potential harm that may be inflicted, an anticipatory attack is permissible only if the other criteria are met. Under the restrictionist view (with or without the adaptation suggested by Travalio and Altenburg), this would require certain or near certain knowledge of an attack that is imminent. Under

---

[48] For example, in 2002–2003, the Bush administration argued that Saddam Hussein's use of chemical weapons against Iraqi Kurds in the 1980s indicated that he would use nuclear or biological weapons against other states if he possessed them (White House, "President Bush Outlines Iraqi Threat: Remarks by the President on Iraq, Cincinnati Museum Center, Cincinnati Union Terminal, Cincinnati, Ohio," Cincinnati, Ohio: The White House, 2002b).

[49] In criticizing the restrictionist approach, Schmitt writes of the right of self-defense being relative to the situation, which implies the need to consider all relevant factors. Schmitt also warns that the threat posed by weapons of mass destruction would cause self-defense miscalculations to have disastrous effects. Thus, it would seem that an important factor would be the degree of harm that would result if a potential attack were successful. Yet, Schmitt's standard does not consider the potential costs of inaction in assessing the right to conduct anticipatory attacks (see Michael N. Schmitt, 2003).

Schmitt's view, it would require certain or near certain knowledge of a future attack and an imminent loss of the ability to forestall it.

Two distinct arguments could be made that international law would permit considering the degree of harm a target state faces when assessing the right of anticipatory self-defense. First, considering the degree of harm would further the purpose of self-defense. If the underlying rationale of permitting states to attack before being attacked is to permit states to help themselves, then one of the reasons for doing so is to prevent harm to a target state. Given that, it would seem that the degree of harm that would result from an attack would be relevant in assessing whether a target state has the right to use force to prevent that attack. Second, whether a potential attacker possesses weapons of mass destruction is a factor in assessing a state's right to conduct an anticipatory attack against it because the international community views such weapons as having a significant role in threatening international peace and security.[50] Thus, the sovereignty of states that possess such weapons and engage in behavior reasonably viewed as threatening should be accorded less respect and be considered more violable than that of states that engage in similar behavior but do not possess such weapons.

The issue then becomes how the degree of harm that a potential target state faces should be included in the assessment of whether the right to anticipatory self-defense has matured. Several different methods could be proffered but those that are most likely to gain broad acceptance will build on what is believed to be the current law. For example, it could be argued that in assessing whether the right to anticipatory self-defense has matured, reference should still be made to a

---

[50] That the international community views weapons of mass destruction in this way is revealed through state practice as determined by broad participation in multinational conventions on the topic. There are several multinational conventions, most of which have extensive international participation, that recognize the threat posed by weapons of mass destruction and work to prevent their proliferation. The major three are the Convention on the Prohibition of the Development, Production and Stockpiling of Bacteriological (Biological) and Toxin Weapons and on Their Destruction, which has 146 state parties; the Convention on the Prohibition of the Development, Production, Stockpiling and Use of Chemical Weapons and on Their Destruction, which has 152 state parties; and the Treaty on the Non-Proliferation of Nuclear Weapons (NPT), which has 189 state parties.

set standard, such as the restrictionist view or Schmitt's more realistic variation of it, but that instead of requiring that a high threshold level for each criterion be met, as the degree of potential harm increases, the thresholds for the criteria should be lowered. For example, the restrictionist standard and Schmitt's variation require certainty or near certainty of a future attack. However, if a potential attacker possessed or was developing nuclear weapons, a greater degree of uncertainty might be permitted. Similarly, for the temporal element of the threshold event—the attack itself under the restrictionist approach and the loss of the ability to forestall the future attack under Schmitt's approach— imminence would not be required and something short of imminence would be acceptable.

Although such an approach would reflect current realities and be legally defensible, it has not been proffered either by international scholars or by states. Specifically, despite appearing to align with the current National Security Strategy and official statements as to when preemption may be employed, the United States has made no obvious attempt to argue that the above approach, or one similar, comports with current international law.

An alternative approach that more significantly departs from the current law was proffered by Michael Walzer in *Just and Unjust Wars* and may gain currency, primarily because of the prominence of the author and his work. As early as 1977, when *Just and Unjust Wars* was published, Walzer recognized the inadequacy of the restriction-

---

The argument proffered is not that a violation of one of these treaties should result, by itself, in the right to use force. First, some states are not parties to the treaties and the treaties themselves may not have become customary international law that binds those states. Thus, some states that act in contravention of the terms of one of the treaties may not be violating it. Second, several remedies for violating a treaty exist, and in many instances, even if all of those remedies prove unsuccessful, the treaty violation still will not justify the use of force. However, although the specific terms of the treaties do not bind all states, they do indicate that it has become customary international law that the proliferation of chemical, biological, and nuclear weapons threatens international peace and security and states that possess such weapons are more likely, all other things being equal, to be considered as threatening international peace and security. This argument would be strongest for states possessing biological weapons, which are proscribed altogether by the relevant treaty, and weakest for nuclear weapons, since the NPT explicitly accepts that some states will possess them, although it does call for their eventual elimination.

ist view's requirement of waiting for an attack to be imminent before responding.[51]

Walzer claimed that the trigger for using force anticipatorily should be whether the state that is the target of anticipatory self-defense had threatened the state acting against it. Under Walzer's view, the relevant criterion was not an imminent attack but rather a "sufficient threat." Walzer intended this admittedly subjective term to cover three criteria: (1) the threatening state manifests an intent to injure the attacking state, (2) there exists "a degree of active preparation that makes that intent a positive danger," and (3) the situation is such that "waiting or doing any other than fighting greatly magnifies the risk." Walzer summed up his formula thus: "States may use military force in the face of threats of war, whenever the failure to do so would seriously risk their territorial integrity or political independence," even in the absence of any immediate intent to attack.[52]

Walzer's three criteria can be evaluated as to how they comport with the requirement of necessity. Recall that necessity can be broken down into three separate elements: the triggering event that invokes the right to self-defense, the degree of likelihood that the triggering event will occur, and the temporal aspect of that triggering event. These elements align with Walzer's criteria.

For Walzer, the triggering event is a manifest intent to injure the state acting in self-defense. Instead of requiring merely a set degree of likelihood of that intent to injure, Walzer requires a form of its proof: "a degree of active participation that makes that intent a positive danger."[53] As for the third criterion of necessity, the temporal aspect of the triggering event, Walzer's first two criteria implicitly require that the threat, specifically the intent to injure, be present. Walzer's third criterion adds another temporal element: If the state waits to act in anticipatory self-defense, this will increase its risk.[54]

---

[51] Michael Walzer, *Just and Unjust Wars: A Moral Argument with Historical Illustrations*, 3rd ed., New York: Basic Books, 2000, pp. 74–85.

[52] Walzer (2000, p. 81).

[53] Walzer (2000, p. 81).

[54] Walzer (2000, p. 81).

Walzer's standard is unquestionably more permissive than the restrictionist standard and may be more permissive than even the alternative standards described previously. Walzer recognized this increased permissiveness, but he considered it necessary as "there are threats with which no nation can be expected to live," but with which the restrictionist view would require nations to live.[55]

Anticipatory Attack Against Nonstate Actors

The preceding discussion on the law of anticipatory self-defense does not distinguish between anticipatory attacks against states and those against nonstate actors. International law, however, accords significantly different treatment to states and nonstate actors. Historically, international law governed relations between states; it was not concerned with nonstate actors or individuals. Although international law unquestionably is broader today, many commentators argue that the law of self-defense and anticipatory self-defense applies only to interstate conflict. Under that view, states can still respond forcefully to terrorism, but the legality of their actions is governed by the law of domestic and international law enforcement.

The response of the international community to the events of September 11, 2001, made it clear that the law of self-defense (and by extension, anticipatory self-defense) applies to nonstate actors. The U.N. Security Council reacted immediately to the attacks. On September 12, it passed Resolution 1368, which labeled the attacks a "threat to international peace and security," and referred to the "inherent right of individual or collective self-defence in accordance with the [U.N.] Charter."[56] The Security Council also referred to self-defense in Resolutions 1373 and 1378, the latter of which was passed after Operation Enduring Freedom began against al Qaeda and the Taliban

---

[55] Walzer (2000, p. 85).

[56] United Nations, *Resolution 1368 (2001) Adopted by the Security Council at Its 4370th Meeting, on 12 September 2001*, S.C. Res. 1368, U.N. SCOR, 56th Sess., 4370th Mtg., U.N. Doc. S/RES/1368, 2001a.

in Afghanistan.[57] Through its references to Article 51, the self-defense provision of the U.N. Charter, it appears the Security Council was acting as if Article 51 applied to nonstate actors. Other international organizations acted similarly. NATO invoked Article V, the collective self-defense provision of its treaty, and the Organization of American States invoked the Rio Treaty's self-defense provision.

Individual states also acted as if the attacks implicated the right of self-defense. The pronouncements of international organizations were also pronouncements of their member states. A Security Council resolution requires an affirmative vote by at least nine of its members. NATO requires a consensus among all 19 of its members to invoke Article V. Other states acted similarly: Australia invoked the collective self-defense provision of the Security Treaty Between Australia, New Zealand, and the United States of America (the ANZUS Treaty).[58] The United Kingdom joined the United States in the initial attacks against al Qaeda and the Taliban. Australia, Canada, the Czech Republic, Germany, Italy, the Netherlands, New Zealand, and Turkey offered ground troops. Georgia, Oman, Pakistan, the Philippines, Qatar, Saudi Arabia, Tajikistan, Turkey, and Uzbekistan provided airspace and facilities. China, Egypt, and Russia announced approval of the action. Other states offered various other forms of support.[59]

Entering Other States to Attack Nonstate Actors

Although it seems clear that the law of self-defense applies to non-state actors, this raises another legal issue. Because nonstate actors by

---

[57] United Nations, *Resolution 1373 (2001) Adopted by the Security Council at Its 4385th Meeting, on 28 September 2001,* S.C. Res. 1373, U.S. SCOR, 56th Sess., 4385th Mtg. at 1, U.N. Doc. S/RES/1373, 2001b; United Nations, *Resolution 1378 (2001) Adopted by the Security Council at Its 4415th Meeting, on 14 November 2001,* S.C. Res. 1378, U.N. SCOR, 56th Sess., 4415th Mtg., U.N. Doc. S/RES/1378, 2001c.

[58] Australia, New Zealand, and the United States of America, *Security Treaty Between Australia, New Zealand, and the United States of America,* San Francisco, Calif., September 1, 1951.

[59] Nora Bensahel, *The Counterterror Coalitions: Cooperation with Europe, NATO, and the European Union,* Santa Monica, Calif.: RAND Corporation, MR-1746-AF, 2003, pp. 55–63.

definition do not have sovereignty over their own territory, attacking them necessarily involves entering or striking into the territory of a state, often without its consent. Even if a state would be legally justified in attacking a nonstate actor in anticipatory self-defense, it does not follow that it may cross into another state to do so.

The right of territorial integrity is both customary international law and treaty law under Article 2(4) of the U.N. Charter. Crossing into a third-party state without its consent violates that state's rights, and thus international law, unless it is justified. For such an action to be justified, the actions of the nonstate actor must be legally attributable to the third-party state, or else the third-party state must have violated some obligation to the state infringing on its territorial integrity.

If the acts of the nonstate actor may be legally attributed to the third-party state, the right of the target state to act in self-defense against the nonstate actor extends so that the target state may also act against the third-party state. The acts of nonstate actors can be attributed to a state only in limited circumstances: either the nonstate actors acted on behalf of, or as agents of, the state, or the state renders such active and regular assistance to the nonstate actors that the state becomes responsible for their actions.

If the third-party state does not consent to the intrusion and the acts of the nonstate actor are not attributable to it, whether the attacker may cross into the third-party state's territory to conduct operations against the nonstate actor depends upon whether the relationship between the nonstate actor and the third-party state falls into one of two categories. The first category includes relationships in which the state assists the nonstate actor, either actively or passively.[60] The second category consists of relationships in which states try, but fail, to prevent nonstate actors from operating in their territory. A review of the law reveals that potential target states very likely can cross into states to attack preemptively nonstate actors that fall into the first category, and probably can cross into states to attack preemptively nonstate actors that fall into the second category.

---

[60] Passive assistance includes acquiescing to the activities of nonstate actors or refraining from using due diligence to prevent them from operating in the state.

A state's obligation to refrain from assisting or acquiescing in terrorist activity has existed for some time. In 1970, the U.N. General Assembly passed Resolution 2625, which states:

> Every State has the duty to refrain from organizing, instigating, assisting or participating in acts of civil strife or terrorist acts in another State or acquiescing in organized activities within its territory directed towards the commission of such acts, when the acts referred to in the present paragraph involve a threat or use of force.[61]

In 1985, the U.N. General Assembly unanimously passed Resolution 40/61, which similarly appealed to states "to fulfill their obligations under international law to refrain from organizing, instigating, assisting, or participating in terrorist acts against other states, or acquiescing in activities within their territory directed towards the commission of such acts."[62] Although these General Assembly resolutions do not, by themselves, constitute statements of the law and are not binding, they are evidence of the attitudes and practices of states, and, as such, may be evidence of, or contribute to, customary international law.

Security Council resolutions, on the other hand, are binding upon member states. Thus, it is significant that in 1992 the Security Council stated:

> In accordance with Article 2, paragraph 4 of the Charter of the United Nations, every State has a duty to refrain from organizing, instigating, assisting or participating in terrorist acts in another State or acquiescing in organized activities within its ter-

---

[61] United Nations, *Declaration on Principles of International Law Concerning Friendly Relations and Cooperation Among States in Accordance with the Charter of the United Nations*, G.A. Res. 2625, U.N. GAOR, 25th Sess., Su No. 28, U.N. Doc. A/8018, 1970, p. 122.

[62] United Nations, *Measures to Prevent International Terrorism Which Endangers or Takes Innocent Human Lives or Jeopardizes Fundamental Freedoms and Study of the Underlying Causes of Those Forms of Terrorism and Acts of Violence Which Lie in Misery, Frustration, Grievance and Despair and Which Cause Some People to Sacrifice Human Lives, in an Attempt to Effect Radical Changes*, G.A. Res. 40/61, U.N. GAOR, 40th Sess., Su No. 53, U.N. Doc. A/40/53, 1985, p. 302.

ritory directed toward the commission of such acts, when such acts involve a threat or use of force.[63]

Through this pronouncement, the Security Council found that this requirement was inherent to the obligation all states have under Article 2(4) of the U.N. Charter to refrain from threatening or using force against other states.[64] The significance of this resolution cannot be overstated. By invoking Article 2(4), the resolution seems to hold that organizing, instigating, assisting, or participating in terrorist acts in another state or merely acquiescing in organized activities directed towards the commission of such acts, are the legal equivalent of the state itself conducting such acts. Not only would this likely permit a target state to cross into a third-party state that failed to fulfill this obligation in order to attack the terrorists in self-defense, it may also permit the target state to attack the third-party state itself.[65]

International law is less clear as to whether it is permissible to cross into a third-party state to attack terrorists defensively if the state tried, but failed, to prevent nonstate terrorists from operating in its territory. Until the events of September 11, 2001, the international community was mostly silent about states that fell into this category. It does not appear that international law had placed affirmative obligations on states to prevent the operations of terrorists, but had only placed prohibitive obligations upon states not to assist terrorists. Thus, if a state did not assist or acquiesce in terrorist activities, even if it failed to prevent such activities, it would not have violated its international obligations.

After September 11, the international community placed additional obligations upon member states. On September 28, 2001, the

---

[63] United Nations, *Resolution 748 (1992) of 31 March 1992*, S.C. Res. 748, U.N. SCOR, 47th Sess., 3063d Mtg., U.N. Doc. S/RES/748, 1992, p. 52.

[64] In 1998, the Security Council reaffirmed this obligation in the wake of the bombings of the U.S. embassies in Kenya and Tanzania (United Nations, *Resolution 1189 (1998)*, S.C. Res. 1189, U.N. SCOR, 52d Sess., 3915th Mtg. at 110, U.N. Doc. S/RES/1189, 1998a, p. 110.

[65] Of course, the permissibility of any defensive action is also contingent upon the maturation of the right to self-defense.

Security Council passed Resolution 1373, which, among other things, required all states to

> [r]efrain from providing any support, active or passive, to entities or persons involved in terrorist acts, including by suppressing recruitment of members of terrorist groups and eliminating the supply of weapons to terrorists; . . . [d]eny safe haven to those who finance, plan, support, or commit terrorist acts, or provide safe havens; . . . [and p]revent those who finance, plan, facilitate or commit terrorist acts from using their respective territories for those purposes against other States or their citizens.[66]

Resolution 1373 places substantial affirmative obligations upon states with respect to terrorists. It does not require merely that states use due diligence to suppress recruitment, eliminate the supply of weapons, deny safe haven, and prevent the use of their territory for terrorist purposes. Instead it requires that states actually accomplish them. A state that tries but fails to do so does not appear to meet the resolution's mandate, and, therefore, fails to fulfill its obligation. According to this interpretation, a state that tries but fails to prevent terrorists from operating within its territory does not insulate itself from the threatened state being legally permitted to cross into its territory to attack the terrorists in self-defense. However, although this interpretation appears to comport with the language of the resolution, the relative recency of these obligations and the dearth of similar pronouncements suggest that it may be premature to draw definite conclusions on this point.

The Significance of Legality

The preceding discussion concerned what international law allows. This section concerns a more fundamental issue: whether the law matters. That is, are questions about the legality of an anticipatory attack merely academic? Does a finding or a conclusion about the legality or

---

[66] United Nations (2001b, p. 1).

illegality of the use of force have any practical effect, either *ex ante* or *ex post*, on a state that considers it necessary to resort to force?

Michael Glennon argues that states no longer consider laws regulating the use of force to be obligatory:

> The international system has come to subsist in a parallel universe of two systems, one *de jure* the other *de facto*. The *de jure* system consists of illusory rules that would govern the use of force among states in a platonic world of forms, a world that does not exist. The *de facto* system consists of actual state practice in the real world, a world in which states weigh costs against benefits in regular disregard of the rules solemnly proclaimed in the all-but-ignored *de jure* system. The decaying *de jure* catechism is overly schematized and scholastic, disconnected from state behavior, and unrealistic in its aspirations for state conduct.[67]

Glennon's argument appears most valid when considering a situation in which a state faces a threat it considers dire. In such a case, a state facing such a threat will be concerned primarily with how best to ameliorate or eradicate the threat. Legality may not be ignored, but it will be, at best, a secondary consideration. A state is not likely to discard what it considers to be the best or most effective policy for responding to a dire threat because of questions about its legality. To the contrary, a state will likely choose its policy and then attempt to convince the international community of the legality of the chosen policy.[68]

A useful example of this is the Cuban missile crisis. In commenting about the discussions that produced the strategy and policy of the United States, Dean Acheson noted the irrelevance of legal considerations. "Judgment centered about the appraisal of dangers and risks, the

---

[67] Michael J. Glennon, "The Fog of Law: Self-Defense, Inherence, and Incoherence in Article 51 of the United Nations Charter," *Harvard Journal of Law and Public Publicy*, Vol. 25, No. 2, 2002, pp. 539–558, p. 540.

[68] That is not to say that the direness of a threat is binary and that international law is irrelevant when a threat is dire and relevant when it is not. The direness of a threat falls along a continuum, and is likely to be inversely proportional to the relevance of international law: The more dire the threat, the less concerned decisionmakers are likely to be about the political consequences of illegally attacking in order to avoid it, and the less dire a threat, the more likely decisionmakers are to be concerned with such consequences.

weighing of the need for decisive and effective actions against considerations of prudence; the need to do enough, against the consequence of doing too much."[69] Yet, despite the lack of consideration about the legality of the various options, once a policy was chosen, the United States publicly defended the legality of its policy.

The wisdom of a policy and its legality, despite being separate concepts, become inextricably intertwined. Evaluating an action's wisdom and legitimacy allows for four possible states: the action is both legal and good policy, illegal but good policy, legal but bad policy, or illegal and bad policy. It should be possible to argue that a use of force is wise but illegal or legal but unwise, yet this rarely happens. In particular, those who argue that a use of force is wise almost always claim that it is also legal. This leads to the impression that legal judgments follow, indeed derive from, policy judgments. If it is true that all uses of force believed to be wise are also claimed to be legal, then the law becomes irrelevant as a separate factor in decisionmaking and evaluating policies. Uses of force believed to be wise will be pursued (and their legality defended) and uses of force believed to be unwise will be abandoned.

Even if it were true that the law is irrelevant in deciding whether to use force, the use of force may have legal consequences if an international institution or tribunal later judges it to be illegal. In addition, perceptions of legality may have immediate practical consequences. As discussed below, perceptions of legality affect perceptions of legitimacy, and legitimacy has tangible effects. These may even affect the feasibility of the attack itself, since other states' decisions regarding the basing or transiting of equipment or personnel may be strongly influenced by the perceived legitimacy of the action.

Whether international institutions or tribunals can assess that a state used force illegally, and what the consequences of such a find-

---

[69] Henkin et al. (1993, p. 39 and note 3, quoting "Address Given at Amherst College," as reported in *The New York Times*, December 10, 1964). In an earlier address about the Cuban missile crisis, Acheson summed up the view of those who argue for the irrelevance of the law in stating, "The survival of states is not a matter of law" (Henkin et al., 1993, p. 40, quoting Dean Acheson, "Law and Conflict: Changing Patterns and Contemporary Challenges—Panel: Cuban Quarantine: Implications for the Future: Remarks," *American Society of International Law Proceedings*, Vol. 57, 1963, pp. 10–14, p. 14.

ing would be, depend on the specific state involved. Historically, the United States has remained free from most such judgments and free from any legal consequences of the rare adverse judgment rendered against it. There is a substantial probability, however, that this will not continue to be the case. Three international bodies have the power to declare that the United States used force illegally: the U.N. Security Council, the International Court of Justice (ICJ), and the recently established International Criminal Court (ICC), but of these only the ICC might reasonably be expected to do so.

The U.N. Security Council

The Security Council is authorized to find that a state has breached the peace and thereby violated Article 2(4) of the U.N. Charter, and to impose remedial action, such as sanctions or the use of force to counter that state's illegal use of force. It is exceedingly unlikely, however, that the Security Council will ever find that the United States used force illegally, for the United States can veto any Security Council resolution.

The International Court of Justice

The International Court of Justice may rule on the legality of the use of force, but only if the states that are parties to the dispute accept the court's jurisdiction. States may accept the ICJ's jurisdiction in one of three ways: They conclude a special agreement whereby they submit the particular controversy to the court; they are parties to a treaty that provides for the court to resolve disputes under the treaty; or both states have accepted the "optional clause," which declares that a state accepts the jurisdiction of the court as compulsory for a dispute with another state that has accepted the optional clause.

It is unlikely that any of the three avenues will enable the ICJ to rule on the legality of a use of force by the United States. First, the United States will probably not agree to have the court adjudicate a specific use of force. Second, the United States is not party to any treaty that would compel it to submit a dispute involving the use of force to the ICJ. Third, the United States no longer accepts jurisdiction under the optional clause, and is unlikely to do so in the near future.[70]

Even if the ICJ somehow held that it had jurisdiction over a dispute involving a U.S. use of force, the United States could refuse to comply with the court's ruling. The sole enforcement mechanism against a state that refuses to comply with a judgment of the ICJ is through the Security Council, and the United States could veto any attempt to enforce an ICJ ruling against it, although such a judgment might still entail significant political consequences.

The International Criminal Court

The International Criminal Court is a new entity,[71] and unlike the Security Council or the ICJ, it presents a real possibility of rendering and enforcing a judgment that the United States used force illegally. This possibility exists despite the fact that the ICC may take jurisdic-

---

[70] At the ICJ's inception, the United States filed with the court its declaration that it accepted the court's jurisdiction under the optional clause. On April 6, 1984, the United States attempted to exclude from this acceptance "disputes with any Central American State or arising out of or related to events in Central America." Days later, Nicaragua brought to the court a dispute against the United States. The ICJ, against the objection of the United States, ruled that it had jurisdiction. The United States withdrew from the litigation and revoked its acceptance of the court's jurisdiction under the optional clause. Despite this, the ICJ ruled on the merits and imposed judgment against the United States (Detlev F. Vagts, "Review: Going to Court, Internationally," *Michigan Law Review*, Vol. 87, No. 6, 1989, pp. 1712–1717).

[71] The ICC is a creation of the Rome Statute of the International Criminal Court (United Nations, *United Nations Diplomatic Conference of Plenipotentiaries on the Establishment of an International Criminal Court, Rome, Italy, 15 June–17 July 1998*, A/CONF.183/9, July 17, 1998b). The Rome Statute provided that it would become effective after 60 states had ratified it, a threshold that was crossed on April 11, 2002. Accordingly, on July 1, 2002, the ICC came into being. As of this writing, 139 states have signed and 100 states have ratified the Rome Statute (parties to the Rome Statute are listed at http://www.icc-cpi.int/statesparties. html as of October 17, 2005).

tion over individuals only, not states,[72] and that the United States is not a party to the ICC.[73]

To adjudicate a matter, the ICC, as is the case for any court, must have two types of jurisdiction: personal jurisdiction and subject matter jurisdiction. Personal jurisdiction refers to a court's power over the parties of a case. Subject matter jurisdiction refers to a court's power to adjudicate a particular type of case.

Personal Jurisdiction. The ICC has personal jurisdiction over individuals who meet any of three criteria. First, the court has jurisdiction over nationals of an ICC party state. Second, the court has jurisdiction over an act by any individual if that act was committed in a party state. Third, the court has jurisdiction over an act by any individual if the act was committed in a nonparty state and the nonparty state requests the court take jurisdiction of the matter.[74]

The ICC cannot take jurisdiction of U.S. nationals under the first criterion, as the United States is not a party state to the ICC; however, both the second and third criteria may grant the court such jurisdiction. If the United States attacks an ICC party state, the ICC would have jurisdiction over all acts involved in that action, and if the United States attacks a nonparty state, that state could request that the ICC take jurisdiction.

Subject Matter Jurisdiction. The ICC has subject matter jurisdiction over the following types of cases: genocide, crimes against humanity, war crimes, and aggression.[75] Genocide is defined as any of several specific acts when "committed with intent to destroy, in whole or in

---

[72] United Nations (1998b, Article 1).

[73] The United States signed, but did not ratify, the Rome Statute. On May 6, 2002, the United States announced that it did not intend to become a party to the treaty and would have no legal obligations arising from having signed the treaty (U.S. Department of State, "International Criminal Court: Letter to UN Secretary General Kofi Annan, Press Statement, Richard Boucher, Spokesman, Washington, D.C., May 6, 2002," Washington, D.C.: U.S. Department of State, 2002a).

[74] United Nations (1998b, Article 12).

[75] United Nations (1998b, Article 5[1]).

part, a national, ethnical, racial or religious group."[76] Crimes against humanity are "any of the following acts when committed as part of a widespread or systematic attack directed against any civilian population, with knowledge of the attack." The listed acts include but are not limited to murder, enslavement, deportation or forcible transfer of population, torture, rape and other forms of sexual violence, and "other inhumane acts of a similar character intentionally causing great suffering, or serious injury to body or to mental or physical health."[77]

War crimes is the most extensive of the categories within the ICC's jurisdiction; it contains 50 separate criminal acts.[78] Many are based on and use identical or very similar language as previous international conventions, such as the Geneva Conventions of August 12, 1949. Examples of these crimes include the willful killing, torture, or taking hostage of those who would be protected persons under the relevant Geneva Convention.[79] The Rome Statute claims that the remaining listed war crimes derive from "the established framework of international law."[80] Some of them do; however, several appear to be changed definitions of crimes that had been well established under international law or to be new crimes for which there is no consensus. At a minimum, many of the listed crimes proscribe acts that are not clearly criminal under current international law.[81]

The Rome Statute also includes the crime of aggression, which, of the ICC's proscribed acts, is the one most directly related to anticipa-

---

[76] United Nations (1998b, Article 6). The acts listed are "killing members of the group, causing serious bodily or mental harm to members of the group, deliberately inflicting on the group conditions of life calculated to bring about its physical destruction in whole or in part, imposing measures intended to prevent births within the group, [and] forcibly transferring children of the group to another group."

[77] United Nations (1998b, Article 7).

[78] United Nations (1998b, Article 8).

[79] United Nations (1998b, Article 8[2][a]).

[80] United Nations (1998b, Article 8[2][b]).

[81] See "Panel Discussion: Association of American Law Schools Panel on the International Criminal Court," *American Criminal Law Review*, Vol 36, No. 2, 1999, pp. 223–264, p. 233 (Professor Halberstam arguing that the Rome Statute alters well-established definitions of crimes, adds new crimes, and is being used for political purposes).

tory attack; however, the crime of aggression has not yet been defined, and thus, currently is outside the court's jurisdiction. Once a definition for the crime of aggression is adopted in accordance with the requirements of the Rome Statute, the court shall exercise jurisdiction over it.[82] Defining aggression faces several problems. First, aggression has never been defined in any multilateral treaty.[83] Second, no commonly accepted definition of aggression exists.[84] Third, aggression has historically been considered to be a crime of a state, not of an individual.[85] Fourth, the crime of aggression equates to finding that there has been an illegal breach of the peace. Under the U.N. Charter, the Security Council has the power to determine whether an act constitutes a breach of the peace, and there may be a reluctance to give that power to the ICC. Depending on the conditions by which the court could take jurisdiction over the crime of aggression, prosecutions could be brought without the Security Council having found that an anticipatory attack constituted a breach of the peace. Thus, the ICC could find that an attack was an illegal act and a breach of the peace even though the Security Council declined to do so.[86] In the face of these

---

[82] United Nations (1998b, Article 5[2]).

[83] United Nations, *Report of the International Law Commission on the Work of Its Forty-Sixth Session*, Draft Statute for an International Criminal Court, U.N. GAOR, 49th Sess., U.N. Doc. A/49/10, 1994, Supp. No. 10, p. 72, Article 20(b).

[84] David Stoelting, "Status Report on the International Criminal Court," *Hofstra Law and Policy Symposium*, Vol. 3, 1999, pp. 233–285, p. 265.

[85] Stoelting (1999, p. 265).

[86] The Rome Statute permits the Security Council to order the ICC, through a resolution adopted under Chapter VII of the U.N. Charter, to defer a prosecution or investigation for a 12-month period; but absent such a resolution, the ICC would be free to proceed (United Nations, 1998b, Article 16). It is unlikely that the Security Council would pass a resolution demanding the ICC defer investigating or prosecuting a U.S. national for participating in, or for acts arising from, an anticipatory attack. The crime of aggression has not been defined but it is likely that, under the definition that eventually emerges, acting with the authorization of the Security Council would preclude a prosecution for aggression. Thus, if the ICC were considering investigating and prosecuting an act of aggression, the action presumably would not have been preauthorized by the Security Council. If the Security Council did not pass a resolution authorizing the attack before it occurred, either because the United States did not seek

problems, a working group on defining aggression is attempting to find a solution.[87]

Broadly, there are two avenues by which an anticipatory attack could result in an ICC prosecution. First, given the uncertain legality of anticipatory attack, it could lead to claims that the civilian officials and military personnel involved in planning, ordering, authorizing, or participating in the attack committed the crime of aggression.[88] Second, a prosecution for genocide, crimes against humanity, or war crimes could be sought for acts committed during an anticipatory attack.[89] If there is a belief that the United States illegally attacked another state, because no prosecution for aggression can yet be maintained, the ICC may seek

---

one or because the Security Council declined to give one, it might well be unwilling to pass a related resolution after an attack. This is especially so given the questionable legality and unquestionable controversy of anticipatory attack. In general, nations on the Security Council have been reluctant to pass such resolutions, even though the only instances in which they have been sought have been for deferring prosecution emanating from U.N. peacekeeping operations (United Nations, *Security Council, Fifty-Eighth Year, 4772nd Meeting, Thursday, 12 June 2003, 10 a.m., New York*, U.N. Doc. S/PV.4772, 2003). In 2003, while passing the resolution, most representatives expressed concerns about voting in favor of the resolution. These included the representatives of France, who abstained in the voting, and the United Kingdom, who voted in favor of ordering the deferral (United Nations, 2003). Their concerns are particularly noteworthy because both nations are permanent members of the Security Council and have the power to veto any resolution. In 2004, despite U.S. efforts to acquire another Security Council resolution requiring the ICC to defer investigation and prosecutions emanating from U.N. peacekeeping operations, the Security Council refused to pass one.

[87] See Daryl A. Mundis, "The Assembly of States Parties and the Institutional Framework of the International Criminal Court," *American Journal of International Law*, Vol. 97, No. 1, 2003, pp. 132–146; Silvia A. Fernandez de Gurmendi, "The Working Group on Aggression at the Preparatory Commission for the International Criminal Court," *Fordham International Law Journal*, Vol. 25, No. 3, 2002, pp. 589–605.

[88] The proposals for defining aggression seemed to share the understanding that only the leading policymakers of a state could be criminally liable for the crime of aggression, but that understanding may be difficult to codify. In the United States, a multitude of individuals have a role in making policy and may be, in part, causally responsible for a particular policy that is eventually enacted. In addition, cleaving between those who make policy and those who execute policy is difficult (Fernandez de Gurmendi, 2002, pp. 598–599).

[89] Committing acts that constitute genocide, a crime against humanity, or a war crime, or that would otherwise violate the laws of war would be illegal under U.S. law. The crimes would not carry the labels genocide, war crimes, or crimes against humanity. Individuals

to prosecute U.S. nationals for one of the above crimes. This possibility is made more probable because the Rome Statute's list of war crimes and their accompanying definitions are sufficiently vague as to allow, and perhaps invite, prosecutions for behavior that is a common, albeit unfortunate, consequence of war.

Although a thorough account of the vagueness of the Rome Statute's crimes is beyond the scope of this discussion, the following example illustrates the potential problem. Article 8, paragraph 2(b)(iv) of the Rome Statute lists as a war crime

> [i]ntentionally launching an attack in the knowledge that such attack will cause incidental loss of life or injury to civilians or damage to civilian objects or widespread, long-term and severe damage to the natural environment which would be clearly excessive in relation to the concrete and direct overall military advantage anticipated.

Encompassed in this one crime are four separate crimes, based on the *jus in bellum* principle of proportionality in the Law of Armed Conflict.[90] For simplicity, only the first of the four will be addressed here:

> Intentionally launching an attack in the knowledge that such attack will cause incidental loss of life . . . to civilians which

---

who committed such acts could instead be liable for various crimes including, but not limited to, murder, torture, kidnapping, false imprisonment, or various violations of the Uniform Code of Military Justice. Any U.S. national who committed one of these would be subject to criminal prosecution in the United States or, in the case of military personnel, a court-martial.

If that occurred, the ICC would not take jurisdiction over the matter. The ICC's jurisdiction is complementary to national jurisdictions. If a state with jurisdiction over the matter prosecutes, or investigates and decides not to prosecute, then the ICC must defer to the state's jurisdiction. This rule, however, is subject to an exception that would permit the ICC to prosecute, discussed in the next subsection of this chapter.

[90] W. Hays Parks, "Air War and the Law of War," *Air Force Law Review*, Vol. 32, No. 1, 1990, pp. 1–226.

would be clearly excessive in relation to the concrete and direct overall military advantage anticipated.[91]

To better understand the crime, it is helpful to separate it into its individual elements.[92] First, the perpetrator launched an attack. Second, the attack was such that it would cause incidental death to civilians. Third, the perpetrator knew that the attack would cause incidental deaths to civilians. Fourth, the attack was such that the extent of the resulting civilian loss of life would be clearly excessive in relation to the concrete and direct overall military advantage anticipated. Fifth, the perpetrator knew that the civilian deaths would be of such an extent.[93] In warfare, a great number of attacks include the first, second, and third elements, for many attacks are launched with the knowledge that they will result in civilian casualties, and this is recognized in the laws of war. Whether such acts are criminal depends on the fourth and fifth elements.

The fourth element, whether the extent of the resultant death would be clearly excessive in relation to the concrete and direct overall military advantage anticipated, depends on valuations of the death caused by the attack and the military advantage anticipated, and whether the former was "clearly excessive" in relation to the latter. Judges who possess no military expertise will be making decisions about such matters, and they will be making these decisions far removed, in both time and location, from the battlefield and from the stresses in which decisions were made. These factors are likely to increase the probability that acts

---

[91] The construction of the four crimes assumes that "incidental" modifies each of the four harms: loss of civilian life, injury to civilians, damage to civilian objects, and environmental damage. The language of the provision may permit other constructions.

[92] The Assembly of State Parties of the ICC drafted elements of crimes to assist the court in interpreting the Rome Statute's provisions (United Nations, *Assembly of States Parties to the Rome Statute of the International Criminal Court, First Session, New York 3–10 September 2002 Official records*, ICC-ASP/1/3, 2002, p. 112). The elements described in the text are derived from those listed in United Nations (2002, p. 132).

[93] An example of the imprecision of the crime's definition is that the elements do not explicitly require that the attack actually resulted in civilian deaths. Although the elements could be interpreted in such a way so that they combine to require that civilian deaths occurred, they also allow for other interpretations.

that previously would have been considered lawful will be found to be criminal.

The fifth element requires that the defendant knew that the civilian deaths would be of a clearly excessive extent. This element may provide the defendant with some protection; however, precisely what the element requires is unclear. Under one interpretation, it requires that a defendant know the extent of the death that would result from an attack, and that the resultant death would be clearly excessive in relation to the military advantage anticipated. A defendant would not be criminally liable for having acted under a mistaken belief that the death resulting from an attack would be less extensive than it turned out to be or that such death would not be clearly excessive. Under this interpretation, a defendant's culpability depends entirely on his own value judgment. If the defendant did not consider the expected loss of life to be excessive, he could not be found guilty. The court's evaluation of the defendant's value judgment as to the excessive character of the death would be irrelevant.[94]

A different interpretation of the fifth element of this war crime would require only that a defendant know the extent of the death that would result from an attack. Whether the extent of the death was of an excessive character would be a legal issue decided by the court. Thus, a defendant would not be criminally liable if the defendant acted under a mistaken belief that the death resulting from an attack would be less extensive than it turned out to be, but a mistaken value judgment as to whether the death was clearly excessive would not preclude liability.

Which interpretation is correct is unclear. At least one scholar claims, with disappointment, that the Elements of Crimes mandates the first interpretation;[95] however, his interpretation may be incorrect. The Elements of Crimes explicitly state that the court is to evaluate the defendant's value judgment.[96] If the defendant's value judgment con-

---

[94] Michael Bothe, "War Crimes," in Antonio Cassese, Paola Gaeta, and John R. W. D. Jones, eds., *The Rome Statute of the International Criminal Court: A Commentary*, Oxford and New York: Oxford University Press, 2002, pp. 379–426, p. 400.

[95] Bothe (2002, p. 400).

[96] United Nations (2002, p. 132, note 37).

trolled, which the first interpretation mandates, then the court would have no cause to evaluate that value judgment. On the other hand, the second interpretation makes relevant the court's evaluation of the defendant's value judgment.[97] Thus, it appears that under the Elements of Crimes, the second interpretation is correct and the court's value judgment as to the excessive character of the attack should control the defendant's liability.

Regardless of the interpretation that should result from the Elements of Crimes, the court is free to disregard it. The Elements of Crimes are merely guidelines to assist the judge in interpreting the crimes listed in the Rome Statute.[98] Thus, the judges in the ICC have substantial authority and discretion in determining not only whether a given activity constituted a crime, but also what activity, in the abstract, could constitute a crime.[99] This single example using part of one of the crimes listed in the Rome Statute illustrates both the complexity of the issues surrounding the court and the breadth of the judges' authority.

Complementarity. The primary limit on the court's jurisdiction results from the Rome Statute's adoption of the principle of complementarity, which mandates that the ICC's jurisdiction is complementary to national jurisdictions. If a state with jurisdiction over the matter prosecutes, or investigates and decides not to prosecute, then the ICC must defer to the state's jurisdiction.[100]

---

[97] The court's evaluation of the defendant's value judgment is the equivalent of the court rendering its own value judgment, which the second interpretation requires.

[98] Rome Statute, art. 9; Mauro Politi, "Elements of Crimes," in Antonio Cassese, Paola Gaeta, and John R. W. D. Jones, eds., *The Rome Statute of the International Criminal Court: A Commentary*, Oxford and New York: Oxford University Press, 2002, p. 447 ("[T]he elements are meant to be used by the judges as simple guidelines in reaching determinations as to individual criminal responsibility.").

[99] This is in keeping with civil law jurisdictions. In the United States, for a defendant to be found guilty of a crime, every element of that crime must be proved beyond a reasonable doubt. In contrast, civil law jurisdictions do not break a single crime into separate elements. Rather, the standard for conviction is "the judge's intimate conviction of the defendant's guilt, based on the totality of the evidence presented" (Politi, 2002, p. 446).

[100] United Nations (1998b, Article 17).

However, this rule contains an exception that has the potential to swallow the rule. The ICC need not defer to a state's jurisdiction if the state is either "unwilling or unable genuinely" to investigate or prosecute.[101] The Rome Statute defines inability by whether the state's judicial system is operating (as opposed to it having collapsed).[102] In contrast, a state's unwillingness to prosecute entails a far more subjective inquiry. To determine unwillingness, the court will assess and consider whether the purpose of the state's judicial proceedings is to shield the individual from criminal liability, whether there has been an unjustifiable delay in the prosecution or investigation, and whether or not the proceedings were or are being conducted independently and impartially.

Thus, the ICC will decide whether a state's investigation into an alleged criminal act emanating from an anticipatory attack was sufficient to preclude the ICC from asserting its jurisdiction.[103] If the ICC finds the state's investigation wanting, for example by ruling that it was not conducted independently or impartially, then the ICC can take jurisdiction over the matter and the individuals involved.

Article 98 Agreements. The current administration has attempted to minimize the effect of the ICC on U.S. nationals by persuading states to sign "Article 98 agreements," which are bilateral agreements through which another state agrees to not cooperate with the ICC regarding a prosecution of a U.S. national. The Department of State reports that it has concluded at least 100 such agreements,[104] but their effect to date appears to be negligible. First, few powerful nations or nations of

---

[101] United Nations (1998b, Article 17).

[102] United Nations (1998b, Article 17[3]).

[103] United Nations (1998b, Article 17[1]).

[104] U.S. Department of State, "U.S. Signs 100th Article 98 Agreement, Press Statement, Richard Boucher, Spokesman, Washington, D.C., May 3, 2005," Washington, D.C.: U.S. Department of State, 2005c. However, the majority of these agreements have been with states that are not parties to the ICC.

strategic importance have signed.[105] Second, of those states that have signed agreements, few have ratified them—news reports indicate that only 31 states have done so, while 11 others have entered into executive agreements that do not require ratification—which leaves the bulk of the agreements ineffective.[106] Third, of the 99 state parties to the ICC, 53 have explicitly refused to sign Article 98 agreements. Fourth, the Article 98 agreements may not be enforceable under both the provisions of the ICC and the terms of the agreements themselves. Thus, states that have signed them may not be bound to refrain from cooperating with the ICC; at most, those states may have only deferred deciding whether they will cooperate until some later date. If and when the ICC seeks the cooperation of such a state in seizing U.S. nationals or otherwise cooperating in an investigation or prosecution, the state may decide that the Article 98 agreement is unenforceable, a decision that may be easier for it to make should the ICC first rule such agreements unenforceable.

Insularity. The opportunity to prosecute U.S. nationals for acts arising from an anticipatory attack is heightened by the court's insularity. The ICC is the sole arbiter of its jurisdiction and the sole arbiter of the propriety of its substantive legal decisions.[107] The court has an appeals process, but it is internal to the ICC. Thus, the ICC alone decides whether a crime was committed, what actions are sufficient to constitute a crime, and whether a state's actions were sufficient to invoke the principle of complementarity and preclude the court from exercising its jurisdiction over a matter.

---

[105]For example, Romania is the most consequential European state to sign an Article 98 agreement but has not ratified it; the European Union has consistently opposed such agreements.

[106]For these data, see Coalition for the International Criminal Court, "Status of U.S. Bilateral Immunity Agreements (BIAs)," 2005.

[107]Article 119(1) of the Rome Statute empowers the ICC alone to resolve all judicial decisions, including decisions relating to jurisdiction, the application of complementarity, and the actions that constitute a crime. Article 19(1) provides that the court should determine whether it has jurisdiction over a matter. Article 17(1) grants the court the power to determine whether the court should decline jurisdiction in accord with the principle of complementarity.

The breadth of the Rome Statute's provisions and its insularity grants the ICC sufficiently broad authority to permit the court to take jurisdiction over U.S. nationals and to rule on the legality of an anticipatory attack, or to otherwise judge as illegal acts arising from that attack. In addition, the ICC has sole authority to act in this area; its insularity ensures that its rulings cannot be appealed to any outside body.

Legitimacy

Even assuming Michael Glennon is correct that states are not primarily concerned with legality when forming policy—instead they choose policies they believe will best further the interests of the state and thus willfully act in contravention of the law[108]—it is demonstrably true that the law is relevant to decisions regarding the use of force. Were it otherwise, states would not be as concerned as they clearly are with asserting the legality of their actions—such concerns arise repeatedly in most of the case studies contained in this volume, and more recently legal justifications for the 2003 invasion of Iraq were energetically proffered by Washington and London in the run-up to that operation. A cynic might claim that being a member of the community of nations requires exhorting respect for the law even when acting in contravention of it. A more practical rationale is that claims of legality are made to achieve legitimacy, and legitimacy has tangible political benefits.

Legitimacy and legality are inextricably linked. The unquestioned legality of an action generally confers legitimacy upon it. Thus, an action is viewed as legitimate if it is expressly authorized (as opposed to implicitly authorized) by the Security Council or if the action was taken in self-defense to repel an ongoing attack. Conversely, actions that are of questionable legality will tend to be of questionable legitimacy as a result. Thus, the legitimacy of an action will inevitably be

---

[108]See Glennon (2002).

questioned when it is based on a claim of anticipatory self-defense[109] or another, less-certain legal justification.[110]

Although legality and legitimacy are linked, they have several important differences. First, legality is rules-based, which causes assessments about an action's legality to be static. The legality of an action is assessed based on whether the facts (that are reasonably believed to exist at the time of the action) justify force in accord with the rules then in existence. For example, the Security Council either authorized a measure or it did not, a state either was attacked or it was not, the facts as they appeared to exist at the time either justified a state to act in self-defense or they did not. Thus, at the time it was taken, the action either was legal or it was not, though different observers may arrive at divergent judgments about the question.

The subsequent discovery of new facts does not alter the legality of an action. An action considered to be legal because the facts that then existed indicated a threat that justified force will not later be considered illegal if it is discovered that the threat was not sufficient to justify the use of force. Conversely, an action considered to be illegal because the facts that then existed did not indicate a threat that justified force will not later be considered legal because it is subsequently discovered that the threat was sufficient to justify force. In contrast, perceptions of the legitimacy of an action often change over time, as new information comes to light or as standards of behavior change.

Because the existing legal standards regarding the use of force are very restrictive, such actions that are perceived to be legal will gener-

---

[109] Scholars disagree on the instances in which states claim anticipatory self-defense to defend their use of force. Compare, for example, Franck (2001, p. 59), providing several instances in which a state claimed it acted out of anticipatory self-defense, including the United States in imposing a naval quarantine on Cuba in 1962 and Israel in attacking Egypt, Jordan, and Syria in 1967, with Christine Gray (2000, pp. 112–113), arguing that a state rarely claims it acted out of anticipatory self-defense and, in particular, that neither the United States nor Israel claimed anticipatory self-defense to justify their actions against Cuba and Egypt, Jordan, and Syria, respectively.

[110] One such justification is that the Security Council implicitly authorized the use of force. See Jules Lobel and Michael Ratner, "Bypassing the Security Council: Ambiguous Authorizations to Use Force, Cease-Fires, and the Iraqi Inspection Regime," *American Journal of International Law*, Vol. 93, No. 1, 1999, pp. 124–154.

ally be considered legitimate as well, but attacks that are not legal by these criteria may also appear legitimate. In particular, an action may well be considered legitimate if it is perceived to be undertaken for a moral purpose even if the action does not strictly accord with the law. For example, the legality of the war in Kosovo was questionable and is still debated;[111] however, many observers viewed the action as being legitimate largely because the perceived purpose of the action was for humanitarian need.[112]

An action's consequences also relate differently to its legality and its legitimacy. The legality of an action is assessed independently of its consequences, but its legitimacy may be assessed from a consequentialist perspective. Thus, an action may be considered legitimate if it produces favored outcomes even if it is viewed as illegal. This consequentialist perspective is one of the factors that allow perceptions of legitimacy to evolve over time. For example, immediately after Israel's 1981 preventive attack against Iraq's nuclear program, the Security Council passed a resolution that "strongly condemn[ed] the military attack by Israel" and judged it to be "in clear violation of the Charter of the United Nations and the norms of international conduct."[113] The members of the Security Council, including the United States, unanimously agreed to the resolution, and it reflected the view of most international legal scholars.[114] In the wake of the Gulf War, however, which revealed an extensive Iraqi nuclear weapons program and increased estimates of

---

[111] The legality of the war in Kosovo has been defended on two separate bases, both of which are questionable: implied Security Council authorization and the doctrine of humanitarian authorization. See Christine Gray (2000, pp. 31–42, 193–95).

[112] It could also be argued that the action was viewed by many as being legitimate because it was conducted by NATO and not because of a perceived moral purpose. This misstates the causation. NATO conducted the action because its member states, among others, approved of the action, and the NATO states approved of the action because its perceived purpose was a moral one. Thus, the support of NATO, and many other nations, did not cause the action to be legitimate. Rather, the perceived moral purpose caused the NATO states to support the action and caused the action to be viewed as legitimate.

[113] United Nations, *Resolution 487 (1981) of 19 June 1981*, S.C. Res. 487, U.N. SCOR, 36th Sess., 228th Mtg., U.N. Doc. S/Res/487, 1981.

[114] Anthony D'Amato, "Israel's Air Strike Against the Osiraq Reactor: A Retrospective," *Temple International and Comparative Law Journal*, Vol. 10, 1996, pp. 259–264.

Saddam Hussein's aggressiveness, many adopted the view that "Israel did the world a great service" by destroying the Osirak reactor.[115] Thus, a decade after the strike, based on new information and the occurrence of new events, the strike's legitimacy increased.

Perhaps the most fundamental difference between legality and legitimacy is that the former is assessed by a relatively small community of specialists whereas the latter is a function of the perceptions of a variety of large and assorted audiences whose opinions have widely varying effects. Uses of force, including anticipatory attacks, are far more likely to be viewed as legitimate among the populations of the states that launch them than among those of the target state and its allies, for a variety of reasons ranging from political bias to being exposed to different portfolios of information about the action. Because it is an intrinsically political matter, governments and other leaders can deliberately shape perceptions of legitimacy, and usually work hard (although not always effectively) to do so. This task is complicated by the fact that, while different messages about an action may be useful for different audiences, it is rarely possible to communicate separately with each, and this is becoming progressively more difficult as sources of news and political opinion become less confined by national borders.

Conclusion

International law regarding anticipatory self-defense tends to be ambiguous at best. Its conditions restrict the legality of anticipatory attack to narrow circumstances that may prohibit nations from acting in self-defense to counter security threats, particularly in the current environment. A trend may be developing toward setting more permissive conditions under which first strikes would be legal, allowing action further in advance of enemy attack and perhaps against threats that are less than certain, but it is too early to draw such a conclusion with certainty.

---

[115] D'Amato (1996, p. 259).

In contrast with legality, legitimacy is a broader, more flexible, and even more ambiguous concept, informed by perceptions of legality but affected by many other factors as well. Consequently, an action taken in anticipatory self-defense is more likely to be considered legitimate than to be considered legal, and its legitimacy is likely to be far more important to decisionmakers than its legality.

CHAPTER FOUR

Preemptive and Preventive Strategies in Future U.S. National Security Policy: Prospects and Implications

Exactly what role preemptive and preventive attacks will play in American foreign policy in the coming decade and beyond is uncertain, most of all because the emergence and development of the threats to which they might be used as a response cannot be predicted precisely. However, examining the theory, practice, and consequences of anticipatory attack, along with past and present U.S. declaratory security policy, does point toward a range of reasonable expectations upon which to base future defense planning. This chapter addresses the prospects for and implications of U.S. first strikes in the near to medium term on two levels: first, considering preemptive and preventive attack as elements of United States grand strategy, and then examining the implications that this holds for military strategists and planners.

The arguments and conclusions that follow draw on the analyses in the preceding chapters, and on the results of the 12 historical case studies listed in Table 1.1 and described in detail in Appendixes A, B, and C. These include both cases in which anticipatory attacks were carried out and cases in which such policy options were considered by national leaders but ultimately rejected. Each of the cases falls into one of the three categories identified earlier as being particularly relevant to future U.S. consideration of anticipatory attack: attacks to eliminate or reduce threats of interstate aggression, attacks against terrorist non-state actors, or attacks to limit the development or spread of dangerous military capabilities.

Striking First: Rhetoric and Reality

The post-2001 U.S. doctrine of anticipatory attack, at least as represented by official documents such as the 2002 National Security Strategy, does not constitute a departure from past U.S. security policy as extreme as some commentators have suggested. As discussed earlier in this monograph, there are no specific conditions under which the United States has stated that it will strike first, and in official documents the possibility of doing so is raised only with respect to threats involving either terrorist adversaries or hard-to-deter states possessing or pursuing weapons of mass destruction. Yet these are categories that encompass the most serious threats likely to face the United States during the near to medium term, so to entertain the possibility of carrying out preventive as well as preemptive attacks against them is very significant: As the case studies in Appendix A describe, past U.S. leaders also occasionally considered but only very rarely launched anticipatory attacks in response to perceived security threats, and situations in which such actions have appeared even moderately attractive have been relatively few and far between.

U.S. presidents and their administrations have varied in their receptivity to preventive attack options. Aversion to striking first was particiularly prominent in the deliberations surrounding the development of NSC-68 during the Truman administration and in Robert Kennedy's expression of reluctance to be compared by history to Japan's Prime Minister Tojo during the Cuban missile crisis even as he perceived powerful political pressures to avoid any settlement of the confrontation that might appear to constitute a diplomatic success for the Soviet Union.[1] Nevertheless, as will be argued below, the recent prominence of preemptive and (though not labeled as such) preventive attack in U.S. policymakers' statements is likely to turn out to be a greater break from past U.S. policy in presentation than in substance.

---

[1]   See Appendix A. The same is true among Israeli leaders, as described in the cases in Appendix B.

Changing Perceptions of Power and Threats

Beneath this rhetorical shift (which is significant in its own right), there does appear to be a substantial change in the inclinations of U.S. security policy. There are at least three general areas in which a combination of changing international conditions and the distinctive attitudes and beliefs of the George W. Bush administration make the United States more likely to carry out anticipatory attacks than it has been in previous decades. Some of these factors might change under a subsequent presidential administration, but others are likely to persist as long as the current security environment obtains.

First, deterrence and defense (using both military and nonmilitary means) appear to offer less adequate protection against some types of security threats than they once did—or, more accurately, the sorts of threats against which they provide the least reliable protection now loom larger than they did in past decades. The perceived inadequacy of deterrence relates primarily to facing adversaries whose actions are not amenable to deterrence because they value nothing more than attacking the United States, or because the United States simply has little or no ability to influence their behavior.[2] Al Qaeda appears to be the exemplar of such an international actor; while it is not the first arguably undeterrable terrorist adversary the United States has ever faced, it is far and away the most capable one. Reduced confidence in the adequacy of defensive measures, on the other hand, is based on the nature rather than the motivation of security threats, and relates mainly to the rise of terrorist threats that are sufficiently destructive to represent problems for national defense rather than law enforcement, and particularly the

---

[2] Deterring an adversary may also be impractical if its behavior is genuinely irrational—for example, if its policies are determined by an utterly deranged leader—but such cases have always been highly exceptional in international politics. It is more common, although still unusual, to face an adversary that makes decisions based upon such distorted (or simply poor) information about its situation that its actions depart profoundly from any pattern that might be expected of a reasonably rational actor; Saddam Hussein's remarkable failure to conciliate the international community during the run up to the 2003 invasion of Iraq despite not possessing weapons of mass destruction would seem to fall into this category; speculation as to the quality of information about the outside world that affects North Korean decisionmaking has been active for years.

possibility of terrorist attacks using nuclear or sophisticated biological weapons.

Second, the unprecedented military preeminence of the United States expands the range of possible uses of military force that American leaders can reasonably consider, including but not limited to conducting a considerable range of preemptive and preventive attacks (although there are still many that would fall into the "too hard to do" column, especially with limited assistance from allies).

Finally, current U.S. leaders have made clear that they feel far less constrained by the possibility of diplomatic fallout from their actions than have those of any other recent administrations. Since preventive attacks are prone to trigger international criticism, fear of which has often proved to be a powerful argument against them, the less one worries about such reactions, the more acceptable striking first is likely to appear.

Persistent Obstacles to Striking First

In spite of the constellation of factors that make preemptive and especially preventive attack a more acceptable policy option for U.S. leaders in the current period than has traditionally been the case, most of the considerations that have caused anticipatory attacks to be infrequent in the past continue to apply today. As a result, although it is possible that such actions will now be seriously considered more often, it is unlikely that there will be a dramatic increase in the frequency with which the United States will actually launch major anticipatory attacks. These constraints fall into two broad categories, corresponding to the two dimensions in Figure 2.1.[3]

First, many threats cannot be addressed by striking first because they are not recognized in time for such an opportunity to exist, or at least to be politically realistic. This can happen because the enemy attack comes as a surprise—either from an entirely unexpected source,

---

[3] The risk averseness of leaders constitutes a third dimension. The more cautious decisionmakers are, the greater will have to be the apparent likelihood of enemy attack and the advantages of striking first in order for anticipatory attack to be attractive to them. However, it is not clear that risk acceptance among current or likely future U.S. leaders is greater—or less—than historical norms.

or more commonly from an adversary recognized to be a potential enemy but whose attack was not foreseen; both the Pearl Harbor and September 11, 2001, attacks against the United States fall into the latter category. In other cases, the threat is recognized in advance, but too late to be averted, due to the time required to decide to undertake an anticipatory attack or the time required to carry it out.

It is possible to reduce the frequency of such surprises by improving intelligence collection and analysis, by increasing the responsiveness of armed forces, and by streamlining national security decision-making, but intelligence will never be perfect because many threats are intrinsically difficult to anticipate. This is true in general, but is particularly so when considering anticipatory attack, because it is not enough to know that an enemy attack is possible; what is required is a high degree of confidence that the adversary *is* going to attack, or at least that there is a strong probability that this will happen. For example, to have averted the Pearl Harbor strike in late 1941 through a preemptive attack against Japan, U.S. leaders would have needed to recognize not only that the Imperial Japanese Navy was capable of launching a massive air strike against Pearl Harbor, but that Tokyo was in fact committed to doing so. Simply being aware that it was theoretically possible would not have been sufficient to make starting a war with Japan a plausible policy option in Washington.

Lowering the threshold of certainty about the threat that one requires before launching a first strike can simplify the intelligence problem to a degree. As discussed in Chapter Two, the more severe a threat is, the more likely leaders will be to entertain the possibility of launching a preventive attack to avert it even when there is some uncertainty as to the inevitability of an enemy attack; the lower the costs of the anticipatory attack and any subsequent conflict are expected to be, the more willing leaders will be to launch it as well. However, the likelihood of an enemy attack can change abruptly, so, in some cases, extending the opportunity for strategic warning may only be possible if highly speculative preventive attacks are acceptable. There is another consideration that limits the extent to which risk acceptance can compensate for intelligence limitations as well: A state that decided that even low-probability attacks were worth preventing by striking first would be likely to find many such candidates, so assuming limited political and military resources, it would still be necessary to be able to distinguish which of these were in fact the most threatening.

The second consideration that continues to limit the policy utility of anticipatory attack is that even when such opportunities do exist they are often militarily unattractive or the military advantages they offer appear meager compared to their potential political costs. In short, a good offense may not be the best defense, or may not be much better than a good defense. Preventive attacks often promise less than decisive results unless the attacker is willing to conquer, occupy, and remake the target state, as the United States concluded when considering attacks against the Soviet Union or China, and is now dealing with in Iraq; in some cases, such as the Osirak raid, a threat may appear so serious that merely delaying its emergence will be worthwhile, but if the costs of striking first are high, marginal benefits will more often be insufficient to justify them.[4] Preemptive attacks are often of only marginal military value, if that, simply because striking first is not greatly superior to allowing the adversary to deliver the first blow. Ironically, this is particularly true for the United States. U.S. military power gives Washington unrivaled ability to launch anticipatory attacks, but it also reduces the need for them: The more powerful a state is, the more likely it will be able to deter or defend itself against the threats it faces, although this depends greatly on the nature of the threat. The world is full of political actors that could attack the United States, but that are extremely unlikely to dare to do so, and which U.S. armed forces could easily deal with if they did. That Israel, in contrast, has been relatively willing to launch anticipatory attacks against its enemies has much to do with its perceived military vulnerability.

Anticipatory Attacks After Operation Iraqi Freedom

The U.S.-led invasion of Iraq in 2003 can be expected on the whole to reduce further the probability of major anticipatory attacks by the United States in the near future, but not reduce it to zero. The central reason for this is that repeating Operation Iraqi Freedom (OIF)

---

[4]   See Appendixes A and B for detailed discussion of these cases.

somewhere else relatively soon would be difficult, on several levels. The occupation of Iraq will presumably continue to require large numbers of American troops for some years to come, leaving fewer combat-ready ground forces available for similar operations elsewhere. Moreover, mustering either domestic or international political support for another operation like OIF and motivated by similar concerns would be extremely difficult in the wake of discovering that Iraq did not in fact possess a large arsenal of biological and chemical weapons or a substantial nuclear weapon development program, the perceived threats of which motivated the U.S. and allied attack. After OIF, the credibility both of intelligence assessments of WMD threats and of U.S. policy-makers advocating anticipatory attacks will be dramatically weaker.[5] It is also possible that the postwar costs of the Iraqi (and Afghan) occupations will further reduce the palatability of military operations likely to lead to similar occupations elsewhere, although this will depend heavily on the course of events in Iraq and Afghanistan over the coming months and years.

Perhaps paradoxically, the likelihood that OIF will be reprised elsewhere may also be reduced by its operational success. The rapid and comparatively easy defeat of the Iraqi regime by a relatively small invasion force should tend to encourage states facing the possibility of attack by the United States in similar circumstances to try to avoid provoking a U.S. attack upon themselves. This does not necessarily mean that they will be deterred from developing weapons of mass destruction (discussed further below), or even from pursuing policies of limited brinkmanship toward the United States, but their incentives to avoid extreme provocations have certainly increased rather than declined, which should on the whole reduce U.S. incentives for future anticipatory attacks.

---

[5] For an analysis of the failure of U.S. intelligence assessments of Iraqi WMD, see Charles Duelfer, *Comprehensive Report of the Special Advisor to the DCI on Iraq's WMD, 30 September 2004*, Baghdad, 2004. For recommendations for reforming U.S. intelligence capabilities, see National Commission on Terrorist Attacks upon the United States, *The 9/11 Commission Report: Final Report of the National Commission on Terrorist Attacks upon the United States*, New York: Norton, 2004.

However, these factors do not mean that anticipatory attack has been removed from the U.S. security policy menu altogether. First, they apply far less powerfully to anticipatory attacks that do not involve large scale, sustained military operations and other OIF-like costs, especially ones that are not only small but also covert, although the effects of the U.S. intelligence community's reduced credibility may be far reaching. Second, even an anticipatory attack larger, riskier, and costlier than the Iraq invasion is conceivable in the event of a sufficiently great provocation. Most conspicuously, a major incident of nuclear terrorism could dramatically increase Americans' willingness to launch anticipatory strikes against states perceived to be potential sponsors or facilitators of similar terrorist attacks in the future.

Anticipatory Attack in Future National Security Strategies

Over the longer term, it is conceivable that the United States could adopt a national security strategy that places considerably greater emphasis on striking first than the present one. As discussed earlier, the "Bush doctrine" is both limited and ambiguous in its embrace of anticipatory attack as a policy instrument. It does not commit the United States to the preventive elimination of all serious threats, or even of all terrorist or rogue state threats. Although the 2002 NSS does state that the United States will seek to deter potential rivals from challenging American military preeminence, it does not even allude to the possibility that rising powers will be attacked if they are not deterred from such rivalry.

Yet pursuing such a strategy is within the bounds of possibility, given the capabilities of the United States. It might take a number of forms, ranging from taking on a global constabulary role, vigorously pursuing all terrorists and international aggressors in order to pacify the world, to a policy of defensive predation, seeking to perpetuate American hegemony by attacking any aspiring challenger. Theoretical justifications and historical precedents for such strategies exist, though most of the latter were neither palatable nor successful. Anticipatory attack cannot realistically be the only element of a national security strategy, but it could grow from being its headline to becoming its true centerpiece. Such a strategy would be ambitious and expensive, however, for many reasons discussed in this monograph, making its successful adoption very unlikely in the current security environment.[6]

Leading Scenarios for U.S. Anticipatory Attack

Traditionally, the most prominent contexts in which anticipatory attacks have been contemplated or executed have been nuclear standoffs, principally that between the United States and the Soviet Union during the Cold War (and, increasingly, India and Pakistan, more recently), and rivalries among states seeking to conquer—or to fend off conquest by—their neighbors, as in Europe in 1914 or the Middle East during the three decades following the British decision to withdraw from Palestine. For the United States today, there are three types of scenarios in which striking first is most significantly a possibility, but within each, major U.S. anticipatory attacks would be highly exceptional rather than something to be routinely expected.

Foiling or Blunting Cross-Border Aggression

The first and most familiar category is preemptive or preventive attack to avert or to reduce the effects of interstate aggression, either in the form of invasion or bombardment by missiles or other weapons. Because the United States does not currently face a serious threat of this sort, such attacks would presumably be employed in order to protect vulnerable allies. Following the elimination of Iraq as a potential adversary, two scenarios along these lines stand out as important possibilities:

---

[6] As suggested by the earlier discussions, such a security strategy would become more attractive under conditions in which the United States and its allies faced serious but relatively narrow security threats that could be readily identified and attacked. It would be more readily affordable if it were a cooperative effort by the United States and other powerful states rather than a largely unilateral one, but, as past collective security efforts have demonstrated, there is a natural tension between increasing the number of actors and expanding the ambitions of their strategy (Richard K. Betts, "Systems for Peace of Causes of War? Collective Security, Arms Control, and the New Europe," *International Security*, Vol. 17, No. 1, 1992, pp. 5–43).

an attack by North Korea against South Korea,[7] or by China against Taiwan. There are other such possibilities, but they either appear far more remote at present (for example, regional aggression by Iran) or are unlikely situations for such assertive American intervention (as in the case of a war between India and Pakistan).

The principal obstacle to launching an anticipatory attack to protect South Korea in the event of a severe crisis on the peninsula is that because effectively disarming North Korea with a conventional first strike is unlikely to be feasible (due to the size of the North's armed forces and the extent of their hardening against air attack), South Korea would be expected to suffer heavy losses in an ensuing Second Korean War. While a U.S. first strike might limit this damage significantly, U.S. leaders would still face the prospect of initiating very costly hostilities, something that would probably appear unacceptable in Washington (and even more so in Seoul) unless it appeared truly certain that a North Korean attack was imminent and could not be averted short of war—a degree of certainty that would in practice be very unlikely until the North Korean attack were actually launched.[8]

The China-Taiwan situation has many parallels to the Korean one. Again, a U.S. preemptive attack to defend its ally would involve the probability of incurring extremely high costs (though these would differ significantly from those involved in a war with North Korea), and China would assuredly not cease to be a threat as a result of a U.S. attack. Therefore, deciding to launch a first strike against China would depend on having near certainty of an inevitable attack on Taiwan; moreover, depending on the nature of the attack and China's efforts to minimize its vulnerability, the marginal military value of a U.S. first strike might be far from great. If China launched a cross-strait inva-

---

[7] The possibility of launching a preventive attack against North Korea to eliminate its nuclear arsenal rather than to protect South Korea (though the two scenarios might overlap) is addressed later.

[8] As described in Appendix B, Israel has often had to base its deliberations about striking first against Egypt on significantly incomplete information, in a relationship where it is safe to assume that Israeli information sources about the actions and intentions of its neighbors are markedly superior to the U.S. intelligence picture regarding North Korea's plans and preparations.

sion as its first hostile act, the picture would look different because there might be a brief window during which Chinese intentions were unambiguous before the actual attack as well as a lucrative target set for preemption;[9] however, barring a massive miscalculation, it seems unlikely that Beijing would launch an obvious invasion force by sea or air if U.S., or even Taiwanese, forces were physically and politically poised to interdict it.

Striking Violent Nonstate Actors to Avert Terrorism

It is not surprising that in the wake of the September 11 attacks, terrorists were the most prominently cited target for possible U.S. anticipatory attack. The idea of attacking terrorists before they strike is of course attractive; against suicide attackers, there is no other time to do so. Deciding to preempt terrorist attacks at the tactical or operational level—for example, to arrest or kill the members of a terrorist cell before they can mount their intended attack—is generally an easy policy decision when the opportunity presents itself, and such preemption frequently occurs. As a rule, when terrorists are able to carry out their attacks, it is not because the authorities lacked the will to preempt them, but because they did not have the opportunity (or were not successful in exploiting it), usually due to a lack of information about the terrorists' identities, locations, or plans.[10] Typically, police forces or military special operations forces carry out such attacks, although conventional military forces may play a supporting role (for example, by providing surveillance capabilities or airlift).

Considering anticipatory attack against terrorists at the strategic level—that is, attacking a terrorist group before it initiates hostilities, not merely striking a particular cell before it attacks—has far more in common with deciding whether to launch an anticipatory attack

---

[9] Although it would take some time for an invasion force to mass for an attack, this would presumably be done under the guise of conducting benign military exercises.

[10] A decade ago this generalization may have been less true, when some law enforcement agencies were not inclined to arrest terrorism suspects before they committed their crimes; such trepidation has become anachronistic in recent years as suicide attacks have become popular and body counts have risen.

against a state.[11] In both cases, the possibility of starting a conflict that might otherwise have been avoided will loom large in policymakers' thinking if the potential adversary is powerful. The United States faced precisely such a choice prior to Operation Iraqi Freedom, when it was suggested that Hizbollah, a large and highly capable terrorist organization but in recent years an active enemy only of Israel, could be expected to turn against the United States when the invasion of Iraq began, and therefore that a preventive attack against Hizbollah would be prudent.[12] This option was not accepted, and in the end Hizbollah did not strike at U.S. targets in response to OIF; in contrast, the Jordanian government did launch an anticipatory attack against Islamist militants in southern Jordan to prevent them from mounting terrorist attacks during the Iraqi invasion (see Appendix C).

If one wishes to prevent the emergence of terrorist groups in the first place, a different set of challenges arises. Because most terrorist groups are spawned from insurgent movements, eliminating insurgencies may halt the evolutionary process (although a lack of battlefield success might also drive insurgents to resort to terrorism as an alternative tactic). However, this naturally means that stopping terrorism before its practitioners become terrorists involves seriously engaging in counterinsurgency warfare—and in a lot of it, if it is not clear which insurgent groups or elements of them are the ones from which terrorist organizations might subsequently be spawned. Thus adopting a policy of attacking terrorism at the source on a broad scale would call for very extensive investment in special operations forces and the other military and nonmilitary tools of counterinsurgency warfare.

---

[11] In practice, determining whether a particular terrorist organization, as opposed to a state, has already initiated hostilities can be an imprecise business, as new groups splinter off from existing ones, members move from one group to another, and terrorist groups form and break informal alliances and cooperative arrangements with each other.

[12] For a more recent discussion of the pros and cons of launching such a preventive war, see Daniel Byman, "Should Hezbollah Be Next?" *Foreign Affairs*, Vol. 82, No. 6, 2003, pp. 54–66.

Attacking States to Limit the Spread of Weapons of Mass Destruction

Finally, attacking states to prevent weapons of mass destruction—specifically nuclear or sophisticated biological weapons—from making their way into terrorist or other undeterrably dangerous hands may be the most important, but also the most challenging, arena for anticipatory attack in the current international environment. Here, too, a number of factors combine to greatly limit the frequency with which such operations are likely to be carried out by the United States.

First, nuclear proliferation in particular is not a widespread phenomenon—some six decades into the atomic age, only nine states possess even rudimentary nuclear weapons,[13] which limits the number of potential targets for preventive attack. Although it is certainly possible that the world is entering a period of accelerated nuclear proliferation in the wake of recent Indian and Pakistani nuclear tests, North Korean claims to have developed atomic weapons, and ongoing Iranian nuclear efforts, it is by no means clear that this is the case.[14] More significantly, states that do have important WMD programs can be expected to take concerted measures to limit their vulnerability to anticipatory attack; biological weapons programs are significantly more common than nuclear ones, but are also less conspicuous.

In this respect, the experience of Iraq in the 1980s serves as a compelling historical lesson for any aspiring nuclear power, at once

---

[13] Counting North Korea as the ninth; one other state (South Africa) developed but no longer possesses them. Of the nine, three (China, North Korea, and Pakistan) have raised serious concerns in recent years about willingly exporting their nuclear technology (similar fears about the security of Russian nuclear weapons and expertise cannot be addressed through preventive attack). In addition to these states and those that have given up nuclear arsenals (South Africa, Ukraine, Belarus, and Kazakhstan), Iraq once possessed an advanced nuclear development program, and Iran has one today.

[14] On factors that motivate states to develop nuclear weapons, see Scott Douglas Sagan, "Why Do States Build Nuclear Weapons? Three Models in Search of a Bomb," *International Security*, Vol. 21, No. 3, 1996, pp. 54–86. For examinations of why so many states that could build nuclear weapons choose not to do so, see Mitchell Reiss, *Without the Bomb: The Politics of Nuclear Nonproliferation*, New York: Columbia University Press, 1988; and Mitchell Reiss, *Bridled Ambition: Why Countries Constrain Their Nuclear Capabilities*, Washington, D.C.: Woodrow Wilson Center Press, 1995.

cautionary and inspirational. Iraq's original nuclear weapons program was based on a highly visible nuclear research facility housing the Osirak nuclear reactor, constructed in the 1970s. In 1980–1981, the air forces of Iran (unsuccessfully) and then Israel (very successfully) mounted raids against Osirak, destroying the reactor and setting the Iraqi nuclear weapons program back by years. Following the Israeli preventive attack, however, the Iraqi nuclear program was rebuilt, this time redundantly and in great secrecy, so that it was only after the 1991 Gulf War, when United Nations inspectors entered Iraq, that the United States realized the extent and sophistication of the Iraqi program. The resulting lesson is that it is likely to be both important and feasible to limit the vulnerability of one's nascent nuclear capability to destruction from the air. As with attacking terrorists, here again it is limitations on intelligence and surveillance capabilities far more than shortcomings in the ability to destroy targets once they are found and identified, that constrains U.S. options for anticipatory attack.

The key consideration for those contemplating preventive attacks to eliminate weapons of mass destruction threats is that under most circumstances inflicting limited damage will not solve the policy problem presented by the adversary's WMD capability, so that completely eliminating the weapons or development programs will require occupation of the target country. In the case of Iraq in 2003, establishing such occupation was not difficult for the United States and Great Britain (though sustaining it has been neither easy nor inexpensive); against Iran, North Korea, or a destabilized Pakistan, doing the same would be a dramatically more ambitious and certainly more costly undertaking.

In some cases simply slowing down an adversary's armament efforts may be sufficient motive for mounting an attack. For example, in 1981 the Israelis perceived the prospect of a nuclear-armed Iraq to be so dangerous to them that even an attack that would delay but not eliminate the threat appeared worthwhile. The vulnerability of Iraq's nuclear program also encouraged the Israelis to strike, keeping the costs of preventive attack low by requiring only an isolated raid, not a war, to destroy the existing nuclear program. Notably, however, Prime Minister Begin expected that in a matter of years another such attack would be required to keep Iraq disarmed, not anticipating that the Osirak raid would not be repeatable. A preventive attack that only buys time by delaying a threat may also be attractive in cases where the attacker expects that the threat will diminish or vanish relatively soon, for example because the hostile regime is unstable and therefore likely to collapse and be replaced by a less dangerous government before the effects of the strike wear off. Although such conditions could exist in Iran or North Korea, it seems unlikely that a U.S. government would consider merely impeding either country's efforts to develop nuclear weapons to be a worthwhile objective for a major preventive attack.

Political Consequences of Anticipatory Attack

When considering striking first, it is critical to consider potential effects on third parties, particularly in cases of preventive attack as a response to threats of WMD proliferation. It is likely that such attacks, at least if they are impressively effective, will intimidate some states, helping to deter them from pursuing the development of weapons that might bring a similar fate down upon themselves.[15] For example, the success of Operation Iraqi Freedom may have contributed significantly to Libya's 2004 decision to abandon its nuclear, biological, and chemical weapons programs, although Libya's compliance with Western coercive demands regarding these and other issues had been developing for years.[16] Similarly, in a non-WMD context, the U.S. invasion of Grenada in 1983 had salutary coercive effects on the behavior of the pro-Cuban government of Suriname.

However, it is also likely that some states will draw the opposite lesson: that U.S. propensity and capability for preventive attack makes it all the more important to possess nuclear weapons or some other powerful deterrent to American attack, especially if the United States

---

[15] For such an argument, see William G. Eldridge, "Why Preemptive Counterproliferation Attack Works: Investigating Third Party Outcomes," paper presented at the International Studies Association, Montreal, Que., 2004.

[16] George Joffé, "Libya: Who Blinked, and Why," *Current History*, Vol. 103, No. 673, 2004, pp. 221–225.

appears unwilling to risk conflict with states, such as North Korea, that do possess nuclear weapons.[17] Both responses are reasonable ones, and which will predominate in the wake of any particular U.S. action will be difficult to predict with confidence beforehand. On the whole, though only as a general tendency, one should expect that weaker states will be relatively susceptible to intimidation, since pursuing WMD might simply attract American bombs, while larger or more powerful ones will be better equipped to develop such weapons in ways that are less vulnerable to attack—it should come as no surprise that Iran has been less inclined to give up its nuclear program since OIF than Libya was. The more the doctrine or the practice of striking first does contribute to nuclear proliferation, the more the U.S. armed forces will need to be prepared to conduct military operations against states that not only possess but also may be willing to use nuclear weapons.[18]

Finally, launching preventive attacks, and to a considerable extent merely advocating them as a legitimate tool of statecraft even without carrying them out, should tend to make other states more inclined to attack their enemies preventively. This is not likely to be a matter of other countries simply imitating the United States, but rather follows from the fact that one of the major factors discouraging preventive attacks is the political costs of violating international norms against them. To the extent that these norms are weakened by U.S. rhetoric and actions, preventive attacks will become a generally more affordable option, and one that the United States will have difficulty criticizing other countries for adopting. This does not imply that one should expect an epidemic of preventive attacks in hotspots around the world, and of course U.S. endorsement of the principle has not been a necessary condition for preventive attacks to occur in the past. However, it would be very surprising if preventive attacks by other states did not become more rather than less common in a world where the United States has

---

[17] The most celebrated such conclusion was the statement by India's foreign minister, following the 1991 Gulf War, that the conflict demonstrated that one should not go to war against the United States without possessing nuclear weapons.

[18] Similarly, conducting preventive attacks against terrorist groups may discourage other groups or some prospective members, but also may hold considerable potential to motivate others to join or support the terrorists' cause.

thrown its diplomatic weight behind the idea that they are potentially acceptable, and it would be prudent to take this prospect of increased regional instability into account in future security policymaking.

Anticipatory Attack and Future U.S. Defense Planning

The preceding discussion of preemptive and preventive attack focused on strategic considerations for U.S. national security policy at the highest levels, but this inevitably has lower-level implications for defense policy in areas such as campaign planning and military force structure development that are the principal concerns for the armed services and joint commands. In general, planners should expect that sizeable anticipatory attacks will be infrequent and those that do occur will tend to have widely varying requirements that are not unique to striking first, so that preparing for such operations is not a key driver for change in U.S. military capabilities.

Anticipatory Attack as a Niche Contingency

For military policymakers, the headline that emerges from analyzing the strategic utility of striking first is that such strategies are likely to be considered more frequently in U.S. national security decisionmaking in the early 21st century than they were in the preceding decades, and may be employed somewhat more often. However, U.S. anticipatory attacks, particularly large-scale ones, will remain relatively infrequent, and most security threats will continue to be addressed in other ways, including the use of anticipatory deterrent and defensive measures. To the extent that the United States does strike first, this will most often take the form of relatively small and, when possible, covert operations, since these will typically involve much smaller costs and risks than attacks such as OIF—although these may still be considerable, especially if covert operations are exposed. Changes in national leadership may affect this pattern significantly, but should not be expected to change it fundamentally.

If striking first is likely to play a relatively small role in U.S. security policy in the future, in order to support the national security strategy the U.S. armed forces, and arguably the U.S. Air Force most of all, will need to be prepared to conduct anticipatory attacks in cases when this can be expected to advance U.S. security interests, but will not have the luxury of being able to optimize for them. Fortunately, anticipatory attacks rarely call for a suite of military capabilities that is fundamentally different from those required for other types of attack on the one hand, or for anticipatory actions other than attacks on the other.

The military requirements for preemptive and preventive attacks, will be highly case- and scenario-specific. That is, preparing to launch, say, a preemptive attack to disrupt a Chinese invasion of Taiwan or a preventive attack to disarm North Korea are very different propositions, although of course many of the same military capabilities would be important in each case. Striking first against a terrorist group such as Hizbollah would be more different still. What is required in each case will depend upon the characteristics of the adversary in question, the details of key target sets, the contributions of U.S. allies, and so on. Therefore, a general inclination toward or against anticipatory attacks on the part of national leaders will tell military planners relatively little about how to prepare for them: What they need to know instead when designing force structures and investing in military capabilities is where the United States is or is not likely to strike first, with what objectives, and under what circumstances.

In fact, whether the United States will strike first may be one of the less important questions. While at the operational level the requirements for launching an anticipatory attack against a particular state or terrorist group will differ greatly from those for attacking a different one, in each case these will not differ profoundly from the requirements for fighting the same adversary in a defensive or retaliatory scenario. To illustrate this point, consider how Operation Iraqi Freedom would have looked if Saddam Hussein had been substantially and demonstrably responsible for al Qaeda's September 11 terrorist attacks, as many Americans incorrectly believed him to be in 2003. In that case, the invasion of Iraq would have been a clearly defensive action rather than a preventive attack, as Operation Enduring Freedom was in 2001. This certainly would have made some differences in the Iraqi campaign. Far more U.S. allies would have been likely to contribute forces or provide other support to the effort, for example, while Iraq might have been somewhat better prepared to face the invasion since Saddam would presumably have expected it to be launched. Yet the campaign to seize and occupy Iraq and install a new government would have looked much the same as OIF actually did, because the same adversary and essentially the same objectives would have shaped the campaign whether or not it was an anticipatory attack.

Because launching a preventive attack against any plausible prospective adversary would look far more like fighting some other type of conflict against the same opponent than it would resemble carrying out an anticipatory attack against a very different enemy, there are severe limits to how much it is possible to generalize usefully about military requirements for anticipatory attack as a whole, especially with respect to capabilities for force application.[19] However, it is worth noting that on the whole the military requirements for striking first will tend to be less demanding than those for purely defensive warfare, not only because initiating the conflict may offer advantages of surprise, but also because seizing the initiative should tend to reduce the need to be prepared for as wide a range of enemy actions as might be faced in a case where the enemy was allowed to strike first or on its own terms. After all, the reason to strike first would be that doing so is likely to be more successful or less expensive than the alternative.

Intelligence Requirements for Striking First
A few broad generalizations are worthwhile, however. Most importantly, anticipatory attack strategies tend to depend particularly heavily on having good strategic intelligence about both the capabilities and the intentions of the adversary, although the sorts of intelligence

---

[19] The situation would be slightly different if the United States adopted a policy under which it planned to conduct preemptive but not preventive attacks quite often, insofar as the former tend to call for the ability to prepare for and attack enemies very quickly in response to the emergence of imminent threats, which would place a premium on investing in certain types of quick-response strike capabilities, for example. However, good opportunities for true preemption tend to be so few and far between that it is difficult to imagine a plausible strategy that would frequently involve preemptive attacks on a large scale.

that are required vary with the circumstances. For preemptive strategies narrowly defined—that is, attacks to foil imminent aggression by the enemy—assessing how certain and how imminent the enemy attack is becomes enormously important for strategic decisionmaking, as many of this monograph's case studies illustrate. Failing to recognize that the enemy is about to strike will eliminate any opportunity for preemption. On the other hand, preemption that is motivated by incorrectly perceiving that one is about to be attacked risks the fighting of an unnecessary war (and perhaps losing it, if the enemy is powerful enough), and may entail high diplomatic costs as well if the preempting state is branded as aggressive as a result.

For preventive attacks, where the goal is to eliminate a less-than-immediate threat, the future capabilities and intentions of the adversary matter most, shifting the central problem from one of collecting and analyzing current intelligence to one of prediction (although current enemy capabilities will also be important for deciding how militarily attractive an anticipatory attack option would be). The less predictable the target's behavior seems to be (or the behavior of states or nonstate actors is in general, if one believes that they all behave more or less similarly), the more difficult this forecasting challenge becomes. On the other hand, anticipating less imminent threats is at least facilitated to the extent that the longer time horizon permits greater deliberation and reduces the need for very rapid analysis and dissemination of intelligence.

The need for better intelligence is, of course, not unique to preemptive and preventive attacks, but rather has become an issue in virtually every aspect of military affairs. However, the relationship between intelligence and striking first is distinctive in two respects. First, although many sorts of military strategies suffer if one's intelligence about the enemy is not sufficiently good, inadequate intelligence makes the coherent use of anticipatory attack impossible by definition: Unless threats can be anticipated, it is not an option. Even when threats can be anticipated to some degree, but with a substantial degree of uncertainty, leaders are unlikely to embrace anticipatory attack due to the potential costs of being wrong about the need for it.

Second, preemptive and preventive attack strategies are particularly dependent upon understanding the enemy's intentions (either current or future, depending on the circumstances), which often presents uniquely challenging problems for collectors and analysts of intelligence because of the limited degree to which intentions can be deduced from observing easily visible objects and behavior. Even when dealing with threats that require the adversary to mobilize or deploy forces conspicuously, determining whether such actions represent preparations for attack or merely feints or defensive measures is likely to depend on collecting closely held information through human or signals intelligence.[20] And this challenge becomes even more problematic if the threat in question is one that can develop covertly or if it still lies far in the future. Of course this does not mean that it is impossible to divine the enemy's intentions or that resources should not be devoted to improving our ability to do so. Rather, the point is that the intelligence problems involved are intrinsically difficult ones that can be reduced but not eliminated, and that strategists' expectations about the utility of striking first should always take this into account.

Meeting these intelligence requirements is to a large degree the responsibility of the United States and allied intelligence communities, both outside and within the Department of Defense. Among the armed services, the Air Force has a particularly large role to play, however. Most obviously, it operates a wide variety of reconnaissance and surveillance systems, both occupied and unoccupied, that are critical for collecting the intelligence required in order to assess potential threats from adversaries and to estimate the prospects for dealing with these through anticipatory attack. However, the Air Force's traditional focus on strategic attack, manifested most recently in its institutional championing of effects-based operations, arguably also places the service in the forefront of thinking about how to collect, analyze, and

---

[20] To a significant degree this parallels the intelligence challenges posed by the ongoing shift toward emphasizing effects-based operations (EBO) in the United States and many allied armed forces, due to EBO's focus on assessing second- and third-order effects beyond the physical destruction of targets.

employ the types of information that are central to anticipatory attack strategies.

Other Military Capabilities for Anticipatory Attack

Beyond the preeminence of intelligence, the distinctive military requirements for striking first vary greatly according to the type of scenario. Of the three categories identified above as being particularly relevant to U.S. security policy in the near future, the most challenging aspect of being prepared to preempt cross-border aggression is the need to strike quickly if the threat is one that could materialize with little warning. To the extent that this is true, it becomes necessary to position and maintain the appropriate forces in a posture that permits the preemptive attack to be launched on relatively short notice, whether through forward basing, rapid deployment, long-range strikes, or a combination of these. If the initial attack is to be merely the opening round in a longer conflict, it will also need to be backed up by the capabilities required for sustained combat operations.

Preventive attacks to address threats of nuclear weapon development or proliferation are less likely to require rapid responses. Instead, they challenge U.S. (or other states') military capabilities because of the typical need to eliminate such threats decisively if they are going to be worth attacking preventively. Permanently removing a state-level nuclear threat using military force will generally require not only destroying weapons and production facilities, but also replacing the regime that sought to develop them, lest they be reconstituted as in post-1981 Iraq; this, in turn, will typically require invasion and occupation (or at least substantial intervention in an ongoing civil war if such an opportunity exists).[21]

If the attacker merely aspires to degrade an enemy nuclear program temporarily, as Israel did in the Osirak raid, more limited force may be sufficient. But even in such cases, in order to be attractive to national leaders the attack usually must be powerful and thorough

---

[21] On the difficulties of causing regime changes through more limited uses of force, see Stephen T. Hosmer, *Operations Against Enemy Leaders*, Santa Monica, Calif.: RAND Corporation, MR-1385-AF, 2001.

enough to cripple the enemy's efforts for a substantial period, not merely to impede them, and in the post-Osirak world no state developing such weapons is likely to make this as easy to do as it was for Israel in 1981. Against a target state that already possesses nuclear weapons, the ability to destroy not just some but all of them in a preventive attack is likely to be a minimum strategic requirement, as it was when the United States contemplated anticipatory attack during the Cuban missile crisis. The greatest constraint on doing all of these things will be having accurate and complete intelligence regarding the targets, but the ability reliably to destroy the elements of the target sets, which are likely to be limited in number but very well protected also looms large (provided the intelligence is good enough for this to matter), and may require powerful defense suppression capabilities and relatively exotic ordnance for attacking hardened or deeply buried targets, or those that may need to be attacked in ways that will minimize nuclear or other environmental contamination.[22]

To the extent that preventive attacks are less likely to be supported by allied and other states than more clearly defensive operations, preparing to carry out such attacks would also call for paying particular attention to forces that could be employed with relatively little in the way of international cooperation, including basing and overflight permission. Depending on the prospective adversary, this consideration would favor investment in reconnaissance, surveillance, strike, and support capabilities with the ability to operate at very long ranges or from platforms at sea, and to reach targets stealthily or by flying above denied terrestrial airspace.

Finally, as was observed earlier in this chapter, the military requirements for anticipatory attacks against terrorists and other dangerous nonstate actors depend both on the frequency with which such operations are to be carried out and on the balance between narrowly targeted attacks against small groups and sustained operations against

---

[22] See Glenn C. Buchan, David Matonick, Calvin Shipbaugh, and Richard Mesic, *Future Roles of U.S. Nuclear Forces: Implications for U.S. Strategy*, Santa Monica, Calif.: RAND Corporation, MR-1231-AF, 2003, Chapter Four; and David A. Ochmanek, *Military Operations Against Terrorist Groups Abroad: Implications for the United States Air Force*, Santa Monica, Calif.: RAND Corporation, MR-1738-AF, 2003, pp. 28–29.

the insurgent groups from which terrorist threats typically emerge. Because counterterrorist operations are primarily the domain of police and, to a lesser degree, special operations forces (SOF), conducting such anticipatory attacks on a limited scale has little effect on military force structure, while doing so with great intensity over the longer term would require substantial increases to SOF force structure, a path down which the United States has begun to move since September 2001. Similarly, anticipatory attacks against insurgent groups do not differ greatly in character from other counterinsurgency warfare, but doing a lot of either would call for corresponding investment increases in U.S. and allied SOF and other military components that are disproportionately required in counterguerrilla, foreign internal defense, and related operations.

The Importance of Operational Preemption

Although this analysis concludes that anticipatory attack at the strategic level will not transform the use of force by the United States, and generates relatively little in the way of unique capability requirements, this does not mean that operational preemption is a similarly marginal issue for defense planners. Striking targets in order to avert future enemy actions within the context of a larger war plays an increasingly important role in contemporary warfare whether the conflict is anticipatory in nature or not, for several reasons. On the supply side of the equation, improving U.S. sensor, intelligence, command and control, and strike capabilities are expanding the opportunities for operational preemption, such as striking enemy land or mobile missile forces before they can move into position to attack or before they disperse into locations that will be difficult to detect or to strike. On the demand side, the proliferation of certain types of military capabilities—nuclear and some biological weapons, ballistic missiles, and advanced air defense systems, for example—and rising expectations that U.S. losses will be kept low increase the range of possible enemy actions that it could potentially be very costly not to preempt. Although it is often subsumed under other rubrics, such as attacking urgent or fleeting targets, operational preemption is already a central consideration in the development of U.S. military capabilities and doctrine, and with good reason.

Dangers of Relying on Preemptive and Preventive Attack

Considering that the strategic utility of anticipatory attack tends to be very constrained, the possibility that generals or policymakers could rely excessively on such strategies in order to address their national security problems might appear improbable. Yet anticipatory attack can be very alluring, and a danger does exist that leaders will place too much store in it. This was certainly the case in several European capitals in 1914, when perceptions of offensive dominance in land warfare contributed both to faulty military doctrines and to pathological crisis behavior, particularly in France and Germany.[23] More recently, and perhaps more surprisingly, the Israeli armed forces responded to their preemptive success in 1967 by assuming that a future war would begin with a similar anticipatory attack, in spite of warnings from national political leaders that again striking first might be too diplomatically expensive to be acceptable. In 1973, this indeed proved to be the case, and Israel was left to fight a defensive war far more improvisationally than would otherwise have been the case.[24] In addition, the more a state finds it politically or militarily necessary to fight as part of a coalition, as the United States typically does, the more its freedom to launch preventive attacks is likely to be constrained.

For a state such as the United States to plan on dealing with all, or even most, of its security threats through anticipatory attack is likely to be possible only under conditions of serious failure in rational policymaking. With sound strategic reasoning it should be impossible to overlook considerations such as the possibility that even militarily attractive options may be politically impractical, or the fact that intelligence will never be perfect. Yet such deliberative failures did occur in Europe in the years before the July Crisis and in Israel prior to the October War. Because anticipatory attack appears to have many attrac-

---

[23] Jack Snyder, *The Ideology of the Offensive: Military Decision Making and the Disasters of 1914*, Ithaca: Cornell University Press, 1984b; and Van Evera (1999, Chapter Seven).

[24] Carter (1998, pp. 52–64).

tive features, and sometimes may indeed be an optimal strategy, decisionmakers considering it need to remain alert to the risk of being seduced into overestimating its potential or ignoring its limitations.

This is particularly true for military leaders, because a doctrine of anticipatory attack, like other offensive strategies, offers certain advantages (such as seizing and retaining the military initiative) that are likely to be particularly resonant for them, while its potential diplomatic or other political costs may appear relatively remote when one is concentrating on planning successful military campaigns. The recent emphasis on anticipatory attack in U.S. security strategy has been propelled primarily by civilian leaders, but it would be unrealistic to assume that American military leaders will necessarily be immune to the unbridled enthusiasm for anticipatory attack that has at times taken hold of generals and admirals in other armed forces.[25]

Preemptive Attack as a Threat to the United States

This analysis has focused on anticipatory attack as a tool of U.S. national security policy. However, preemptive attacks may also figure increasingly prominently in U.S. national security policy as part of the constellation of future threats against the United States. Put simply, states or other actors expecting to be attacked by the United States may perceive powerful incentives to strike first; dangerous though it is to start a war against the world's only superpower, allowing the United States to attack on its own terms is likely to be even worse. Because war against the United States is indeed so dangerous, it is only when a U.S. attack appears to be inevitable that a state should be willing to initiate such a war itself as a defensive measure. However, if such certainty appears to exist, striking first may appear to be the only way for a weaker adversary to compensate for its military disadvantage—recall

---

[25] For example, until very recently, the transformation plans of the U.S. Army were based on developing forces whose tactical and operational survival depended upon what was at times described as "near-perfect battlespace awareness" in order to be able to fire first in encounters with the enemy, even though it was vanishingly rare to find military experts not directly involved in that planning who believed that such a goal was attainable.

that Israel's repeated uses of anticipatory attack have been motivated in large part by its sense of vulnerability, not by its military strength. Thus it is far from surprising that contemporary Chinese military doctrinal writings have raised the possibility of striking first against U.S. forces in the event of a confrontation over Taiwan.

U.S. foreign policy behavior is one factor that should affect states' inclination to strike first, since the perception that U.S. attack is inevitable could be increased by American policy statements emphasizing the merits of preventive attack, or (probably more powerfully) by demonstrations of U.S. willingness to initiate wars for anticipatory or other reasons. However, preemptive attacks against the United States are a threat that American policymakers would still need to consider even if the Bush doctrine were soon abandoned, since U.S. military capabilities pose an existential threat that potential targets cannot ignore regardless of Washington's declared or actual intentions.

As a result, for U.S. military planners, anticipatory attack may ironically have far more important policy implications for defensive than for offensive operations. As discussed previously, preparing the capabilities required to strike first in cases where such strategies will advance American security interests does not appear to call for major reshaping of the U.S. armed forces, both because such cases will be relatively infrequent, and because anticipatory attack creates few unique operational requirements. In contrast, the possibility of being subjected to anticipatory attack and the resulting need to deter or defend against adversary first strikes have important implications for U.S. military planning, particularly in areas such as force protection, basing, and expeditionary deployment. First strikes against the United States or its allies might focus on disrupting their military operations by damaging critical forces or operating bases, or on impeding the deployment of U.S. forces into the theater by attacking vital transport or communications nodes. Alternatively, such attacks could be designed to cause political disruption, such as striking civilian targets in allied states in order to discourage their governments from cooperating with the United States.

Deterring such preemption by threats of escalation or retaliation is unlikely to be fruitful, at least when facing enemies who expect to suffer regime changes or other catastrophic losses to an uninhibited U.S. attack, since they will have little to lose. Therefore, dealing with these threats will depend heavily on various combinations of active and passive defenses, depending on the capabilities of the adversary and the nature of the targets. The goal of making preemptive attacks against U.S. military targets less appealing, and thus less probable, is one that should figure prominently in thinking about future U.S. defense postures and about the direction and shape of U.S. and allied military transformation efforts, which could either considerably reduce or increase vulnerability to enemy first strikes. This in turn may affect the pattern of defense investment by potential adversaries: To cite but one example, acquiring antisatellite capabilities that would primarily be useful in a first strike becomes far more attractive to such states if U.S. military operations depend heavily on fragile space systems than if they are enabled by satellite constellations and other communications networks that are robust and redundant.

The Nexus of Politics and War

Nowhere is the Clausewitzian dictum that war is an extension of politics, and inseparable from it, truer than in the realm of anticipatory attack. The interweaving of military and political considerations conspicuously pervades both the theories and the case studies addressed in this analysis.[26] One of its consequences is that the more inclined one is to consider launching anticipatory attacks, the more important it is to have good ongoing communications between the leaders of the nation and of its armed forces.

---

[26] It is also prominent in cases not among those analyzed in detail here. The most famous of these is the July Crisis of 1914, when German policymakers were unaware that although they were desperately seeking to keep Great Britain out of the incipient European war for which they were mobilizing their forces, the very act most likely to trigger British intervention, the violation of Belgian neutrality, was a key feature of the German Army's mobilization plan (Van Evera, 1984, especially pp. 93–95). See also Snyder (1984a), regarding other incompatibilities between Germany's diplomatic and military strategies.

Military planners and leaders need to know what their political leaders have in mind with respect to anticipatory attack. In part this means understanding their intentions, which may or may not correspond to the policy statements that appear in the published National Security Strategy and elsewhere. Even if the declaratory policy does accurately reflect the thinking of the President and administration, it is virtually certain to be publicly expressed in terms that are too vague to provide adequate guidance for decisions about programs and force structure because, as discussed above, these are affected far more by the details of specific contingencies than by a general inclination toward or away from anticipatory attack as a whole.

For their part, senior military officers need to keep national decisionmakers familiar with the extent and limits of their capabilities. This is true far beyond the realm of anticipatory attack, of course, but is particularly relevant if preemptive options are going to be considered in conditions where the time available for making strategic choices is limited. This is illustrated vividly by the case of the Cuban missile crisis, when President Kennedy's Executive Committee of the National Security Council (ExComm) had been deliberating about the possibility of an anticipatory strike against Soviet missile sites in Cuba for some time before requesting and receiving a sobering military estimate regarding how effective an attack could be expected to be. Such information should ideally be in the hands of decisionmakers not only at the beginning of a crisis, but beforehand, since an understanding of the extent and limits of the possible should be taken into account even during normal, peacetime policymaking.

U.S. Preventive Attack Cases

U.S. Consideration of Preventive War Against the USSR

The question of whether to adopt a strategy of anticipatory attack is not a new one in U.S. policy debates. Striking first was a recurrent theme in early Cold War strategic thought, and a handful of military leaders, civilian policymakers, academics, and journalists advocated launching a preventive war against the Soviet Union at several junctures during the late 1940s and early 1950s. This case study examines the arguments advocates and opponents of preventive attack strategies put forward to see how they might inform debate today over the virtues of anticipatory attacks. It reviews the geopolitical conditions that fostered a perception of threat potent enough to spur a small but vocal group to urge the Truman and Eisenhower administrations to initiate preventive war. It illuminates the complex strategic dilemmas the administrations faced; examines the options they considered; describes why, ultimately, neither president elected to take this course of action; and evaluates the short- and long-term results of their decisions.

The Situation

Despite the ability of the United States, the United Kingdom, and the Soviet Union to work together to defeat the Axis Powers in the Second World War, the postwar environment was one of uncertainty and trepidation. With their common enemies eliminated, conflicting interests and ideological differences, the "Grand Alliance" quickly dissolved amid mutual suspicion and contradictory worldviews.[1] Within months of the war's end, Soviet rhetoric became markedly more aggressive, and many Western leaders, having witnessed the consequences of America's isolationism and Europe's initial acquiescence to Nazi aggression, believed Soviet belligerence should be confronted early, lest it lead to a more costly war in the future.[2] As the Soviet Union consolidated its hold on Eastern Europe, Americans became convinced the nation's security depended on defending the badly weakened democracies of Western Europe. But the United States was rapidly demobilizing its military forces, and though Moscow too had begun a substantial demobilization, American leaders were growing fearful of Soviet military power.

The American security debate was also influenced by tensions within the domestic policy environment, where intense interservice rivalry was inflamed by massive postwar budget cuts. After enduring two world wars in less than half a century and having just witnessed a sobering demonstration of the destructive power of atomic weapons, military and civilian leaders generally agreed that the nation's security should be anchored on efforts to deter future wars; however, the military services disagreed on how best to achieve that objective. General George C. Marshall and the Army advocated instituting universal military training to provide a large manpower pool for supporting the

---

[1] For an eloquent discussion of the mistrust between East and West during and after the war, see John Lewis Gaddis, *We Now Know: Rethinking Cold War History*, New York: Oxford University Press, 1997, pp. 15–25; a good overview of the first few years after World War II is provided by Melvyn Leffler, *A Preponderance of Power: National Security, the Truman Administration, and the Cold War*, Stanford, Calif.: Stanford University Press, 1992.

[2] Academics now refer to this mindset as either heeding the "lessons of Munich" or, alternatively, being swayed by the "Munich analogy." Winston Churchill invoked the Munich analogy repeatedly in the late 1940s, as did several American policymakers. For compelling analyses of how this and other historical analogies have influenced political decisionmaking, see Richard E. Neustadt and Ernest R. May, *Thinking in Time: The Uses of History for Decision-Makers*, New York: Free Press, 1986; and Yuen Foong Khong, *Analogies at War: Korea, Munich, Dien Bien Phu, and the Vietnam Decisions of 1965*, Princeton, N.J.: Princeton University Press, 1992.

United Nations and to demonstrate American resolve.[3] Navy Secretary James V. Forrestal and chief naval planner Admiral Harry Yarnell argued that a larger, more active Navy would deter "future Pearl Harbors" by providing a visible defense-in-depth.[4]

While each of these proposals had a degree of merit, the first failed to account for an emerging geostrategic environment in which threats might materialize more quickly than a citizen army could be deployed to meet, and the second was out of step with the fiscal realities of postwar budget retrenchment. Therefore, both were vulnerable to Army Air Forces commander General Henry H. Arnold's argument that capitalizing on the combined technological advances in air power and atomic weapons would not only be more affordable, but would also be a more effective deterrent. Arnold and other air power advocates argued that these advances made intercontinental strategic bombing feasible, and only air power could respond to foreign aggression quickly. As a result, political leaders would likely turn to air power before relying on surface forces, making an independent air force armed with atomic weapons a more credible deterrent than a large standing army or navy.[5] Indeed, as RAND analyst Bernard Brodie foresaw in 1946, political leaders would come to regard the atomic bomb as the "absolute weapon."[6] Over the course of multiple studies, commissions, and hearings conducted between 1945 and 1950, the decision to focus the main thrust

---

[3] U.S. Senate, *Hearings on Universal Military Training*, Washington, D.C., 79th Congress, 2nd Session, 1946, pp. 569–574.

[4] Michael S. Sherry, *Preparing for the Next War: American Plans for Postwar Defense, 1941–45*, New Haven: Yale University Press, 1977, p. 93; Vincent Davis, *Postwar Defense Policy and the United States Navy, 1943–1946*, Chapel Hill, N.C.: University of North Carolina Press, 1966, pp. 23–24; and Kenneth J. Hagan, *This People's Navy: The Making of American Sea Power*, New York: Free Press, 1991, p. 335.

[5] Russell D. Buhite and W. Christopher Hamel, "War for Peace: The Question of an American Preventive War Against the Soviet Union, 1945–1955," *Diplomatic History*, Vol. 14, No. 3, 1990, pp. 367–384, p. 371; Herman S. Wolk, "The Quest for Independence," in Bernard C. Nalty, ed., *Winged Shield, Winged Sword: A History of the USAF*, Vol. I, Washington, D.C.: Air Force History and Museums Program, 1997, pp. 371–398.

[6] See Bernard Brodie, ed., *The Absolute Weapon: Atomic Power and World Order*, New York: Harcourt, Brace and Company, 1946.

of America's security on the deterrent strength of air power armed with atomic weapons took shape and won support among policymakers.[7]

First Calls for Preventive War. While policymakers and military leaders were growing certain that atomic weapons held the key to America's search for affordable security, most of them also realized that the United States would not enjoy its nuclear monopoly indefinitely. Sooner or later, the Soviet Union would get the bomb. Anticipating that eventuality, military planners began arguing for a policy of preventive attack as early as September 1945. That month the Joint Chiefs of Staff (JCS) endorsed a memorandum from the State-War-Navy Coordinating Committee (SWNCC) stating that if an enemy appeared to be preparing for war, the nation "should demonstrate its readiness and determination to take prompt and effective military action abroad to anticipate and prevent an attack on the United States."[8]

Army Air Forces Generals were more explicit. In 1945, General Arnold's annual report to the War Department asserted that "the only certain protection against aggression is to meet it and overcome it before it can be launched or take full effect."[9] In early 1946, when a *New York Times* interviewer asked how the United States would defend itself once the Soviet Union got atomic weapons, Arnold stated that there was only one way to defend against the atomic bomb, "hit it before it starts" and then went on to say: "I don't like the word 'defense.' We should shoot to insure the security of the Americas. . . . This coun-

---

[7] For detailed discussions of how American policies on deterrence developed, see David Alan Rosenberg, "American Atomic Strategy and the Hydrogen Bomb Decision," *The Journal of American History*, Vol. 66, No. 1, 1979, pp. 62–87; and Rosenberg (1983). Also see Robert Frank Futrell, *Ideas, Concepts, Doctrine: Basic Thinking in the United States Air Force*, Maxwell Air Force Base, Ala.: Air University Press, 1989, pp. 217–237.

[8] State-War-Navy Coordinating Committee, "Basis for the Formulation of a U.S. Military Policy," SWNCC 282, 1945, in Thomas H. Etzold and John Lewis Gaddis, eds., *Containment: Documents on American Policy and Strategy, 1945–1950*, New York: Columbia University Press, 1978, pp. 39–44.

[9] Henry H. Arnold, *Second Annual Report of the Commanding General of the Army Air Force to the War Department*, Washington, D.C.: U.S. Air Force, 1945, quoted in Russell D. Buhite and W. Christopher Hamel, "War for Peace: The Question of an American Preventive War Against the Soviet Union, 1945–1955," *Diplomatic History*, Vol. 14, No. 3, 1990, pp. 367–384, p. 373.

try should capitalize on the atomic bomb, if necessary to assure world peace."[10] Later that year, Arnold's deputy, Lt. Gen. Ira C. Eaker, told reporters that

> the next war will be a short war of unparalleled destruction, that the first blows would be struck through the air, and that to prevent destruction of this country in event of such an attack we must strike the enemy first. . . . If we are to prevent the launching of atom bombs, guided missiles, or super-rockets against our industrial establishments, we must have a force ready to destroy these weapons before they are launched.[11]

These officers were among the most vocal advocates of anticipatory attack, and policymakers were well aware that they had a parochial interest in favoring a strategy that would require investing in air power at the expense of the other military services. Yet calls for preventive war did not come from the Air Force ranks alone. In September 1945, Army General Leslie R. Groves, commander of the wartime Manhattan Project and military liaison to the Atomic Energy Commission, told *The New York Times* that if Moscow did not accept the Baruch Plan for international control of atomic weapons, the United States should consider attacking the Soviet Union's research facilities to maintain the American atomic monopoly.[12] He followed that interview with a letter to Congress in January 1946, in which he insisted that there were only two acceptable alternatives regarding atomic weapons: Either there must be a "hardboiled, realistic enforceable world agree-

---

[10] *The New York Times*, January 14, 1946, quoted in Alfred Vagts, *Defense and Diplomacy*, New York: Kings Crown Press, 1956, p. 330; *The New York Times*, February 14, 1946, quoted in Alfred Vagts, *Defense and Diplomacy*, New York: Kings Crown Press, 1956, p. 330.

[11] *The New York Times*, November 21, 1946, quoted in Alfred Vagts, *Defense and Diplomacy*, New York: Kings Crown Press, 1956, p. 330.

[12] "Keep Atomic Bomb Secret, Gen. Groves Urges: Atomic Bomb Project Director Honored," *The New York Times*, September 22, 1945, p. 3.

ment" outlawing them, or the United States and its allies "must have an exclusive supremacy in the field."[13]

As the destructive power of atomic weapons became more widely known, an increasing number of flag officers concluded that allowing an enemy to strike first was unacceptable. After witnessing the 1946 atomic tests on Bikini Atoll, an evaluation board that included Army General Joseph Stilwell, Lt. Gen. Albert Wedemeyer, and Admirals Ralph Oftsie and William Parsons reported to the JCS that an atomic attack, if used in conjunction with other weapons of mass destruction, would "depopulate vast areas of the earth's surface, leaving only vestigial remnants of man's material works."[14] Because absorbing the first blow of such an attack would be so devastating, the report stated that Congress needed to change its

> traditional attitudes toward what constitutes acts of aggression . . . [and employ] every practical means to prevent surprise attack. Offensive measures will be the only generally effective means of defense, and the United States must be prepared to employ them before a potential enemy can inflict significant damage upon us.[15]

Military officers were not the only people who saw a Hobbesian choice presented by atomic weapons. As Soviet relations with the West worsened after 1945, a small but growing number of statesmen, academics, and journalists proposed using the U.S. atomic monopoly to compel Moscow to moderate its aggressive behavior and accept international control of atomic weapons. Their arguments frequently con-

---

[13] Leslie R. Groves, "Our Army of the Future—As Influenced by Atomic Weapons," January 2, 1946, in U.S. Department of State, *Foreign Relations of the United States*, Vol. I: *General: The United Nations*, Washington, D.C.: U.S. Department of State, 1972, pp. 1197–1203, p. 1198.

[14] Joint Chiefs of Staff, "Evaluation of Effect on Soviet War Effort Resulting from the Strategic Air Offensive," May 12, 1949, JCS 1953/1, in Steven T. Ross and David Alan Rosenberg, eds., *America's Plans for War Against the Soviet Union, 1945–1950: A 15-Volume Set, Reproducing in Facsimile 98 Plans and Studies Created by the Joint Chiefs of Staff*, New York: Garland, 1989a, Vol. 11.

[15] Joint Chiefs of Staff (1949).

cluded that if such efforts led to war, then fighting it before the Soviets had atomic weapons was far preferable to allowing them to arm.[16]

Meanwhile, encouraged by Maj. Gen. Orvil Anderson, the commander of Air University and one of the most ardent advocates of preventive war, the faculty and students of the Air War College began assessing the strategic implications of nuclear weapons as early as 1947. First concluding that "the initial blow suffered by any nation from an atomic attack can be decisive," they analyzed what they perceived to be the potential Soviet threat and, in June 1948, surmised that

> [a]ll measures short of direct military action to contain the threat of Communist domination are of doubtful effect in meeting other exacting requirements in preserving our national life. Military action using weapons of mass destruction, prior to the Soviet development of these weapons, in final essence appears to be the only ultimate means of attaining security for our nation and the world.[17]

Yet, outspoken as the preventive war advocates were, they never amounted to more than a small minority in America's postwar political

---

[16] The most hawkish preventive war advocates included Winston Churchill and former U.S. Ambassador to Moscow William C. Bullitt. Those advancing the compellence argument included philosopher Bertrand Russell, New York University philosophy professor James Burnham, University of Chicago government professor Herbert Finer, political columnists Joseph Alsop and Stewart Alsop, and political analyst George Fielding Eliot. See Joseph Alsop and Stewart Alsop, "If Russia Grabs Europe," *The Saturday Evening Post*, Vol. 220, No. 25, 1947, pp. 15–17 and 62; William C. Bullitt, *The Great Globe Itself: A Preface to World Affairs*, New York: C. Scribner's Sons, 1946; James Burnham, *The Struggle for the World*, New York: The John Day Company, Inc., 1947; George Fielding Eliot, *If Russia Strikes*, Indianapolis: Bobbs-Merrill Co., 1949; Herman Finer, *America's Destiny*, New York: Macmillan Co., 1947; Gaddis (1997, p. 91); Ray Perkins, "Bertrand Russell and Preventive War," in Alan Schwerin, ed., *Bertrand Russell on Nuclear War, Peace, and Language: Critical and Historical Essays*, Westport, Conn.: Praeger, 2002, pp. 3–14; Marc Trachtenberg, "A 'Wasting Asset': American Strategy and the Shifting Nuclear Balance, 1949–1954," *International Security*, Vol. 13, No. 3, 1988, pp. 5–49, quoting Lord Moran's diary; Charles McMoran Wilson Moran, *Winston Churchill: The Struggle for Survival, 1940–1965*, London: Constable, 1966, p. 315; and House of Commons, *Parliantary Debates: House of Commons Official Report*, January 23, 1948, p. 561.

[17] Air University, Air War College, Student Composite Solution, Problem Numbers 9 and 12, quoted in Futrell (1989, p. 285).

arena, and Washington's elder statesmen soundly rejected their arguments. One of the first to speak out against talk of preventive war was a former U.S. ambassador to Moscow, Joseph E. Davies, who denounced "a few militarists—not among the great war leaders—in this and other countries who advocate war with Russia now rather than later."[18] He considered their talk "insanity" and the equivalent of "throwing dynamite around."[19] Likewise, Commerce Secretary Henry Wallace complained that "a school of military thinking" was calling for "a preventive war, an attack on Russia now before Russia has atomic bombs."[20] Wallace considered such talk "not only immoral, but stupid."[21] While Davies and Wallace hardly qualified as elder statesmen, former Secretary of War Henry Stimson did. He declared the call for preventive war "worse than nonsense" and said "it results from a cynical incomprehension of what the people of the world will tolerate from any nation." He went on to say, "We could not possibly take that opportunity without deserting our inheritance. Americans as conquerors would be terribly miscast."[22] John Foster Dulles declared that it was unthinkable that the United States would start a preventive war because doing so would expose its free institutions "to the utmost peril." He granted that the world situation demanded that "military factors [not] be ignored, but [insisted that] in accordance with American tradition, [the military must] be an instrument of national policy, and *not* itself a maker of that policy."[23]

Pressures for Preventive War Intensify During East-West Confrontations. During the late 1940s, the preventive war lobby made no headway with President Truman or his closest advisors. However, during several

---

[18] *The New York Times*, November 15, 1945, quoted in Alfred Vagts, *Defense and Diplomacy*, New York: Kings Crown Press, 1956, p. 330.

[19] *The New York Times* (1945).

[20] Alfred Vagts (1956, p. 330).

[21] Alfred Vagts (1956, p. 330).

[22] *Time*, April 4, 1948, quoted in Alfred Vagts, *Defense and Diplomacy*, New York: Kings Crown Press, 1956, p. 332.

[23] *The New York Times*, January 18, 1948, quoted in Alfred Vagts, *Defense and Diplomacy*, New York: Kings Crown Press, 1956, p. 332, emphasis in original.

of the East-West confrontations that marked the first ten years of the Cold War, well-placed officials in both the Truman and Eisenhower administrations urged their presidents to launch preventive strikes on the Soviet Union. Both chief executives resisted these pressures, but Eisenhower, at least, seems to have given the idea some amount of consideration.

In the spring of 1948, the Soviets began interfering with Allied road and rail traffic to Berlin and, though the JCS had drawn up preliminary plans for launching an atomic offensive against the Soviet Union, the Truman administration had not yet developed policies regarding what circumstances would justify executing those plans or what level of authority was necessary for the release of atomic weapons. Still hoping the world community would outlaw their use, and worried that the American people would not tolerate their employment for "aggressive purposes," President Truman ordered the Joint Chiefs to table their nuclear war planning that May and, instead, develop plans for a conventional conflict.[24] But as relations with Moscow deteriorated, Secretary of Defense James Forrestal, along with Army and Air Force Secretaries Kenneth Royall and W. Stuart Symington and Air Force Chief of Staff Gen Hoyt S. Vandenberg, began pressing the Administration to define its nuclear policies, and on July 28, Forrestal directed the Joint Chiefs to reinstitute planning for the atomic offensive. On September 16, 1948, President Truman approved NSC-30, a policy statement drafted by the Air Force and endorsed by the State Department and the National Security Council (NSC), recognizing that "the military must be ready to utilize promptly and effectively all appropriate means available, including atomic weapons" in the event of

---

[24] Rosenberg (1979, pp. 68–69; 1983, p. 12).

war, but "the decision as to the employment" of those weapons would rest solely with the Chief Executive.[25]

There is no evidence to support some historians' claims that Forrestal, Symington, and Vandenberg urged President Truman to launch a preventive war during the Berlin Blockade—though Forrestal's diary maintains that the President assured him on September 13 that he was prepared to use atomic weapons "if it became necessary"—nor is there anything to suggest that calls for preventive war increased in the immediate wake of the Soviet Union's first atomic test in August 1949.[26] To the contrary, although America's unexpectedly early loss of the atomic monopoly shocked Truman enough to persuade him both to accelerate the production of fission bombs and to approve the development of vastly more powerful thermonuclear weapons, it also prompted him to order a joint State-Defense study that he approved as NSC-68 in April 1950: a policy that, among other things, emphatically renounced preventive war as a strategy option for the United States.[27]

However, when the Korean War began in June 1950, the question of whether to launch an atomic offensive against the Soviet Union resurfaced within the Truman administration. Seeing the North

---

[25] National Security Council, "United States Policy on Atomic Warfare," 1948, in U.S. Department of State, *Foreign Relations of the United States, 1948*, Vol. I: *General: United Nations*, Washington, D.C.: U.S. Department of State, 1975, pp. 624–628; Rosenberg (1983, p. 13; 1979, p. 69); David R. Mets, "Technology, Thought, Troops: Gen. Carl A. Spaatz and the Dawn of the Nuclear Age," in Rebecca Hancock Cameron and Barbara Wittig, eds., *Golden Legacy, Boundless Future: Essays on the United States Air Force and the Rise of Aerospace Power: Proceedings of the Aim High Symposium Held on May 28–29, 1997 at the Double Tree Hotel, Crystal City, Virginia*, Washington, D.C.: Air Force History and Museums Program, 1997, pp. 179–240, p. 220.

[26] Rosenberg (1979, p. 69). Regarding allegations of pressure for preventive war during the Berlin Blockade, see Buhite and Hamel (1990, pp. 375–376).

[27] Gaddis (1997, pp. 99–101); Rosenberg (1979, pp. 78–87); Scott Douglas Sagan, "The Perils of Proliferation: Organization Theory, Deterrence Theory, and the Spread of Nuclear Weapons," *International Security*, Vol. 18, No. 4, 1994b, pp. 66–107, p. 78; Marc Trachtenberg, *A Constructed Peace: The Making of the European Settlement, 1945–1963*, Princeton, N.J.: Princeton University Press, 1999, pp. 11–15; National Security Council, "Objectives and Programs for National Security," 1950a, in U.S. Department of State, *Foreign Relations of the United States, 1950*, Vol. I: *National Security Affairs; Foreign Economic Policy*, Washington, D.C.: U.S. Department of State, 1977, pp. 234–292.

Korean aggression as an act prompted by Moscow, U.S. officials met with their British counterparts in July and discussed whether, if the Chinese intervened, the United States should respond with an attack on the Soviet Union.[28] Receiving no support for such a move from their principal ally, they quickly dismissed the notion; yet when the Chinese did cross the Yalu in November, Central Intelligence Agency (CIA) Director Walter Bedell Smith asked his NSC colleagues "to what point will the U.S. be driven [before it will] attack the problem at its heart, namely Moscow, instead of handling it on the periphery as at present," and on January 3, 1951, the JCS issued a paper arguing that it was "militarily foolhardy" to fight a land war against China while the "heart of aggressive COMMIE power remained untouched."[29]

In the meantime, several prominent officials began openly lobbying for preventive war. On August 25, 1950, Navy Secretary Francis Matthews addressed a large crowd assembled at the Boston Navy Yard, calling on the United States to fulfill its "inescapable role" by initiating an atomic attack to destroy the Soviet Union's will to wage war and thereby "become the first aggressor for peace."[30] Several days later, a *New York Times* article speculated that Matthews' speech was a trial balloon sent up by Defense Secretary Louis A. Johnson "who has been selling the same doctrine of preventive war in private conversations around Washington."[31] In November and December, former Air Force Secretary W. Stuart Symington, then chairman of the National Security Resources Board, exchanged letters with Bernard Baruch arguing for war against the Soviet Union; the following month, he sent President Truman a memo proposing a strategy shift from purely defensive

---

[28] "Summary of the United States–United Kingdom Discussions," July 20–24, 1950, in U.S. Department of State, *Foreign Relations of the United States, 1950,* Vol. VII: *Korea,* Washington, D.C.: U.S. Department of State, 1976, p. 463, as cited in Trachtenberg (1999, p. 19).

[29] "Minutes of the 71st Meeting of the NSC, November 9, 1950," and JCS 1776/180, January 3, 1950, "Records of the Joint Chiefs of Staff," cited in Trachtenberg (1999, p. 19, emphasis in original).

[30] Buhite and Hamel (1990, p. 376); Sagan (1994b, p. 77); Trachtenberg (1999, p. 20).

[31] Trachtenberg (1999) notes that Marquis Childs wrote a similar report in his column in *The Washington Post* on August 31, 1950.

efforts to localize and contain communist aggression to a "clear and positive" policy. His preferred policy would entail a strategy of withdrawing from Korea, directly engaging China in an air and naval war, and, if Moscow became involved, conducting an "atomic bombardment of Soviet Russia itself."[32] In Congress, Senator John L. McClellan had advocated preventive war against the Soviet Union even before the North Koreans attacked. Once the war began, he and Senator Paul H. Douglas argued openly for taking the fight to Moscow, and Senator Eugene D. Millikin and Representative Henry S. Jackson were said to have supported the idea.[33]

As for the President, in July 1950, he publicly warned that Chinese intervention "might well strain to the breaking point the fabric of world peace," and he became more pointed in September when he said that "communist imperialism" might "expand to a general war"

---

[32] Buhite and Hamel (1990, p. 377); Trachtenberg (1999, pp. 25–26); W. Stuart Symington, "Current History of National Planning Policy—Diplomatic, Economic and Military; and Reasons Why It Is Essential That These Three Segments of National Security Be Further Integrated: Memorandum by the Chairman of the National Security Resources Board (Symington) to the President," undated, in *Foreign Relations of the United States, 1951*, Vol. I, *National Security Affairs; Foreign Economic Policy*, Washington, D.C.: U.S. Government Printing Office, 1980, pp. 21–33; and W. Stuart Symington, "Recommended Policies and Actions in Light of the Grave World Situation," January 11, 1951, NSC 100, in U.S. Department of State, *Foreign Relations of the United States, 1951*, Vol. I, *National Security Affairs; Foreign Economic Policy*, Washington, D.C.: U.S. Government Printing Office, 1980, pp. 7–18. The Symington-Baruch correspondence is available in the Baruch Papers, Box 95, Seeley G. Mudd Library, Princeton University, cited in Trachtenberg (1999, p. 26, note 79).

[33] Trachtenberg (1999, p. 20 and note 62). For references to prewar congressional interest in preventive war, see Jack K. McFall, "Memorandum by the Assistant Secretary of State for Congressional relations (McFall) to the Under Secretary of State (Webb)," January 26, 1950, in U.S. Department of State, *Foreign Relations of the United States, 1950*, Vol. I: *National Security Affairs; Foreign Economic Policy*, Washington, D.C.: U.S. Department of State, 1977; and *Newsweek*, February 13, 1950, p. 20. For McClellan's remarks after the war began, see "Both Parties Back Truman's Arms Call: All-Out Support for Proposal of 3,000,000-Man Force Generally Approved," *The New York Times*, September 3, 1950, p. 11. See *Time*, December 18, 1950, pp. 20–21, for Douglas's recommendation for the United States, in the event of new communist aggression, to "unleash such power as we have directly on Russia itself."

if new armies enter the fray.[34] As Marc Trachtenberg points out, these statements might have been bluffs or responses to mounting Republican pressure to be more assertive, given the fact that Truman had just approved NSC-73/4, which argued for keeping the conflict localized, but his diary reflections reveal that he considered trying to end the war during that period by issuing Stalin with a nuclear ultimatum.[35] Whatever his motives, he ultimately rejected any temptation to threaten war against Moscow. He chided Matthews for his Boston speech, rebuffed Symington's memos, and had the Air Force relieve Maj. Gen. Anderson from his post as Air University commander for telling a reporter from the *Montgomery Advertiser* that he stood ready to launch an atomic offensive against the Soviet Union.[36]

By the time Eisenhower became president, several aspects of the strategic situation had changed. Energized by the Korean War, U.S. production of conventional arms had risen dramatically. By mid-1952, the monthly production of "military end items" was five to six times what it had been only a year before, and the trend was accelerating

---

[34] Harry S Truman, "Special Message to the Congress Reporting on the Situation in Korea," 1950, in U.S. Department of State, *Foreign Relations of the United States, 1951*, Vol. I: *National Security Affairs: Foreign Economic Policy*, Washington, D.C.: U.S. Department of State, 1980, pp. 527–537; Trachtenberg (1999, p. 19); "Truman Speaking to the World Last Night," *The New York Times*, 1950, p. 4.

[35] Trachtenberg (1999, pp. 19–20); see James S. Lay, Jr., "Note by the Executive Secretary to the National Security Council on the Position and Actions of the United States with Respect to Possible Further Soviet Moves in the Light of the Korean Situation," August 24, 1951, NSC 73/4, in U.S. Department of State, *Foreign Relations of the United States, 1950*, Vol. I: *National Security Affairs; Foreign Economic Policy*, Washington, D.C.: U.S. Department of State, 1977, pp. 375–389.

[36] Truman characterized Symington's arguments as "bunk" and "drivel" and responded to the memo with a short note that said: "Dear Stu, this is [as] big a lot of Top Secret malarky as I've ever read. Your time is wasted on such bunk as this. H.S.T." (Symington, undated, quoted in Trachtenberg, 1999, p. 26). Anderson told the *Advertiser*: "Give me the order to do it and I can break up Russia's five A-bomb nests in a week! When I went up to Christ I think I could explain to him that I had saved civilization" (quoted in Buhite and Hamel, 1990, pp. 377–378, and cited in Trachtenberg, 1999, p. 20). Also see the quote in "General Removed Over War Speech," *The New York Times*, September 2, 1950.

sharply.[37] Likewise, spurred by the Soviet Union's 1949 atomic test, U.S. production of fissionable materials, atomic weapons, and bombers had soared, leaving Moscow's nuclear warfare capabilities far behind, at least temporarily.[38] Most important, the Korean conflict had settled into a stalemate around the 38th parallel, evolving into a costly war of attrition. The American people had become increasingly frustrated with the situation, and Eisenhower had taken office on the promise of ending it.

These factors led the Eisenhower administration to take a more aggressive approach to dealing with the Korean conflict, including threatening the use of atomic weapons against Chinese cities in Manchuria, despite the fact that Beijing had a mutual defense treaty with Moscow.[39] This apparent "window of opportunity" also encouraged U.S. leaders to consider more assertive policies for dealing with the Soviet Union and fostered in some a renewed interest in various aspects of a possible preventive attack.[40] In a May 1953 NSC meeting to discuss strategies for ending the Korean War, Vice President Richard Nixon argued that their course of action should be decided "only in the context of the longer-term problem which would confront us when the Soviet Union had amassed a sufficient stockpile of atomic weapons to deal us a critical blow and to rob us of the initiative in the area of for-

---

[37] James S. Lay, "NSC Staff Study on Reappraisal of United States Objectives and Strategy for National Security: Annex to a Report to the National Security Council by the Executive Secretary," August 22, 1952, NSC 135/1 Annex, in U.S. Department of State, *Foreign Relations of the United States, 1952–1954*: Vol. II, *National Security Affairs*, Washington, D.C.: U.S. Department of State, 1984, p. 89.

[38] According to David Alan Rosenberg, estimated Soviet strategic capabilities in 1952 were limited to about 50 atomic bombs and 800 short-range Tu-4 bombers. The United States is estimated to have had about 250 bombs in 1950 and 1,000 by the summer of 1953. See Rosenberg (1983, p. 23).

[39] Gaddis (1997, p. 107). See JCS discussion of use of atomic weapons in Manchuria in Joint Chiefs of Staff, memorandum, May 19, 1953, in U.S. Department of State, *Foreign Relations of the United States, 1952–1954*, Vol. XV: *Korea*, Washington, D.C.: U.S. Department of State, 1984, p. 1061.

[40] Trachtenberg (1999, pp. 31–33).

eign policy." Eisenhower agreed and added that Project Solarium "was being initiated with this precise problem in mind."[41]

Project Solarium was a policy exercise in which three handpicked teams of experts were asked to explore alternative strategies for dealing with the Soviet threat. Team A was given the task of defending the current policy of containment. The team developed a strategy designed to "wage peace" by focusing on negotiations and avoiding risks of general war. Team B was told to accept containment as a viable strategy, but to be less tentative about its implementation. The recommendation it produced consisted of drawing a geographical line and threatening massive retaliation if the Soviets crossed it—in essence, a forceful version of containment. Team C was asked to devise a way to "roll back" Soviet expansion—that is, halt then reverse Moscow's ability to hold territory outside Russia's traditional borders. Its recommendations were the most dramatic, concluding, "The U.S. cannot continue to live with the Soviet threat. So long as the Soviet Union exists, it will not fall apart, but must and can be shaken apart. Time has been working against us. This trend will continue until it is arrested and reversed by positive action." The team proposed substantially increasing the defense budget and "exploit[ing] to the fullest, use of military forces as instruments of national policy to achieve political, propaganda, and prestige objectives by both military and diplomatic means." They were careful to stipulate that the nation should not initiate a general war, but insisted that the United States should be willing to risk one to reverse the tide of Soviet communism.[42]

The President's top foreign policy advisors summarily rejected the Project Solarium Steering Committee's spring 1953 recommendation that a fourth policy alternative be considered: Give Moscow an ultimatum to come to terms with Washington within two years or face the

---

[41] "Minutes of NSC Meeting, May 13, 1953," 1953, in U.S. Department of State, *Foreign Relations of the United States, 1952–1954*, Vol. XV: *Korea*, Washington, D.C.: U.S. Department of State, 1984, p. 1016, cited in Trachtenberg (1999, pp. 32–33).

[42] "Summary of Points Made in Discussion Following Presentation by Task Forces," July 16, 1953, in U.S. Department of State, *Foreign Relations of the United States, 1952–1954*, Vol. II: *The United Nations; The Western Hemisphere*, Washington, D.C.: U.S. Department of State, 1976, p. 434.

prospect of general war.[43] Moreover, very little of the hawkish Alternative C found its way into the October 1953 statement of basic national security policy, NSC-162/2, or the one that followed in January 1955, NSC-5501.

However, a heightened sense of urgency animated the policy debate after the Soviet Union exploded its first two-stage bomb in August 1953. That month, Air Force Chief of Staff General Nathan F. Twining briefed the JCS on the results of a study the Air Force had conducted entitled "The Coming National Crisis," which argued that a time was rapidly approaching when the nation would find itself in a "militarily unmanageable" position. Before that time arrived, the United States would have to decide whether to trust its future to the "whims of a small group of proven barbarians" in Moscow, or "be militarily prepared to support such decisions as might involve general war."[44] Members of the JCS Advanced Study Group were more direct in May 1954, when they briefed President Eisenhower on a paper they had produced arguing that the United States should consider "deliberately precipitating war with the USSR in the near future—that is before the USSR could achieve a large enough thermo-nuclear capability to be a real menace to the Continental U.S."[45] The President's response to this briefing was noncommittal, but several records indicate that he, too, had been wrestling with how to handle the prospects of an extended confrontation with an emerging nuclear superpower that seemed irreconcilably hostile to the United States.

Soon after the August 1953 Soviet test, President Eisenhower had discussed the implications of the enlarged nuclear threat with Secre-

---

[43] Rosenberg (1983, p. 33).

[44] Chief of Staff, U.S. Air Force, "The Coming National Crisis," memorandum to the Joint Chiefs of Staff, August 21, 1953, Twining Papers, Series 2, Topical Series, Nuclear Weapons 1952–1961 folder, Colorado Springs, Colo.: U.S. Air Force, 1953, cited in Sagan (1994b, pp. 79–80); Robert M. Lee, "The Coming National Crisis," memorandum for the Chief of Staff, U.S. Air Force, August 21, 1953, 1952–1957 Subject File, Box 121, Nathan F. Twining Papers, Library of Congress, cited in Rosenberg (1983, p. 33).

[45] Matthew Ridgway, "Memorandum for the Record," May 17, 1954, Historical Record, January 15 to June 30, 1954, Box 30, Ridgway Papers, U.S. Army Military History Institute, quoted in Sagan (1994b, p. 79) and in Rosenberg (1983, p. 34).

tary of State John Foster Dulles, and he summarized his thoughts in a memo to Dulles on September 8. He surmised that, as the Soviets had blocked all efforts to place atomic weapons under international control, they must be contemplating using them for aggressive purposes. Consequently, American policy could no longer be oriented toward simply avoiding "disaster during the early 'surprise' stages of a war." Rather, the nation would "have to be constantly ready, on an instantaneous basis, to inflict greater loss on the enemy than he could reasonably hope to inflict upon us." Such a state of readiness would be the backbone of deterrence, but sustaining it for an extended period of time would create other problems:

> If the contest to maintain this relative position should have to continue indefinitely, the cost would either drive us to war—or into some dictatorial form of government. . . . In such circumstances, we would be forced to consider whether or not our duty to future generations did not require us to initiate war at the most propitious moment we could designate.[46]

The thought of preventive war crossed President Eisenhower's mind at least twice more in the next several months. In a December 1953 conference with Winston Churchill in Bermuda, the British Prime Minister remarked that if they believed the Russians were really bent on destroying the world's free nations, perhaps the allies ought to take action before Moscow had as many atomic bombs as the United States. The President responded that perhaps, logically, it ought to be considered.[47] Six months later, when Dulles raised concerns in an NSC meeting that the alliance system might unravel in the face of ever-stiffening U.S. resistance to the growth of Soviet power, Eisenhower said that, if that were indeed the situation, "we should perhaps come back to the very grave question: Should the United States now get ready to

---

[46] Dwight D. Eisenhower, "Memorandum to Dulles," September 8, 1953, in U.S. Department of State, *Foreign Relations of the United States 1952–1954*, Vol. II: *National Security Affairs*, Washington, D.C.: U.S. Department of State, 1984, p. 461, cited in Rosenberg (1983, p. 34) and in Trachtenberg (1999, p. 39, emphasis in original).

[47] Trachtenberg (1999, p. 39).

fight the Soviet Union?" He then pointed out that "he had brought up this question more than once at prior Council meetings, and he had never done so facetiously."[48]

Yet, despite his deep concern about the mounting political, economic, and psychological costs of deterrence, President Eisenhower, like Truman before him, ultimately proscribed preventive war as an acceptable option for the nation's security strategy. On January 6, 1955, he approved a statement of basic national security policy that said unequivocally, "the United States and its allies must reject the concept of preventive war or acts to provoke war."[49] Instead, he would stay the course already set in his "New Look" policy which emphasized containment of communist expansion through a network of bilateral and multilateral alliances and sought to deter Soviet aggression with the nation's "great capacity to retaliate, instantly, by means and at places of our own choosing," thereby incorporating selected elements of Project Solarium recommendations A and B.[50]

On the other hand, neither Truman nor Eisenhower ruled out the option of launching a preemptive strike, should an attack by the Soviet Union appear imminent. Truman's public and private statements about whether he would ever authorize a preemptive attack were always vague, perhaps by design.[51] Yet NSC-68, the basic national security policy he endorsed, was very straightforward in saying, "The military advantages of landing the first blow become increasingly important with modern weapons, and this is a fact which requires us to be on the alert in order to strike with our full weight as soon as we are attacked, and, if possi-

[48] "Notes of NSC Meeting" June 24, 1954b, in U.S. Department of State, *Foreign Relations of the United States 1952–1954*, Vol. II: *National Security Affairs*, Washington, D.C.: U.S. Department of State, 1984, p. 696, cited in Trachtenberg (1999, p. 39).

[49] National Security Council, "Basic National Security Policy," NSC 5501, January 6, 1955, quoted in Rosenberg (1983, p. 34).

[50] "Secretary Dulles' Address, 12 January 1954," *Current History*, Vol. 26, 1954, pp. 308–309, cited in Futrell (1989, p. 428).

[51] Rosenberg (1983, pp. 26–27).

ble, before the Soviet blow is actually delivered."[52] In 1952, amid growing concern that Moscow's emerging atomic capability might threaten the survival of Strategic Air Command's (SAC's) retaliatory bombing force, the NSC staff studied the issue and briefed the President in September. Truman was "startled" by hearing the extent of American vulnerability to surprise attack and concluded that "there wasn't much of a defense in prospect except in a vigorous offense."[53]

Eisenhower was much more open about his willingness to preempt an impending attack. In January 1954, he told a group of Congressmen that if it appeared the Soviets were about to strike, his action would "be a very quick thing as fast as Congress can meet" then added, "if you were away and I waited on you (before taking retaliatory action), you'd start impeachment proceedings against me."[54] Yet, he was not sanguine about his ability to launch a preemptive strike, given constraints in the American political system. In January 1956, he received a Net Evaluation Subcommittee report indicating that, even with a month's advance warning, there was no civil or military defense the nation could employ that would avert catastrophic losses in a Soviet nuclear attack. Deeply disturbed, the President recorded in his diary:

> The only possible way of reducing these losses would be for us to take the initiative sometime during the assumed month in which we had the warning of an attack and launch a surprise attack against the Soviets. This would be not only against our traditions, but it would appear to be impossible unless the Congress would meet in a highly secret session and vote a declaration of war which

---

[52] "NSC-68: United States Objectives and Programs for National Security (April 14, 1950): A Report to the President Pursuant to the President's Directive of January 31, 1950," April 7, 1950, in U.S. Department of State, *Foreign Relations of the United States, 1950*, Vol. I: *National Security Affairs; Foreign Economic Policy*, Washington, D.C.: U.S. Department of State, 1977, pp. 281–282.

[53] "Minutes of NSC Meeting, 3 September 1952," 1952, in U.S. Department of State, *Foreign Relations of the United States, 1952–1954*, Vol. II: *National Security Affairs*, Washington, D.C.: U.S. Department of State, 1984, p. 121, cited in Trachtenberg (1999, p. 34).

[54] L. A. Minnich, "Minutes, BiPartisan Legislative Meeting, 5 January 1954," Staff Notes, January–December 1954 Folder, Box 54, Dwight D. Eisenhower Diary, Dwight David Eisenhower Library, quoted in Rosenberg (1983, p. 34).

would be implemented before the session was terminated. It would appear to be impossible that any such thing would occur.[55]

In an effort to deal with these difficulties, the President signed NSC-5602/1, a revised basic national security policy, on March 15, 1956. Among other things, the new policy reiterated the rejection of preventive war, called for flexibility, and emphasized the importance of keeping local conflicts limited; however, it also declared that "nuclear weapons will be used in general war and in military operations short of general war as authorized by the President."[56] Interpreting the revised policy for the JCS on March 30, he explained that he considered "any war in which Russian troops were involved directly against United States forces or the United States" to be a "general war," and in the case of general war, he would launch SAC "as soon as he found out Russian troops were on the move." He would simultaneously request that Congress declare war, and the planes could be recalled if necessary, but he would not risk leaving them on the ground where they "might not ever get off."[57] Fortunately, neither president's resolve to launch a preemptive attack was ever tested.

The Threat

As Soviet-American relations soured after the Second World War, U.S. policymakers came to believe that Moscow was threatening the United States and the free world with ideological subversion, political domination, and ultimately, national destruction. These threats were first physically manifested in the strength of the Soviet Army, its repressive occupation of Eastern Europe, and the menace that prospects of further communist expansion presented for the democracies of the West. American leaders recognized U.S. dependence on Western Europe, and

---

[55] Dwight D. Eisenhower, *The Eisenhower Diaries*, New York: Norton, 1981, p. 312.

[56] National Security Council, "Basic National Security Policy," NSC 5602/1, March 15, 1956, Basic National Security Policy Folder, NSC Series, Public Policy Subseries, Box 17, WHO-SANSA, Dwight D. Eisenhower Library, pp. 1–11, cited in Rosenberg (1983, p. 42).

[57] Andrew J. Goodpaster, March 30, 1956, dated April 2, 1956, April 1956-Goodpaster Folder, Dwight D. Eisenhower Diaries, Box 15, Ann C. Whitman File, Dwight D. Eisenhower Papers as President (ACWF-EPP), quoted in Rosenberg (1983, p. 42).

they perceived the spread of Soviet communism as a threat to strangle the American economy and isolate the United States as the world's sole surviving great democracy. American leaders believed that communist aggression in Asia was instigated by Moscow, and they interpreted it as further evidence of the Soviet Union's malign intent. As Moscow acquired atomic weapons and became a growing nuclear power, the sense of peril to the American homeland grew. The depth of these fears was most clearly reflected in NSC-68, which said:

> [T]he Soviet Union, unlike previous aspirants to hegemony, is animated by a new fanatic faith, anti-thetical to our own, and seeks to impose its absolute authority over the rest of the world. Conflict has, therefore, become endemic and is waged, on the part of the Soviet Union, by violent or non-violent methods in accordance with the dictates of expediency. With the development of increasingly terrifying weapons of mass destruction, every individual faces the ever-present possibility of annihilation should the conflict enter the phase of total war. . . . [A]ny substantial further extension of the area under the domination of the Kremlin would raise the possibility that no coalition adequate to confront the Kremlin with greater strength could be assembled. It is in this context that this Republic and its citizens in the ascendancy of their strength stand in their deepest peril. The issues that face us are momentous, involving the fulfillment or destruction not only of this Republic but of civilization itself.[58]

While this general sense of menace was enduring, it was not constant in intensity throughout the period examined here. Episodes of Soviet agitation, expansion, or repression in Eastern Europe temporarily raised Western anxieties, as did the surprising advances in Soviet nuclear weapon technology in 1949 and 1953. Josef Stalin's bellicose rhetoric also increased Western fears, raising questions not only about his intentions, but also about his rationality. Most significantly, the East-West confrontations during the Berlin Blockade and the Korean War created perceptions of crisis in Washington.

---

[58] National Security Council, "United States Objectives and Programs for National Security (April 14, 1950): A Report to the President Pursuant to the President's Directive of January 31, 1950," NSC 68, Washington, D.C., 1950b, p. 237.

Policy Options

The range of policy options American leaders considered for dealing with the Soviet threat included building up powerful conventional military forces to protect American interests; capitalizing on America's technological advantage in air power and nuclear weapons to deter aggression by threatening atomic devastation; containing Soviet expansion by creating a network of alliances and strengthening U.S. allies through economic and military support; attempting to "roll back" Soviet domination through covert and conventional military, diplomatic, and economic "positive actions"; waging a preventive war by means of an "air-atomic offensive"; and launching a preemptive strike should a Soviet attack appear imminent. A few policymakers also considered trying to find an accommodation with the Soviets, as typified in Secretary of State Dulles' 1953 memorandum proposing that the United States make an effort to reach a modus vivendi with Moscow.[59]

The Decision to Renounce Preventive War

No single decision is responsible for producing America's broad strategy of relying on air power and atomic weapons to deter Soviet attack while containing communist expansion by developing a network of alliances with capitalist states strengthened by economic development. Rather, deterrence strategies and containment policies evolved over the first decade of the Cold War as decisionmakers struggled through the political, economic, and strategic exigencies of the challenges at hand.

President Truman believed maintaining a large conventional force was impractical given postwar fiscal realities. The Korean War did compel the United States to rebuild its military forces to some extent, but America and its allies could never hope to match the combined personnel reserves of the Soviet Union, China, and their satel-

---

[59] See John Foster Dulles, memorandum to Dwight D. Eisenhower, September 6, 1953, in U.S. Department of State, *Foreign Relations of the United States, 1952–1954*, Vol. II: *National Security Affairs*, Washington, D.C.: U.S. Department of State, 1967, pp. 457–460, where he worries whether the allies will continue to stand strong with the United States and concludes, "[W]e cannot avoid a major reconsideration of the collective security concepts." He then recommends that the United States make a "spectacular effort to relax world tensions on a global basis" in order to achieve détente with Moscow.

lite states, nor could they afford to redirect from their own economic development the vast amounts of capital that large standing forces and, potentially, a conventional arms race would have required. President Eisenhower also recognized this dilemma, and his "New Look" echoed the previous administration's efforts to maintain conventional military austerity. Deterrence through air power and nuclear weapons appeared to be an affordable alternative to larger conventional force investments in both administrations.

Likewise, the alliance system and policy of containment did not leap fully grown from the minds of postwar decisionmakers. George Kennan developed a skeletal framework for containment in his February 1946 "long telegram" from Moscow, a monumental document that directly informed the formulation of the Truman Doctrine.[60] Yet the muscle and sinew of the containment strategy took shape over time as Western policymakers became increasingly fearful of communist expansion and recognized the interdependence of the nations threatened by it. As in the case of deterrence, the substance of the Truman Doctrine was also reaffirmed in Eisenhower's New Look.

As deterrence and containment strategies developed and matured, concern arose, particularly in military circles, about their passive nature. They might stave off immediate disaster, but they seemed to offer little means to defuse or defeat the long-term threat. The few ideas offered for mitigating that threat through accommodation, such Dulles' proposal to seek a modus vivendi with Moscow, gained little traction with decisionmakers imbued with the "lessons of Munich" and averse to any policy that might resemble appeasement. On the other hand, neither Truman nor Eisenhower was receptive to the "positive actions" their advisors occasionally proposed for rolling back the Soviets and reversing the tide of communist expansion. Western conventional forces were wholly inadequate to challenge the Soviet Army's hold on Eastern Europe, and the costs of general war, particularly after

---

[60] Kennan introduced the concept of containment to the American public in the now-famous July 1947 "X" article in *Foreign Affairs*. See X (George F. Kennan), "The Sources of Soviet Conduct," *Foreign Affairs*, Vol. 25, No. 4, 1947, pp. 566–582.

Moscow acquired atomic weapons, were too high to risk provocative adventures.

Likewise, Truman firmly rebuffed all proposals for preventive war, and though Eisenhower seems to have given the matter at least passing thought, it is almost certain that he never came close to considering it a reasonable policy option. There are multiple reasons why neither president would venture down such a path.

The first and, perhaps most obvious, is that the United States lacked the capability to carry out such a strategy throughout most, if not all, of the period in which it was considered. In the late 1940s, when calls for preventive war were most frequent, America's stockpile of atomic weapons was very small and growing at a remarkably slow pace. As historian David Alan Rosenberg notes, "there were only two weapons in the stockpile at the end of 1945, nine in July 1946, thirteen in July 1947, and fifty in July 1948."[61] Moreover, even if the United States had possessed the numbers of bombs called for in JCS war plans, the Air Force lacked the capability to deliver them. In December 1946, America's strategic bomber force included only 30 atomic-capable B-29 bombers. As the combat radius of these aircraft was limited to about 2,000 miles, they could only have flown one-way missions to many targets in the Soviet Union, even from overseas bases.[62] By 1948, the Air Force had let production contracts for the B-50, B-47, and the intercontinental-range B-36, and it had begun developmental work on aerial refueling, but none of these capabilities would be available in significant numbers before the early 1950s.[63] Complicating matters, in this era before the U-2 or other advanced overhead reconnaissance assets were available, American planners had little more intelligence to guide their targeting efforts than prewar maps of Russia and information the Germans had collected during the war.[64]

---

[61] Rosenberg (1983, p. 14).

[62] Walter S. Moody, *Building a Strategic Air Force*, Washington, D.C.: Air Force History and Museums Program, 1996, pp. 96 and 125; Rosenberg (1983, p. 15).

[63] Moody (1996, pp. 76–86).

[64] Gaddis (1997, p. 89); Rosenberg (1983, p. 15).

In late 1948, harboring doubts about whether the Air Force could successfully carry out an air-atomic offensive against the Soviet Union and whether such a strategy would lead to Moscow's capitulation as its advocates claimed, Defense Secretary Forrestal directed the JCS to undertake a detailed analysis of the matter.[65] The newly formed Weapons Systems Evaluation Group (WSEG) examined the first question, and on January 28, 1950, its director, Army Lt. Gen. John E. Hull, briefed President Truman, his cabinet, the service secretaries, and the JCS on the study's findings. The WSEG concluded that if the entire bomber force were launched in a massive attack, 70 to 85 percent would reach their targets (depending on weather, Soviet defenses, and other variables), but only 50 to 70 percent would return home. Even where bombs were dropped, only between one half and two thirds of industry in the immediate vicinity would be destroyed, due to limitations in bombing accuracy.[66]

The second question became the focus of a study conducted by a committee of two flag officers each from the Army, Navy, and Air Force and headed by Air Force Lt. Gen. Hubert R. Harmon. Its final report was even more pessimistic. After examining such variables as target selection, physical and psychological weapons effects on Soviet civilians and military personnel, and potential impacts on cities, industry, and the Soviet economy, the committee delivered its unanimous findings to the JCS on May 12, 1949. The Harmon Committee reported that, although an atomic attack would cause an estimated 6 to 8 million casualties and reduce Soviet industrial capacity by 30 to 40 percent, it would not "per se, bring about capitulation, destroy the roots of communism, or critically weaken the power of Soviet leadership to dominate the people." In fact, the committee opined, "for the major-

---

[65] Joint Chiefs of Staff (1949), cited in Rosenberg (1979, pp. 71–72).

[66] WSEG conclusions are provided in Joint Chiefs of Staff, "p. 152–96, Plus Letter from Lieutenant General Hull to Joint Chiefs of Staff: Evaluation of Effectiveness of Strategic Air Operations, 13 January 1950, and Enclosures C, D, E, F, G, H, and K," February 10, 1950, JCS 1952/11, in Steven T. Ross and David Alan Rosenberg, eds., *America's Plans for War Against the Soviet Union, 1945–1950: A 15-Volume Set, Reproducing in Facsimile 98 Plans and Studies Created by the Joint Chiefs of Staff*, New York: Garland, 1989a, Vol. 13, cited in Rosenberg (1979, pp. 83–84).

ity of the Soviet people, atomic bombing would validate Soviet propaganda against foreign powers, stimulate resentment against the United States, unify the people, and increase their will to fight." Worst of all, the study found that the atomic offensive planned by the JCS and Air Force would not seriously impair the Soviet Army's ability to advance quickly into Western Europe, the Middle East, and Asia, though its ability to maneuver thereafter would be limited by fuel and lubricants shortages as a result of damage to the Russian petroleum industry.[67]

These findings were reflected in policy the following year when the President signed NSC-68, which included this statement:

> The ability of the United States to launch effective offensive operations is now limited to attack with atomic weapons. A powerful blow could be delivered upon the Soviet Union, but it is estimated that these operations alone would not force or induce the Kremlin to capitulate and that the Kremlin would still be able to use the forces under its control to dominate most or all of Eurasia. This would probably mean a long and difficult struggle during which the free institutions of Western Europe and many freedom-loving people would be destroyed and the regenerative capacity of Western Europe dealt a crippling blow.[68]

American capabilities grew dramatically in the early 1950s as a result of the Korean War and anxieties created by Moscow's successful atomic test in August 1949. By July 1953, the American atomic stockpile is estimated to have consisted of about 1,000 bombs, and it was twice that large by 1955 when the Soviet atomic arsenal was estimated at between 190 and 426 bombs. In March 1954, SAC had 150 long-range B-36s, 685 medium bombers (mostly B-47s), and 540 tankers.[69]

---

[67] Joint Chiefs of Staff (1949), cited in Rosenberg (1979, pp. 72–73).

[68] National Security Council (1950b, p. 281).

[69] William B. Moore, "Memorandum Op-36C/jm," memorandum from Executive Assistant to the Director of Op-36, the Atomic Energy Division, Office of the Chief of Naval Operations, to Rear Admiral George C. Wright USN, Director of Op-36C, March 18, 1954, in David Alan Rosenberg and W. B. Moore, "'Smoking Radiating Ruin at the End of Two Hours': Documents on American Plans for Nuclear War with the Soviet Union, 1954–55," *International Security*, Vol. 6, No. 3, 1981, pp. 3–38, p. 18.

Yet, even with this dramatic increase in capability, prospects for success in a preventive war against the Soviet Union were far from certain.

In July 1954, the JCS tasked the WSEG to analyze the probable impacts of a coordinated atomic offensive by SAC and U.S. tactical forces in Europe and the Middle East on the Soviet Union's warfighting capacity. Once again, despite the size advantage of the U.S. atomic arsenal in that era, the findings reported in February 1955 were not encouraging. Due to inadequate intelligence on Soviet dispersal airfields and uncertainties regarding the ability to destroy Soviet aircraft before they could be launched, the WSEG concluded that "the atomic offensives do not provide a high degree of assurance of neutralizing the Soviet atomic capability." Although the attack would cause 77 million casualties (60 million of them fatal) and "virtually wipe out the Soviet Bloc industrial capabilities," the Soviets might have adequate military stockpiles to conduct sustained operations for four to seven months. Allied success would depend on the ability to achieve air superiority, provide adequate defense in depth to preclude Soviet penetrations, and fight effectively enough to compel Soviet forces to concentrate and present targets for atomic weapons; yet, due to the "slow buildup capability of the allies compared to the Soviets, it appear[ed] unlikely that the Soviets could be contained in Central Europe for more than one or two months with the present allocation of atomic weapons." The WSEG estimated that with 100 more weapons for use against "troop targets," the allies would have a "fair chance of holding for some five or six months" assuming air superiority and the ability to force Soviet concentrations.[70]

Ironically, in the early years, these limitations played a smaller role in the preventive attack debate than one might expect. Due to the veil of secrecy that concealed details about the atomic stockpile and capabilities to deliver the weapons, most opponents of preventive war were unaware of the deficiencies, while some of the most vocal advocates—

---

[70] "Briefing of WSEG Report No. 12," provided in Rosenberg and Moore (1981, pp. 29-38). The report emphasized that maintaining air superiority was essential for any chance of success. At the same time, it was pessimistic about the ability to do so, anticipating that Soviet atomic strikes on allied airfields would disrupt allied fighter operations.

namely the Air Force generals and a handful of other military flag officers—were among the privileged few who knew how meager America's early strategic capabilities really were. Even President Truman was not formally briefed on the size of the atomic stockpile until April 1947, and was "shocked to discover that it was only a fraction as large as he had thought."[71] By the time of the Eisenhower administration, the first WSEG study and the Harmon Committee report had given decision-makers a more realistic view of the nation's atomic warfare capabilities, but even then, opposition to preventive war was largely based on factors other than the uncertainty of success.

One of those factors was the apparent inability of civilian and military leaders, including those advocating preventive war, to fathom what the United States would do after such a conflict, even if it won. Forrestal once said, "Conquering the Russians is one thing [but] finding out what to do with them afterward is an entirely different problem."[72] Eisenhower echoed that sentiment when he observed, "The colossal job of occupying the territories of the defeated enemy would be far beyond the resources of the United States at the end of such a war."[73] At one point he even said, "The only thing worse than losing a global war was winning one."[74]

Another factor was the stiff resistance such thinking generated from U.S. allies. The Truman Administration acknowledged some of their concerns in NSC-68 when it said, "Many would doubt that it was a 'just war' and that all reasonable possibilities for a peaceful settlement had been explored in good faith particularly in Western Europe. . . . It would, therefore, be difficult after such a war to create a satisfactory international order among nations."[75] But the Europeans also had pragmatic reasons for fearing a preventive war. As the first outlines of

---

[71] Rosenberg (1979, p. 66).

[72] Gaddis (1997, p. 89).

[73] "Notes of NSC Meeting," March 4, 1954a, in U.S. Department of State, *Foreign Relations of the United States 1952–1954*, Vol. II: *National Security Affairs*, Washington, D.C.: U.S. Department of State, 1984, p. 636, quoted in Trachtenberg (1999, p. 40).

[74] Quoted in Trachtenberg (1999, p. 40).

[75] National Security Council (1950b, pp. 281–282).

a nuclear arms race began to emerge in the early 1950s, they became increasingly uneasy about the prospects of being caught between the superpowers in a conflict that would be catastrophic for them. These concerns raised fears in Washington that a Soviet-American confrontation might lead to neutralization of America's frontline allies in both Europe and Asia.[76]

But the main impediment that made preventive war such an unattractive option to American policymakers was the fact that so many of them and their constituents considered it an immoral act, one inconsistent with American tradition. In June 1950, Secretary of State Dean Acheson publicly acknowledged that preventive war was a conceivable policy option, but declared, "All responsible men must agree that such a course is unthinkable for us. It would violate every moral principle of our people."[77] Referring to Francis Matthews' call for preventive war in his Boston Navy Yard speech, President Truman wrote in his memoirs: "I have always been opposed to even the thought of such a war. There is nothing more foolish than to think that war can be stopped by war. You don't 'prevent' anything by war except peace."[78] Years later, when Army Chief of Staff General Matthew Ridgway heard the JCS Advanced Study Group propose that the United States provoke a war with Moscow before the Soviet thermonuclear capability became a serious threat, he denounced the idea as "contrary to every principle upon which our Nation has been founded" and "abhorrent to the great mass of American people."[79] He was right about public opinion. In July 1950, a Gallup poll indicated that only 14 percent of Ameri-

---

[76] Dulles was especially concerned about the alliance system unraveling, but the JCS also worried that fear of atomic war might drive the allies to neutrality. See "JCS to Wilson, 23 June 1954," in U.S. Department of State, *Foreign Relations of the United States 1952–1954*, Vol. II: *National Security Affairs*, Washington, D.C.: U.S. Department of State, 1984, pp. 680–686, cited in Trachtenberg (1999, p. 41).

[77] Dean Acheson, "Address Before the Civic Federation of Dallas and the Community Course of Southern Methodist University," Dallas, Tex., June 13, 1950, quoted in Dean Acheson, *The Pattern of Responsibility*, Boston: Houghton Mifflin, 1952, p. 25.

[78] Harry S Truman, *Memoirs by Harry S Truman: Years of Trial and Hope* (Vol. 2), New York: Doubleday, 1956, p. 383.

[79] Ridgway (1954), quoted in Rosenberg (1983, p. 34).

cans felt the United States should respond to the invasion of South Korea with a declaration of war on the Soviet Union.[80] In September 1954, a Gallup poll asked whether Americans agreed with the statement, "[W]e should go to war against Russia now while we still have the advantage in atomic bombs and hydrogen bombs." Less than 14 percent of respondents agreed, while 75 percent disagreed.[81] Perhaps Secretary of State Dulles captured the prevailing sentiment best when he said, "No man should arrogate to himself the power to decide that the future of mankind would benefit by an action entailing the killing of tens of millions of people."[82]

The Results

The thirty-odd years of Cold War history that followed these events testify that the containment and deterrence strategies developed during the Truman and Eisenhower administrations were sound. While Marxist or procommunist movements won occasional victories in the Third World, communism was largely contained, and by the end of the 1980s, it had lost its economic viability and popular appeal in most of the world. Likewise, despite early fears that an atomic-armed Soviet Union might be irrationally aggressive—akin to contemporary U.S. concerns about the behavior of nuclear-armed rogue states—Moscow proved to be surprisingly careful in most of its dealings with Washington. Though confrontations did occur, most notably the Berlin crises and the Cuban missile crisis (discussed below), when they did, both sides behaved in a cautious, measured manner and deterrence held sway.

Deterrence and containment strategies ultimately cost the United States trillions of dollars, but they were not nearly as expensive as a pre-

---

[80] Gallup Poll News Service, *The Gallup Poll No. 458*, July 7, 1950, Question qn15, "Do you think the United States should declare war on Russia now?" cited in Trachtenberg (1999, p. 5, note 2).

[81] Gallup Poll News Service, *The Gallup Poll No. 536*, August 24, 1954, Question qn6c, "Some people say we should go to war against Russia now while we still have the advantage in atomic bombs and hydrogen bombs. Do you agree or disagree with this point of view?" cited in Trachtenberg (1999, p. 5, note 2).

[82] Quoted in Trachtenberg (1999, p. 44).

ventive war would have been. Launching an air-atomic offensive on the Soviet Union before Moscow acquired atomic weapons would almost certainly have cost millions of lives, not only in Russia and Eastern Europe, but in the probable Soviet invasion of Western Europe as well. The ultimate outcome would likely have been Soviet domination of continental Europe, crippling the United States economically and prolonging the East-West confrontation, if not tipping the long-term balance in Moscow's favor. Attacking the Soviets in the 1950s, after the United States had stockpiled a thousand or more bombs and Moscow had hundreds, would have increased the carnage in Russia enormously and probably would have cost the lives of millions of Americans. It might well have resulted in massive destruction of U.S. cities and industry, and the probable subsequent Soviet domination in Europe would have denied America the lifeblood of Western trade that would be essential for economic recovery. In either era, deliberately provoking a war or launching a surprise attack would likely have cost the U.S. government its moral legitimacy with the American people, and would in all probability not have eliminated the threat that inspired it.

This case offers several implications for those considering anticipatory attack strategies today. First, the cost-benefit tradeoffs of resorting to preventive attack appear increasingly attractive when an adversary is perceived to be implacably hostile and potentially irrational. The expected benefits of preventive war rise when a weaker adversary approaches the threshold of a substantial increase in power, such as a major advance in weapon technology. Most advocates of anticipatory attack recognize that such a strategy entails costs, but they believe the costs of their preferred strategy will be less than those incurred by waiting for the adversary to become more powerful or to strike first. Anticipatory attack is seen as a way to limit damage, when some amount of damage is believed to be inevitable.

None of these insights is new, but what this case reveals is that advocates of anticipatory attack may fail to evaluate all the costs their proposed strategy would incur. In this case, they tended to base their cost-benefit analyses solely on first-order tradeoffs—that is, arguing that attacking promptly would result in fewer casualties than would be incurred if the enemy were granted the initiative, but not taking into account second-order political, economic, and moral costs, or even the follow-on military implications of the war they wished to initiate. None of the advocates of preventive war had an answer for the question of what to do with the Soviet Union after the conflict. Strangely, many of them argued for war in spite of knowing that deficiencies in American capability made its success unlikely. Moreover, none of them seemed to consider the impacts such an act would have had on the alliance system or America's position in world affairs, or addressed the long-term implications of the precedent such an act would have set in the world. None seemed to consider how launching a preventive attack would have affected civil relations within the United States, or America's traditions and sense of moral legitimacy—in essence, its national conscience. Fortunately, Presidents Truman and Eisenhower, and less bellicose policymakers in both administrations, did take these costs into consideration.

U.S. Consideration of Preventive Attack Against China

In the early 1960s, as Beijing strove to develop nuclear weapons, American policymakers wondered whether a nuclear-armed People's Republic of China (PRC) would be a responsible world citizen and what implications that development might portend for further nuclear proliferation. President Kennedy, in particular, worried that Mao Zedong might be more aggressive and less susceptible to deterrence than Soviet leaders appeared to have been to date. At the same time, growing antipathy between Mao and Nikita Khrushchev suggested to Kennedy and his advisors that Washington and Moscow might share an interest in constraining China's nuclear ambitions. Acting on that impression, they sought a nuclear test–ban treaty with the Soviets, hoping that agreement would, in addition to dampening the Soviet-American nuclear arms race, generate international pressure to forestall Beijing's nuclear development and aggravate already strained Sino-Soviet relations.

Although Khrushchev showed little interest in signing a treaty at first, he warmed to the idea after the Cuban missile crisis. Encouraged by Moscow's new tone, Kennedy hoped the Soviet Union would pressure China to abandon its nuclear ambitions, and some evidence suggests he may have envisioned the possibility of a combined Soviet-American military strike on China's nuclear research facility if Beijing could not be constrained by diplomatic pressure alone. Records indicate this idea lived on into the Johnson administration, until late 1964.

This case study examines these events to see how they might inform thinking about the virtues and dangers of anticipatory attacks today. It reviews the geopolitical environment in the early 1960s, assesses the arguments advanced for and against taking military action to prevent Chinese nuclear development, and explains why neither Kennedy nor Johnson chose to use force against China. Finally, it considers the short- and long-term outcomes of these decisions and weighs the implications for situations in the future where anticipatory attacks are seen as an option.

The Situation

By the time John F. Kennedy assumed the Presidency in January 1961, the People's Republic of China (PRC) was well advanced in its effort to develop nuclear weapons. Having received technical assistance from the Soviet Union from 1955 until Mao's bellicosity and recklessness in the Taiwan Straits convinced the Soviets to stop helping them in 1959, the Chinese had built an extensive research facility and test site at Lop Nor in western China.[83] The Kennedy administration monitored China's nuclear progress with growing concern. It also followed the widening rift in Sino-Soviet relations as Beijing increasingly challenged Moscow's leadership of the world communist movement and rebuked the Russians for not taking a more militant stand against the West.

Encouraged by intelligence assessments that the Soviet Union and China shared few common interests beyond ideology, President Kennedy and his key staff became intrigued by the prospects of cleav-

---

[83] For an interesting account of how China's shelling of Quemoy in 1958, followed by Mao's proclamations about China's ability to absorb an American nuclear attack, shocked the Russians into terminating their assistance, see Gaddis (1997, pp. 249–253).

ing the Sino-Soviet relationship.[84] They believed the United States and Soviet Union, as the world's nuclear superpowers, shared a "condominium of interests" in maintaining peace and stability in Europe and Asia, and constraining Beijing's nuclear development might be one of those mutual interests. Consequently, Moscow might be receptive to the prospects of entering a nuclear test–ban agreement with the United States as a means of bringing international pressure to bear on Beijing. The President decided that he should try to meet with Khrushchev at the earliest possible date to explore this issue, among others.[85]

President Kennedy met with Khrushchev in Vienna that June, but to his disappointment, the Soviet leader did not embrace the condominium of interests the Americans had envisioned. In fact, discussions between the President and Chairman turned confrontational across a wide range of topics. Khrushchev showed no interest in coming to terms with the United States on a nuclear test ban, and he lectured Kennedy about Washington's longstanding refusal to recognize the PRC.[86] This rebuff turned out to be only a foretaste of the tensions that were building between Washington and Moscow. Over the next year and a half, Soviet-American relations grew steadily worse, culminating in the Cuban missile crisis in October 1962.

That event appears to have sobered both nations to the risks of nuclear war, and with that new sobriety came a renewed interest in

---

[84] "National Intelligence Estimate: Estimate of the World Situation," NIE 1-61, January 17, 1961, in U.S. Department of State, *Foreign Relations of the United States 1961–1963*, Vol. V: *Soviet Union*, Washington, D.C.: U.S. Department of State, Doc. 6, 1998.

[85] McGeorge Bundy, "Notes on Discussion of the Thinking of the Soviet Leadership," Cabinet Room, February 11, 1961, cited in Gordon H. Chang, *Friends and Enemies: The United States, China, and the Soviet Union, 1948–1972*, Stanford, Calif.: Stanford University Press, 1990, pp. 229–230.

[86] Alexander Akalovsky, "Memorandum of Conversation: Vienna Meeting Between the President and Chairman Khrushchev," June 3, 1961a, 3:00 p.m., Vienna, in U.S. Department of State, *Foreign Relations of the United States, 1961–1963*, Vol. V: *Soviet Union*, Washington, D.C.: U.S. Department of State, Doc. 85, 1998; Alexander Akalovsky, "Memorandum of Conversation: Meeting Between the President and Chairman Khrushchev in Vienna," June 4, 1961b, Vienna, in U.S. Department of State, *Foreign Relations of the United States, 1961–1963*, Vol. V: *Soviet Union*, Washington, D.C.: U.S. Department of State, Doc. 87, 1998.

reaching an agreement on a nuclear test ban. In meetings with Soviet Ambassador Anatoly Dobrynin in late 1962 and early 1963, American representatives discussed what the superpowers might do to relieve tensions and normalize relations. Encouraged by Dobrynin's constructive tone and subsequent statements from Moscow, in April 1963, President Kennedy and British Prime Minister Harold Macmillan sent Khrushchev a joint proposal to set up a high-level conference to negotiate a nuclear test–ban treaty. Moscow did not respond at first, and Dobrynin reemphasized Soviet objections to Washington's previous test-ban proposals in a May meeting with Special Assistant for National Security Affairs McGeorge Bundy, but Khrushchev surprised American leaders on June 7 by accepting the April conference proposal.[87]

Meanwhile, Sino-Soviet relations continued to deteriorate. Beijing castigated Moscow for provoking the Cuban missile crisis on the one hand and for backing down to the Americans on the other. An open propaganda war ensued, in which Beijing and Moscow attacked each other so bitterly that other communist leaders worried whether the world communist movement might be irreparably damaged. To make matters worse, the ongoing border conflict between China and India put the Soviet Union in an awkward position, as it was nominally allied with Beijing, but was friendly to New Delhi. In the midst of the quarrelling, Chinese harassment forced Moscow to close its last two consulates in China.[88]

Talk of a Preventive Strike. As the Kennedy administration's hopes of getting a nuclear test–ban treaty gained new life, so did expectations that Soviet cooperation might somehow be used to constrain China's

---

[87] Dobrynin restated the standing Soviet objection to onsite inspections. When Bundy reminded him of the Administration's concern about a nuclear-armed China, Dobrynin pointedly countered that Moscow was concerned about U.S. intentions to arm NATO with nuclear weapons that could end up in German hands. See McGeorge Bundy, "Memorandum of Conversation Between the President's Special Assistant for National Security Affairs (Bundy) and the Soviet Ambassador (Dobrynin)," May 17, 1963, Washington, D.C., in U.S. Department of State, *Foreign Relations of the United States, 1961–1963*, Vol. V: *Soviet Union*, Washington, D.C.: U.S. Department of State, Doc. 322, 1998.

[88] See Central Intelligence Agency, "Current Intelligence Weekly Review," October 12, 1962, Washington, D.C., in U.S. Department of State, *Foreign Relations of the United States, 1961–1963*, Vol. V: *Soviet Union*, Washington, D.C.: U.S. Department of State, Doc. 244,

nuclear weapons program. When the President addressed the National Security Council on January 22, 1963, he expressed concern once again about the prospects of a nuclear-armed China and his opinion that a test-ban agreement might produce pressure against development of such a capability. "Any negotiations that can hold back the Chinese Communists are important, he said, because they loom as our major antagonists in the late 60s and beyond."[89]

Encouraged by these remarks, W. Averill Harriman wrote Kennedy the following day, saying "the most important matter in the interest of our security which you touched upon was the question of attempting to prevent Red China from obtaining nuclear capability, and the possibility of working with the Soviets to this end." He went on to say he had spoken to several Russians on this matter and one had told him that "if the United States and the Soviet Union agreed, world opinion would prevent China from acting independently." Because of "the earnest manner in which he spoke," Harriman had the impression that "what the Kremlin had in mind was that with such an agreement, together we could compel China to stop nuclear development, threatening to take out the facilities if necessary."[90]

The conference was scheduled to take place in Moscow in mid-July 1963. Kennedy appointed Harriman to head the American negotiating team and told him to "go as far as he wished in exploring the

---

1998, pp. 3–4; Central Intelligence Agency, "Current Intelligence Weekly Review," January 18, 1963a, Washington, D.C., in U.S. Department of State, *Foreign Relations of the United States, 1961–1963, Volume V: Soviet Union*, Washington, D.C.: U.S. Department of State, Doc. 280, 1998, pp. 1–3; Central Intelligence Agency, "Current Intelligence Weekly Review," June 21, 1963b, Washington, D.C., in U.S. Department of State, *Foreign Relations of the United States, 1961–1963, Volume V: Soviet Union*, Washington, D.C.: U.S. Department of State, Doc. 334, 1998, pp. 2–4.

[89] "Editorial Note," in U.S. Department of State, *Foreign Relations of the United States, 1961–1963*, Vol. XXII: *China, Korea, Japan*, Washington, D.C.: U.S. Department of State, Doc. 164, 1996.

[90] Quoted in U.S. Department of State, *Foreign Relations of the United States, 1961–1963, Vol VIII: National Security Policy*, Washington, D.C.: U.S. Department of State, 1996a, pp. 457–462.

possibility of a Soviet-American understanding with regard to China."[91] As the conference date approached, the administration began assembling briefing books to prepare the team for the negotiations. Among the papers included in those books was one written in the Arms Control and Disarmament Agency discussing possible Soviet responses to a U.S. proposal to "take radical steps, in cooperation with the USSR, to prevent the further proliferation of nuclear capabilities." The paper asserted that if Moscow accepted the proposal, "they would be obliged to see it through to the very end," which might require "Soviet, or possibly joint US-USSR, use of military force" against China.[92]

The American team arrived in Moscow on July 14, 1963, and negotiations began the following day with Harriman and Britain's Lord Hailsham meeting with Khrushchev. Later that day, Harriman reported to Washington that Khrushchev had immediately ruled out the possibility of a comprehensive treaty and on-site inspections, but seemed interested in reaching a three-environment agreement. When Harriman raised the issue of China, Khrushchev said it would be years before Beijing became a nuclear power, so he was not particularly concerned.[93] In response, Kennedy wired Harriman telling him he was convinced the Chinese problem was more serious than Khrushchev's comments allowed. He urged Harriman to press the question in a private meeting and "try to elicit Khrushchev's views of means of limiting

---

[91] Arthur Meier Schlesinger, *A Thousand Days: John F. Kennedy in the White House*, Boston: Houghton Mifflin, 1965, p. 825, quoted in Chang (1990, p. 241).

[92] Arthur Barbar, "Briefing Book on US-Soviet Non-Diffusion Agreement for Discussion at the Moscow Meeting," June 12, 1963, Kennedy Papers, NSF, Box 265, U.S. Arms Control and Disarmament Agency, *Disarmament*, Vol. 1, pp. 1–7, quoted in Chang (1990, pp. 244–245). Chang maintains that a not-yet-declassified section of the briefing book also exists, entitled "Military and Other Sanctions Against Communist China."

[93] W. Averill Harriman, "Telegram from the Embassy in the Soviet Union to the Department of State," Moscow, July 15, 1963a, 10:00 p.m., in U.S. Department of State, *Foreign Relations of the United States, 1961–1963*, Vol. VII: *Arms Control and Disarmament*, Washington, D.C.: U.S. Department of State, Doc. 325, 1995.

or preventing Chinese nuclear development and his willingness either to take Soviet action or accept U.S. action aimed in this direction."[94]

There is no record that Harriman ever raised the issue of a preventive strike with Khrushchev in any meeting, private or otherwise. However, on July 18, 1963, he informed Washington he had decided to play down further "nondissemination" discussions, although he had used them "as one approach to hammer away at China." He said Khrushchev and Foreign Minister Andrei Gromyko had shown no interest in such discussions and, in fact, "brushed them off on several occasions." He felt that if he pursued the issue, the Soviets might link it to U.S. nuclear weapons in Europe.[95] The President agreed and told Harriman to ask Hailsham to downplay it as well.[96]

After taking several additional days to work out such issues as how to handle violations, how to add new signatories to the treaty, and rights of withdrawal, the negotiators initialed their agreement on July 25 and signed the treaty on August 5, 1963. The diplomatic record suggests little more was said about China during the final days of negotiation; however, on July 19, 1963, Harriman speculated that stiff Soviet objections to the American team's proposed wording on a party's right to withdraw should another country conduct a test reflected their belief that acceptance of such a clause "would constitute open admission [of]

---

[94] John F. Kennedy, "Telegram from the Department of State to the Embassy in the Soviet Union," Washington, July 15, 1963a, in U.S. Department of State, *Foreign Relations of the United States, 1961–1963*, Vol. VII: *Arms Control and Disarmament*, Washington, D.C.: U.S. Department of State, Doc. 326, 1995, p. 801.

[95] W. Averill Harriman, "Telegram from the Embassy in the Soviet Union to the Department of State," Moscow, July 18, 1963b, 5:00 p.m., in U.S. Department of State, *Foreign Relations of the United States, 1961–1963*, Vol. VII: *Arms Control and Disarmament*, Washington, D.C.: U.S. Department of State, Doc. 331, 1995.

[96] John F. Kennedy, "Telegram from the Department of State to the Emassy in the Soviet Union," Washington, July 18, 1963b, in U.S. Department of State, *Foreign Relations of the United States, 1961–1963*, Vol. VII: *Arms Control and Disarmament*, Washington, D.C.: U.S. Department of State, Doc. 332, 1995, p. 813.

US pressure on Sovs to do something about [the] Chinese nuclear threat." He said they were unwilling to make such an admission.[97]

While it is unclear how far Kennedy hoped to go with the Soviets to constrain Beijing's nuclear weapon program, records suggest that several members of his administration wondered about the viability of a military strike even after the limited test-ban treaty was signed, and staff work on this idea carried over into the Johnson administration. On July 31, 1963, Acting Assistant Secretary of Defense for International Security Affairs William Bundy sent a memorandum to the Chairman of the Joint Chiefs of Staff requesting a contingency plan for an attack with conventional weapons on the Chinese nuclear production facilities. This attack would be designed to "cause severest impact on and delay in the Chinese nuclear program." On December 14, the JCS responded with a memorandum indicating that such an attack was feasible, but recommending nuclear weapons be considered for it.[98]

Meanwhile, an interdepartmental group of representatives from the Departments of State and Defense, the CIA, and the U.S. Information Agency (USIA) assembled to study the military and political implications of China achieving a nuclear capability, and on October 15, 1963, Secretary of State Dean Rusk held a policy planning meeting to discuss the paper that group produced. It argued that such a development would not pose a substantial military threat and would only "heighten already existing issues rather than pose wholly new problems." Concluding that the challenge presented by China's nuclear development would be more diplomatic than military, it ruled out consideration of

---

[97] W. Averill Harriman, "Telegram from the Embassy in the Soviet Union to the Department of State," Moscow, July 19, 1963c, 8:00 p.m., in U.S. Department of State, *Foreign Relations of the United States, 1961–1963*, Vol. VII: *Arms Control and Disarmament*, Washington, D.C.: U.S. Department of State, Doc. 333, 1995.

[98] Joint Chiefs of Staff, memorandum, JCSM-986-63, December 14, 1963, Washington National Records Center, RG 330, OSD Files: FRC 91-0017, 471.61 China Reds; and William Bundy, memorandum, July 31, 1963, Washington National Records Center, RG 330, OSD Files: FRC 91-0017, 471.61 China Reds; both referenced in Robert W. Komer, "Memorandum from Robert W. Komer of the National Security Council Staff to the President's Special Assistant for National Security Affairs (Bundy)," Washington, D.C., February 26, 1964a, Johnson Library, National Security File, Komer Files, China (CPR), Nuclear Explosion/Capability.

a U.S. preventive attack. The individuals at Rusk's meeting generally agreed with the findings, but noted that a Chinese nuclear capability might create more difficulties for Taiwan than the paper allowed. They also suggested that it would not take a large nuclear arsenal to terrorize and coerce China's Asian neighbors, but concluded that the U.S. nuclear deterrent "would act as a major restraint" on Beijing.[99]

Robert Komer of the NSC staff reported this discussion to McGeorge Bundy and, at Walt Rostow's urging, gave him a copy of the paper. William Bundy also sent a copy to the JCS for comment. Noting that the meeting consensus was that the Chinese would behave cautiously even after they obtained a few nuclear weapons, Komer saw little incentive to look for ways to "'strangle the baby in the cradle' before the Chinese developed a capability." However, the JCS responded with a memo recommending an interagency group be established "to consider ways and means for impeding the Chinese Communist nuclear development program." In any event, NSC Executive Secretary Bromley Smith felt the Chinese nuclear capability was "so far down the road" that he did not think the President should be troubled with it again that year. McGeorge Bundy apparently agreed.[100]

Consideration of Preventive Attack by the Johnson Administration. President Kennedy did not live to address the issue again, and seeing no urgency in the October 15 paper, Komer "sat on it" until Rostow pressed him to send the conclusions to President Johnson. In a February 26, 1964, note to McGeorge Bundy, Komer offered to distill the paper into a one-pager for the President and complained that the December 14 JCS memo recommending that they consider the use of

---

[99] See "Highlights of Secretary Rusk's Policy Planning Meeting," October 15, 1963, *Foreign Relations of the United States, 1961–1963*, Vol. XXII: *Northeast Asia*, Washington, D.C.: U.S. Department of State, Doc. 191, 1996. Interestingly, someone at the policy planning meeting said, "Prevention of a ChiCom nuclear capability is one important goal that we share in common with the Soviets," then speculated, "The USSR may mobilize all the means at its disposal to forestall the ChiComs from acquiring a nuclear capability."

[100] Robert W. Komer, "Memorandum from Robert W. Komer of the National Security Council to the President's Special Assistant for National Security Affairs (Bundy)," November 5, 1963, Washington, D.C., in U.S. Department of State, *Foreign Relations of the United States, 1961–1963*, Vol. XXII: *China, Korea, Japan*, Washington, D.C.: U.S. Department of State, Doc. 193, 1996.

nuclear weapons against the Chinese production facilities further complicated the picture. He also complained that Rostow was "also poking around in the pre-emptive action field" and asked if they wanted that. Bundy jotted back, "I'm for this."[101]

Staff work on the China nuclear weapons development issue appeared to culminate in April 1964. That month, Rostow sent McGeorge Bundy a Policy Planning Council paper arguing that the Chinese capability would not be significant enough to "justify the undertaking of actions which would involve great political costs or high military risks." The paper asserted that it was unlikely the United States could "develop a viable political basis for action" against the Chinese, and pointed out that, due to the inability to locate all the production facilities with certainty, even a successful strike might not keep China from producing a bomb within the next few years.[102] A few days later, Rostow sent President Johnson a separate paper that he said summarized a "major planning exercise" the Policy Planning Council had conducted over the previous year. This paper said a Chinese nuclear test could occur any time (but probably not before late 1964 or later), but the effects of such a development would be more psychological than military, so no major policy change was required. It said "pre-emptive military action" would be undesirable except, possibly, as part of a "general action against the mainland in response to a major ChiCom aggression." Although Rostow's cover memo said the issue would be the subject of "further intensive staffing on a particularly secure basis," records available to date do not suggest that such staffing occurred.

Though the option of launching a preventive attack seemed to have been abandoned in April, it suddenly resurfaced in late 1964 when intelligence indicated a Chinese nuclear test was imminent. Meeting at the State Department on September 15, 1964, Rusk, McGeorge

---

[101] Komer (1964a).

[102] Robert Johnson, "Paper Prepared in the Policy Planning Council: An Exploration of the Possible Bases for Action Against the Chinese Communist Nuclear Facilities," April 14, 1964, in U.S. Department of State, *Foreign Relations of the United States, 1964–1968*, Vol. XXX: *China*, Washington, D.C.: U.S. Department of State, Doc. 25, 1998.

Bundy, Defense Secretary Robert McNamara, and CIA Director John McCone laid out a position they would take to the President later that afternoon. They agreed they were not in favor of "unprovoked unilateral U.S. military action against Chinese nuclear installations" at that time. However, they believed there were

> many possibilities for joint action with the Soviet Government if that Government [was] interested. Such possibilities [included] a warning to the Chinese against tests, a possible undertaking to give up underground testing and to hold the Chinese accountable if they test in any way, and even a possible agreement to cooperate in preventive military action.[103]

They felt Rusk should explore the matter with Ambassador Dobrynin as soon as possible. The President met with Rusk, McNamara, and Bundy in the Cabinet Room that afternoon and approved their proposal.[104]

Two days later, Henry Rowan, from the Defense Department's International Security Affairs Office, challenged the interdepartmental planning group's "excessively cheery" view of the imminent Chinese nuclear expansion. He admitted that the short-term threat of China's rudimentary capability would be small, but he insisted the longer-term implications were "horrendous." He pointed out how small the Soviet capability had been initially, but how much its subsequent growth had affected American policies in the 15 years that followed. The Chinese could develop a crude intercontinental ballistic missile (ICBM) within 15 years, triggering costly U.S. antiballistic missile or civil-defense efforts. Moreover, he argued, Chinese nuclear weapons might prompt

---

[103] McGeorge Bundy, "Memorandum of Conversation: Memorandum of Conversation with Ambassador Dobrynin," September 25, 1964b, 1–3:30 p.m., in U.S. Department of State, *Foreign Relations of the United States, 1964–1968*, Vol. XXX: *China*, Washington, D.C.: U.S. Department of State, Doc. 54, 1998.

[104] McGeorge Bundy (1964b).

India to go nuclear, and Beijing might offer nuclear technology to others, such as Egypt's President Nasser.[105]

Rowan believed that the United States ought to consider conducting a limited, nonnuclear air attack to destroy China's two key nuclear installations, in hopes of setting the Chinese program back two to five years and deterring them from rebuilding. He thought the Soviets might publicly protest such an act, but would secretly approve of it, and there was a chance Washington could "bring them around in advance." Robert Johnson, author of the previous papers arguing moderation, rebutted Rowan's arguments, asserting that the Soviet-Chinese analogy was faulty. American nuclear superiority would deter Chinese aggression, and U.S. antiballistic missile and civil-defense decisions would not be so sensitive to Chinese developments. He judged Rowan's proliferation argument to be the strongest, but countries like Israel might have reasons to seek nuclear weapons regardless of what China did. Contending a "one-time attack wouldn't do the job" anyway, Johnson stood by his earlier conviction that the United States should rely on arms control and diplomacy to limit the impact of Chinese nuclear developments rather than resort to a first strike.[106]

Others' opinions were more tentative than Rowan's and Johnson's. Komer noted that, while U.S. defense decisions might not be sensitive to Chinese developments, a more likely scenario would entail the Chinese program triggering Soviet antiballistic missile and civil-defense efforts, thus triggering U.S. spending. Rostow felt the Chinese would be more cautious once they got nuclear weapons. He said if Washington and Moscow had just agreed on a major arms-control agreement, the conditions might be right for a preemptive strike, but he and Komer questioned what kind of precedent such an attack might create. "Would preemption of [the] ChiComs encourage Nasser to take out Israeli nuclear facilities? Would it encourage the Soviets to play similar

---

[105]Robert W. Komer, "Memorandum from Robert W. Komer of the National Security Council Staff to the President's Special Assistant for National Security Affairs (Bundy)," September 18, 1964b, Washington, D.C., in U.S. Department of State, *Foreign Relations of the United States, 1964–1968*, Vol. XXX: *Chiina*, Washington, D.C.: U.S. Department of State, Doc. 51, 1998.

[106]Komer (1964b).

games?" Rostow concluded by saying that if the Chinese attacked in Southeast Asia, the United States would have an overwhelming case for preemption; otherwise, the planning group should consider it only the context of a broader modus vivendi with Moscow in an effort to isolate Beijing. If that would occur, the international reaction to preemption would be considerably less.[107]

Secretary Rusk did not meet with Dobrynin in the days immediately following these meetings, but on September 25, 1964, McGeorge Bundy met with him over lunch and made a "principal effort to direct the Ambassador's attention to the problem of Communist Chinese nuclear weapons." He made it plain that Washington was ready for "private and serious talk" about what to do about the problem "if there were any interest in the Soviet government." Dobrynin avoided the issue and gave Bundy the impression "that in the thinking of the Soviet Government the Chinese nuclear capability was already, in effect, taken for granted."[108]

Bundy's impression was probably correct. On October 16, 1964, China exploded its first nuclear device at the Lop Nor test site. The Johnson administration released a public statement intended to minimize the event's psychological impact in the international community.[109] The Soviet Union was remarkably silent on the occasion. Moscow was probably preoccupied with other concerns—Alexei Kosygin had replaced Khrushchev as chairman of the Council of Ministers the day before. In meetings with the Soviets during the weeks following the test, discussions focused on what positions the new Soviet leadership would take on a wide range of policy issues. When Americans brought

---

[107] Komer (1964b). Komer adds as an aside that when Rostow asked Richard Helms his view, he said he had raised the preemption question at the White House several times and had been told to "keep his mouth shut." He and other attendees felt there was some secretive planning afoot. Komer said, "If so, or if there ought to be, the best cover for it might be simply to put out the word that we've taken a negative decision on the matter."

[108] McGeorge Bundy (1964b).

[109] McGeorge Bundy, "Memorandum for Record: Meeting of an Executive Group of the National Security Council," October 16, 1964d, in U.S. Department of State, *Foreign Relations of the United States, 1964–1968*, Vol. XXX: *China*, Washington, D.C.: U.S. Department of State, Doc. 57, 1998.

up the Chinese, Ambassador Dobrynin downplayed the significance of the nuclear test and Foreign Minister Gromyko emphasized that it was time for the United States to reevaluate its policies regarding nonrecognition of Beijing and the PRC's admittance to the United Nations.[110] In fact, discussions in Washington focused on those very issues, though such policy changes would not occur until the Nixon administration. On the other hand, what was notably absent from the American policy debate after the Chinese test was further talk of a preventive attack on China's nuclear production facilities.

The Threat

President Kennedy believed a nuclear-armed China would be a direct threat to U.S. forces, allies, and friends in Asia. Although Beijing's initial capability would be rudimentary, he was convinced it would grow quickly enough to make China America's principal enemy in the late 1960s and beyond.[111] Kennedy saw Mao Zedong as a fanatically aggressive communist and apparently thought he was irrational. Witnesses reported hearing the President tell France's Minister of Culture Andre Malraux that the Chinese "would be perfectly prepared to sacrifice hundreds of millions of their own lives" to carry out Mao's militant policies, and that China would be a "great menace in the future to humanity, the free world, and freedom on earth."[112]

Neither his staff nor anyone in the Johnson administration seemed to share Kennedy's level of apprehension, though some appreciated the short- and long-term threats China's nuclear program presented. All of them acknowledged that the short-term threats were more political and psychological than military. While China's initial capability would

---

[110] See "Memorandum of a Conversation: Chinese Communist Nuclear Detonation," October 20, 1964, 6:10 p.m., Washington, D.C., in U.S. Department of State, *Foreign Relations of the United States, 1964–1968*, Vol. XXX: *China*, Washington, D.C.: U.S. Department of State, Doc. 61, 1998; Foy D. Kohler, "Telegram from the Embassy in the Soviet Union to the Department of State," November 11, 1964, 10:00 p.m., Moscow, in U.S. Department of State, *Foreign Relations of the United States, 1964–1968*, Vol. XIV: *Soviet Union*, Washington, D.C.: U.S. Department of State, Doc. 70, 2001.

[111] "Editorial Note" (1996).

[112] William R. Tyler, oral history, March 7, 1964, quoted in Chang (1990, p. 236).

not pose a direct military threat, it might give Beijing some degree of coercive leverage over its neighbors, yet even that could be mitigated by reassuring friends and allies that the United States would meet its security commitments in Asia. At most, nuclear capability might gain the PRC a degree of political stature at the expense of the United States and its noncommunist friends.

Others argued that, while China's nuclear capability might not present a military threat in the immediate future, it would pose a serious long-term danger. China's nuclear development might prompt India to seek nuclear weapons. China might proliferate its nuclear technology to other states, such as Egypt. And even a rudimentary nuclear capability might embolden Beijing to be more aggressive in its use of conventional military forces. Finally, once China's nuclear threat did become more potent, it might trigger defensive investments in Washington and Moscow that could result in an expensive arms race.

Policy Options

President Kennedy sought a nuclear test–ban treaty in hopes it would generate enough international support to pressure China to abandon its nuclear ambitions. He expected the treaty to aggravate already troubled Sino-Soviet relations, and if Beijing resisted abiding by its restrictions, he thought Moscow might join Washington in attempting to compel Chinese compliance through diplomatic pressure and, perhaps, combined military action. Soviet leaders may have encouraged these expectations. They apparently sought a test-ban treaty hoping it would give them a means of vilifying China in the eyes of the world communist movement.

As it became apparent that the treaty would have no effect on Beijing's determination to develop nuclear weapons, the Kennedy administration began staffing other options for dealing with the impending Chinese nuclear threat, and this work continued in the Johnson administration. Some officials in the Defense Department were interested in conducting air strikes with conventional weapons to destroy China's nuclear production facilities, hoping thereby to set Beijing's program back several years. The State Department–chaired Policy Planning Council and interdepartmental planning group, on the other hand, believed a military strike would be too politically costly and offered too little certainty of success. They advised no major policy change. The JCS favored finding ways to impede China's nuclear development and said a conventional air strike was feasible, but recommended that the use of nuclear weapons be considered instead. No one seemed willing to do so. When the Chinese test was imminent, the Johnson administration ruled out any consideration of unilateral American action, but once again opted to seek Soviet cooperation in preventive diplomacy or military action to block the Chinese nuclear program.

Policy options not considered included efforts to woo stronger Soviet cooperation with guarantees to keep West Germany from going nuclear, offers to withdraw U.S. tactical nuclear weapons from Europe, or offers to accept Soviet positions on recognition of East Germany, a nonaggression pact in Europe, or general disarmament. American leaders also did not consider trying to deter Beijing from testing by threatening to provide India or Taiwan with nuclear weapons in response, or trying to compel Moscow's cooperation by threatening to provide West Germany with nuclear arms. All of these options were so contrary to American policies that they were beyond consideration.

The Decision Not to Attack China

Preventive attack was not an acceptable policy option for either administration because its expected political costs were too high while its benefits were far from certain. Without the legal foundation of a broadly accepted treaty or a mandate from the United Nations, launching an unprovoked attack on a sovereign state would have damaged America's reputation in the international community, antagonizing allies and alienating friends. It would have provided the world communist movement with enormous fodder for its propaganda mill and might have catapulted some nonaligned states into the communist camp. Such an act would have set a dangerous precedent that might have encouraged similar attacks against U.S. allies in the future. Launching such an attack and failing would have been embarrassing for U.S. leaders, resulting in domestic turmoil and a loss of American credibility abroad.

There was also good reason to expect that such an effort would fail. The Lop Nor nuclear research facility was located deep in China's western interior, more than 1,000 miles from any potential staging base for an American attack. A preliminary technical analysis suggested a moderately heavy conventional air attack might put the installation out of operation, assuming the attacker knew the locations of all the production facilities, but that was an assumption U.S. decisionmakers could not make.[113] It is little wonder that, while the JCS conceded such a strike was feasible, they recommended that policymakers consider doing it with nuclear weapons. Yet, crossing the nuclear threshold would have raised the political costs substantially without guaranteeing success, given the uncertainty of having found all the targets. Such a recommendation was neither politically realistic nor morally palatable. Moreover, even a successful attack would have disrupted the Chinese nuclear program but would not have prevented China from resuming its efforts, and thus would merely delay the threat rather than eliminate it.

Ironically, the greatest impediment to a U.S. decision to launch an anticipatory attack seems to have been the inability to get Soviet cooperation. Key members of both administrations surmised that attacking the Chinese might be politically acceptable if Moscow would participate in, or at least not object to, the act. But Soviet leaders were not interested in taking such a step, either in the Kennedy era or afterward. During the test-ban negotiations, Harriman theorized that Khrushchev was interested in signing the treaty so he could use Mao's refusal to do so against him in their contest for leadership of the world communist movement.[114] That was a reasonable conclusion, but while Khrushchev may have been eager to attack Mao politically, he was not willing to side with the leader of the capitalist world in a military attack on a fellow communist state. Doing so would have damaged his standing among communist leaders and risked starting a costly war against a country with an immense army deployed on the long Sino-Soviet border.

---

[113] Johnson (1964).

[114] Harriman (1963b).

The Results

The Kennedy and Johnson administrations' reluctance to launch a preventive attack on China's nuclear facilities was prudent given the high costs and the limited benefits that were expected. Although China developed nuclear weapons and, eventually, ICBMs capable of threatening the American homeland, Beijing never invested in more than a basic strategic deterrent (and focused more on developing nuclear missiles for possible use against the Soviet Union than on threatening the United States), and China's limited capability probably had no appreciable impact on U.S. nuclear defense spending. Beijing did not brandish nuclear weapons in an effort to coerce its neighbors or the United States, and though the Chinese did encourage and support communist aggression in Southeast Asia, they probably would have done so even had they not developed nuclear weapons.

China's effect on nuclear proliferation is harder to assess. Although India had the technological potential to develop nuclear weapons soon after China, and conducted a nuclear test explosion in 1974, New Delhi chose not to demonstrate an overt nuclear weapons capability until May 1998. Pakistan tested its first nuclear device days after India, and though China signed the nuclear nonproliferation treaty in 1992, reports indicate that it supported Pakistan's nuclear program and may have also provided Iran and Algeria with prohibited technology.[115] Pakistani aid, in turn, may have been behind North Korea and Libya's efforts to develop nuclear weapons.[116] Yet, none of this, occurring long after China's first successful test, suggests that attempting a preventive strike on China's nascent nuclear program would have been prudent policy.

Perhaps the greatest effect of China's emergence as a nuclear-capable state was one that appears to have been unanticipated in Washington until after the detonation at Lop Nor. Within two weeks of that

---

[115] Rodney W. Jones, Mark G. McDonough, and Leonard S. Spector, *Tracking Nuclear Proliferation: A Guide in Maps and Charts, 1998*, Washington, D.C.: Carnegie Endowment for International Peace, 1998, pp. 3, 6–7.

[116] Patrick E. Tyler and David E. Sanger, "Pakistan Called the Libyans' Source of Atoom Design," *The New York Times*, January 6, 2004, p. A1; David E. Sanger, "Pakistani Says He Saw North Korean Nuclear Devices," *The New York Times*, April 13, 2004, p. A12.

event, key members of the administration began to realize that Washington's longstanding policy of nonrecognition of the PRC was becoming unsupportable. Although the United States put off conceding the issue until the Nixon administration, Beijing's nuclear capability helped make the communist regime's permanence in China even more undeniable, and American policymakers began to realize that U.S. refusal to accept that reality and acquiesce to the PRC's admittance to the United Nations might ultimately hurt America's prestige.[117] Yet, it is difficult to attribute the U.S. policy realignment primarily to China's nuclear test. The nonrecognition policy had been in place for 15 years, and opposition to it had been growing in the international community, even among U.S. allies. At most, the detonation at Lop Nor was a catalyst that forced Johnson and his advisors to realize that U.S. recognition of the PRC was no longer a question of "if," but of "when."[118]

No one can say with certainty what would have resulted from an American preventive attack against the Chinese nuclear program. However, it is extremely unlikely that even an operationally successful attack—even a nuclear one—would have done more than temporarily delay China's acquisition of nuclear weapons, and it would have done that at enormous political cost on many levels. In this case, a preventive attack appeared to make little sense at the time, and the decision against it was revealed to be even sounder in retrospect.

---

[117] See, for instance, James C. Thomson, Jr., "Memorandum from James C. Thomson, Jr., of the National Security Council Staff to the President's' Special Assistant for National Security Affairs (Bundy): The U.S. and Communist China in the Months Ahead," October 28, 1964, Washington, D.C., in U.S. Department of State, *Foreign Relations of the United States, 1964–1968*, Vol. XXX: *China*, Washington, D.C.: U.S. Department of State, Doc. 63, 1998.

[118] See J. Harlan Cleveland, "Memorandum from the Assistant Secretary of State for International Organization Affairs (Cleveland) to Secretary of State Rusk: China and the UN," November 5, 1964, in U.S. Department of State, *Foreign Relations of the United States, 1964–1968*, Vol. XXX: *China*, Washington, D.C.: U.S. Department of State, Doc. 64, 1998; and Samuel E. Belk, "Memorandum for the Record: Meeting with the President on United Nations Matters," November 18, 1964, 1:00 p.m., Washington, D.C., in U.S. Department of State, *Foreign Relations of the United States, 1964–1968, Volume XXX: China*, Washington, D.C.: U.S. Department of State, Doc. 66, 1998.

The Cuban Missile Crisis, 1962

In October 1962, an American U-2 reconnaissance aircraft discovered sites under construction for Soviet intermediate- and medium-range ballistic missiles in Cuba. How much the presence of these missiles might have upset the strategic nuclear balance remains unclear, but U.S. officials worried that ignoring this brazen act within the American sphere of influence would undercut the country's international reputation. This brief case study explores the American decisionmaking about how best to respond to Soviet missiles in Cuba. For 13 days, President Kennedy's Executive Committee (ExComm) navigated the ups and downs of a crisis that could have escalated to a nuclear war. Although they ultimately relied on a naval blockade and back-channel diplomacy to bring the crisis to a successful conclusion, they did consider the value of an anticipatory attack to prevent nuclear weapons from becoming a permanent fixture in Cuba. This episode thus offers instructive lessons for American policymakers considering using force to prevent a contemporary opponent from acquiring weapons of mass destruction.

The Situation

The Cuban missile crisis took place against the backdrop of larger Cold War disputes, especially over the fate of Berlin. On three occasions from 1958 to 1961, Soviet Premier Nikita Khrushchev threatened war if the United States did not negotiate an end to the Western presence in Berlin. From the Soviet perspective, the divided city in the heart of East Germany remained a thorn in the side of the communist bloc. Each of these threats, however, went largely unanswered. Over time, Khrushchev's inability to force a favorable settlement on the United States undermined his position at home and abroad. Within the Soviet Union, he began to look like an ineffectual leader who had not only failed to deal with a languishing economy, but also had not followed through on his international threats. His East German allies, in particular, pressured him to take a harder stance over Berlin.[119]

While the Soviet Union failed to make gains in Europe, it was making inroads in Latin America. In a stunning diplomatic victory, Moscow had managed to woo the new Cuban government of Fidel Castro into the Soviet orbit in 1960. One year later, the failure of the "Bay of Pigs" invasion by insurgents financed and trained by the United States prompted Khrushchev to send greater conventional military aid to the Castro regime. He also issued a public warning that an American invasion of Cuba would risk war with the Soviet Union. American officials made it equally clear that they did not want nuclear weapons in Cuba. It was Khrushchev's failure to impress on Kennedy the need to resolve the situation in Berlin and the presence of American missiles in Turkey, close to the Soviet border, that finally prompted the Premier in May 1962 to send nuclear weapons to Cuba.[120] Khrushchev could present Kennedy with a fait accompli and secure the diplomatic victory he so desperately sought. To improve his chances of catching the Americans by surprise, Khrushchev even reassured Kennedy that he would not create problems internationally until after the November 1962 elections, but that subsequently they would need to resolve Berlin.

The first inkling that the Soviet Union might have placed nuclear weapons in Cuba came in August 1962, two months before the actual crisis.[121] At that time, American surveillance flights had discovered the presence of Soviet surface-to-air missile (SAM) batteries in several locations across the island. Central Intelligence Agency director

---

[119] These concerns over Berlin are summarized in Trachtenberg (1999, Chapters Seven and Eight); and Michael R. Beschloss, *The Crisis Years: Kennedy and Khrushchev, 1960–1963*, New York: Edward Burlingame Books, 1991.

[120] Nikita Sergeevich Khrushchev, *Khrushchev Remembers: The Last Testament*, Strobe Talbott, trans., Boston: Little, Brown, 1974.

[121] The following summary relies on Robert F. Kennedy, *Thirteen Days: A Memoir of the Cuban Missile Crisis*, New York: W. W. Norton, 1969; A. A. Fursenko and Timothy J. Naftali, *One Hell of a Gamble: Khrushchev, Castro and Kennedy, 1958–1964*, New York: Norton, 1997; and Graham T. Allison and Philip Zelikow, *Essence of Decision: Explaining the Cuban Missile Crisis*, 2nd ed., New York: Longman, 1999.

John McCone thought that these SAM sites were potentially guarding something valuable, perhaps nuclear weapons. His own analysts at the CIA, including Sherman Kent, considered it unlikely that the Soviets would engage in such risky behavior. Evidence for McCone's hunch arrived on October 14, 1962, when an American U-2 photographed Soviet medium-range ballistic missile (MRBM) sites under construction in Cuba. Two days later, Special Assistant for National Security Affairs McGeorge Bundy informed the President about the presence of Soviet missiles in Cuba.

President Kennedy immediately assembled a close group of advisors to help him decide how to respond. The group, later called the Executive Committee (ExComm), met in the morning of October 16, 1962, to begin their deliberations. By October 17, they knew that the Soviets planned to install not only MRBMs but longer-ranged intermediate-range ballistic missiles (IRBMs) as well. These missiles could reach beyond the U.S. eastern seaboard to cover the rest of the United States. With the gravity of this threat in mind, over the next several days the ExComm debated a list of options that spanned the escalatory ladder. Doing nothing, diplomacy, and a naval blockade of Cuba were among the less provocative moves they considered. At the other extreme, they examined the possibility of various types of air strikes or a ground invasion to prevent the missiles from being deployed.

The Kennedy administration quickly concluded that it needed to act to remove the Soviet missiles from Cuba, even if doing so risked a nuclear war. According to their calculation, they faced enormous domestic pressure to do something, especially with an election looming. How could President Kennedy admit to the American public, they reasoned, that he did nothing while he permitted the installation of Soviet missiles that could menace the United States? They also worried that failing to respond would damage U.S. international credibility in future crises. Standing up to Khrushchev today would pay dividends if the Soviets tried to alter the status quo tomorrow.

Ultimately, on October 20, the ExComm narrowly agreed on a naval quarantine as the best short-term course of action. At the same time, many members of the ExComm believed that it might be necessary to resort to their secondary option, air strikes that would probably be followed by a ground invasion. While many committee members regarded it as likely to fail, the quarantine at least bought time for more diplomacy. On October 21, American reconnaissance planes discovered the presence of Soviet Il-28 light bombers and MiG-21 fighter aircraft in Cuba. The next day, members of the U.S. Senate vigorously urged President Kennedy to reconsider air strikes or an invasion instead of a naval quarantine. As they debated, American ships began to reach their positions for the blockade. That evening, President Kennedy addressed the nation to reveal American knowledge of the threat, to announce the U.S. blockade in response, and to demand that Khrushchev remove the Soviet missiles from Cuba. The blockade would require American vessels to board ships en route to Cuba to search for and, if necessary, to seize weapons and materials for completing the Soviet missile sites.

The Threat

Soviet missiles in Cuba had both symbolic and practical effects on the strategic nuclear balance. The presence of Soviet nuclear weapons off the coast of the United States allowed Khrushchev to demonstrate a point about similar American weapons in Turkey. Now the Americans, Khrushchev believed, would learn how it felt to have a knife held close to their soft underbelly. In concrete terms, the missiles in Cuba did improve the nuclear balance for the Soviet Union, but not dramatically. At the time, the United States held an overwhelming lead in nuclear warheads and delivery vehicles. Most glaringly, the Soviets lacked an intercontinental land-based missile force of any sophistication and their ballistic-missile submarine force trailed far behind American capabilities. This forced the Soviets to rely on a bomber force to deliver a retaliatory strike against the United States. Although the IRBMs were first-strike weapons, they could not have disarmed U.S. nuclear forces and provided only marginal value for damage limitation.[122] The MRBMs and IRBMs in Cuba, then, would augment Soviet second-strike capa-

---

[122]While some scholars argue that the Soviets had a sufficient supply of MRBMs and IRBMs to cover most of the United States if launched from Cuba, they did not have enough to be used effectively as first-strike weapons. Those arguing the possibility of the Soviet first-strike include Richard M. Pious, "The Cuban Missile Crisis and the Limits of Crisis Management," *Political Science Quarterly*, Vol. 116, No. 1, 2001, pp. 81–105.

bilities, but only marginally. With their respective ranges of 1,000 and 2,200 nautical miles, the Soviets could use them to reach targets deep in the United States. However, it was clear to both sides that the Soviets could already do this to a limited but nevertheless deterrent degree even after an American strategic nuclear first strike. The true value of these missiles lay in the possibility that Khrushchev could use them as bargaining chips for Berlin.

How imminent was the threat posed by Soviet nuclear weapons in Cuba? There are two potential answers to this question. In terms of the certainty of their use against the American homeland, it seemed unlikely the Soviets would use these missiles to strike the United States unprovoked. The real question of urgency surrounded their permanent installation in Cuba. American analysts calculated that Soviet technicians would complete the MRBM sites in one week. The IRBMs they

Figure A.1
The Soviet Missile Threat from Cuba

SOURCE: James H. Hansen, "Soviet Deception in the Cuban Missile Crisis," *Studies in Intelligence: Journal of the American Intelligence Professional*, Vol. 46, No. 1, 2002, Unclassified Edition.
RAND *MG403-A.1*

estimated would come on line in December. Although an enemy attack was not imminent, a Soviet nuclear capability was, and once the Soviet missiles were operational, both an air strike and an invasion would be far riskier for the United States.

Policy Options and the Virtues of a Naval Quarantine

The ExComm debated five options for dealing with the Soviet missile threat in Cuba, with two falling into the category of preventive attack. Members of the committee quickly ruled out doing nothing. Even if the missile threat did not significantly change the strategic nuclear balance, as McNamara argued, it could undermine American credibility abroad and outrage public opinion at home. Public and private diplomacy offered one potential way to get Soviet missiles out of Cuba. However, the ExComm concluded that without a threat underpinning U.S. diplomatic efforts, they would have nothing with which to bargain.

On the very first day of the crisis, then, most members became resigned to using force. Initially, they discussed the possibility of having the Air Force conduct limited or "surgical" strikes against the missile sites and their attached air-defense batteries. As they investigated this option more closely, however, the President and his advisers became more convinced that a limited air attack might not remove the missile threat. Even with the advantage of surprise, Kennedy's military experts could not guarantee that a so-called surgical strike would work. The ExComm next contemplated a large air campaign against multiple targets across Cuba. This more ambitious plan, however, risked a wider war and still would not assure removing the threat. A further danger with the air-strike option was that it risked provoking a nuclear attack by the Soviets. Rather than lose the missiles to an American air attack, their commander might choose to use them.

Finally, the ExComm became increasingly convinced that the crisis would end with an American ground invasion of Cuba. Only then could they truly guarantee the removal of the missile threat. Unfortunately, they realized that sending U.S. forces into Cuba risked a bloody struggle with high American casualties. There was also a chance that the Soviets, pressured by their Cuban allies, might strike with their nuclear-armed MRBMs, in effect causing what the invasion was ultimately intended to prevent.[123] Moreover, a large-scale invasion would presumably cause a Soviet military response where they had the conventional advantage, in Europe and specifically against Berlin. Such an event would spark a much larger conflict, perhaps ending in a nuclear exchange.

In effect, the United States did not have a first-strike advantage against the Soviet missile threat. The possibility of escalation almost certainly made a preventive attack of any size extremely dangerous. Most worrisome was that the use of force against Cuba risked a superpower exchange at the strategic nuclear level. Although the Soviet Union was at a disadvantage in terms of the strategic nuclear balance, American forces could not achieve a disarming strike to spare the United States and U.S. allies from a devastating retaliatory response. The inability of the United States to limit damage to an acceptable level stemmed in part from its nuclear doctrine, poor targeting information, and inaccurate weapons.[124] The only instance in which the United States might have held a first-strike advantage in this crisis was in the face of an imminent attack from Soviet missiles in Cuba. Should this unlikely scenario have arisen—very improbable because the Soviet homeland would suffer from retaliation—then by striking preemptively the

---

[123]It also appears that the Soviet forces in Cuba possessed short-range FROG missiles with tactical nuclear warheads, although U.S. leaders did not realize this at the time. Some scholars have concluded that the local Soviet commanders had been given authority to use these weapons against a U.S. invasion force; however there is still a debate regarding whether the authority to use these missiles was in fact predelegated. Those arguing this possibility include James G. Blight and David A. Welch, *On the Brink: Americans and Soviets Reexamine the Cuban Missile Crisis*, New York: Hill and Wang, 1989. Skeptical about this argument is Mark Kramer, "Tactical Nuclear Weapons, Soviet Command Authority, and the Cuban Missile Crisis," *Cold War International History Project Bulletin 3*, Washington, D.C.: Woodrow Wilson Center, 1993.

[124]On the strategic nuclear balance see Scott Douglas Sagan, "SIOP-62: The Nuclear War Plan Briefing to President Kennedy," *International Security*, Vol. 12, No. 1, 1987, pp. 22–51; and more recently, Francis J. Gavin, "The Myth of Flexible Response: United States Strategy in Europe During the 1960s," *International History Review*, Vol. 23, No. 4, 2001, pp. 847–875.

United States could greatly limit the damage done to the American homeland.[125]

Members of the ExComm also expressed great concern about the moral and political implications of striking first, especially by using the element of surprise. The President's brother, Attorney General Robert Kennedy, expressed his doubts about an attack by writing in a note, "I now know how Tojo felt when he was planning Pearl Harbor."[126] He would later recall that the ExComm spent the most time debating the moral implications of striking first. These policymakers recognized that while American credibility for carrying out deterrent threats was at stake, the country's reputation as a law-abiding nation could also suffer by using force too precipitously. To offset the potential damage done to the U.S. image abroad, American diplomats sought and eventually won the support of the Organization of American States (OAS) for the blockade of Cuba.

While the deliberations of the ExComm did not occur as methodically as this discussion suggests, in due course the committee decided on a naval blockade. Through their long discussions weighing both military and political risks, the committee split the difference and concluded that a quarantine of Cuba would represent the best course of action, at least in the short term. Most ExComm members, including the President, were not sanguine about their ability to avoid using force. They reasoned, however, that this step would buy them more time and possibly open a space for diplomacy. They could have chosen to launch a surprise air strike, but this seemed too risky a strategy given that it could not guarantee the complete removal of the missile threat. Quarantine, especially with the imprimatur of the OAS, also would avoid a use of force that might tarnish the country's image. At the very least, the United States could proclaim to the international community that it had given diplomacy one last, clear chance. In each of these ways, then, a naval blockade, while not free of risks, gave Khrushchev and the ExComm more time to bargain before the United States resorted to preventive attack.

---

[125]Sagan (1987).

[126]Robert F. Kennedy (1969, p. 9).

The Results

In response to the announcement of the blockade, the Soviet Premier proclaimed that the weapons sent to Castro were defensive in nature and warned of dire consequences should the United States invade Cuba. On October 23, 1962, Kennedy dispatched a letter to Khrushchev urging that they should both work together to ensure that things did not spin out of control. The following day, October 24, as the blockade was almost ready to take effect, 16 of 19 Soviet ships turned back from Cuba, two slowed down, and only the tanker *Bucharest* continued towards its destination. The ships thought to contain Soviet missiles were among those that turned away, prompting Secretary of Dean Rusk to comment, "We're eyeball to eyeball and I think the other fellow just blinked."[127] Later that evening, however, Khrushchev wrote to Kennedy, informing him that the Soviet Union would not submit to "arbitrary" American demands.

One day later, on October 25, as both sides began to worry about how the crisis might escalate, Kennedy transmitted another letter to Khrushchev warning him not to underestimate American determination to eliminate the missiles from Cuba. While this correspondence was taking place, the ExComm received word that Soviet personnel appeared to have stepped up their efforts in Cuba to finish work on the MRBM sites and to prepare for an American attack. The same day, Kennedy rebuffed overtures from the United Nations to suspend the quarantine.

As it appeared the two sides were on a collision course, Khrushchev took the first step in avoiding war. Kennedy finally received a letter from the Soviet Premier on October 26 offering to withdraw the missiles in exchange for a pledge from the United States not to invade Cuba. The long and rambling letter suggested Khrushchev had become unhinged by the crisis. He expressed his concern that if the two leaders continued on the present course they risked nuclear war. A second letter from Khrushchev arrived later the same day offering to exchange U.S. missiles in Turkey as well as a no-invasion pledge for the removal

---

[127]Recounted in Mark J. White, *Missiles in Cuba: Kennedy, Khrushchev, Castro, and the 1962 Crisis*, Chicago: Ivan R. Dee, 1997, p. 120.

of Soviet missiles from Cuba, suggesting that the Soviet leader had reconsidered his bargaining position. The following day, on October 27, Kennedy agreed in public to the first offer of a no-invasion pledge, but he also privately relented in consenting to remove the Turkish missiles. While making these concessions, Kennedy also threatened to attack Cuba if the nuclear weapons were not dismantled and returned to the Soviet Union.

As the politicians were working to end the crisis, military events beyond their control risked turning the quarantine into a wider war. On the morning of the same day Kennedy was replying to Khrushchev's offer, an American U-2 reconnaissance aircraft crossed into Soviet airspace near Alaska, triggering Russian air defenses.[128] Luckily no shots were fired, but the episode demonstrated how alerted forces from both sides could stumble into war. Later that afternoon, surface-to-air missiles shot down a U-2 over Cuba, a possibility that had always worried the ExComm. A few hours after the downing of the U-2, U.S. Navy F-8 Crusaders took antiaircraft fire as they flew over Cuba. This time, however, no aircraft were lost.

Events fortunately cooled down on October 28, with Khrushchev's public announcement that the Soviet Union would remove its missiles from Cuba. The quarantine had apparently succeeded in convincing the Soviets that the United States was determined to see the missiles removed. At the same time, Khrushchev had won a pledge from Kennedy that the United States would not conduct another invasion to oust the Castro regime. In November, the United States also began steps to remove its Jupiter IRBMs from Turkey. However, Khrushchev failed to achieve the fait accompli he had thought would finally win him a favorable settlement in Berlin.

Several broad lessons emerge from this episode that are relevant for policymakers contemplating anticipatory attacks in response to sudden changes in the military balance. These lessons should have relevance for dealing with adversaries on the verge of acquiring nuclear weapons or those that have already done so. Although the same fears of

---

[128]See Allison and Zelikow (1999, pp. 240–241); Scott Douglas Sagan, "Nuclear Alerts and Crisis Management," *International Security*, Vol. 9, No. 4, 1985, pp. 99–139, pp. 118–121.

escalation that moderated American and Soviet behavior will not likely exist in every such case, future policymakers will still need to weigh the military as well as the political costs of striking first.

First, it is easier to defend the status quo than to change it. American policymakers gambled that they could manipulate the risk of a wider war to prevent the Soviets from changing the military balance in Cuba. A naval blockade put the onus on Soviet policymakers to avoid war. This insight would become an important element of deterrence theory.[129] The choice of quarantine also illustrates that anticipatory attacks represent only one category of anticipatory options. In this case, the Americans found a coercive strategy that allowed them to avoid the use of force. Perhaps in the future, other coercive threats, like sanctions, in combination with incentives could persuade some countries to forego weapons of mass destruction.[130] It is important to recall that in return for removing their missiles from the Caribbean, the Soviets won a similar U.S. concession in Turkey as well as an American pledge to not invade Cuba.[131]

Second, fear of inadvertent escalation made communication between the sides in the crisis crucial. Not only did the exchange of messages allow both sides to bargain, it also let them express a desire to avoid war. Finally, anticipatory strikes require good intelligence. Members of the ExComm expressed reluctance to use air strikes against the missiles not only because they offered little guarantee of entirely removing the threat but because a less than completely effective strike might trigger a nuclear attack by the Soviet troops operating them. Even in an era of precision-guided munitions with superb accuracy, the United States still needs to know where crucial targets are before they can be attacked.

---

[129] This is one of the key insights of Schelling (1966, Chapter One).

[130] Libya's recent renunciation of its nuclear arsenal suggests this possibility. See Martin S. Indyk, "The Iraq War Did Not Force Gadaffi's Hand," *Financial Times*, March 9, 2004.

[131] On the coercive use of conditional rewards, see David A. Baldwin, "The Power of Positive Sanctions," *World Politics*, Vol. 24, No. 1, 1971, pp. 19–38.

The Invasion of Grenada, 1983

The 1983 invasion of Grenada was the only sizable anticipatory attack actually launched by the United States during the Cold War, though it is a rather marginal case. While it did not involve preventing the acquisition of nuclear, biological, or chemical weapons, Operation Urgent Fury was motivated in part by the desire to prevent an adversary from acquiring a bothersome new military capability, in this case a Soviet and Cuban military base in the eastern Caribbean. That this would have been a relatively minor strategic development compared to, say, the placement of nuclear missiles in Cuba 20 years earlier, this was offset by the low expected costs of striking first to prevent it. Therefore, understanding why the United States did launch a preventive attack against Grenada is of considerable relevance when considering such cases in the current policy environment, especially given the dearth of other U.S. first strikes.

The Situation

In 1979, five years after Grenada became independent from British colonial rule, the nation's government was overthrown in a coup d'état by the socialist opposition New Jewel Movement (NJM), led by Maurice Bishop.[132] The new government was kept at arm's length by the United States due to its refusal to restore democracy and its ties with Cuba and the Soviet Union.[133] The U.S. government was particularly troubled by the expansion of Grenada's army and by the presence of Cuban construction workers and military personnel on the island to construct a 10,000-foot runway at Point Salines for a new international airport to facilitate tourist travel to the island. President Ronald Reagan had been concerned about Grenada at least since attending a conference in Barbados in 1982, where eastern Caribbean leaders had expressed their fears that Grenada would become a base for communist

---

[132]On the background to the invasion, see Mark Adkin, *Urgent Fury: The Battle for Grenada*, Lexington, Mass.: Lexington Book, 1989; and Robert J. Beck, *The Grenada Invasion: Politics, Law, and Foreign Policy Decisionmaking*, Boulder, Colo.: Westview Press, 1993.

[133]George Pratt Shultz, *Turmoil and Triumph: My Years as Secretary of State*, New York: Scribner's, 1993, p. 327.

subversion in the region;[134] in a March 1983 address about U.S. defense policy, he stated that

> The rapid buildup of Grenada's military potential is unre-
> lated to any conceivable threat to this island country of under
> 100,000. . . . The Soviet-Cuban militarization of Grenada, in
> short, can only be seen as power projection into the region.[135]

However, on October 13, 1983, Grenada's hard-line communist Deputy Prime Minister, Bernard Coard, and the commander of the Grenadian army, Hudson Austin, led a bloody military coup against the government, which was followed by civil disorder, the deaths of dozens of civilians, the imposition of martial law, and on October 20, the assassination of Bishop.[136] Fearing for the safety of 800 American students at the St. George's School of Medicine, and concerned about the possibility of Grenada now becoming even more actively aligned with Cuba and the USSR, U.S. leaders considered launching an invasion of the island, and ultimately decided to do so in response to a request from the Organization of Eastern Caribbean States (OECS).[137]

The Threat

Washington had several concerns about the situation in Grenada. The most immediate, and the one given most attention in the press, was the safety of the American medical students. This was also the most uncertain, because no threat had been made against them.[138] However, their situation could change suddenly, particularly under conditions as chaotic as those prevailing on the island following the coup and the

---

[134]Julie Wolf, "The Invasion of Grenada," *The American Experience*, undated Web page.

[135]Ronald Reagan, "Address to the Nation on Defense and National Security," March 23, 1983.

[136]Shortly before the coup, Bishop had visited Washington and met with American officials in an effort to improve relations with the United States.

[137]The larger Organization of American States (OAS), however, did not endorse the invasion of Grenada.

[138]In retrospect it appears that the students were in little danger, though Washington could not be confident of this at the time (Adkin, 1989, pp. 108–109).

killing of the ousted Prime Minister. The possibility that they might be taken hostage was made particularly vivid by the fact that less than three years had elapsed since the Iranian embassy hostage crisis had finally ended after preoccupying the United States for more than 14 months.

Less pressing, but more certain in the eyes of U.S. administration decisionmakers, was the threat of Grenada becoming a base for Cuban-sponsored subversion in the region and potentially even for Soviet military forces, with the new airport serving at a minimum to allow transport aircraft from Cuba to deliver military supplies, and at a maximum becoming an operational base for Soviet and Cuban military aircraft.[139] It is often assumed that more remote threats are consequently less certain than more proximate ones, and while this is a reasonable generalization, it does not always obtain in particular cases, and certainly did not with respect to Grenada, where it was the more speculative danger (along with the ongoing killings) that gave the crisis its urgency, and the longer-term threat that made Grenada a matter of serious national security concern for the Reagan administration.

Policy Options

U.S. leaders had three principal policy options. One was to take no military action against Grenada in the near term, waiting to deal with security threats posed by the new government once they materialized. This would avoid both the direct costs of a military operation, and any resulting outrage from the international community. However, it would neither physically protect the medical students nor stop the civil disorder and the deaths of Grenadians, would not of course solve the longer-term threat of a pro-Soviet regime in Grenada, and might be interpreted as evidence of U.S. weakness in the international security

---

[139]Constantine Menges, then a newly appointed Special Assistant for National Security Affairs and an early advocate of attacking Grenada, even argued that the Soviet Union might use Grenada as a base for nuclear forces in order to offset the deployment of U.S. theater nuclear missiles in Europe (Constantine Christopher Menges, *Inside the National Security Council: The True Story of the Making and Unmaking of Reagan's Foreign Policy*, New York: Simon and Schuster, 1988, p. 70).

arena, an impression that the White House was particularly keen to avoid.

The second option was limited military action, launching a non-combatant evacuation operation (NEO) to rescue the students without occupying the island. This would solve the immediate problem of averting a possible hostage crisis, and would have been sufficient if this had been Washington's only concern, but would leave in place a regime whose hostility to the United States would presumably be much increased by the experience.[140]

The third alternative was to seize the island and establish a new, more palatable government there, rescuing the medical students in the process. This would address both the immediate and longer-term threats, and would serve as a show of American strength as well. The last of these considerations may have loomed larger by the time the final decision to carry out the invasion was made. A suicide truck bomb attack destroyed the U.S. Marine barracks in Beirut on October 23, killing 241 Marines and convincing Washington to abandon its unsuccessful peace enforcement intervention in Lebanon, but by that point the invasion option had already essentially been approved. The direct costs of an invasion were not expected to be high, given the limited defensive capabilities of the Grenadian army, and the Reagan administration did not perceive potential international objections to an invasion as a particularly serious problem, given that it would have the support of Grenada's immediate neighbors.

The Decision to Attack
Compared to the three cases described in this appendix, the stakes in Grenada were not remotely as high for the United States. However, the expected costs of preventive attack against such a weak opponent were lower still. Invading Grenada promised to resolve a long-standing security concern, to eliminate the uncertain but troubling possibility of the American students becoming the center of a new hostage crisis, and to demonstrate U.S. capability and willingness to roll back communist influence in the Americas, all at relatively low cost. President Reagan

---

[140]Menges (1988, p. 70).

made the final decision to go ahead with the attack on October 24, and the invasion began the following day.

Operation Urgent Fury involved attacks by some 1,900 U.S. troops supported by helicopters, carrier-based A-7 attack aircraft, AC-130 gunships, and naval gunfire.[141] Rangers parachuted onto the Point Salines airfield, securing it for the subsequent arrival of units of the 82nd Airborne Division, while a Marine Amphibious Unit landed in the north of the island to secure the American students and Navy SEAL teams rescued the Governor General, who was being held captive. In spite of the attacking forces' massive military superiority, the operation did not go smoothly, but the objectives were taken successfully, and the United States declared that hostilities were over on November 2.[142] Nineteen U.S. troops died in the attack, not counting an undisclosed additional number of deaths among special operations forces, and 152 were wounded. Twenty-four Cubans were killed, along with an estimated 67 Grenadian soldiers and civilians.[143] The last U.S. forces withdrew from Grenada in 1985.

The Results

The invasion of Grenada was a military success notwithstanding the problems that occurred during its execution, and all of its objectives were achieved. The American students' safety was secured, although what would have happened to them if the attack had not been carried out necessarily remains uncertain. Grenada was occupied and the disorder that had followed the October 13 coup was ended. The invasion was widely condemned around the world, including by Great Britain, which expressed outrage at the United States having attacked a sover-

---

[141] For details of the operation, see Adkin (1989). The invasion and subsequent peacekeeping force finally grew to some 5,000 personnel, including 300 from OECS member states.

[142] Adkin (1989, especially pp. 333–340) identifies several points at which only good luck prevented far more serious reverses for the invaders—Fidel Castro was not pleased by the performance of Cuban troops in the conflict, either (pp. 313–318); see also H. Norman Schwarzkopf and Peter Petre, *It Doesn't Take a Hero: General H. Norman Schwarzkopf, The Autobiography*, New York: Bantam Books, 1992, p. 258.

[143] Adkin (1989, pp. 308–309).

eign member of the Commonwealth.[144] However, this was not particularly costly to Washington, not least because the attack was consistent with perceptions of the Reagan administration that already prevailed and which it was not seeking to reverse, and the decision to invade was widely popular in the United States.

A new, elected government was installed in Grenada following the invasion, eliminating the threat that the island would become a base either for the spread of communist influence in the eastern Caribbean or for the deployment of Soviet or Cuban forces. The attack also appeared to have a deterrent effect on other states, most notably Suriname, which severed its close ties with Cuba and expelled the Cuban contingent from Suriname within days after the end of Operation Urgent Fury.[145] In the long run, of course, the threat posed by the possibility of Grenada doing the bidding of Moscow and Havana turned out to be far less severe than U.S. leaders had supposed, for the simple but unforeseen reason that the Soviet threat would itself disappear before the end of the decade as the Cold War came to an end. Ironically, the resource drain from supporting its expensive, far-flung allies, such as Washington had feared Grenada would become, was one of the factors that contributed to the Soviet Union's eventual collapse from within.[146]

---

[144]Beck (1993, Chapters Six and Seven); and Reynold A. Burrowes, *Revolution and Rescue in Grenada: An Account of the U.S.-Caribbean Invasion*, New York: Greenwood Press, 1988, pp. 89–95.

[145]Shultz (1993, p. 344). In early 1983, the United States had briefly considered launching a covert attack to remove the pro-Cuban Surinamese government of Desi Bouterse, but international support was scarce, and the unilateral plans that were considered appeared prohibitively risky (Shultz, 1993, pp. 295–297).

[146]John E. Mueller, *Retreat from Doomsday: The Obsolescence of Major War*, New York: Basic Books, 1989, pp. 196–211.

Israeli Preemptive and Preventive Attack Cases

Introduction

Israel faces a unique set of structural security disadvantages vis-à-vis its neighbors.[1] It lacks strategic depth, especially to the north and east. The relatively small size of its population necessitates a standing army much smaller than those of its Arab neighbors and imposes a dependence on the rapid mobilization of reserves in times of conflict.[2] This in turn renders Israel strategically vulnerable to surprise attacks and economically vulnerable to extended operations. Israel must further contend with a high probability of outside intervention in the event of major conflict. These geographic, demographic, economic, and political realities have in turn shaped Israel's strategic doctrine.

---

[1] For a thorough discussion, see Yoav Ben-Horin and Barry Posen, *Israel's Strategic Doctrine*, Santa Monica, Calif.: RAND Corporation, R-2845-NA, 1981.

[2] Key works on the Israeli Defense Force (IDF) and its predecessors include Martin L. Van Creveld, *The Sword and the Olive: A Critical History of the Israeli Defense Force*, New York: Public Affairs, 1998; Edward Luttwak and Dan Horowitz, *The Israeli Army*, Cambridge, Mass.: Abt Books, 1983; and Zeev Schiff, *A History of the Israeli Army (1870–1974)*, San Francisco: Straight Arrow Books, 1974.

Population size remains a problem for Israel. Today, Israel maintains armed forces with 167,000 active members and 358,000 personnel. In comparison, the Egyptian military consists of 450,000 active members and 410,000 reservists, and the Syrian armed forces include 319,000 active members and 354,000 reservists. These disparities in manpower reflect differences in total population: 6.1 million people in Israel, 74.7 million in Egypt, and 17.6 million in Syria (Institute for Strategic Studies, *The Military Balance, 2003–2004*, London, 2003; Central Intelligence Agency, *The World Factbook*, undated Web page).

The objective of Israel's strategic doctrine is twofold: to deter Arab attacks, and to deliver a resounding defeat against its enemies should deterrence fail. Decisive victories are viewed as essential for Israeli deterrence in both the short and long terms. According to the logic underpinning this doctrine, painful defeats give Israel's enemies pause when contemplating the renewal of hostilities, while the cumulative effect of costly losses should eventually resign Israel's enemies to the state's existence. A set of operational preferences—including anticipatory attacks—has evolved within Israel's strategic doctrine to help it achieve decisive military victories.

Israel's strategic doctrine has displayed a strong preference for anticipatory attacks. In addition to helping deter Israel's enemies and achieve decisive victories, striking first has also helped to circumvent the constraints within which Israel must operate. Fighting on the offensive allows Israel to control the location, speed, and duration of operations. Battles may thus be fought on enemy territory rather than on Israel's, reserves mobilized in advance, and objectives achieved before political pressures abroad and economic pressures at home become too high.[3] Consequently, Israeli planners have seen many significant benefits to anticipatory attacks.

The historical record both bears out Israel's preference for striking first and illustrates the limits the state has faced in doing so. In 1956, with the help of France and Britain, Israel launched a preventive war against Egypt. In 1967 Israel preempted what many of the state's decisionmakers believed was an imminent Arab attack. In 1973, however, Israel passed up the opportunity to preempt what was known to be an impending Arab attack due to fears of the diplomatic consequences of striking first as well as an increased confidence in Israel's ability to absorb a first blow. In 1981, Israeli aircraft successfully carried out a preventive attack against Iraq's fledgling nuclear weapons program. The following sections describe each of these events in turn.

---

[3] Quick victories are even more attractive from an Israeli perspective because they help minimize casualties and allow Israel to rout one enemy before moving on to another in wars of more than one front (John J. Mearsheimer, *Conventional Deterrence*, Ithaca: Cornell University Press, 1983, p. 135).

The Sinai Campaign, 1956

The Situation

In July 1952, a group of Egyptian military officers led by Gamal Abdel-Nasser overthrew the country's monarchy, leading to a radical shift in Egypt's domestic and foreign policies. Israeli decisionmakers viewed Nasser's new regime—committed to socialism at home and anti-imperialism abroad—with alarm. Prime Minister David Ben-Gurion in particular believed Nasser to be the primary threat facing the young Israeli state, seeing in him a potential combination of Saladin and Ataturk, able both to unite and to lead the Arabs.[4] In 1954, after conducting a three-month study of Israel's security picture, Ben-Gurion concluded that the Arabs would be ready for war in terms of equipment, training, and unity of command some time in 1956.[5]

Fueling these concerns, both Egypt and Israel had embarked on concerted efforts to increase the quantity and quality of their military arsenals through purchases from the Western powers. This search for external armaments helped lead France, the United Kingdom, and the United States to conclude a "Tripartite Agreement" to monitor and control weapons sales to the region. Frustrated with its inability to secure sufficient purchases from these suppliers, Egypt broke with the regime in 1955 and turned to the Soviet Union for weapons. Israel viewed the resulting "Czech" arms deal—so named to disguise the Soviet source of the weapons—as a watershed development in its relations with Egypt, and a clear threat to the region's delicate military balance.

The Threat

Although Egypt had always enjoyed a quantitative superiority over Israel in terms of military supplies, Israel had always been able to count on a qualitative advantage in terms of equipment and particularly of personnel. The large numbers of advanced aircraft, tanks, artillery pieces,

---

[4] Avi Shlaim, *The Iron Wall: Israel and the Arab World*, New York: W. W. Norton, 2000, p. 135.

[5] Shlaim (2000, p. 93).

surface ships, submarines, and small arms included in the Czech arms deal, however, threatened to give the Egyptians not only significantly more arms than the Israelis, but better ones as well.[6] Defense officials worried that superior levels of Israeli training and motivation could not overcome the limitations of fundamentally inferior systems. Consequently, Israeli decisionmakers expected that Egypt's military capabilities would soon surpass their own.

The impending shift in the air balance was particularly threatening to Israel. After the initial deal, two subsequent rounds of Soviet sales added still more advanced jet fighters to Egypt's arsenal. Once the Egyptians were able to integrate these new systems—Israeli estimates anticipated this happening sometime between October 1956 and early 1957—the Israeli Air Force (IDF/AF) would no longer be able to defend the country's cities and civilian population from Egyptian air strikes. Having experienced the Blitz of 1940 in London, Ben-Gurion was particularly sensitive to any potential weakness in the air. Cabinet records quote him as saying, "If they [the Egyptians] really get MiGs, I will be for bombing them."[7]

Israeli decisionmakers' concern over the Czech arms deal extended beyond its implications for the Israeli-Egyptian balance. Nasser's purchase of Soviet arms was seen as opening the door to greater Soviet involvement and influence in the Middle East, a highly disadvantageous development from Israel's perspective. With the Western powers adhering to the precepts of the Tripartite Agreement, a potential regional arms race had thus far been avoided. The Soviet Union, on the other hand, was not viewed as similarly restrained and, further, was likely to supply only the Arab states to Israel's detriment. Nasser had characterized the arms deal as one between Egypt and Czechoslovakia because he had foreseen the concern such a sizeable Soviet role in the region would provoke.[8]

---

[6] Levy and Gochal (2001, p. 18).

[7] Levy and Gochal (2001, p. 25).

[8] Michael Brecher, *Decisions in Israel's Foreign Policy*, New Haven, Conn.: Yale University Press, 1975, p. 257, footnote 1.

While Israeli decisionmakers were primarily concerned with the impending shift in regional military capabilities, Egyptian intentions appeared threatening as well. Nasser's pan-Arabist rhetoric was broadcast throughout the region and included stridently anti-Semitic pronouncements. Palestinian guerrilla attacks from Egyptian-controlled territory had become official policy in early 1955 and were occurring with greater frequency. Finally, Nasser nationalized the Suez Canal in July 1956, having earlier closed the Straits of Tiran to Israeli shipping. The number of Egyptian troops in the Sinai increased dramatically. All of these developments pointed to increasing Egyptian "self-assurance and assertiveness."[9] As a result, some Israeli decisionmakers viewed a "second round" of war as simply a matter of time, and if the war came at a time when Egypt was capable of decisively defeating the Israeli Defense Force (IDF), Israel's national survival would be in jeopardy.

Nasser's aggressive policies, however, did not come without costs. His decision to nationalize the canal brought Great Britain, France, and Israel together in agreement that something had to be done about his regime. France and Britain wished to regain their financial interests in the canal, as well as to reassert their role as regional powers. Israel saw a need to prevent Egypt from gaining military supremacy. The nationalization of the canal, then, became the catalyst that prompted the three countries to begin military planning to push Egypt out of the Sinai and potentially overthrow Nasser.[10]

Policy Options

Israel tried four main options in seeking to address the threat posed by Nasser's Egypt in the mid-1950s. In chronological order, though some overlap did occur, they were warning Nasser while seeking arms in an effort to deter him; seeking arms in order to more successfully attack Egypt; provoking a war in order to avoid the appearance of launching a preventive war; and launching a preventive war. One option that

---

[9] Brecher (1975); also see Chaim Herzog, *The Arab-Israeli Wars: War and Peace in the Middle East*, New York: Random House, 1982, pp. 111–114.

[10] For a summary of events leading up to the 1956 war, see Ahron Bregman, *Israel's Wars, 1947–93*, London and New York: Routledge, 2000, pp. 55–61.

was not considered was doing nothing. Ben-Gurion believed that "a negative attitude of 'waiting it out' is not enough. In the long run, doing nothing may be far more dangerous than any bold deed—such as fomenting a war."[11]

Though all Israeli decisionmakers believed Nasser posed a serious threat, there were disagreements as to how to respond. Moshe Sharett[12] wanted to warn Nasser of the consequences of his actions while embarking on an expanded arms search. Sharett believed Israel should focus its procurement efforts on the United States while others in the government such as Ben-Gurion and his supporters centered their efforts on France. The United States was not willing to sell Israel significant amounts of arms without a pledge to abstain from launching any attacks, a condition many in the government found intolerable. France, on the other hand, became increasingly willing to arm Israel as Nasser grew more belligerent and Soviet arms flowed into Egypt in ever-greater quantities.[13] Yet Israel's purchases of aircraft and other equipment from the French, while helping to redress the qualitative imbalance caused by Cairo's access to Soviet weaponry, were still not sufficient to keep pace with Egypt's military buildup.[14]

Ben-Gurion and his supporters wanted to improve Israel's capabilities also, but as a prelude to military action rather than to increase the state's deterrent power vis-à-vis Egypt. Israeli Defense Minister Moshe Dayan wrote in his diary, "Supreme efforts must be made to acquire more arms and ammunition until the date of the clash," but stressed that "one thing must not be made dependent on the other."[15]

---

[11] Levy and Gochal (2001, p. 33).

[12] Sharett served as Foreign Minister from 1949 to 1956 and as Prime Minister as well during 1954 and 1955.

[13] Zach Levey, *Israel and the Western Powers, 1952–1960*, Chapel Hill, N.C.: University of North Carolina Press, 1997, pp. 68–70.

[14] Herzog (1982, p. 112); Zach Levey, "Israeli Foreign Policy and the Arms Race in the Middle East, 1950–1960," *Journal of Strategic Studies*, Vol. 24, No. 1, 2001, pp. 29–48, p. 37.

[15] Quoted in Shlaim (2000, pp. 141–142).

In the view of some planners, then, Israel should have contemplated war even if its armament efforts had failed.

However, Israeli decisionmakers, including the most hawkish, were uncomfortable with the idea of launching a preventive attack. Ben-Gurion's earlier comment about "fomenting a war" revealed a preference for an Arab instigation of hostilities. He feared that if Israel started the war it would be penalized by Western arms suppliers afterward, leaving it isolated and weak for an expected future third round of fighting, a concern that would haunt Israeli leaders in subsequent crises and wars as well. Even Dayan, who had been advocating a preventive attack against Egypt for at least two years prior to the Czech arms deal, had qualms. He wrote that "[a] preventive war means an aggressive war initiated by Israel directly" and that "Israel cannot afford to stand against the entire world and be denounced as the aggressor."[16] Only as the window of opportunity began to close did Ben-Gurion decide to strike.

The Decision to Attack

Israeli war plans had been hindered by three problems: the need for more and better arms to narrow the gap with Egypt, the need for diplomatic support so Israel would not be isolated and thus unable to procure additional arms for future rounds of conflict, and the need for an aerial umbrella to protect Israeli cities from Egyptian bombing during the war. French arms sales solved the first problem, while the agreement of France and the United Kingdom to participate in the conflict under the guise of imposing a settlement solved the second and third.[17] Further facilitating the decision to attack was the resignation of Sharett, a long-time opponent of any large-scale preventive attack.[18] With these problems successfully addressed, Ben-Gurion decided on

---

[16] Cited in Shlaim (2000, pp. 141–142).

[17] For an account of the British and French roles in the war, see Avi Shlaim, "The Protocol of Sevres, 1956: Anatomy of a War Plot," *International Affairs*, Vol. 73, No. 3, 1997, pp. 509–530.

[18] Having failed to secure significant arms sales from the United States, Sharett left the Israeli government in 1956.

war in July 1956, presenting his plan to the cabinet only after making the decision to strike.

The plan for a preventive attack against Egypt had three military objectives and three political goals. Militarily, Israel aimed to destroy the Egyptian army, to end the blockade of Israeli shipping in the Straits of Tiran and the Suez Canal, and to stop guerrilla raids in Egyptian-controlled territory. Politically, it hoped to bring about the end of Nasser's regime, to acquire additional territory (particularly the Sinai peninsula), and to remake the region's political map, which was based on the unacceptable borders of 1948. How to achieve the war's political goals received considerably less attention than how to accomplish its military objectives, possibly due to the lack of debate in the cabinet about the plan.

On October 29, 1956, Israel struck. Paratroopers landed deep inside Sinai to give the appearance of a threat to the Canal while ground forces drove across the peninsula. The next day, the United States sponsored a Security Council resolution calling for an immediate Israeli withdrawal, which was vetoed by Britain and France. The same day, as planned, the two European powers suggested establishing a 10-mile-wide buffer along both sides of the Canal, ostensibly to separate the two sides' forces. Nasser predictably refused, and French and British forces began carrier- and land-based air strikes against Egypt on October 31, followed by an amphibious invasion on November 5. The war was over two days later when U.S. coercive pressure compelled the British, and consequently the French and Israelis, to halt their offensive and consent to a cease-fire and eventual withdrawal of their forces from Egypt.[19]

The Results

Israel achieved its military objectives, successfully seizing the Sinai peninsula, but failed to accomplish its political goals for the campaign. The preventive attack defeated (though it did not destroy) the Egyptian army, opened the Straits of Tiran (though not the Suez Canal) to

---

[19] Jonathan Kirshner, *Currency and Coercion: The Political Economy of International Monetary Power*, Princeton, N.J.: Princeton University Press, 1995, pp. 63–82.

Israeli shipping, and stopped guerrilla raids from Egypt for the next 11 years. The war did not bring about Nasser's downfall, however; indeed, it strengthened him considerably both in Egypt and in the Middle East as a whole. Israel was forced to return all the territory it had gained with the exception of one small area along the border. Consequently, Israel did not succeed in creating a stable regional political order, and war erupted again a decade later. Despite impressive military success, therefore, Israel was denied any significant political benefits in its disputes with its Arab neighbors.

More broadly, the war damaged Israel's relations with both superpowers. Israel's attack on Egypt surprised and angered President Eisenhower. The United States threatened to halt all U.S. assistance to Israel, the imposition of U.N. sanctions, and Israeli expulsion from the United Nations. One of the few tangible benefits Israel did secure was a U.S. pledge to maintain freedom of navigation in the Gulf of Aqaba, but that promise was revealed to be hollow in 1967. During the conflict, the Soviet Union threatened to intervene on Egypt's behalf and after the war's conclusion became the Arab states' main military supplier and diplomatic backer. The conflict represented one of the lowest points in the emerging U.S.-Israeli relationship and ended the already weak ties between the Soviet Union and Israel.

The war also solidified the parameters of the Arab-Israeli conflict. For the Arabs, the war confirmed Israel's aggressive intentions and reinforced their conviction that the Jewish state's continued existence was unacceptable. Egypt's armed forces regained and even surpassed their prewar levels within a few years, spurred on by the now significantly increased perception of an Israeli threat and aided by considerable Soviet assistance. Palestinian guerrillas, meanwhile, were denied Egypt as a staging ground by the postwar interposition of the United Nations Emergency Force (UNEF) along the border. Therefore they shifted their efforts farther afield, culminating in the formation of the Palestine Liberation Organization, which was to become a decades-long problem for Israel.

The preventive attack against Egypt thus appears to have had mixed results for Israel. On the one hand, due to the imposition of the UNEF in Sinai, the war gave Israel a quiet southern border for 11 years—a significant achievement considering that Egypt was its largest, most populous, and potentially most threatening neighbor. On the other, it strengthened Israel's primary enemy, granted the Arabs a strong and committed ally in the Soviet Union, sparked one of the darkest periods in Israel's relationship with the United States, and led to unexpected innovations in the Palestinian guerrilla movement. At the time, the potential costs seemed worth the expected benefits. Viewed with the benefit of hindsight, however, it appears that Israel's anticipatory attack catalyzed Tel Aviv's adversaries in ways that made future conflict more likely.

The Six-Day War, 1967

The Situation

In 1967, following a decade of relative calm, developments in Syria and the Palestinian movement combined with Israel's responses to them to usher in a third round of Arab-Israeli fighting. The rise to power of the extreme leftist and stridently anti-Zionist Ba'ath party in Syria in February 1966 contributed greatly to Syrian-Israeli tensions. Three main points of contention complicated relations between the two states: the demilitarized zones along their common border, control of the headwaters of the Jordan River, and the activities of Palestinian guerrillas. The latter two were of particular importance, as the Syrians attempted to reduce the amount of water reaching Israel, and organized guerrilla raids into Israeli territory.[20]

As violence along the Syrian-Israeli border mounted throughout the early months of 1967, Israel decided to step up its response.[21] On April 7, a skirmish along the border escalated into an aerial engagement as Syrian MiGs intercepted Israeli bombers. The IDF/AF shot down six Syrian fighters, including some over Damascus—a particularly humili-

---

[20] Shlaim (2000, p. 228).

[21] Michael B. Oren, *Six Days of War: June 1967 and the Making of the Modern Middle East*, New York: Ballantine Books, 2003, p. 44.

ating development for the Syrians.[22] Rather than reduce Syrian support for the Palestinian guerrillas however, the April incident increased it.[23] By mid-May, a growing number of Israeli decisionmakers felt something needed to be done about the Syrian problem, and on May 12, Israeli Chief of Staff Yitzhak Rabin made a statement interpreted by some as indicating an Israeli intention to topple the Syrian regime. Though Rabin was reprimanded for his comments, others in the government, including Prime Minister Levi Eshkol, followed with equally bellicose pronouncements.[24] These statements and the border incidents underlying them led many in the Arab world to believe an Israeli attack on Syria was likely.

During this period of heightened tensions, the Egyptian government received a warning from the Soviet Union that Israeli troops were massing to invade Syria. The Soviets claimed on May 13 that 10 to 12 IDF brigades had assembled along the border, and gave the date of attack variously as sometime between May 16 and May 22.[25] Though the Soviets had already warned several times over the past year of pending Israeli invasions—and the Syrians themselves had been making similar claims since the April 7 engagement—the tone of recent Israeli statements and the specificity of the Soviet warning combined to give this particular round the ring of truth.[26] The Syrian Defense Minister, Hafez al-Assad, requested immediate Egyptian action to deter an Israeli attack. Nasser responded by dispatching the Egyptian Chief of Staff to Damascus to verify the Israeli troop deployment. Nasser's envoy reported back on May 15 that he had seen nothing to confirm Syrian fears, but by then Egyptian troops were already moving into the Sinai.[27]

---

[22] Benny Morris, *Righteous Victims: A History of the Zionist-Arab Conflict, 1881–2001*, New York: Vintage Books, 2001, p. 304.

[23] Oren (2003, p. 53).

[24] Shlaim (2000, pp. 236–237); and Morris (2001, p. 304).

[25] Morris (2001, p. 305); and Oren (2003, p. 54).

[26] Oren (2003, pp. 43, 55).

[27] Morris (2001, p. 305).

The Threat

Nasser had managed to keep Egypt out of the recent disputes, preferring to wait until the Arabs were stronger militarily before making any provocative moves against Israel. His pragmatic approach was difficult to sustain, however, in the face of Jordanian accusations that he was "hiding behind UNEF's skirts" and Syrian pressure to honor the terms of the November 1966 defense treaty between the two states.[28] "There is general agreement among commentators that Nasser neither wanted nor planned to go to war with Israel," writes one historian of the conflict. "What he did was embark on an exercise in brinkmanship that was to carry him over the brink."[29] By mid-May, Nasser felt he had to act, both in order to maintain his own credibility and to restrain the Syrians. On May 14, the Israelis detected Egyptian troops crossing the Suez Canal and moving into the Sinai Peninsula. Three days later Nasser demanded the withdrawal of UNEF. On May 22, he announced his intention to close the Straits of Tiran, and did so the following day. While Nasser estimated that closing the Straits had raised the chance of war to over 50 percent, the Israelis viewed this act as a clear casus belli.[30]

Coloring Israeli threat perception were fears of attack against the nuclear reactor at Dimona in the Negev desert, close to the Egyptian border and potentially vulnerable to aerial bombardment, where Israel was secretly developing nuclear weapons. Israeli decisionmakers assumed this was a motivating factor in Nasser's actions, though he avoided any mention of it during the crisis. Over the previous several years, however, numerous statements by Nasser and those close to him had raised Israeli fears of a possible preventive attack on the reactor. In 1964, Nasser had warned the United States that an Israeli nuclear capability "would be excuse for war, no matter how suicidal."[31] In 1965, his confidant had written that Israel was only three years from

---

[28] Morris (2001, p. 303); and Oren (2003, p. 31).

[29] Shlaim (2000, p. 237).

[30] Oren (2003, p. 83).

[31] Oren (2003, p. 76).

producing an atomic bomb and that the Arabs would need to take action. In 1966, Nasser repeated that if Israel developed the bomb, Egypt's response would be "preemptive war."[32] Two separate Egyptian photographic reconnaissance missions over the facility led some Israeli decisionmakers to believe a strike on the reactor was imminent.

Policy Options

The Israeli government had four main options in dealing with the threat posed by Egypt's mobilization. It could (1) rely on international diplomatic efforts to end the crisis, (2) initiate a major mobilization of its own to deter Egypt from attacking and to prepare for war in case deterrence failed, (3) absorb a possible Egyptian first strike and then counterattack, or (4) strike first. Israel pursued a diplomatic solution, while also mobilizing its forces, for a surprisingly long period before finally deciding to attack. The notion of absorbing an Arab first strike was quickly discarded and, as in 1956, doing nothing was not considered, as the damage this might do to Israel's deterrent ability was perceived to be prohibitive.

From the beginning of the crisis, U.S. officials stressed the importance of a diplomatic solution and warned Israel against any anticipatory attack. Such warnings had a disturbing resonance for Israeli decisionmakers who remembered Washington's hostile response to the Sinai Campaign in 1956.[33] Unable to provide Israel with the security guarantee it sought, U.S. officials instead pledged to organize an international armada to break the blockade of the Straits of Tiran. While this option, named Operation Red Sea Regatta, had the advantage of Washington's support, it proved unattractive for two reasons. First, as some Israeli military leaders noted, Regatta might reopen the Straits but would do nothing to restore Israel's deterrent power.[34] Second, the U.S. plan offered no solution to the broader Egyptian military threat

---

[32] Quoted in Morris (2001, p. 307).

[33] Oren (2003, p. 77).

[34] Shlaim (2000, p. 240).

or to Palestinian guerrilla raids.[35] While the disinclination of key countries to participate effectively ended the Regatta effort, it never represented a viable solution from the Israeli point of view.

Israel acted upon a second option—mobilization—early in the crisis as well. Upon first learning of the Egyptian deployment, Rabin wanted to call up large numbers of reserves in hopes of deterring an Egyptian attack, and in preparation for one in the event that deterrence failed. Prime Minister Eshkol refused Rabin's first request, fearful of provoking a war before diplomatic efforts had been given sufficient chance to succeed, but reluctantly agreed to a limited mobilization several days later.[36] This early action had the advantage of giving the IDF ample time to prepare for the eventual attack on Egypt, but it also increased the likelihood of war at a time when, as Ben-Gurion noted, Nasser was seeking to avoid hostilities and Israel was isolated diplomatically.[37] Further, keeping the reserves mobilized while Eshkol was committed to pursuing diplomatic options caused morale problems among the soldiers and large-scale disruption of the economy.

Deliberately absorbing an Arab first strike was not seriously considered. Israeli Foreign Minister Abba Eban was warned against any Israeli anticipatory attack during a trip to Washington in late May but was given no firm U.S. security commitment. The message seemed to leave Israel with little choice except to wait and place its trust in either diplomatic efforts that appeared to have stalled or the IDF's ability to counter any Arab attack quickly. Absorbing the first blow would deny the Soviets any pretext for intervening on behalf of their Arab allies during the fighting and would insulate Israel from political backlash following the war's conclusion, but it would also mean fighting at least the early stages of the war on the enemy's terms as well as sustaining higher levels of casualties.[38] The military costs seemed clearly to outweigh the political benefits, with one cabinet member asking upon

---

[35] Oren (2003, p. 123).

[36] Oren (2003, pp. 62–63).

[37] Morris (2001, p. 307); Shlaim (2000, p. 239).

[38] Oren (2003, p. 104).

Eban's return, "Does anyone . . . really think that we should let the enemy strike first just to prove to the world that they started it?"[39]

An Israeli first strike was the only option that remained. By May 19, Rabin was already considering a preemptive attack, specifically a comprehensive strike on the Egyptian Air Force. The IDF/AF had a well-developed plan, code-named Focus, in place for just this objective and Rabin was confident that it would work.[40] Even the Prime Minister believed that "the first five minutes [of any war] will be decisive. The question is who will attack the other's airfields first."[41] Eshkol had held the military back for more than two weeks while he tried to secure U.S. action to end the crisis, but by the first week of June, Israeli decisionmakers concluded that they could expect little help, but also little resistance, from the United States. U.S. acquiescence to an Israeli preemptive strike would take care of the more pressing potential costs by checking Soviet involvement and providing Israel with diplomatic and possibly military support. With this key hurdle overcome, after three weeks of waiting, Israel struck on the morning of June 5.

The Decision to Attack

Launching an anticipatory attack in 1967 was a more difficult proposition than it had been in 1956. In the run-up to the Sinai Campaign, the IDF had been numerically stronger than the Egyptian forces in the Sinai and Israel had been allied with two major powers against a single enemy. In 1967, however, the opposing forces were approximately equal in size, and Israel would be fighting a two- and possibly three-front war alone.[42] Two additional factors absent in 1956 further complicated Israeli calculations during the 1967 crisis: the initial opposition of the United States to any anticipatory attack and the relatively diffuse Israeli decisionmaking process. The combination of these factors, along with

---

[39] Oren (2003, p. 122).

[40] Oren (2003, p. 80).

[41] Oren (2003, p. 82).

[42] Mearsheimer (1983, pp. 145–146).

indications that outside powers might solve the situation, led Israel to focus on the diplomatic route until June.

By June, a shift in the U.S. position increased the political feasibility of an Israeli attack, while the June 1 appointment of Moshe Dayan as Defense Minister increased the likelihood of one. To avoid a repeat of the 1956 experience, Israel needed to secure U.S. acquiescence for any military action.[43] The cabinet had therefore refrained from authorizing any attacks throughout the May crisis period for fear of the potential political repercussions.[44] By June, however, Israel began receiving what some have called a "yellow light" from the United States.[45] The arrival of Dayan, a proponent of immediate military action, helped tilt the cabinet balance in favor of war, leaving only the questions of timing and objectives. On June 2, Dayan altered the objective from one of limited aims to the total destruction of the Egyptian military. The IDF would focus its initial efforts on Egypt and turn to Jordan and Syria only if necessary and after the Egyptians had been defeated.[46] On June 4, the cabinet voted for war and Israel struck the following morning, beginning with a large, precisely coordinated air attack that largely destroyed Egypt's air force on the ground, and then subjected Syria's to the same fate in rapid succession.

The Results

The Six-Day War was an overwhelming military victory for Israel. In less than one week, Israeli armed forces conquered the Golan Heights, the West Bank, the Gaza Strip, and the Sinai Peninsula, resulting in an Israel three-and-a-half times its prewar size and with control of an undivided Jerusalem.

This stunning accomplishment was tempered with a decidedly mixed political outcome. The newly conquered territories placed an additional 1.1 million Palestinians under Israeli control, almost qua-

---

[43] Mearsheimer (1983, p. 144).

[44] Reiter (1995, pp. 17–18).

[45] See William B. Quandt, "Lyndon Johnson and the June 1967 War: What Color Was the Light?" *Middle East Journal*, Vol. 46, No. 2, 1992, pp. 198–228.

[46] Morris (2001, pp. 318–319).

drupling their prewar numbers and making Israel the country with the single largest Palestinian population. With this quantitative surge came a qualitative change as well. For the previous two decades, the conflict had been one between Israel and its Arab neighbors, with the Palestinian issue largely dormant. The Six-Day War changed that, reawakening Palestinian identity and stimulating nationalist aspirations throughout the occupied territories and beyond. The conquest of the West Bank and the Gaza Strip also led to the settler movement that, like the Palestinian movement, would complicate Israeli efforts to achieve peace for decades to come.[47]

Postwar developments farther afield were even less encouraging. While the key goal of the war—the destruction of the enemy armed forces—had seemingly been achieved, increased postwar Soviet support quickly rebuilt the Egyptian and Syrian arsenals. By October 1968, Egypt's armed forces were better equipped than they had been at the war's outbreak in June 1967. In Syria, Hafez al-Assad, one of the war's key instigators, became Prime Minister in a two-stage coup and then President.[48] More broadly, the defeat spurred retrenchment in the Arab world, not reform as some Israeli decisionmakers had hoped. The war did fatally undermine pan-Arabism, but added fuel to the fires of Arab discontent, contributing to the rise of Islamic fundamentalism. The war also cost Israel its relations with the Soviet Union and most of the Eastern Bloc, and caused France to stop supplying weapons to Israel, leaving it entirely dependent upon U.S. arms exports.[49]

The Six-Day War, even more than the Sinai Campaign 11 years earlier, combined a clear military victory with ambiguous political results. Nasser's moves of mid-May effectively overturned all of Israel's gains in the 1956 war, severely undermining the state's deterrent power and necessitating a strong response. The war left Israel in control of territories formerly belonging to three separate Arab states, providing it with important strategic buffer zones but also creating fuel for fur-

---

[47] Morris (2001, pp. 329–336, 343–344, 363).

[48] Morris (2001, p. 345).

[49] All Eastern Bloc countries except Romania but including Yugoslavia broke relations with Israel (Morris, 2001, p. 344; and Shlaim, 2000, p. 250).

ther conflict, and forcing it to deal with large numbers of Palestinians who would pose a challenge to either Israel's democratic nature or its demographic basis. After three wars in less than two decades, the basic parameters of the conflict had not improved but rather had hardened.

The October War, 1973

The Situation

Egypt's recovery from its defeat in the 1967 war took far less time than Israel expected. Within months the Soviets had replaced all the equipment lost during the war and within several years the Egyptians had replaced all their casualties. Nasser believed that Israel's overwhelming victory in that war rendered any negotiated return of captured territories unlikely. Therefore, he opted for a form of limited warfare designed to play to Egyptian strengths and Israeli weaknesses, chiefly Egypt's greater ability to sustain a steady stream of casualties. When what came to be called the War of Attrition of 1969–1970 ended inconclusively with a U.S.-assisted cease-fire agreement, each side believed it had emerged the victor. The Israelis assumed that the Egyptians now grasped the military imbalance and thus the irrationality of starting another war from such a markedly inferior position.[50] The Egyptians on the other hand realized that military initiatives—even those unlikely to succeed on the battlefield—could achieve political results, in large part by bringing about superpower intervention.

After succeeding Nasser upon his death in September 1970, Egyptian President Anwar Sadat made a series of statements explicitly offering peace in return for an Israeli withdrawal from the territories it had conquered in 1967. Israel turned down these offers, and by May 1971 Sadat was convinced that war was his only option.[51] Despite newly bellicose rhetoric, 1971 passed without war, and with the Soviet Union

---

[50] Morris (2001, pp. 347–348, 363).

[51] Israel's Prime Minister Golda Meir stated in early 1971 that the Sinai's key city, Sharm al-Sheik, and an access road leading to it from the Israeli port of Eilat had to remain under Israel's control. Defense Minister Moshe Dayan stated famously that he preferred "Sharm

continuing to stall on fulfilling Egyptian requests for more sophisticated weaponry. Sadat began to view the approximately 15,000 Soviet advisers in Egypt as a constraint on his war plans and an obstacle to improved relations with the United States, which he saw as the only state able to influence Israel.[52] In July 1972, he announced the expulsion of the advisers, hoping both to jolt the Soviet Union into giving Egypt the support it sought and to improve relations with the United States. Outside observers interpreted the move as a sign that Sadat had given up on the option of war, however, since the expulsion significantly weakened Egyptian air and antiaircraft capabilities, both crucial to any plans for war.

The Threat

Israeli intelligence assessments claimed war was "improbable" or "highly improbable" all the way from late 1970 until the night before hostilities finally began in October 1973. Israeli decisionmakers did not view Sadat as a cause for great concern—an impression confirmed by his many unfulfilled threats about going to war—and they believed that the Syrians would not attack without the Egyptians.[53] The many threatening actions taken by both Arab states in the run-up to the war were similarly dismissed as either part of a regular large-scale military exercise in Egypt's case, or prompted by fears of an Israeli attack in Syria's, given a recent incident involving the downing of several Syrian planes by Israeli fighters.[54]

Four developments finally combined to undermine this optimistic view of Arab intentions: the sudden departure of the families of the Soviet advisers from Cairo and Damascus, the receipt and analysis of

---

al-Sheik without peace to peace without Sharm al-Sheik." Sadat announced his willingness in June 1971 "to sacrifice a million Egyptian soldiers to recover lost lands" and later that month, called 1971 "the year of decision" (Morris, 2001, pp. 388–389).

[52] Morris (2001, pp. 390–391).

[53] Morris (2001, p. 395).

[54] Abraham Rabinovich, *The Yom Kippur War: The Epic Encounter That Transformed the Middle East*, New York: Schocken Books, 2004, p. 56; Richard K. Betts, *Surprise Attack: Lessons for Defense Planning*, Washington, D.C.: Brookings Institution, 1982, p. 69.

aerial photographs taken on October 4 showing Arab deployments, the departure of Soviet ships from Egyptian waters, and the arrival of two messages from a highly placed and very reliable Egyptian source that war was about to break out. The first came on October 4 and said war was imminent; the second came at midnight on October 5–6 and said the attack would come the following day before dark.[55]

Policy Options

The Israeli government had only two basic options in responding to the threat posed by Egypt's and Syria's impending initiation of hostilities. It could either strike first and preempt the Arab offensive or simply mobilize and absorb the attack.

Preempting the attack would confer on Israel all of the military advantages and political disadvantages of striking first. It would allow Israel to fight according to its own plans rather than react to Arab initiatives and would minimize Israeli casualties.[56] However, it would also undermine U.S. support, vital both during and after the war. Furthermore, given that the United States was not convinced of a pending Arab attack, striking first would leave Israel with no way of proving that such an attack had in fact been coming. The Arabs, and their Soviet patron, could then claim that the resulting Egyptian and Syrian attacks were merely responses to an Israeli initiation of hostilities.[57]

Preparations for war also posed a set of strategic trade-offs for Israeli military planners. Mobilizing the reserves—the bulk of Israel's armed forces—would help Israel limit the damage of the first blow and speed the launch of a counterattack. The military benefits of a full mobilization would be less than those of preemption, while the political costs might be nearly as significant: A complete and open mobilization could itself be interpreted as an act of war. Again Israel would open itself to charges of initiating hostilities. A sharply limited mobilization—

---

[55] Morris (2001, pp. 399–400).

[56] After 1967, the Israeli Air Force based its planning for the next war on the militarily optimistic assumption that Israel would strike first again, in spite of warnings from national leaders that this might be politically impossible. See Carter (1998, pp. 52–64).

[57] Morris (2001, pp. 400–401).

enough to handle only defense—while uncontroversial politically, would have little value militarily.

The Decision Not to Attack

Prime Minister Meir decided against preemption because it was still not completely clear that an attack was coming and, more important, because Israel feared a negative U.S. reaction.[58] Defense Minister Dayan and Chief of Staff Elazar had met early on the morning of October 6 to discuss options. Elazar favored complete mobilization, which would involve some 200,000 troops, and preemptive strikes on Syrian surface-to-air missile (SAM) sites and airfields early in the afternoon.[59] Dayan wanted only about 50,000 men called up, arguing that if the IDF fully mobilized, the Arabs could argue they had felt threatened and preempted an imminent *Israeli* attack.[60] Dayan also opposed preemption, noting, "We're in a political situation in which we can't do what we did in 1967."[61] They presented these options to Meir, who supported a compromise mobilization of 100,000 to 120,000 men and rejected any preemption, noting, "If we strike first, we won't get help from anybody."[62]

The Results

The 1973 war marked a departure from past rounds of Arab-Israeli fighting. Egypt and Syria initially achieved their limited military objectives, with the Egyptians crossing the Suez Canal and entrenching themselves on its east bank under a SAM umbrella before negotiations began and the Syrians likewise recapturing portions of the Golan Heights.[63] Although the Israelis finally turned the tide of the war, scor-

---

[58] Mearsheimer (1983, p. 164).

[59] The Egyptian source said only that the attack would come "by dark" on October 6, but as the message was passed through the Israeli leadership that phrase was somehow changed to the fixed time of 6:00 p.m.

[60] Morris (2001, pp. 400–402).

[61] Rabinovich (2004, p. 87).

[62] Rabinovich (2004, p. 89).

[63] Shlaim (2000, p. 320).

ing major battlefield victories and driving deep into Egypt and Syria before hostilities ended, the Arab states achieved their larger political goal of breaking the political deadlock by provoking an international crisis that would in turn force superpower intervention. Their respectable showing after so many crushing defeats restored Arab honor and made dialogue with Israel possible.[64] Israel, on the other hand, achieved none of its traditional strategic aims in war aside from bloodying the enemy forces, neither denying the enemy any military gain nor achieving advantageous cease-fire lines, and suffered its largest number of casualties in any war to date.[65]

The negative domestic repercussions in Israel were a function of the intelligence failures leading up to the war rather than the decision not to preempt when a window of opportunity presented itself. A high-level commission led by the President of the Supreme Court, Justice Shimon Agranat, was convened to satisfy public pressure to investigate the events leading up to the war and the war's conduct.[66] The Agranat Commission issued an interim report in April 1974, in which it recommended the dismissal of several senior intelligence and military officers but did not address the issue of "ministerial responsibility," thereby effectively exonerating Meir and Dayan.[67] Public outcry led to the Prime Minister's resignation, which meant the resignation of the entire cabinet, later that month. Neither was included in the successor government. The war had therefore led, within six months of its conclusion, to the removal from office of, among others, Israel's two most prominent political leaders, the IDF's commander, and the country's chief intelligence officer.

---

[64] Morris (2001, p. 437).

[65] Ilan Pappé, *A History of Modern Palestine: One Land, Two Peoples*, Cambridge, UK, and New York: Cambridge University Press, 2004, p. 209; and Shlaim (2000, p. 320).

[66] Shlaim (2000, p. 442).

[67] The interim report called for the resignation of Chief of Staff Gen. Elazar, Chief of Intelligence Gen. Zeira, his deputy, the head of military intelligence's Egyptian desk, and the commander and the chief intelligence officer of Southern Command (Rabinovich, 2004, p. 502; and Morris, 2001, p. 443).

The principal cost of Israel's decision not to preempt was a higher number of casualties and a longer war than the state would otherwise have had to sustain. Whether preempting on the morning of October 6 would have significantly altered the course of the war by denying Egypt and Syria their military and thus political objectives is unclear.[68] Any benefit vis-à-vis the Arabs would have had to have been weighed against the political costs Israel would have sustained in its relationship with the United States. A shorter war would likely have meant less need for U.S. resupply and therefore alienating the United States would not have had immediately dire consequences for the actual fighting of the war. U.S. support would still have been needed in the postwar negotiations and beyond, however. Therefore, not preempting made sense for Israel, particularly given the Arabs' limited war aims and Israel's territorial buffer.

The Osirak Raid, 1981

The 1981 Israeli air strike against Iraq's Osirak nuclear reactor facility[69] is among the most prominent—and arguably precedent-setting—of all anticipatory attacks, and is particularly instructive for policymakers considering preventive attacks against states seeking to develop nuclear weapons or other threatening military technologies. Among the more theoretically noteworthy features of the case is the way in which the perceived international legitimacy of the Israeli raid has changed during the years since it occurred.

---

[68] Had Israel ultimately been unsuccessful at dealing with the attacks, and had its enemies been more ambitious, it might have been faced with the prospect of launching a nuclear attack in order to prevent being overrun.

[69] Strictly speaking, Osirak was the name of the small, French-built Tammuz 1 nuclear reactor, but is the name by which the entire facility is best known and so will be used here; the other key components of the complex were the larger Tammuz 2 reactor, also supplied by France, and an Italian-built "hot cell" for plutonium separation.

The Situation

In the 1970s, Saddam Hussein's Iraq embarked on an ambitious program to develop and build nuclear weapons. The centerpiece was the Osirak (or Tammuz) reactor facility, 12 miles southeast of Baghdad, where the fissile material for the weapons would be produced.[70] In 1979, Israeli intelligence estimated that, by 1982, the Iraqis would have acquired all the equipment and materials required to build nuclear weapons, and that a crude Iraqi nuclear device would be ready to test by 1985.[71]

Israel sought energetically to persuade France and other European states not to provide the reactor and associated equipment to Iraq, or at least to supply only low-grade nuclear fuel that would not be usable for building nuclear weapons, but neither diplomacy nor the work of Israeli intelligence agents succeeded in impeding Iraq's efforts substantially. Neither did an unsuccessful bombing attack on the Osirak facility by two Iranian F-4 aircraft in September 1980, early in the Iran-Iraq war. By early 1979, Israeli Prime Minister Menachem Begin had come to believe that an anticipatory attack against Osirak was necessary in order to prevent Iraq from becoming a nuclear-armed state, and that such an attack would have to be launched before the main reactor was fully fueled and activated.

---

[70] Shelomoh Nakdimon, *First Strike: The Exclusive Story of How Israel Foiled Iraq's Attempt to Get the Bomb*, New York: Summit Books, 1987, Chapters Five through Nine; Dan McKinnon, *Bullseye One Reactor*, San Diego, Calif.: House of Hits, 1987, especially Chapter Nine; Timothy L. H. McCormack, *Self-Defense in International Law: The Israeli Raid on the Iraqi Nuclear Reactor*, New York: St. Martin's Press, 1996, Chapter Two; Khidhr `Abd al-`Abbas Hamzah and Jeff Stein, *Saddam's Bombmaker: The Terrifying Inside Story of the Iraqi Nuclear and Biological Weapons Agenda*, New York: Scribner, 2000.

[71] Nakdimon (1987, pp. 107–108).

The Threat

Israeli fears were straightforward: that once armed with nuclear weapons, Saddam Hussein might well attack Israel with them.[72] Unlike the United States, Israel was highly vulnerable to nuclear attack in the sense that a handful of atomic weapons successfully delivered against its major cities would be sufficient to destroy the State of Israel for all practical purposes.[73] Moreover, Saddam Hussein appeared to be if not undeterrable, then at least more likely to engage in risky aggression than Soviet or Chinese leaders, potentially willing to accept serious retaliatory damage to Iraq in order to achieve the destruction of Israel, and with it the presumptive leadership of the Arab world. In short, national survival appeared to be at issue, and Israeli leaders considered the situation under the shadow of the experience of 1973, when fears of political repercussions deterred them from launching an anticipatory attack against Egypt, leading to heavy military losses.

Policy Options

As Israeli efforts to persuade France and Italy to pull the plug on the Iraqi weapon program proved fruitless, Israel was left with two basic policy options: to launch an anticipatory attack against Osirak in order to cripple the Iraqi nuclear program, or to take no action in the near term, allowing Iraqi nuclear development to continue, and to deter an Iraqi nuclear attack once the weapons became operational. Neither alternative was altogether attractive.

Deterrence would involve no immediate costs, since some years would elapse before Iraq would be able to produce nuclear weapons. Moreover, Israel possessed a substantial nuclear arsenal of its own and thus could pose a massive and credible threat to retaliate in the event of an Iraqi nuclear attack. However, Israel's vulnerability and Hussein's perceived recklessness made relying on deterrence appear to be a

---

[72] In this respect, Israeli fears differed from those of the United States when it was contemplating preventive war against Iraq in 2002–2003, where concerns focused on the possibility that Hussein would transfer weapons to terrorists or engage in nuclear blackmail against his neighbors rather than attack the United States directly.

[73] The same is true of many other Middle Eastern states. See Shai Feldman, *Israeli Nuclear Deterrence: A Strategy for the 1980s*, New York: Columbia University Press, 1982.

less satisfactory policy option than it was for the United States during U.S. considerations of preventive attack to prevent Soviet or Chinese nuclearization.

A preventive attack, on the other hand, offered the prospect of eliminating the threat, but involved considerable risk. First, an air strike against Osirak might fail to hit or to destroy the target. Second, the political costs of such an attack, whether successful or not, might be extremely high: If the United States were sufficiently angered by the attack to cut its political support and its billions of dollars per year in foreign aid to Israel, the effects would be devastating, leaving Israel without any significant ally. As in Israeli deliberations about launching a preemptive attack in 1973, this factor loomed extremely large in 1980–1981. Opponents of the strike also feared that it might reestablish anti-Israeli unity among the Arab states, reversing the gains of the Camp David accords, or even prompt a reconciliation between Iraq and Iran. They also suggested that it might establish a norm that could encourage the Soviet Union to consider launching an attack against Israel's nuclear capabilities.[74]

The final problem with attacking was that a preventive strike could at best be expected to buy time, delaying Iraq's nuclear progress by destroying its existing facilities, but could not prevent Baghdad from eventually rebuilding the program. While an attack might make European states less willing to assist Iraq to fulfill its nuclear ambitions, it could not realistically be expected to reduce Hussein's desire to possess nuclear weapons, and if anything would be likely to have the opposite effect.

If a preventive attack was to be launched against Osirak, Israeli leaders believed that it would have to be carried out before July 1981, when the Tammuz 2 reactor was predicted to be fully fueled and operational. After that time, an attack breaching the reactor was expected to release large amounts of nuclear fallout, causing casualties to the Iraqi civilian population that would be prohibitively costly to Israel's relationships with the rest of the world, as well as morally unacceptable in their own right. As a result, Israeli leaders faced temporal pressure akin

---

[74] Nakdimon (1987, pp. 95–96, 113–114, 160, 194–195).

to that for preemptive attack in their decisionmaking even though the Iraqi nuclear threat still lay years in the future. Prime Minister Begin also felt a sense of urgency because his Likud party appeared likely to lose the mid-1981 general election, and he expected that a Labour government would be unwilling to carry out an attack against Osirak.

The Decision to Attack

Prime Minister Begin already considered an anticipatory attack to be necessary in spring 1979, and the Israeli Air Force began developing plans for a strike against Osirak that year. However, many influential Israeli leaders opposed the option, including Foreign Minister Moshe Dayan, Defense Minister (until late May 1980) Ezer Weizman, and Deputy Prime Minister Yigael Yadin. The principal difference between the hawks and doves on this issue lay in their estimation of the likely international political costs of an air strike, with Begin and his supporters, including Agriculture Minister Ariel Sharon, being far less pessimistic than their opponents about the potential diplomatic consequences.[75] Over the ensuing year and a half, Begin was able to build support for his position, and in October 1980 the Israeli cabinet (with Dayan absent) finally voted 10-6 in favor of launching the attack.

Following a series of delays, the air strike was carried out on Sunday, June 6, 1981. A force of eight newly delivered F-16A fighter-bombers, each carrying two 2,200-pound bombs, escorted by six F-15A fighters, flew more than 650 miles across Jordanian and Saudi airspace and into Iraq at low level in order to avoid detection by Iraqi air defense radars and U.S. airborne warning and control system (AWACS) airborne early warning patrols over Saudi Arabia. They struck the target at dusk, taking its defenses by surprise and destroying the facility, then returned to base without loss. Nine Iraqis were killed or injured by the attack, and one French technician was killed.[76]

---

[75] Sharon cited the mild international reaction to Iran's unsuccessful air strike on Osirak in September 1980 as one indicator that the political costs of a preventive attack would not be excessive (Nakdimon, 1987, p. 159).

[76] For details of the operation, see McKinnon (1987).

The Results

The Osirak attack was a complete military success, and achieved its goal of wrecking the existing Iraqi nuclear program, requiring its facilities to be rebuilt essentially from scratch. The domestic political response to the success was predictably favorable, and following the raid Likud won the 1981 general election.

International reaction was condemnatory. Attitudes toward the attack varied within the United States government, but it was declared not to have been a legitimate act of self-defense, and therefore to have violated Israel's agreement to use U.S.-supplied weapons only for defensive purposes. In response, the United States briefly suspended further exports of fighter aircraft to Israel,[77] but Washington's condemnation was far milder than the attack's opponents had feared it might be, presumably due in some degree to an energetic public relations offensive led by Begin to justify the attack. In subsequent years, the attack has come to be viewed more favorably in many quarters, particularly in the wake of revelations about Iraq's post-Osirak nuclear weapon program following the 1991 Gulf War.

Begin's expectations proved to be incorrect regarding the long-run military effects of the attack, however. At the time, he estimated that Iraq's nuclear program had been delayed by five years, and recognized that his successors would eventually have to deal with similar threats from Iraq. "Resting on the precedent we set, I am sure that every prime minister, and every government in Israel, will destroy the reactor before it becomes operational," he predicted.[78] However, Iraq did not rebuild its nuclear program according to the previous model. Instead, Hussein's regime invested in developing a vast and diverse nuclear program, employing multiple paths for producing fissile material, housed in well-concealed facilities that were not vulnerable to destruction in a repeti-

---

[77] The embargo was poised to be lifted in July 1981, when Israel used American-made jets to attack targets in Beirut in retaliation for a terrorist attack, prompting the suspension to be extended into August. President Reagan was reported to have remarked, "That guy Begin makes it very difficult to help him" (Nakdimon, 1987, p. 281).

[78] Nakdimon (1987, p. 334).

tion of the Osirak raid.[79] During the 1991 Gulf War, only a few of these facilities were known to U.S. campaign planners, and the unexpected scope and the advanced state of the Iraqi nuclear program were revealed only as a result of the postwar weapon inspections.

These discoveries did much to improve the standing of the Osirak raid in international eyes by suggesting that, if the Israelis had not launched their attack, it would presumably have been a nuclear-armed Iraq that would have confronted the West in 1990. On the other hand, had Hussein not invaded Kuwait, leading to the destruction of his nuclear program following Iraq's defeat in Operation Desert Storm, Israel would have faced the nuclear-armed Iraq that Begin had so dreaded later in the 1990s, likely without having had the opportunity to launch a further attack to prevent it. Moreover, it is far from clear that the Osirak raid actually delayed the Iraqi nuclear weapon program overall: While it destroyed the program's rudimentary infrastructure as it existed in 1981, it also may have increased Hussein's interest in developing nuclear weapons and led to substantially greater resources being devoted to the effort.[80]

---

[79] Hamzah and Stein (2000).

[80] Richard K. Betts, "Nuclear Proliferation After Osirak," *Arms Control Today*, Vol. 11, 1981, pp. 1–7, pp. 1, 2, 7; Dan Reiter, "Preventive Attacks Against Nuclear Programs and the 'Success' at Osiraq," *The Nonproliferation Review*, Vol. 12, No. 2, 2005, pp. 355–371.

Counterterrorist Anticipatory Attack Cases

Introduction

The desire to attack terrorist organizations before they strike is central to the U.S. preemption doctrine, and as terrorists become potentially more powerful and traditional security threats from state adversaries decline in importance within the constellation of security threats facing the United States, it is likely that counterterrorist cases will constitute a large proportion of the scenarios in which U.S. leaders will consider launching preventive attacks in the near future. Yet visible anticipatory attacks against such nonstate actors have been rare in the past, not least for the simple reason that terrorist groups usually are not identified as threatening until they mount their first attack, after which attacking them no longer involves striking first—although preempting subsequent terrorist acts at the operational level is generally a very high priority when possible.

Because the universe of first strikes against terrorists does not feature archetypal cases such as the Six-Day War, the Osirak raid, or U.S. consideration of preventive war with the Soviet Union in the late 1940s, this appendix presents four historical cases that involve elements associated with first strikes against terrorist groups. Each is, to a greater or lesser degree, a marginal rather than an ideal example of this genre, yet together they help illuminate the subject as a whole.

Of the cases that follow, two are more or less genuine first strikes. The U.S.-Albanian raids on Islamist organizations in Tirana in 1998 come closest to the ideal type of preventive attack against a nonstate actor; although the targeted groups were associated with al Qaeda, they had not yet mounted terrorist operations against the United States or its allies. The Jordanian government's crackdown against Islamists in the city of Ma'an in late 2002 was more preemptive in nature—it sought to quash in advance a wave of militant unrest that Amman expected to face when the U.S.-led invasion of Iraq began several months later—although it was action taken against internal rather than foreign enemies.[1]

The other two cases were operationally but not strategically preemptive, involving attacks against opponents with whom the attacker was already effectively at war. However, in each case—Israel's 1997 attempted assassination of a Hamas leader in Jordan and the 2002 U.S. attack on al Qaeda terrorists in Yemen using an armed Predator drone—the action involved extending the attacking state's war against the terrorists across the border of a third-party state in a situation where this was an act of great strategic sensitivity, raising it above the level of being a question purely of military policy.

The Israeli Assassination Attempt Against Khaled Mishal, 1997

Israel's Counterterrorism Strategy

Israel has faced attacks from Palestinian groups since the state's inception. In response, it has developed a three-pronged counterterrorism strategy that places heavy emphasis on preemption and prevention.[2] Offensive measures seek to disrupt attacks during their planning stages; defensive measures seek to create obstacles for attackers already en route to their targets; and punitive measures are aimed at deterring future

---

[1] As noted earlier in the report, prior to Operation Iraqi Freedom there were voices in the United States that predicted the invasion would lead to retaliatory attacks against American targets by Hizbollah, and advocated that the United States strike Hizbollah first in order to secure this flank prior to striking Iraq. It is not clear whether this possibility was seriously considered by U.S. leaders at the time.

[2] David Eshel, "Israel Refines Its Pre-Emptive Approach to Counterterrorism," *Jane's Terrorism and Security Monitor*, September 1, 2002; Boaz Ganor, "Israeli Counter-Terrorist Policy," January 1, 1997, The Institute for Counter-Terrorism Web site.

attacks by punishing those involved directly or indirectly in terrorism. Israel has used targeted killings—for both operational preemption and coercive punishment—with particular consistency and increasing frequency over the years, though the target groups and locations selected for such attacks have varied.[3]

Targeted killings are believed to offer a number of operational benefits. They can disrupt attacks in their preparation stages, degrade a group's long-term capabilities, and force terrorists to divert time and resources to self-protection.[4] When a key terrorist leader is eliminated, a group may flounder without its head or alternatively may succumb to internal power struggles.[5] Targeted killings can also cause substantially less collateral damage than other potential strategies to remove particular individuals, such as ground incursions or aerial bombardments.[6] As a result, some observers view targeted killings as Israel's "least undesirable option" in combating terrorism.[7]

Targeted killings also carry a number of potential costs. The most prominent of these include the risk to intelligence sources and methods, the risk of retaliation from the targeted groups, and the danger to the state's image abroad.[8] There is also a danger of diverting intelligence resources away from more strategic threats, such as hostile states. Some commentators cite Israel's focus on hunting down Palestinian terrorists following the attack on its athletes at the 1972 Munich Olympics

---

[3] Jeffrey T. Richelson, "When Kindness Fails: Assassination as a National Security Option," *International Journal of Intelligence and Counterintelligence*, Vol. 15, No. 2, 2002, pp. 243–274, p. 248; Steven R. David, *Fatal Choices: Israel's Policy of Targeted Killing*, Israel: Bar-Ilan University, Mideast Security and Policy Studies No. 51, 2002, pp. 1–26.

[4] Boaz Ganor, "Targeting Terrorists: A Cost-Benefit Analysis," August 1, 2001, The Institute for Counter-Terrorism Web site.

[5] The classic example in the Israeli counterterrorism context of a group collapsing in the wake of its leader's death remains the experience of Palestine Islamic Jihad (PIJ) following the targeted killing of PIJ head Fathi Shiqaqi, discussed further below.

[6] Eshel (2002).

[7] See, for example, Michael Eisenstadt, "'Preemptive Targeted Killings' as a Counterterror Tool: An Assessment of Israel's Approach," *PeaceWatch*, No. 342, 2001.

[8] Ganor (2001).

as a factor in the failure to anticipate the 1973 war.[9] An unsuccessful assassination attempt can also severely hurt the prestige of a state's intelligence services, providing succor to its enemies and reducing its deterrent power.[10]

The Situation

Following the Oslo negotiations between Israel and the Palestine Liberation Organization (PLO) in 1993, high-ranking figures in Hamas and Palestine Islamic Jihad (PIJ) replaced those from PLO-affiliated groups as Israel's main targets. On October 26, 1995, PIJ leader Fathi Shiqaqi was shot and killed in Malta.[11] No clear successor emerged, and the group drifted along for several years without staging any major attacks. This targeted killing is viewed as one of the most successful in the policy's history, both for the cleanness of the strike and the impact it had on the targeted terrorist group.

The next high-profile attack against Palestinian Islamists had more mixed results. Following six months without any Hamas attacks, on January 6, 1996, the group's chief bombmaker Yahya Ayyash was killed in the Gaza Strip by explosives planted in a cell phone he was using.[12] While operationally successful, the targeted killing ushered in a series of Hamas suicide bombings that claimed almost 60 Israeli

---

[9] David (2002, p. 10).

[10] On the importance of deterrence in Israeli strategic thinking, see Efraim Inbar and Shmuel Sandler, "Israel's Deterrence Strategy Revisited," *Security Studies*, Vol. 3, No. 2, 1993, pp. 330–358; and Uri Bar-Joseph, "Variations on a Theme: The Conceptualization of Deterrence in Israeli Strategic Thinking," *Security Studies*, Vol. 7, No. 3, 1998, pp. 145–181.

[11] Shyam Bhatia, "Israel Accused of Jihad 'Execution,'" *The Observer*, October 29, 1995, p. 22.

[12] Serge Schmemann, "Palestinian Believed to Be Bombing Mastermind Is Killed," *The New York Times*, January 6, 1996, p. A3; Patrick Cockburn, "Killing of Hamas Bomber Delights Israel," *The Independent*, January 6, 1996, p. 9.

lives over the succeeding two months.[13] Leaflets referring to Ayyash assumed responsibility for the bombings.[14]

The third strike of this series was directed against Hamas political figure Khaled Mishal in Amman, Jordan. On the morning of September 25, 1997, two agents from Israel's foreign intelligence service, the Mossad, were apprehended after attempting to spray poison into Mishal's ear.[15] The failed assassination attempt damaged Israeli relations with allies Jordan and Canada, and strengthened Hamas and other enemies of the peace process. Amir Oren, a leading expert on Israel's intelligence services, called the operation "probably the worst disaster in the history of the Mossad," noting that it showed "astonishing errors, not just in the failure of its execution but in its very conception."[16]

The Threat

By 1997, Hamas[17] had become the most prominent Palestinian group rejecting the peace process with Israel. The group was founded at the beginning of the first intifada in 1987 as an offshoot of the Palestin-

---

[13] All Israeli casualty figures and other attack data are from "Suicide and Other Bombing Attacks in Israel Since the Declaration of Principles (Sept 1993)," April 6, 1994 [sic], Israel Ministry of Foreign Affairs Web site.

[14] Shaul Mishal and Avraham Sela, *The Palestinian Hamas: Vision, Violence, and Coexistence*, New York: Columbia University Press, 2000, pp. 75–76.

[15] See the three-part Arabic News Special Report on the event: "Special Report Part 1: The Release of Sheikh Yassin," *ArabicNews.com*, October 1, 1997; "Special Report Part 2: The Release of Hamas's Spiritual Leader, Sheikh Yassin," *ArabicNews.com*, October 1, 1997; and "Special Report Part 3: The Downfall of Netanyahu: Mossad's Assassination Fiasco in Jordan," *ArabicNews.com*, October 3, 1997.

[16] Cited in Ed Blanche, "Israeli Intelligence Agencies Under Fire," *Jane's Intelligence Review*, Vol. 10, No. 1, 1998, p. 18.

[17] Hamas is an acronym for Harakat al-Muqawamah al-Islamiyyah, the Islamic Resistance Movement. The word itself also means "enthusiasm," "rapture," "zeal," "elan," or "fighting spirit" (Hans Wehr and J. Milton Cowan, *A Dictionary of Modern Written Arabic: Arabic-English*, 4th ed., Ithaca, N.Y.: Spoken Language Services, 1994, p. 239).

ian branch of the Muslim Brotherhood.[18] Its charter states in part that the Palestinian question can be solved only through violence and that Islam will one day displace Israel.[19] Its military wing[20] first focused on killing Palestinians suspected of cooperating with the Israeli authorities, but quickly moved on to target Israelis as well.[21] Hamas has since conducted more suicide bombings than any other Palestinian group and poses a serious threat to both the secular Palestinian leadership and to Israel.[22]

Two consecutive Hamas suicide bombings in a Jerusalem market on July 30, 1997, provided the immediate context for the plan to strike Mishal in Amman. Coming after four months of calm, the double bombing killed 16 Israelis and wounded 178 others. Israeli intelligence assessments suggested Mishal had played a role in planning the attacks.[23] Hamas carried out a third suicide bombing in western Jerusalem on September 4, 1997, as the anticipatory attack against Mishal was in its final planning stages. This bombing killed five and wounded 181. A Mossad team was sent to Amman and the strike took place three weeks after the September bombing.

Policy Options

The Israeli government likely had four main options in choosing how to deal with Mishal in the fall of 1997. It could wait, request Jordanian

---

[18] On the origins of Hamas, see Khalid Harub, *Hamas: Political Thought and Practice*, Washington, D.C.: Institute for Palestine Studies, 2000, Chapter One; and Mishal and Sela (2000, Chapter One).

[19] Harub (2000, pp. 267–291).

[20] The Izz-ad-Din al-Qassam Brigades were formed in 1991 and named after the celebrated resistance leader of a 1936 anti-Zionist revolt in Palestine (Harub, 2000, p. 11).

[21] See Ian Black and Benny Morris, *Israel's Secret Wars: A History of Israel's Intelligence Services*, New York: Grove Weidenfeld, 1991, pp. 472–479; Dan Raviv and Yossi Melman, *Every Spy a Prince: The Complete History of Israel's Intelligence Community*, Boston: Houghton Mifflin, 1990, pp. 379–404.

[22] For the official Israeli recording of post-Oslo attacks, see "Suicide and Other Bombing Attacks in Israel Since the Declaration of Principles (Sept 1993)" (1994).

[23] Gordon Thomas, *Gideon's Spies: The Secret History of the Mossad*, New York: St. Martin's Press, 1999, p. 133.

action against Mishal, seek Jordanian permission for Israeli action, or move against him without the involvement or knowledge of the Jordanian government. Only the last option appears to have been seriously considered.

Waiting, in effect doing nothing, was an unlikely course for Israel to pursue by September 1997. A previous plan for a strike on Mishal in the summer of 1996, while he attended an Islamic conference in Turkey, had been cancelled for fear of damaging Israel's deepening relations with Ankara.[24] Since then there had been three more suicide bombings, at a cost of 24 more Israeli lives, with more likely in the future. Already a target before these attacks, Mishal most likely took on increased importance after them.

Requesting Jordanian action would also have been an unlikely choice at the time, though there is a small chance it might have succeeded. The Hamas political bureau operated openly in Amman despite quiet cooperation between the Israeli and Jordanian authorities against Palestinian Islamists. However, in 1999, two years after the failed attempt on Mishal, the Jordanians did issue a warrant for his arrest while he was out of the country, in effect denying him reentry.[25] Thus, given existing high levels of Jordanian cooperation and future Jordanian actions, there may have been an unappreciated opportunity for the Israelis to have negotiated a similar, earlier Jordanian effort in 1997.

Attempting to secure Jordanian permission for Israeli operatives to capture or kill Mishal in Jordan would also have been an unlikely course of action and almost certainly would have failed had Israel pursued it. The longstanding domestic combination of sensitivity to Israeli

---

[24] Turkey, along with Iran and Ethiopia, had long been a key pillar in what became known as Israel's "periphery" doctrine, whereby the state would seek alliances with non-Arab or non-Muslim states or groups along the region's edges to help balance against its hostile Arab neighbors (Black and Morris, 1991, pp. 182–188). On the cancelled attack, see Blanche (1998).

[25] Sana Abdallah, "Jordan Cracks Down on Hamas," *United Press International*, August 30, 1999a; Sana Abdallah, "Jordan Decides to Deport Hamas Leader," *United Press International*, September 22, 1999b; Patrick Cockburn, "Jordan Closes HQ of Hamas Militants," *The Independent*, August 31, 1999, p. 11.

incursions and popular support for Palestinian rejectionist groups would have severely constrained the Jordanian government's ability to cooperate with Israel against Hamas so overtly.[26] It could also have sparked Hamas attacks against Israeli targets in the Kingdom, or against the Jordanian monarchy itself, neither of which had previously occurred. There is little chance the Jordanian government would have risked allowing Israel to act against a group that was not threatening Jordan directly.

A targeted killing appears to be the only option that was seriously considered. Israel was greatly limited in the ways it could carry out the attack due to Mishal's presence in a friendly foreign country. Therefore, a synthetic opiate used successfully in the past by the Mossad was reportedly selected for the attempt rather than a higher-profile tactic. The poison, fentanyl, can kill within 48 hours and leaves no trace, granting Israel plausible deniability for the attack.[27]

The Decision to Attack

The double suicide bombing of July 30, 1997, provided the immediate context for the decision to target Mishal in Amman. Following the bombings, Israel's Prime Minister Binyamin Netanyahu called an emergency cabinet meeting, at which the cabinet approved authorization to target Hamas military leaders abroad. It is unclear how Mishal, a member of the group's political bureau, was selected for assassination. Some Israeli decisionmakers believed he had been involved in the planning of the suicide bombings, although a number of observers questioned his role in anything beyond the group's political activities.[28]

Netanyahu restricted the decision to target Mishal in Amman to a very small number of people, bypassing key individuals and committees. The Defense Minister, the head of the internal intelligence

---

[26] On the complex triangular relationship among Jordan's national interests, Palestinian residents, and relations with Israel, see Marc Lynch, *State Interests and Public Spheres: The International Politics of Jordan's Identity*, New York: Columbia University Press, 1999, especially Chapters Four and Six.

[27] Blanche (1998).

[28] Thomas (1999, p. 133).

agency, the head of military intelligence, and the IDF Chief of Staff all expressed anger at having been left out of the decisionmaking process.[29] Reports suggest the Mossad chief of station in Amman learned of the strike only after it had failed and members of the assassination team were on their way to the Israeli Embassy.[30] The two committees charged with selecting assassination targets were bypassed as well. Some accounts suggest the Prime Minister chose Mishal personally; others suggest Mossad director Daniel Yatom provided Mishal's name as one of several possible targets.[31]

It is unclear what benefits the Prime Minister expected from a successful strike against Mishal. Given his position as a political rather than military figure in Hamas, his elimination should not have led to any reduction in terrorist activity through depriving the group of a key individual. While Netanyahu did appear to believe that Mishal had played a role in planning the recent bombings, an expected reduction in the level of violence was not extensively discussed as a reason to target him. Instead, a perceived need to respond to the recent suicide bombings, combined with Mishal's accessibility in neighboring Jordan, appear to have been more important factors in the decision to attack.

The Results

The failed strike carried a number of costs for Israel. The government was forced to provide an antidote for Mishal and to release Sheikh Ahmed Yassin, one of the founders of Hamas and its spiritual leader, to secure the return of its agents in Amman. Israel subsequently released several dozen other Palestinian prisoners as well. Yassin, one of the most prominent Palestinian Islamists, had been sentenced to life in prison in 1989 for his role in the kidnapping and murder of two Israeli soldiers. His release had been a longstanding Palestinian demand and

---

[29] "Israeli Mossad Report on Amman Fiasco: Background," *ArabicNews.com*, February 16, 1998.

[30] Blanche (1998). Other reports suggest he knew of the plan in advance but counseled against it for fear of jeopardizing the important counterterrorism work his station carried out in coordination with Jordanian authorities (Thomas, 1999, p. 133).

[31] Blanche (1998).

provided a particularly significant boost to Palestinian morale. Freeing Yassin and dozens of other Palestinian prisoners also undermined Israel's counterterrorism efforts.

The loss of the Mossad's Amman station following the attack seriously undermined Israel's intelligence-gathering against both regional terrorist groups and states such as Iran, Iraq, and Syria. The station had been in place since 1994, when a peace treaty was signed between the two countries and an Israeli embassy opened in Jordan. The treaty included security accords and Israel and Jordan had developed a strong working relationship in that sphere. Following the attack on Mishal, however, King Hussein ordered all Mossad personnel out of Jordan and cut off security cooperation with Israel, despite the fact that regional Islamists posed as large a threat to his monarchy as they did to Israel.

Israel's ties with Canada were damaged by the incident as well. Canada recalled its ambassador to Israel over the Mossad team's use of Canadian passports in the strike against Mishal.[32] Following the discovery that Canadian passports had been used in a failed 1973 Mossad operation, Canada had redesigned its passports and extracted an Israeli agreement not to use Canadian travel documents in the future.[33] The strike on Mishal revealed that Israel had violated that agreement, compounding the damage to Israeli-Canadian relations. When a second agreement was negotiated between the two countries in the wake of the 1997 incident, some Canadian decisionmakers cited the earlier violation in questioning the new agreement's value.[34]

---

[32] Howard Schneider, "Canada Pulls Ambassador from Israel; Reputed Murder Plot Stirs Diplomatic Protest," *The Washington Post*, October 3, 1997a, p. A29.

[33] In 1973, Mossad operatives traveling on Canadian passports were caught after killing a North African waiter in Lillehammer, Norway, having mistaken him for the chief of operations of Black September, the Palestinian group suspected of carrying out the attack on Israel's athletes at the 1972 Munich Olympics (see Black and Morris, 1991, pp. 269–277; and Alexander B. Calahan, *Countering Terrorism: The Israeli Response to the 1972 Munich Olympic Massacre and the Development of Independent Covert Action Teams*, M.M.S. thesis, Marine Corps Command and Staff College, 1995).

[34] Howard Schneider, "Israelis Apologize to Canada; Forged Passports Case Had Strained Relations," *The Washington Post*, October 11, 1997b, p. A17.

Domestically, opposition leaders and segments of the press called for the resignation of the Prime Minister and the Mossad chief.[35] The latter did resign after a commission appointed by Netanyahu to study the failure laid most of the blame for the failure on him. The prestige of Israel's foreign intelligence service, widely believed to be the most capable in the region, also suffered following the failed attack, as regional Islamists were able to turn the failed attempt on Mishal into significant political capital.[36]

The planned attack on Mishal thus appears to have been a strategic as well as an operational failure. The damage to Israel's relations with its most important Arab ally seems to have outweighed any benefits Israel might have reasonably expected to gain by killing Mishal. The failed strike cost Israel not only significant counterterrorism cooperation against groups such as Hamas, but also a key intelligence post against threatening enemies such as Iran, Iraq, and Syria. It undermined the Israeli public's confidence in its government and undermined the Mossad's deterrent power throughout the region. These significant costs could have been foreseen, and risking them seems ill-conceived in exchange for the vague and relatively insignificant potential benefits of the attack.

The Tirana Raids, 1998

In the summer of 1998, Albanian authorities, with the help of the American CIA and Federal Bureau of Investigation (FBI), conducted a series of raids that disrupted an Islamist effort to establish a terrorist network in Albania. The raids, conducted on June 2, June 29, and July 16, resulted in the arrests of an Arab of French citizenship for murder and three Egyptians for possession of illegal arms and document-forging materials. During his murder trial, the Frenchman admitted to

---

[35] See, for example, the media round-up in Doron Avigad, "An Amateur, Not Up to the Job," *Globes*, October 6, 1997.

[36] Patrick Cockburn, "Netanyahu 'Over-Ruled' Mossad Chief," *The Independent*, October 6, 1997, p. 10.

trying to establish a relationship between the Kosovo Liberation Army (KLA) and al Qaeda. The Egyptians had ties to Islamic Jihad and were wanted for terrorist bombings in the United States and attacks in Egypt. Follow-up actions netted another ten Egyptians involved in subversive activities. All were associated with Islamic charities in Albania.

The Situation

Albania was governed as a reclusive, one-party communist state until 1990, when its regime toppled in the wave of revolutions that swept Eastern Europe. As in many of the former communist countries, Albania's efforts to liberalize its political and economic systems caused considerable domestic turmoil. Aggressive efforts to reform the socialist economy resulted in high inflation and unemployment accompanied by widespread organized crime. Conflict in the former Yugoslavian states between Muslims, Orthodox Serbs, and Catholic Croats added to domestic strain and tensions between Tirana and its Christian neighbors. Financially destitute, the new government initially looked to the West for developmental assistance, but few investors were willing to brave Albania's climate of economic instability.

Unable to attract sufficient economic assistance from the West, Albania's first freely elected president, Sali Berisha, decided to draw on the country's Islamic cultural heritage and appeal to the Muslim world to help Albania's struggling economy. Without consulting Parliament, he submitted Albania's application to become a member of the Organization of the Islamic Conference (OIC), petitioned oil-rich Middle Eastern states for development assistance, and opened Albania's doors to Islamic charities.[37] These moves alarmed many Albanians. Although nearly two-thirds of the nation's three million citizens are Muslim, most consider themselves European and few adhere to strict Islamic religious and social guidelines or identify with Middle Eastern sociopolitical perspectives. Yet Berisha's strategy met with a degree of success. By late 1992, the Islamic Relief Agency was distributing medical supplies and food in Albania and the Islamic Development Bank had

---

[37] Teodor Misha, "Albania Denies Terrorist Links," Institute for War and Peace Reporting, Balkans Crisis Report No. 283, September 26, 2001.

agreed to grant Tirana credit and invest in all sectors of the Albanian economy. Other Muslim charities and financial institutions followed suit soon afterward.[38]

While providing some immediate relief, Berisha's strategy only contributed to the mounting political problems he and his Democratic Party faced over the next five years. Their main opposition, the Socialist Party, voiced a widely held opinion that courting Islam was a backward step in the nation's struggle to establish itself as a modern state.[39] This argument punctuated a larger debate about Berisha's continuing inability to put the nation's economy on a sound footing or deal with its rampant corruption. The demise of the authoritarian communist government and the poverty caused by the faltering economy had combined to create an environment in which organized crime thrived. This problem had both domestic and international ramifications, as mafia groups sprang up across the country and exploited its porous borders in a lucrative trade in weapons, drugs, illegal immigrants, and women from Albania to other destinations in southeastern Europe.[40] Socialists and independent observers frequently charged that officials within the Berisha administration and parliament had not only allowed these problems to fester, but in many cases were personally involved in the corruption.[41]

Political Turmoil. By the mid-1990s, Albania's domestic political climate had turned bitter, with vicious infighting between the Democratic Party and the Socialists, and Berisha was becoming increasingly heavy-handed in repressing his political opponents. The economic growth Albania had managed to achieve between 1992 and 1995 leveled off in 1996, with an inflation rate of 20 percent and many citizens

---

[38] International Crisis Group, *Bin Laden and the Balkans: The Politics of Anti-Terrorism*, Belgrade and Brussels: International Crisis Group, 2001, pp. 4–5.

[39] International Crisis Group (2001, p. 5).

[40] Groupe d'Etats Contre la Corruption, Directorate General I, Legal Affairs, Department of Crime Problems, *First Evaluation Round, Evaluation Report on Albania, Adopted by GRECO at Its 12th Plenary Meeting (Strasbourg, 9–13 December 2002)*, Strasbourg: Groupe d'Etats Contre la Corruption, 2002, p. 4.

[41] Fred Abrahams, "Albania," *Foreign Policy in Focus*, Vol. 2, No. 33, 2001, pp. 1–4, p. 1.

still unemployed.[42] These stresses fed mounting popular frustrations, leading to civil disorder and fueling a steady stream of refugees to Greece and Italy, further straining Tirana's relations with those states. Finally, in the spring of 1997, the Socialist Party's persistent charges of corruption in Berisha's government appeared to be confirmed when a series of government-endorsed pyramid investment schemes collapsed, revealing links between individuals close to the president and organized crime. The crisis sparked widespread rioting, during which hundreds of thousands of weapons, including hand grenades and land mines, were looted from police headquarters and army garrisons around the country.[43] Berisha attempted to stabilize the situation with a mix of repression and conciliatory gestures, but he was ultimately forced to resign and subsequent elections brought a Socialist-led coalition to power with Rexhep Meidani as president and Socialist Party Chairman Fatos Nano as prime minister.[44]

Fatos Nano had long castigated the Berisha administration for its ineptitude and corruption, yet at first, the Meidani-Nano coalition government proved equally incapable of solving Albania's most pressing problems. Following the 1997 riots, the rate of violent crimes escalated sharply as order broke down across much of Albania. The change of government brought little improvement in early 1998. Berisha and his followers refused to accept the legitimacy of the new administration or obey its laws. Local mafia groups, now heavily armed, intimidated citizens and police alike. Prosecutors and police were deterred from vigorously fighting corruption, because when they made arrests, suspects frequently named powerful government officials or members of parliament as co-conspirators in their crimes.[45]

---

[42] After a 50-percent decline in real GDP between 1989 and 1992, Albania's economy grew 8–11 percent annually in 1993–1995, achieved negligible growth in 1996, and declined in 1997. Inflation reached 50 percent in 1997. See U.S. Department of State, "Background Note: Albania," 2005a.

[43] "The State of Albania," Tirana: International Crisis Group, ICG Balkans Report No. 54, 1999, p. 5.

[44] Abrahams (2001, p. 2).

[45] "The State of Albania" (1999, p. 4).

Amidst this chaotic, politically charged environment, the coalition government suspended its OIC membership and moved to strengthen its relations with the United States and European nations.[46] Though not as dramatic a change as it might at first appear to be—even under Berisha, Albania had joined NATO's North Atlantic Cooperation Council in 1992 and began conducting combined military exercises with the United States in 1995—the coalition government broadened Albania's relationship to include intelligence collaboration with the United States and other Western states. It was only then, according Fatos Klosi, director of Albania's intelligence service (ShIK), that Tirana discovered the extent to which militant Islamists had penetrated Albania and used its semi-anarchic territory as a safe haven and gateway for sending terrorists into the rest of Europe.[47]

Nano and other Socialists in the coalition government charged that Berisha and his followers had allowed Albania to become a breeding ground for terrorists. According to Foreign Minister Paskal Milo, extremists used the Islamic charitable foundations that Berisha ushered into the country "to cover their secret activities . . . [and their] relations and links with other Islamic organizations outside Albania." He maintained that Albania had been a "roof for them to stay under" while they obtained visas, passports, and other documents enabling them to travel between the Middle East and Europe.[48] Klosi echoed those allegations and pointed out that Bashkim Gazidede, his predecessor as ShIK director under Berisha, had been head of the Albanian Association of Islamic Intellectuals. Klosi and others inside and outside the Albanian government maintained that Osama bin Laden had, at

---

[46] "Albanian President Wants OIC Status Clarified," *Radio Free Europe/Radio Liberty*, Vol. 2, No. 204, 1998. This gesture was somewhat symbolic, as the parliament had never ratified Albania's membership in the OIC (see Gyorgy Lederer, *Conemporary Islam in East Europe*, Individual Democratic Institutions Research Fellowship [IDIR], 1999, p. 13).

[47] Klosi claims the ShIK could not monitor the infiltration and activities of illegal militants because the 1997 riots had "torn apart and destroyed [his agency] materially and spiritually" (see R. Jeffrey Smith, "Albania Expands Crackdown on Arabs: Officials Say Islamic Groups Used the Nation as Haven, Gateway for Terrorism," *The Washington Post*, August 29, 1998c, p. A10).

[48] Smith (1998c).

Berisha's and Gazidede's invitation, visited Albania in 1994 claiming to represent a wealthy humanitarian agency eager to help Albania's poor. Klosi further claimed that bin Laden and other terrorists had sent units to fight in the KLA and used Albania as a base for infiltrating terrorists into other parts of Europe.[49]

Allegations that the Berisha government had been culpable in allowing Albania to become a sanctuary for terrorists must be considered in the context of Tirana's acrimonious political climate and the inability of either Berisha's government or the Socialist-led coalition to govern effectively in 1997 or early 1998. Few Albanian Muslims, given their secular European cultural orientation, are prone to religious extremism. But insecurities stemming from poverty, civil disorder, and the proximity of civil war in neighboring states, in which the antagonists identified themselves and each other largely along religious lines, may have made some Albanians receptive to extremist ideologies. The Berisha administration had liberally granted Albanian citizenship to Middle Eastern immigrants, and the evidence suggests that militant Islamists established a presence in Albania, working through Islamic charities and financial institutions.[50]

However, a more serious problem lay in Tirana's inability to control its borders or police its territory effectively. This problem became apparent soon after the collapse of the communist regime and worsened during Berisha's tenure, but it reached crisis proportion after the 1997 uprising. Not only did the subsequent anarchy cripple the state's immigration control and law enforcement mechanisms, but in May 1998, the Interior Ministry concluded that as many as 100,000 blank Albanian passports had been stolen during the riots, along with a variety of official government seals. These items appeared on the black

---

[49] Chris Stephen, "Bin Laden Opens European Terror Base in Albania," *The Sunday Times*, November 29, 1998, p. 23; Scott Taylor, "Bin Laden's Balkan Connections: Al-Qaeda Fighters Have Been Quietly Infiltrating the Ranks of Ethnic Albanian Guerrilla Forces in Macedonia Croatia, Bosnia and Kosovo for Years," *The Ottawa Citizen*, December 15, 2001, p. B3.

[50] R. Jeffrey Smith, "U.S. Probes Blasts' Possible Mideast Ties; Alleged Terrorists Investigated in Albania," *The Washington Post*, August 12, 1998a, p. A19.

market immediately afterward, and Albanian and U.S. officials believe many of them fell into the hands of al Qaeda and other terrorists.[51]

Regardless of whether Albanians were vulnerable to Islamist subversion, the country's economic deprivation, rampant corruption, anarchic condition, and open borders made it fertile ground for terrorist exploitation as a sanctuary and transit node for other destinations. Though none of Albania's complex problems could be solved easily, the coalition government decided to take action, in cooperation with the United States, to thwart the Islamist threat while working to develop better intelligence capabilities and tighter control over its borders and immigration.

The Raids. On June 2, 1998, CIA and Albanian authorities raided the Tirana home of French citizen Claude Sheik-bin-Abdel Kader and arrested him for the murder of his Albanian translator. Security officials found false papers, automatic weapons, and ammunition in his residence. During interrogations, Kader admitted to being a member of a group directed by Osama bin Laden and said he had been sent to give weapons to the KLA. Kader also said that four other bin Laden operatives remained at large in Albania.[52]

Later that month, CIA, FBI, and Albanian authorities arrested religious scholar Maged Mustafa and accountant Muhamet Houda, both Egyptians, for falsifying documents. At Mustafa's home, security officials found an automatic rifle and ammunition, a bag of forged papers, and official Albanian government stamps needed to get past customs and police checkpoints.[53] According to ShIK officials, Mustafa and Houda had organized a camp in Elbasan to recruit and train

---

[51] "The State of Albania" (1999, p. 4); International Crisis Group (2001, p. 5); Smith (1998c); Stephen (1998); Scott Taylor (2001).

[52] International Crisis Group (2001, p. 5). Kader was convicted of murder and, on November 14, 1998, sentenced to 20 years in prison. See "Islamist Murder Suspect Sentenced in Albania," *Radio Free Europe/Radio Liberty Newsline: Southeastern Europe*, November 16, 1998.

[53] "Albanian Police Detain Egyptians Falsifying Documents," *Albanian Telegraphic Agency*, June 29, 1998.

Islamic youths to fight in Kosovo. Their objective was to give the war in the Serbian province "a powerful religious character."[54]

During their interrogations, Mustafa and Houda implicated a third Egyptian in terrorist activities. Subsequently, authorities arrested Muhammad Hasan Mahmud, director of the Islamic Revival Foundation (IRF), a suspected fundraising organization for al Qaeda.[55] The IRF provided aid to poor Muslim families and orphans in Albania and was closely linked with several other Islamic charitable and educational organizations in the country. Like other charitable groups operating in Albania, the IRF obtained funds from an organization known as the Kuwait Joint Relief Committee, which was suspected of funneling money and resources to terrorist organizations in Albania and elsewhere. Like Mahmud, Mustafa and Houda were associated with the IRF.[56]

On August 19, twelve days after al Qaeda terrorists bombed the U.S. embassies in Kenya and Tanzania, U.S. and Albanian officials launched a nationwide search for other suspected Islamist terrorists. Within two days, Albanian police arrested ten foreign nationals in Tirana and Elbasan. In these raids, they seized communications equipment, bulletproof vests, weapons, and forged documents including passports.[57]

The Threat

The threat the Islamist presence in Albania posed was not entirely clear in 1998. With the exception of Klosi's allegations, all open-source reports suggested the cells in Tirana were primarily used to recruit and train fighters for the KLA. Yet the existence of a terrorist logistical pipeline threatened the United States and its allies even if that organi-

---

[54] "Detained Islamists Aimed at Giving Religious Character to War in Kosova, Daily Said," *Albanian Telegraphic Agency*, July 14, 1998.

[55] "Third Egyptian Accused of Terrorism Arrested in Tirana—Paper," *Albanian Telegraphic Agency*, July 21, 1998.

[56] Smith (1998a).

[57] Fabian Schmidt, "No Welcome Mat Here," *Transitions*, Vol. 4, No. 10, 1998.

zation's principal function then was to support operations against some other adversary.

If, as Klosi claimed, the Tirana financial network was also used to funnel personnel and resources to the rest of Europe, then it was a serious threat indeed. European al Qaeda cells have been implicated in a wide range of terrorist operations around the globe, including the September 11, 2001, attacks in the United States. Even if the Tirana network did not directly support other European cells at that particular time, redirecting its support from the KLA to those cells would have been a simple matter.

But the greatest threat that Albania posed in 1998 may have been the sanctuary its permissive, semi-anarchic environment offered for a wide range of radical Islamist activities. As early as 1992, at least three fundraising organizations with suspected ties to al Qaeda operated there. Until the 1998 raids, individuals wanted for terrorist attacks in other countries moved openly in the streets of Tirana. Postcommunist Albanian authorities were never able to control their borders effectively, and after the 1997 riots, the region was a virtual cornucopia of illicit weapons and forged documents. Ultimately, whether the specific individuals arrested or the networks dismantled in the 1998 raids were explicitly anti-Western was only one part of a larger security issue. The permissive environment itself represented a threat to America's European allies, U.S. interests in Europe, and ultimately to the security of the United States itself.

Policy Options

American policymakers had several options available to them when intelligence revealed the growing Islamist presence in Albania and Tirana's new coalition government expressed its willingness to move against the militants. The first question was whether to attempt to disrupt the network immediately or wait and continue monitoring its activities. Given a decision to move against the Islamists, U.S. officials would then have to choose from three alternative courses of action: urging Albania to combat the Islamist network on its own, supporting Tirana's efforts with intelligence but leaving operations against the

Islamists to the Albanian authorities, or providing intelligence support and also participating in operations against suspected militants.

The Decision to Raid the Albanian Cells

Washington's decision to move against the Islamist cells in Albania probably resulted from the coincidence of two factors: the escalation in subversive activity observed there after the 1997 riots and the window of opportunity to act that improved relations with Tirana afforded. Albania's semi-anarchic conditions and the increase in militant activity following the 1997 riots presented a threat to American interests that Washington would have been unwise to ignore. Deferring action in hopes of collecting useful intelligence would have been risky, given the permissive environment for illicit activities that Albania's chaotic conditions had created. Yet, without Tirana's cooperation, the United States could not move against this threat without violating Albanian sovereignty. It is uncertain whether the Berisha administration knowingly fostered ties with Islamists, but even if it did not, it was clearly not inclined to move against them. Only after the Meidani-Nano coalition government came to power in January 1998 did the level of cooperation between Tirana and Washington make such an operation possible.

Given an opportunity to move against the Islamist threat in Albania, an operation combining the efforts of U.S. and Albanian intelligence authorities was the most promising approach for both governments. The first alternative, leaving Albania to fight the Islamist network on its own, offered little probability of success given the Albanian security forces' low competence and morale. Relying on them would have been politically risky for the Meidani-Nano administration, as a botched operation would only have underscored the government's inadequacies. Such an outcome would benefit neither the United States nor Albania's coalition government.

Chances of the second option succeeding were also poor, as the ShIK's shortcomings were broader and more serious than mere gaps in intelligence. Providing the ShIK with good information would not overcome its lack of training or poor morale. Beyond that, "spoon-feeding" the ShIK with intelligence would do little to develop the agency's own collection capabilities.

The third option was optimal for several reasons. American participation in the raids and access to Western intelligence increased the operation's chance of success. Moreover, the level of security cooperation this effort entailed would benefit both governments. Having the CIA and FBI work with the ShIK would gain the United States an intelligence presence in a critical region of Europe, in a country that had not been particularly cooperative with Washington prior to 1998. In return, the CIA could train and provide field guidance to Albania's own security and intelligence service, and this too would serve U.S. interests. In May 1998, CIA Director George Tenet expressed particular concern about Albanian security deficiencies at an unpublicized meeting with Klosi in Washington.[58]

The Results

The Tirana raids were a tactical success for Washington and a turning point in the Albanian government's struggle to establish domestic order and the rule of law. The initial raids disrupted the Islamist network in Tirana and Elbasan and led to a general crackdown on subversive activity throughout the nation.[59] While the raids almost certainly did not eradicate Islamist subversion in Albania, they were a significant first step in denying terrorists an uncontested sanctuary in which to organize and fund their violent activities and a transit node from which to export them abroad.

However, not all short-term developments were positive. Islamic organizations in London and Paris criticized the United States and

---

[58] Smith (1998c).

[59] Not all the raids were successful, yet even the tactical failures had some positive effect. For instance, intelligence gathered in the initial raids revealed that the Islamic Salvation Army (ISA), an Algerian extremist group, was operating a cell in Tirana. But before a raid could be organized against this cell, ShIK officials boasted to the Albanian press of their recent successful cooperation with the CIA and FBI, thus alerting ISA operatives of the imminent danger. By the time U.S. and Albanian officials moved against the Algerian cell, all its members had fled the country. No arrests were made, but an extremist cell had been removed, nonetheless (see Smith, 1998a).

Albania for returning the Egyptian suspects to Cairo, where they later died in police custody. Fear of reprisal led the United States to temporarily shut down its embassy in Tirana, and several key U.S. officials cancelled trips to Albania in the ensuing months.[60] On August 7, terrorists bombed the U.S. embassies in Kenya and Tanzania. As the attacks closely followed a threat from Osama bin Laden's right-hand man, Ayman al Zawahiri, to exact retribution for the extradition of Egyptians arrested in the Tirana raids, some authorities speculated that the events were connected.[61] But investigations later revealed that preparations for the embassy bombings were underway at least a month before the first Tirana raid took place.[62]

Developments since the Tirana raids have reinforced early indications that the cooperative effort yielded positive results. Albania's security relationship with the United States has grown over time. American officials helped Albania draft new laws increasing the ShIK's authority to monitor the activities of suspected terrorists.[63] Albanian officials launched an investigation of the Arab-Albanian Bank and several other Islamic financial institutions and charities.[64]

After the September 11 attack, Tirana eagerly cooperated with U.S. investigators to determine whether any aspect of the plot had been organized on or supported from Albanian soil. In late September 2001, Albania's chief of counterterrorism, Colonel Bilbil Mema, and newly appointed Foreign Minister Arta Dade announced that no links had been found between Muslims living in Albania and terrorist organiza-

---

[60] International Crisis Group (2001, p. 5).

[61] Smith (1998a); R. Jeffrey Smith, "U.S. Embassy Threatened in Albania: Warning Against Americans Follows Crackdown on Extremists," *The Washington Post*, August 15, 1998b, p. A11; Scott Taylor (2001).

[62] U.S. Department of Justice, "FBI Executive Summary: Bombings of the Embassies of the United States of America at Nairobi, Kenya, and Dar es Salaam, Tanzania, August 7, 1998, US Dept. of Justice, Federal Bureau of Investigation, Washington, D.C. 20535, November 18, 1998, Orcon/Law Enforcement Sensitive," *Frontline: Hunting bin Laden*; Benjamin Weiser, "U.S. to Offer Detailed Trail of bin Laden in Bomb Trial," *The New York Times*, January 13, 2001, p. A1.

[63] Smith (1998c).

[64] "The State of Albania" (1999, p. 4); Schmidt (1998).

tions involved in the attacks on the United States. American Ambassador to Albania Joseph Limprecht agreed with their assessment, stating that, while it is U.S. policy to not comment on intelligence operations, he could at least say that "no terrorist cells or individuals [connected with the September 11 attack] have been identified or located in Albania."[65]

Albania still has significant problems. One of the poorest countries in Europe and hampered by weak institutions, it continues to be troubled by widespread corruption.[66] Organized crime remains a serious problem, and the nation's borders remain permeable to smugglers.[67] Consequently, Albania will likely remain vulnerable to Islamist exploitation for the foreseeable future. Nevertheless, the Tirana raids offer an example of a successful preventive attack, and the subsequent security cooperation between the United States and Albania has been beneficial for both nations.

Hellfire Strike in Yemen, 2002

On November 3, 2002, a CIA-operated Predator drone fired an AGM-114 Hellfire missile at a car on a highway in a rural area of Marib province, Yemen, destroying it and killing six militant Islamists. One of the victims was Qaed Senyan al-Harethi, a prime suspect in planning and authorizing the October 2000 bomb attack against the destroyer USS *Cole* and believed to be al Qaeda's senior man in the country. The other casualties included four Yemeni members of the Aden-Abyan Islamic Army and a Yemeni-American who, according to authorities, had set up an al Qaeda sleeper cell near Buffalo, New York, and recruited volunteers in the United States to attend terrorist training camps.

---

[65] Jolyon Naegele, "Albania: Country Free of Terrorists, Officials Say," *Radio Free Europe/Radio Liberty*, September 23, 2001.

[66] Groupe d'Etats Contre la Corruption (2002, p. 24).

[67] For a report on Albania's current level of stability, see Commission of the European Communities, *Commission Staff Working Paper: Albania: Stabilisation and Association Report 2003*, Brussels: Commission of the European Communities, 2003.

The Situation

The Republic of Yemen has made substantial political progress since its 1990 birth from the unification of the northern Yemen Arab Republic (YAR) and southern People's Democratic Republic of Yemen (PDRY). In attempting to forge a democracy with the most open political system on the Arabian Peninsula, Yemeni leaders have exhibited a commitment to becoming a modern state. But pressures from inside and outside the young nation have aggravated domestic tensions and remain serious sources of instability. These pressures first led President Ali Abdullah Saleh to court Islamic extremists, then persuaded him to support the U.S.-led war on terrorism, much to the consternation of his religiously conservative political base. It is in the context of these conflicting pressures that he allowed the CIA, probably with the help of Yemeni intelligence, to execute a preemptive strike against Islamist terrorists in his country.

Promise and Tension in a Fragile State. Much of Yemen's instability is rooted in political fissures that have persisted since unification. International expectations were guardedly optimistic when the tribally dominated, religiously conservative YAR peacefully unified with the more socially progressive, former communist regime in the south. A five-member committee appointed YAR President Ali Abdullah Saleh as president of the new state with the former PDRY Chairman as vice president, and governing power was temporarily shared in a 39-member transitional Council of Ministers. In 1991, a national constitution laid the groundwork for what some have called the most liberal political system in the Arab world, and parliamentary elections were held in 1993. But the outcome of those elections disappointed southern leaders, reopening old wounds and aggravating growing strains in the new republic. Reflecting the demographic realities of a more populous north and a rise in religious conservatism, President Saleh's General People's Congress (GPC) and the northern Islamist party, Islah, won a combined total of 185 seats in parliament, with the southern Yemeni Socialist Party (YSP) taking only 55 seats and smaller parties and independent candidates another 47. Feeling underrepresented and increasingly intimidated by northern militant Islamists agitating in southern cities, YSP leaders declared independence as civil war erupted in May 1994.[68]

President Saleh managed to put down the revolt and reunify the country by the end of July, but in doing so, he revealed both the strength and volatility of his political base. Relying heavily on the efforts of Yemeni "Afghan" veterans to help defeat the southern forces, he incurred a "blood debt" on which many Islamists came to believe he reneged later in the decade. Indeed, Saleh has a history of courting Islamic extremism. During the Soviet war in Afghanistan, he opened the YAR to the mujahideen for training, then welcomed Afghan veterans of all Arab nationalities into the country after the conflict. In subsequent years, he allowed the Afghans to operate freely from northern Yemen as they exported extremism to other countries and employed them to attack his political enemies in the south both before and after national unification. This relationship, while mutually beneficial for many years, became increasingly untenable in the changing political and economic landscape after unification.[69]

Militant Islam is but one of many sources of strain in Yemeni society. More fundamental concerns include rapid population growth and widespread poverty. The citizens of Yemen are among the poorest and the most heavily armed in the world. Weapons are carried openly in rural areas, and violence is endemic in the countryside. Smuggling has been rampant along the state's porous borders. Tribal leaders command their own militias. Consequently, the central government has difficulty extending its authority outside the cities, and President Saleh has had to patronize some sheiks to maintain their loyalty while coercing submission from others. Widespread belief that he has favored his own tribal confederation in the award of government jobs and development projects fuels resentment and further instability. In these fer-

---

[68] Jane's Sentinel Security Assessment, The Gulf States, "Internal Affairs, Yemen," September 4, 2003b; International Crisis Group, *Yemen: Coping with Terrorism and Violence in a Fragile State*, Amman and Brussels: International Crisis Group, Middle East Report No. 8, 2003b, p. 7.

[69] Amy W. Hawthorne, "Yemen and the Fight Against Terror," *Policywatch*, No. 572, 2001; Sheila Carapico, "Yemen and the Aden-Abyan Islamic Army," *Middle East Report Online*, October 18, 2000; "External Affairs, Yemen," *Jane's Online*, September 4, 2003.

tile conditions, religious schools have extolled militant extremism, and Islamist groups, both foreign and homegrown, have vied for the hearts of discontented young people.[70]

International events have complicated Saleh's efforts to manage domestic tensions. In 1990, yielding to popular pressure, Yemen became one of the few countries to oppose openly the use of force to expel Iraqi troops from Kuwait. In response, Saudi Arabia immediately sent 700,000 migrant Yemeni workers home, cutting an important source of revenue and placing a heavy burden on Yemen's state social services.[71] Likewise, in January 1991, Washington reduced its annual aid to Sanaa from $20.5 million to $2.9 million, and Gulf Cooperation Council (GCC) states suspended $200 million in development aid over the next several years.[72] Sanaa sought and received economic assistance from other sources, but these too carried costs. Structural adjustments demanded by the donor community, the World Bank, and the International Monetary Fund caused sharp price increases for food and fuel, putting many Yemenis in financial jeopardy.[73] President Saleh also paid a heavy political price for refusing to support the Gulf War. Saudi Arabia and most other GCC states discreetly supported the secessionists during the 1994 civil war. The GCC also rejected Sanaa's bid to join their organization that year, as did the British Commonwealth in 1997.[74]

A New Policy Direction. Chastened by the political and economic consequences of his Gulf War stance, Saleh attempted to take a moderate position when al Qaeda's October 2000 attack on the USS *Cole*

---

[70] International Crisis Group (2003b, pp. i–ii, 6–16).

[71] Other GCC states sent Yemeni workers home soon afterward, bringing the total of suddenly unemployed workers to over 1 million.

[72] Jane's Sentinel Security Assessment (2003b).

[73] In 1990, Yemen's currency traded at 10 Yemeni ryals per U.S. dollar; by 1996 the exchange rate was 150 ryals to the dollar. In 2000, annual income in Yemen was approximately $300 per capita (see International Crisis Group, 2003b, p. 7; European Parliament, Directorate General for Research, Division for Agriculture, Regional Policy, Transport, Development, *Note on the Political and Economic Situation in Yemen*, 2002).

[74] Jane's Sentinel Security Assessment (2003b). South Yemen had been a British colony until becoming independent in 1967.

in the Yemeni port of Aden led Washington to seek Sanaa's help in hunting the perpetrators. He promised to cooperate, but he did not want to antagonize his conservative, anti-American constituents. And though he had already begun distancing himself from the country's more radical Islamists, he still hoped to avoid having to confront the many heavily armed militants living in Yemen's rural, tribal provinces. Consequently, Saleh first denied that the *Cole* attackers had any link to al Qaeda and offered only grudging assistance to U.S. investigators.[75] But that changed dramatically after September 11, 2001. Realizing that Washington's newfound determination to destroy the al Qaeda network might put Yemen on the U.S. target list as a state harboring terrorists, President Saleh pledged full cooperation in the war on terrorism and backed up his words with an aggressive crackdown that rounded up more than 200 suspected al Qaeda members by September 2002.[76] Moreover, despite assurances to his anti-American constituents in September 2001 that he would not permit foreign troops in Yemen, in March 2002, Saleh agreed to let a small contingent of U.S. military advisors enter the country to train Yemeni security forces.[77]

The motivation for the latter policy change may have originated in the inadequacies of his own forces and the difficulties they were having coping with the growing threat Sanaa faced as a result of its changing relationship with militant Islam. The Yemeni army's shortcomings were highlighted in December 2001 when it launched an operation to capture al Qaeda suspects in al-Hosun, a village in the Marib region 100 miles east of Sanaa. Though government forces mounted a concerted air and ground assault, the operation failed when local tribesmen responded with automatic rifle fire and rocket propelled grenades, killing 18 soldiers. Four villagers were also killed and the suspects

---

[75] Jane's Sentinel Security Assessment (2003b); Hawthorne (2001); Thom Shanker and Eric Schmitt, "Threats and Responses: The Hunt; U.S. Moves Commandos to Base in East Africa," *The New York Times*, September 18, 2002.

[76] Scott Peterson, "Yemen Quakes in Cole's Shadow," *Christian Science Monitor*, September 21, 2001; Jane's Sentinel Security Assessment (2003b).

[77] Nick Pelham, "Yemen: Centre Stage of War on al-Qaeda," *BBC News*, March 14, 2002a; Richard Engel, "Yemen Cautious on Battle Against al-Qaeda," *BBC News*, January 23, 2002.

escaped.[78] Two months later, Yemeni police were embarrassed when they tried to detain a suspect in a suburb of Sanaa, only to have him escape in a taxi before accidentally blowing himself up with a hand grenade. On October 13, 2002, Islamist terrorists struck back at Sanaa when a small boat rammed the French-registered tanker *Limburg* and exploded, damaging the hull and killing one crewmember. The event was an important signpost: While the attack on the *Cole* had been a blow against the United States, the suicide bombing of the *Limburg* was aimed more directly at the Yemeni economy, and inflicted heavy damage on the country's oil and shipping industries.[79]

The Strike and Its Immediate Aftermath. On Sunday, November 3, 2002, Qaed Senyan al-Harethi and five other militant Islamists, including one who was an American citizen, set out from a farm in rural Marib province, Yemen.[80] As they drove slowly down a badly potholed road, their car exploded, killing all six men. Early reports by Yemen's official news agency said only that the car had blown up, suggesting it might have been carrying a bomb that accidentally exploded.[81] But the American news media soon began speculating that the CIA had destroyed the car using an armed Predator drone.[82]

Washington and Sanaa first tried to avoid confirming the strike, but American officials folded quickly. When Defense Secretary Donald

---

[78] Faye Bowers and Philip Smucker, "Antiterror Allies: US and Yemen Test the Limits," *Christian Science Monitor*, November 29, 2002; Vicki Mabrey, "Culture Clash in Yemen," *60 Minutes II*, April 10, 2002; Shanker and Schmitt (2002).

[79] Immediately after the *Limburg* attack, insurance costs for vessels using Yemeni ports tripled and shipping dropped approximately 50 percent (see International Crisis Group, 2003b, p. 7).

[80] Authorities believe the U.S. citizen was Kamal Derwish, a Yemeni-American cited in federal court papers as the ringleader of a terrorist sleeper cell in Lackawanna, New York, outside Buffalo (see Azadeh Moaveni, "They Didn't Know What Hit Them," *Time*, Vol. 160, No. 21, November 18, 2002, p. 58).

[81] Knut Royce and Craig Gordon, "A Blow to Al-Qaida: CIA Missile Kills a Leading Target of the U.S. War on Terror," *Newsday*, November 5, 2002.

[82] According to *IslamOnline*, speculation began on CNN Television and NBC News (see "U.S. Takes Anti-Terror Fight in Yemen into Its Own Hands," *IslamOnline.net*, November 5, 2002).

Rumsfeld was questioned about it on November 4, he simply replied that al-Harithi was "an individual that has been sought after as an al Qaeda member as well as a suspected terrorist connected to the USS *Cole*, so it would be a very good thing if he were out of business."[83] Likewise, President Bush did not comment on the affair directly, but reiterated his determination to break up al Qaeda, adding, "And the United States of America is doing just that."[84] But the following day, Deputy Secretary of Defense Paul Wolfowitz told CNN that the Yemen event was "a very successful tactical operation" and said the United States must "keep the pressure on" terrorists wherever they are.[85]

The press accepted that statement as implicit confirmation of U.S. involvement and immediately published a flood of reports filling in details and citing unnamed officials. According to most accounts, al-Harethi's location was determined through intercepts of calls made on his cell phone.[86] Yemeni and American intelligence operatives then kept him and the other suspects under surveillance at the farm for some time and tipped off the CIA when they departed in their car.[87] One widely repeated news story alleged that U.S. Ambassador to Yemen Edmund Hull bribed local tribesmen to reveal the Islamists' location, which he, in turn, relayed to the CIA. The CIA denied the story, and Ambassador Hull declined comment.[88] But all Western news reports agreed on the essential facts: The CIA was operating an armed Predator aircraft over Yemen. At some point, they determined that al-Harethi's car was at the Marib province farm and positioned the Predator overhead. When the Islamists left the farm, the CIA fired at least one and

---

[83] "Predator Drone Kills Six Al Qaeda Suspects," *ABCNews.com*, November 5, 2002.

[84] Royce and Gordon (2002).

[85] "U.S. Missile Strike Kills Al Qaeda Chief: CIA Drone Launched Missile," *CNN*, November 5, 2002.

[86] "No Hiding Place: How Unmanned U.S. Spy Plane Homed in on Satellite Phone Call to Wipe Out Al Qaeda Gang with Missile," *London Daily Mail*, November 6, 2002, p. 21.

[87] Royce and Gordon (2002).

[88] Philip Smucker, "The Intrigue Behind the Drone Strike," *Christian Science Monitor*, November 12, 2002, p. 1. *IslamOnline* notes that Hull was in Marib at the time of the strike (see "U.S. Takes Anti-Terror Fight in Yemen into Its Own Hands," 2002).

possibly two Hellfire missiles from the drone, destroying the car and killing its occupants. Finally, they had done all of this with permission and with some degree of cooperation from the Yemeni government.[89]

For a week after Wolfowitz's interview, Yemeni officials refused to comment on Washington's confirmation, saying only that the blast was under investigation.[90] On Tuesday, November 5, President Saleh said in a nationwide broadcast speech that he would ensure the safety of al Qaeda members in the country if they "repent and express regret for their sins against the homeland." His cabinet also released a statement urging citizens to cooperate with security forces against terrorists who were targeting Yemen, its people, and its national economy.[91] But within days, Sanaa quietly confirmed U.S.-Yemeni cooperation in the clandestine action and expressed anger over both Ambassador Hull's "freelancing" in the countryside during the intelligence-gathering phase of the operation and how Washington so quickly violated its agreement to keep the affair secret.[92] In an interview with *The Christian Science Monitor*, GPC Deputy Secretary General Yahya M. al-Mutawakel said, "This is why it is so difficult to make deals with the United States. . . . This is why we are reluctant to work closely with them. They don't consider the internal circumstances in Yemen."[93]

The Threat

Since September 11, 2001, U.S. authorities have perceived a direct threat in the very existence of al Qaeda. Any individuals associated with that organization are assumed to be enemies of the United States, either as active terrorists or as part of an extensive network dedicated to

---

[89] "Predator Drone Kills Six Al Qaeda Suspects" (2002), "U.S. Missile Strike Kills Al Qaeda Chief" (2002), Craig Hoyle and Andrew Koch, "Yemen Drone Strike: Just the Start?" *Jane's Defence Weekly*, November 8, 2002; Moaveni (2002).

[90] Charlie Aldinger and Mohammed Sudam, "U.S. Hails Attack on Cat, Yemen Silent," *Reuters*, November 6, 2002; "U.S. Takes Anti-Terror Fight in Yemen into Its Own Hands" (2002).

[91] Aldinger and Sudam (2002).

[92] Bowers and Smucker (2002).

[93] Smucker (2002).

supporting terrorism against the American homeland and U.S. forces and interests abroad. Qaed Senyan al-Harethi was considered particularly dangerous. Not only was he implicated in the bombing of the USS *Cole*, but he was believed to be one of Osama bin Laden's key lieutenants and the top al Qaeda member in Yemen, a country U.S. officials identified as second only to the Taliban's Afghanistan in degree of al Qaeda penetration. The Aden-Abyan Islamic Army (AAIA), to which four of the others killed in the Predator attack belonged, was believed to be responsible for numerous terrorist acts in Yemen, including the kidnapping of 16 U.S., British, and Australian tourists in 1998 and the bombing of the British Embassy in Sanaa in 2000.[94] While it is unclear whether U.S. and Yemeni authorities knew the identity of the sixth passenger in the car at the time of the strike, Kamal Derwish (also known as Ahmed Hijazi) had been implicated in setting up an al Qaeda sleeper cell near Buffalo.[95]

Threat perceptions in Sanaa were more complex. Until after the 1994 civil war, President Saleh had considered the mujahideen and other militant Islamists in Yemen to be allies in his struggle against the socialists of the former PDRY. In the latter half of the 1990s, however, changing political and economic conditions forced him to distance himself from terrorists and attempt a moderate stance, balancing between his religiously conservative tribal constituents and Western sources of economic assistance. This shift antagonized the radical Islamists in Yemen, resulting in an increase in terrorism within the country. When Washington focused its attention on Sanaa after September 11, 2001, Saleh realized that the external threat the United States could present to his regime was greater than the risk of offending both the conservatives and the militant Afghans within Yemen, so he pledged his support for the U.S.-led war on terrorism. That, in turn,

---

[94] U.S. Department of State, *Patterns in Global Terrorism*, Washington, D.C.: Government Printing Office, 2002b, p. 120.

[95] Moaveni (2002); James Risen and Marc Santora, "Threats and Responses: The Terror Network; Man Believed Slain in Yemen Tied by U.S. to Buffalo Cell," *The New York Times*, November 10, 2002, p. A17.

made President Saleh an apostate in the eyes of al Qaeda and other radical Islamists. They declared war on him and his government.

Policy Options

American leaders had a variety of options available to them when the CIA learned that al-Harethi and five other Islamists were at the Marib province farm. The first question was whether to move against the militants or keep them under surveillance in hopes of collecting intelligence about the al Qaeda network and its plans. Given the decision to act, the possible options fell into three categories: trust the government of Yemen to apprehend the individuals; conduct a unilateral American operation, with or without Sanaa's permission; or engage in some kind of cooperative action to eliminate the threat. American participation in either of the second two alternatives could have involved anything from a conventional military air strike to a covert operation using agents on the ground. Prominent options included deploying commandos from Djibouti or a ship offshore to "snatch" or kill the militants—special operations forces had been prepositioned in both places for just such a contingency—and launching a clandestine air strike from a Predator drone.[96]

Theoretically, Sanaa's options mirrored those of Washington. When informed of al-Harethi's location, Yemeni officials could have acted (or not acted) alone, turned the problem over to the United States, or worked with American authorities in a combined operation. In reality, however, Sanaa's options were far more constrained. Yemeni security forces lacked the range of capabilities available to U.S. forces, and problems encountered in previous operations called their competence into question. Moreover, President Saleh's eagerness to placate U.S. officials and his unfortunate position caught between a belligerent superpower, a militant and religiously conservative tribal constituency,

---

[96] The United States had at least 800 military personnel in Djibouti, including special operations forces, and some number of commandos standing ready aboard the amphibious assault ship USS *Belleau Wood* off the Yemeni coast. See Shanker and Schmitt (2002); Smucker (2002); Robert Schlesinger, "In Djibouti, US Special Forces Develop Base Amid Secrecy," *The Boston Globe*, December 12, 2002, p. A45.

and a vengeful network of Islamist terrorists reduced his range of plausible options considerably.

The Decision to Strike

Washington's decision to kill a carload of suspected terrorists with an armed Predator drone reveals how highly motivated American leaders were to strike back at al Qaeda after the September 11 attack. Deferring action in hopes of collecting useful intelligence on al Qaeda was not considered a viable option. Qaed Senyan al-Harethi was considered to be too dangerous a terrorist to risk losing for the uncertain benefit of gathering an unknown quantity of information. His meeting with four AAIA terrorists suggested that some kind of cooperative operation was being planned, and the presence of an American operative was even more ominous, though authorities may not have known Derwish was with them when they elected to strike. Finally, al-Harethi was wanted in connection with the bombing of the USS *Cole*; passing up an opportunity to move against him might have suggested that the United States was not committed to punishing the perpetrators of that attack.[97]

American authorities probably would have liked to apprehend the six Islamists. Such an accomplishment would have preserved the rule of law and made the suspects available for intelligence exploitation. But taking them alive presented a challenge. Yemeni security forces had proven unreliable in such a mission, given the belligerence of the heavily armed tribes in Marib. American commandos were available, but employing them in Yemen's rural backcountry might have provoked a spontaneous uprising against the U.S. force and potentially a tribal backlash against the Yemeni government. Many of the same considerations constrained U.S. options for killing the terrorists. A conventional air strike or a commando raid would have called Yemeni

---

[97] American authorities may also have been sensitive to charges of excessive timidity as a result of their failure to strike Mullah Omar when an armed Predator drone observed him leaving Kabul in a motor convoy on the first night of air strikes on Afghanistan during Operation Enduring Freedom (see "US Military 'Missed' Taleban Leader," *BBC News*, October 15, 2001; Tony Karon, "Yemen Strike Opens New Chapter in War on Terror," *Time*, November 5, 2002).

sovereignty into question and jeopardized President Saleh's delicate relationship with tribal authorities, Islah, and his own ruling party. At the very least, it would have seriously damaged his credibility in the eyes of Yemeni citizens.

Given those constraints, the clandestine Hellfire strike appeared to offer the greatest probable benefit for a level of political risk Washington and Sanaa were willing to bear. The Predator drone, with its long loiter time and low-observable profile, offered an ideal platform for monitoring the terrorists while waiting for them to congregate and move to a location away from witnesses and potential victims of collateral damage. The Hellfire missile provided a highly lethal weapon with the necessary ability to strike a moving vehicle reliably. Most importantly, the clandestine strike offered Washington and Sanaa a way to remove a threat with plausible deniability that an attack had occurred, thus keeping U.S. involvement secret and preserving President Saleh's credibility. All things considered, American decisionmakers probably concluded the clandestine strike option offered a high potential benefit with little risk—at least to them.

Yemeni leaders may have had little choice in the matter. Caught between Washington's determination to fight al Qaeda in their country and al Qaeda's subsequent vow to avenge Sanaa's cooperation in that effort, President Saleh was probably more than happy to see six militant Islamists neutralized, provided it could be done in a way that did not appear to violate Yemeni sovereignty, ruffle tribal authorities, or jeopardize his support from conservatives in the GPC and Islah. A clandestine strike carried more risk for Sanaa than it did for Washington, but given the latter's determination to attack the militants one way or another, Saleh probably considered the Hellfire strike to be the alternative with the lowest probable cost.

The Results

The Predator strike was an impressive tactical success. It removed a key al Qaeda leader and five other militant Islamists, four of whom were confirmed terrorists in Yemen and the fifth a suspected al Qaeda organizer in the United States. The operation demonstrated notable advances in remote warfare and international, interagency coordination, enabling success in this instance and raising expectations of success in future strikes against time-sensitive targets. The strike also exacted a measure of retributive justice for the 2000 al Qaeda attack on the USS *Cole* and the 1998 AAIA kidnapping of Americans, Britons, and Australians, and demonstrated the effective use of operational pre-emption to foil terrorist operations in the making.

The strike was probably a strategic success as well. Though the full extent of its long-term effects cannot be known without detailed knowledge of what the terrorists were planning, it probably disrupted one or more future al Qaeda operations, and those operations might have been consequential, considering the identities and past actions of the individuals planning them. Moreover, removing one of Osama bin Laden's key lieutenants may have caused secondary and tertiary impacts on al Qaeda. At the very least, the capability demonstrated in this strike complicates al Qaeda's efforts to plan, organize, and train for future terrorist operations.[98]

Yet the success of this strategy was achieved at considerable political cost for the U.S. and Yemeni governments. As the strike was executed outside any formally recognized war zone, critics in the United States and abroad likened it to political assassination.[99] Many compared it to Israel's targeted killings in the West Bank, making U.S. criticism of those strikes sound hypocritical. In fact, Washington's use of such tactics makes restraining similar Israeli behavior more difficult, and it may have set an undesirable precedent in the international community— American officials presumably would not want to see Russia, China, or

---

[98] One must remember, however, that although this strike was in some ways an isolated incident, it was but one move in a long-term struggle against al Qaeda and groups associated with it. Following the attack, on December 30, 2002, a gunman associated with the Yemeni Islamic Jihad murdered three American missionaries and critically wounded a fourth in Jibla, Yemen, and in June 2003, Islamists attacked a Yemeni military medical team, triggering an army siege on an AAIA stronghold in southern Yemen (see Neil MacFarquhar, "Threats and Responses: Terror; Three U.S. Citizens Slain in Yemen in Rifle Attack," *The New York Times*, December 31, 2002, p. A1; "Militants Killed by Yemeni Forces," *BBC News*, June 25, 2003).

[99] James D. Zirin, "When States Turn Assassin," *The Times (London)*, February 11, 2003, p. 10.

India conducting similar strikes on their enemies abroad.[100] Finally, the strike raised questions about Washington's regard for the sovereignty of other states. When news of the event first surfaced, critics suspected Yemen's sovereignty had been violated, and even after Sanaa admitted involvement, some assumed U.S. officials had coerced Saleh's reluctant acquiescence to an act that was not in his best interest.[101]

More serious, perhaps, are the legal questions raised by the attack. Historically, the United States has considered acts of terrorism mainly in judicial terms—law enforcement authorities have arrested perpetrators who were then afforded due process of law. Some terrorists have been killed, of course, but legal standards require that lethal force be used as a last resort when armed suspects resist arrest. The scale of the September 11, 2001, attacks and the subsequent war on terrorism, however, have shifted the ground rules in Washington, and not everyone agrees the changes are legal or appropriate. No effort was made to arrest the individuals targeted in the Hellfire strike. Critics maintain they were summarily executed without due process and note that some of them had not even been charged with a specific crime. Such concerns are particularly serious in the case of Kamal Derwish, an American citizen.[102]

On the other hand, those who argue that the United States should aggressively prosecute the war on terrorism maintain that the Hellfire strike was a legal combat operation consistent with the National Security Strategy of "preempting" terrorists before they strike. They argue that those killed in this attack were combatants in an organization at war with the United States, and that the strike was legal because Congress passed a joint resolution authorizing the President to use "all necessary and appropriate force" against "persons he determines planned,

---

[100]David Tucker, "Hellfire," Ashbrook Center for Public Affairs at Ashland University Web site, November 2002.

[101]Jim Lobe, "Sovereignty Takes Major Hits in Yemen, Mauritius," *Inter Press Service*, November 8, 2002.

[102]Dana Priest, "CIA Killed U.S. Citizen in Yemen Missile Strike: Action's Legality, Effectiveness Questioned," *The Washington Post*, November 8, 2002, p. A1. For examples of widespread criticism in foreign media, see "CIA Yemen Operation: Many See 'Assassination Without Jury, Judge,'" *GlobalSecurity.org*, November 18, 2002.

authorized, committed, or aided the terrorist attacks that occurred on September 11, 2001," after which President Bush signed an executive order authorizing lethal covert action against al Qaeda. They maintain that it was done in self-defense because al-Harethi was behind the attack on the USS *Cole*. Finally, it met traditional standards for discrimination, proportionality, and military necessity.[103]

Legal or not, the government of Yemen may have to bear the greatest burden of cost for this anticipatory attack. Whether it was coerced or acting on its own volition, cooperating in this action risked painting Saleh, in the eyes of opponents and constituents alike, as a pawn of the United States, thereby weakening his legitimacy. The full impact of such an effect remains to be seen, but the attack at least jeopardized Saleh's precarious balance in trying to support the war on terrorism without alienating Yemen's conservative factions or unifying them against him.[104]

Many of the costs incurred in this operation may have been unnecessary; preserving the secrecy of the clandestine attack might have shielded the United States and Yemen from them.[105] Denying responsibility in Washington's "leaky" political environment would have been difficult, but policymakers needed to weigh that risk against the more tangible costs of disclosure. Perhaps they did so after media speculation began, and a sober evaluation of the political risk of lying in the face of media exposure is what led to Wolfowitz's implicit admission of responsibility. Yet, if ever a case existed when the risks of "plausible deniability" were manageable, this would seem to have been it. Sanaa controlled the investigation and media reporting in Yemen, and Yemeni authorities were highly motivated to suppress the story. Had U.S. officials held to the silence they promised Sanaa, media specu-

---

[103] David Johnston and David E. Sanger, "Fatal Strike in Yemen Was Based on Rules Set Out by Bush," *The New York Times*, Late Edition East Coast, November 6, 2002, p. A16; Pamela Hess, "Experts: Yemen Strike Not Assassination," *United Press International*, November 8, 2002.

[104] International Crisis Group (2003b, pp. 25–27).

[105] In contrast, although it is widely presumed that the assassins of Iraqi-employed supergun inventor Gerald Bull were Israeli agents, this has never been confirmed by Israel.

lation might have died away—or it might have grown more intense. Either way, policymakers need to factor such risks and costs into their decision calculations before acting and before committing to secrecy with a foreign government. Otherwise, the credibility of U.S. foreign policy is placed at risk.

The Jordanian Crackdown in Ma'an, 2002

On November 9, 2002, a police operation to apprehend an Islamist cleric in the city of Ma'an, Jordan, escalated into a military siege followed by eight days of sporadic gun battles between security forces and armed citizens. When followers of Mohammed Chalabi (also known as Abu Sayyaf) resisted police efforts to arrest him, the Jordanian government deployed thousands of regular and special forces, supported by tanks and helicopters, to seal off the city and apprehend what it alleged was a lawless gang of arms and drug smugglers. In the week that followed, the army cut off all road, telephone, and radio communications with the rest of the country and conducted house-to-house searches to confiscate weapons and arrest militants. These moves, in a city where carrying arms is a tribal custom, provoked a series of gun battles with citizens that left at least six locals and several soldiers dead. While residents of Ma'an admitted their city had a history of semilawlessness, a condition long tolerated by local officials, they believed the government's sudden harsh repression was meant to send a stark message to the nation that Amman would tolerate no civil unrest in response to its pro-United States stance regarding the anticipated war in Iraq. Unofficially, Jordanian authorities confirmed that assessment.

The Situation
The Hashemite Kingdom of Jordan has long struggled to maintain a balance between the anti-Israeli sentiments of its Arab population and its need to maintain peace with Israel and good relations with the United States. Created when Britain's mandate for Palestine and Transjordan ended in 1946, the kingdom joined other Arab states in the 1948 war against Israel, during which it seized the West Bank. King

Abdullah I annexed that territory in 1950, but his grandson, King Hussein, lost it in the humiliating Arab defeat of 1967. The loss of the West Bank sent a wave of displaced Palestinians east, swelling refugee camps in Jordan and filling the ranks of armed resistance units, or fedayeen, until their power and defiance threatened the kingdom's sovereignty and security. In 1970, fighting erupted between the Jordanian Army and the most notable fedayeen group, the Palestine Liberation Organization (PLO). Claiming that its leader, Yasser Arafat, was attempting to create "a state within a state," King Hussein drove out the PLO and destroyed the remaining guerilla bases in Jordan in early 1971.[106]

Those events marked a turning point in Jordanian policy, as Amman began a long-term effort to normalize its relations with Israel and seek greater political and economic support from the United States. Although Jordan sent a brigade to fight against Israeli forces in Syria during the 1973 war, no fighting occurred along the 1967 ceasefire line on the Jordan River, and King Hussein assumed a moderating role in regional politics in the years that followed. Jordan's moderate stance led to closer relations with the United States, and Washington favored Amman with considerable economic assistance in the years that followed.[107]

That relationship was temporarily disrupted, as was Jordan's relations with other Arab states, when the King refused to condemn Iraq's 1990 invasion of Kuwait or endorse the U.S.-led coalition that expelled Iraqi forces. That misstep, a result of pressure from pro-Iraqi Jordanians and the fact that Baghdad was Amman's closest trading partner, cost the Hashemite Kingdom hundreds of millions of dollars in aid from the United States and Gulf Cooperation Council (GCC) members. However, Jordanian-GCC relations improved as Amman began distancing itself from Baghdad in 1993, and U.S. ties warmed considerably when Jordan signed a peace treaty with Israel the following year. In 1999, Amman pleased Israel and the United States by making

---

[106]U.S. Department of State, "Background Note: Jordan," 2005b; see also Herzog (1982, p. 222).

[107]Alfred B. Prados, *Jordan: U.S. Relations and Bilateral Issues*, Washington, D.C.: Congressional Research Service, June 2, 2003, p. 1.

a concerted effort to stop the terrorist group Hamas from launching operations from Jordanian soil, closing the group's offices in the kingdom and expelling four of its key leaders.[108] Relations between Amman and Washington became particularly close after September 11, 2001, as King Hussein's son and successor, King Abdullah II, not only strengthened antiterrorist laws and pursued al Qaeda suspects in Jordan, but also endorsed U.S. actions in Afghanistan and sought to persuade other Arab states to support the antiterrorism campaign.[109]

Straining the Balance. Hashemite kings have had to manage multiple sources of tension in Jordan. Balancing the pressures of an anti-Israeli citizenry against the need to maintain positive relations with that country and the United States has been the most visible source of strain, but internal fault lines exist as well. The periodic influxes of West Bank refugees have created a situation in which Palestinian residents now outnumber traditional East Bank Jordanian subjects. This demographic trend has been a source of chronic friction. Palestinians complain of employment discrimination and oppression from an East Bank–dominated bureaucracy and security system; traditional subjects resent the strain less affluent Palestinians have placed on social services. The Islamic revival has created new sources of tension, as urban Islamists lobby for a militant anti-Israeli/anti-American foreign policy and struggle against the largely promonarchy political dominance of the tribally oriented rural regions. The economic crises, peace treaty with Israel, and pro-U.S. diplomatic initiatives that followed the 1991 Gulf War have all exacerbated these strains.[110]

King Hussein and King Abdullah II have tried to relieve some of their subjects' discontent as well as assuage criticism from Western governments by taking initial steps to liberalize Jordan's economy and

---

[108] Gil Sedan, "Jordan's King Puts His Foot Down on Hamas Activity," *Jewish Telegraphic Agency*, October 1, 1999; Lamis Andoni, "Consequences of an Expulsion," *Al-Ahram Weekly Online*, No. 457, November 25, 1999.

[109] Prados (2003, pp. 4, 6–7).

[110] Jonathan Schanzer, "Jordan's War Worries: Saddamistan, Palestinians, and Islamism in the Hashemite Kingdom," *PolicyWatch*, No. 680, November 22, 2002.

democratize its political system.[111] Yet these moves have, in their own ways, added to the tension. Trade liberalization caused dramatic price hikes for essential goods, placing many citizens in greater economic difficulty. Tentative steps toward democratization raised expectations of greater freedom that were dashed when King Abdullah dissolved parliament, cancelled elections, and enacted tough—some say repressive— antiterrorism laws in the wake of September 11, 2001.[112]

The city of Ma'an has experienced many of these stresses and has also suffered from other sources of tension. Once a prosperous hub of communications and trade on the hajj (pilgrimage) route between Damascus and the holy cities of Mecca and Medina, the city of some 30,000 fell into decline after the Desert Highway was rerouted to bypass it in 1982 and the pilgrims' rest station was moved to an outlying area. Soon afterward, the Hijaz Railway stopped carrying passenger traffic to Ma'an, and changes in trucking regulations damaged one of the city's principal industries. Sharp rises in fuel prices coupled with a decline in freight transit following the 1991 Gulf War magnified these impacts to make the region one of the poorest in Jordan.[113]

As the city's economy withered, residents felt increasingly alienated from Amman. The region has strong tribal connections with Saudi Arabia, and local sentiment held that Ma'an's economic difficulties were largely the result of the Jordanian government's callous policies. As family fortunes declined, Ma'anis increasingly turned to smuggling and other illicit activities to augment their dwindling incomes. Local officials largely turned a blind eye to this behavior, but were less tolerant of the increasingly frequent public expressions of discontent. A protest by truckers in 1989 turned violent, leaving 16 dead. In 1996, Amman sent troops to put down riots that erupted following a sharp increase in bread prices. Ma'anis demonstrated in 1998 to protest the U.S. bombing in Iraq and in November 2001 to protest the U.S. cam-

---

[111] Prados (2003, pp. 3–4).

[112] Jillian Schwedler, "Occupied Maan: Jordan's Closed Military Zone," *Middle East Report Online*, December 3, 2002.

[113] International Crisis Group, *Red Alert in Jordan: Recurrent Unred in Maan*, Amman and Brussels: International Crisis Group, 2003a, p. 6.

paign in Afghanistan. In January 2002, as demonstrators expressed support for Osama bin Laden and called for the release of a man being held by police for organizing a previous, unauthorized protest, a 16-year-old boy died in custody after police apprehended him for theft. Over the next several days, armed citizens burned the police station and the governor's car and clashed with police, leaving one policeman dead and 19 other people injured.[114]

Jordanian authorities exercised surprising restraint in this instance, relying on tribal elders to clear the streets and restore order, but there were signs that Amman's patience was growing short. As international events in 2002 pointed to the growing probability of a U.S. war against Iraq, statements coming from the capital suggested the government would "no longer tolerate the pro-Iraq or pro-Palestinian sympathies of either Islamists or pan-Arabists taking precedence over the interests of the kingdom."[115]

Murder of a U.S. Diplomat Triggers a Violent Chain of Events. On October 28, 2002, U.S. Agency for International Development (USAID) official Lawrence Foley was gunned down in front of his Amman residence, triggering a nationwide manhunt for the unknown killers. The following day, police stopped Islamist cleric Mohammed Chalabi, known to his followers as "Abu Sayyaf," at a routine checkpoint on the highway from Amman to Ma'an, and attempted to detain him for questioning regarding the Foley case. Chalabi fled and drove back to Ma'an, exchanging gunfire with police and receiving a gunshot wound in the shoulder in the process. Calling his followers by cell phone en route, he was met in Ma'an by about 50 armed men who escorted him to a hospital for treatment, then to his father's house.[116]

Jordanian officials first tried to work through tribal elders to bring Chalabi and 48 of his followers into custody, but the cleric refused to surrender and the elders were powerless to act against the group of armed militants. After a three-day grace period expired, police moved

---

[114] International Crisis Group (2003a, pp. 4–5).

[115] "Deadly Jordan Crackdown Seen as Stark Warning for Pro-Iraq Uprising," *IslamOnline*, November 11, 2002.

[116] Schwedler (2002).

in and a gunfight erupted. It quickly became apparent that local police could not quell the growing conflict, and Amman sent in the army. Over the next several days, repeated clashes occurred between security forces and armed citizens. The city was blockaded, a curfew was imposed, and all communications between residents and the outside world were cut.[117]

The operation soon expanded beyond efforts to round up the original group of militants, as authorities declared Ma'an a "no-weapons zone" and police and soldiers began conducting house-to-house searches in the al Tour district to confiscate weapons.[118] The army responded to automatic gunfire at security forces with heavy-caliber machinegun fire at buildings from tanks and helicopters. Several houses were burned, including Mohammed Chalabi's. Security forces subdued the disturbance and the curfew was lifted in about a week, but the army maintained an intimidating presence in Ma'an for weeks afterward. Ironically, though Jordanian officials took more than 150 people into custody, including several of Chalabi's men, and captured a cache of illicit weapons and bomb-making materials, the cleric and his inner circle eluded arrest and are believed to be hiding in the mountains east of the city.[119]

Throughout the crisis and afterward, the Jordanian government insisted it was attempting to apprehend a gang of armed thugs and smugglers.[120] Officials also said they had acted to restore order in an increasingly lawless city, as they had "received complaints from Ma'ani citizens and notables about harassment and violence throughout 2002, including attacks against dormitories and cars belonging to women students and staff at the local Hussein Bin Talal University."[121] But interviews conducted by the Brussels-based International Crisis Group

---

[117] International Crisis Group (2003a, p. 3).

[118] The al Tour district, where Mohammed Chalabi lived, was considered one of the most militant neighborhoods in the city.

[119] Schwedler (2002); International Crisis Group (2003a, pp. 3–4).

[120] See "Jordan Security Sweep Nets Militants," *BBC News*, November 13, 2002.

[121] International Crisis Group (2003a, p. 3).

(ICG) in December 2002 revealed that many Ma'anis believed the show of force was a statement that the government would not tolerate regional defiance of its policies, and some believed it was designed to please the United States by demonstrating its resolve against terrorism and that it would not brook any protest against the war in Iraq.[122] Numerous press reports tend to confirm that assessment, citing unnamed officials who said the crackdown was "a preventative measure to limit the impact on internal stability of a military strike against a country which is enormously popular in Jordan."[123]

The Threat

Jordan faced several threats in the months leading to the 2003 invasion of Iraq. The first was the risk of offending Washington if Amman spoke out against U.S. plans to attack the Ba'athist regime or failed to provide some level of support. King Abdullah seemed determined to avoid repeating his father's mistake in opposing the first Gulf War, but efforts to placate the United States would increase other threats. Iraq was Jordan's principal trading partner and source of oil, which Baghdad sold to Amman at a large discount.[124] Offending the Iraqis or supporting a war that crippled the Iraqi economy would almost certainly have deleterious effects on the already troubled Jordanian economy.

In fact, economic and social stresses had already raised levels of tension within the kingdom, yet there were two issues on which nearly all Jordanians agreed: They were anti-Israeli and sympathetic to Iraq. Both of these issues made Jordanians in all the main political groups—monarchist and opposition, East Bank and Palestinian, urban Islamist and rural tribalist—negatively predisposed to U.S. policy. Jordan's policy of supporting the United States risked uniting these factions against the monarchy in the event of a U.S. attack on Iraq. Against

---

[122]International Crisis Group (2003a, p. 3).

[123]Suleiman al-Khalidi, "Jordanian Troops Battle Do-or-Die Islamists," *Reuters*, November 12, 2002; see also "Thousands of Jordanian Troops Control Town," *Reuters*, November 11, 2002; and "Deadly Jordan Crackdown Seen as Stark Warning for Pro-Iraq Uprising" (2002).

[124]Prados (2003, p. 8).

this backdrop, the advent of open defiance to police by an armed group in a city with a history of violent dissent against the government must have made the incident in Ma'an appear to be a serious threat to the kingdom's sovereignty and security. Indeed, in mid-November, as Jordanian troops enforced the curfew and imposed peace on the city, Information Minister Mohammed Adwan told reporters in Amman, "We will not tolerate a state within a state," echoing the pronouncement King Hussein made when he drove the PLO out of Jordan more than 30 years earlier.[125]

Policy Options

As the U.S.-led war against Iraq approached, Jordan traversed several decision points, each with a different set of policy options. The first question was how Amman should posture itself in the confrontation between Washington and Baghdad. Options included speaking out against Washington's stance and refusing to support U.S. operations in the event of war, openly declaring support for the American effort to disarm Iraq, or trying to find some middle ground that would placate the United States without antagonizing the Jordanian populace. As the probability of war increased in late 2002 and Jordanians protested their government's acquiescence to U.S. policies with increasing frequency and vehemence, Amman was forced to decide whether to repress such dissent or permit it in the spirit of free speech and democratization.

Finally, when an American diplomat was murdered and efforts to detain Mohammed Chalabi were met with armed resistance, the Jordanian government faced a new dilemma: how to meet this challenge to its sovereignty in a way that would best preserve national unity and protect the monarchy. Options included negotiating with Chalabi and his group, either directly or through tribal elders; relying on police to apprehend the suspects; deploying the army to support police operations, but constraining their numbers and actions to minimize impacts to the surrounding community; and employing an overwhelming

---

[125] Nick Pelham, "Jordanian Attack on Militants Reveals a National Rift," *Christian Science Monitor*, November 15, 2002b, p. 7.

amount of military force not only to quell the unrest in Ma'an, but to deter further dissent nationwide.

The Decision to Employ Overwhelming Force

Amman's move to repress dissent in Ma'an violently appears to have resulted more from a series of incremental decisions than from any preconceived plan. As it became apparent that Washington was determined to draw to a close its long-running standoff with Saddam Hussein, King Abdullah publicly attempted to tread a middle path between the United States and Iraq. He repeatedly expressed his hopes that the confrontation would be settled by means other than war and denied the presence of any U.S. troops in the kingdom, maintaining that Jordan would not be a "launching pad" for military operations against Iraq.[126] Yet he was careful to not speak out against U.S. policies, and that may have contributed to the growing level of dissent openly expressed by Jordanian citizens. Amman responded to the public's mounting dissatisfaction in a firm but measured way, allowing legal demonstrations in support of Iraq while promoting a "Jordan First" campaign to engender patriotism and support for the monarchy.[127]

Amman tried to handle the Chalabi incident with the same measured firmness, but changed its approach in midcourse. When Chalabi fled to Ma'an and fortified himself behind his armed followers, Jordanian officials attempted to resolve the standoff using a method that had become customary for dealing with problems in that unruly community—they turned to local tribal elders in hopes they could negotiate the militants' surrender. When that failed, Amman trusted the apprehension effort to local police, but it quickly became apparent they were not up to the task. At that point, it was clear that authorities would have to turn to the army, but options still existed regarding the kinds of forces to employ, their numbers, and what rules of engagement

---

[126]Prados (2003, p. 7). In February 2003 Jordanian officials admitted that several hundred U.S. Army personnel were in Jordan to operate Patriot surface-to-air missile batteries, and during the war *The Washington Post* estimated there were 3,000 U.S. troops in the kingdom, which served as a base for conducting special operations into western Iraq.

[127]Schanzer (2002); see also Jane's Sentinel Security Assessment, Eastern Mediterranean, "Internal Affairs, Jordan," June 27, 2003a.

would govern their actions. Amman might have assembled a special operations force tailored to capture or kill the militants with minimal impact to the surrounding community, and then have escalated the operation as necessary. Instead, Jordanian officials called up thousands of troops and laid siege to the city from the outset, forcefully searching houses in the neighborhood where Chalabi lived, and employing heavy weapons when they faced resistance. The level of force suddenly employed in Ma'an suggests the government had concluded that their careful effort to balance tensions in Jordan was not succeeding. Events in Ma'an presented both a challenge to state sovereignty and an opportunity to set an example to the rest of the nation demonstrating that Amman would not tolerate defiance of its authority or civil instability in response to a war in Iraq.

The Results

The Jordanian government's preventive crackdown in Ma'an was effective in quelling the rising tide of open dissent and instability in the months leading to the invasion of Iraq. Security forces imposed an uneasy peace on Ma'an, and nationwide expressions of protest subsided significantly in the ensuing months. While one might have expected the operation to trigger an outcry from political groups opposed to the monarchy, particularly the Islamists, in fact, it had the opposite effect. Jordan's largest political party, the Islamic Action Front (IAF), took a conciliatory stance, offering its services to help restore calm according to the principles of law, due process, and nonviolence.[128] In sum, Amman's gamble that force would quell instability rather than aggravate it paid off, at least for the short term.

The long-term outlook in Jordan is less clear. The social and economic strains that fostered nationwide discontent before the crisis still exist. Interviews conducted by the ICG after the crackdown suggest the episode "aggravated the feeling among Ma'anis and other Jordanians that the government relied too heavily on security measures to resolve issues rooted in political, social and economic conditions."[129]

---

[128]International Crisis Group (2003a, p. 4).

[129]International Crisis Group (2003a, p. 4).

By March 2003, billboards in Ma'an publicizing the "Jordan First" campaign had all been defaced.[130] Yet Jordan remained relatively quiet throughout the war in Iraq, and in June 2003, King Abdullah allowed the long-promised parliamentary election to take place. This time the IAF took part—they had boycotted the previous election, held in 1997, to protest what they alleged to be discriminatory election laws—winning 17 out of 110 seats in parliament.[131] It appears that King Abdullah will continue using minor democratic reform as a means to tap his state's internal political pressures. How well that will work over the long run remains to be seen.

---

[130]Kareem Fahim, "Jordan's South Rises, Again," *Village Voice*, March 18, 2003.

[131]Jane's Sentinel Security Assessment (2003a).

NSS Statements on Preemptive and Preventive Attack

The following excerpts comprise all of the statements in the 2002 National Security Strategy that relate to striking first:[1]

> Our enemies have openly declared that they are seeking weapons of mass destruction, and evidence indicates that they are doing so with determination. The United States will not allow these efforts to succeed. . . . And, as a matter of common sense and self-defense, America will act against such emerging threats before they are fully formed. History will judge harshly those who saw this coming danger but failed to act. In the new world we have entered, the only path to peace and security is the path of action. (p. v)

> Our goals on the path to progress are clear: political and economic freedom, peaceful relations with other states, and respect for human dignity. . . . To achieve these goals, the United States [must]: . . .

> - strengthen alliances to defeat global terrorism and work to prevent attacks against us and our friends; . . .
> - prevent our enemies from threatening us, our allies, and our friends, with weapons of mass destruction; . . . (p. 1)

> Our priority will be first to disrupt and destroy terrorist organizations of global reach and attack their leadership; command, control, and communications; material support; and finances. This

---

[1] George W. Bush (2002a).

will have a disabling effect upon the terrorists' ability to plan and operate. . . .

While we recognize that our best defense is a good offense, we are also strengthening America's homeland security to protect against and deter attack. (pp. 5–6)

We must be prepared to stop rogue states and their terrorist clients before they are able to threaten or use weapons of mass destruction against the United States and our allies and friends. . . .

Given the goals of rogue states and terrorists, the United States can no longer solely rely on a reactive posture as we have in the past. The inability to deter a potential attacker, the immediacy of today's threats, and the magnitude of potential harm that could be caused by our adversaries' choice of weapons, do not permit that option. We cannot let our enemies strike first. . . .

For centuries, international law recognized that nations need not suffer an attack before they can lawfully take action to defend themselves against forces that present an imminent danger of attack. Legal scholars and international jurists often conditioned the legitimacy of preemption on the existence of an imminent threat—most often a visible mobilization of armies, navies, and air forces preparing to attack.

We must adapt the concept of imminent threat to the capabilities and objectives of today's adversaries. Rogue states and terrorists do not seek to attack us using conventional means. They know such attacks would fail. Instead, they rely on acts of terror and, potentially, the use of weapons of mass destruction—weapons that can be easily concealed, delivered covertly, and used without warning. . . .

The United States has long maintained the option of preemptive actions to counter a sufficient threat to our national security. The greater the threat, the greater is the risk of inaction—and the more compelling the case for taking anticipatory action to defend ourselves, even if uncertainty remains as to the time and place of the enemy's attack. To forestall or prevent such hostile acts by our adversaries, the United States will, if necessary, act preemptively. The United States will not use force in all cases to preempt emerging threats, nor should nations use preemption as a pretext for aggression. Yet in an age where the enemies of civilization openly and actively seek the world's most destructive technologies, the United States cannot remain idle while dangers gather. . . .

The purpose of our actions will always be to eliminate a specific threat to the United States or our allies and friends. The reasons for our actions will be clear, the force measured, and the cause just. (pp. 14–16)

References

Abdallah, Sana, "Jordan Cracks Down on Hamas," *United Press International*, August 30, 1999a.

————, "Jordan Decides to Deport Hamas Leader," *United Press International*, September 22, 1999b.

Abrahams, Fred, "Albania," *Foreign Policy in Focus*, Vol. 2, No. 33, 2001, pp. 1–4.

Acheson, Dean, "Address Before the Civic Federation of Dallas and the Community Course of Southern Methodist University," Dallas, Tex., June 13, 1950.

————, *The Pattern of Responsibility*, Boston: Houghton Mifflin, 1952.

————, "Law and Conflict: Changing Patterns and Contemporary Challenges—Panel: Cuban Quarantine: Implications for the Future: Remarks," *American Society of International Law Proceedings*, Vol. 57, 1963, pp. 10–14.

Adams, James, *Bull's Eye: The Assassination and Life of Supergun Inventor Gerald Bull*, New York: Times Books, 1992.

Adkin, Mark, *Urgent Fury: The Battle for Grenada*, Lexington, Mass.: Lexington Books, 1989.

Akalovsky, Alexander, "Memorandum of Conversation: Vienna Meeting Between the President and Chairman Khrushchev," June 3, 1961a, 3:00 p.m., Vienna, in U.S. Department of State, *Foreign Relations of the United States, 1961–1963*, Vol. V: *Soviet Union*, Washington, D.C.: U.S. Department of State, Doc. 85, 1998. Online at http://www.state.gov/www/about_state/history/vol_v/80_85.html as of December 22, 2005.

————, "Memorandum of Conversation: Meeting Between the President and Chairman Khrushchev in Vienna," June 4, 1961b, Vienna, in U.S. Department of State, *Foreign Relations of the United States, 1961–1963*, Vol. V: *Soviet Union*, Washington, D.C.: U.S. Department of State, Doc. 87, 1998. Online at http://www.state.gov/www/about_state/history/vol_v/86_89.html as of December 22, 2005.

al-Khalidi, Suleiman, "Jordanian Troops Battle Do-or-Die Islamists," *Reuters*, November 12, 2002.

"Albanian Police Detain Egyptians Falsifying Documents," *Albanian Telegraphic Agency*, June 29, 1998. Online at http://www.telpress.it/ata/1998/jun_98/hdarch29.htm#06 as of October 25, 2005.

"Albanian President Wants OIC Status Clarified," *Radio Free Europe/Radio Liberty*, Vol. 2, No. 204, 1998. Online at http://www.rferl.org/newsline/1998/10/4-see/see-211098.asp as of October 25, 2005.

Aldinger, Charlie, and Mohammed Sudam, "U.S. Hails Attack on Car, Yemen Silent," *Reuters*, November 6, 2002.

Allison, Graham T., Albert Carnesale, and Joseph S. Nye, eds., *Hawks, Doves, and Owls: An Agenda for Avoiding Nuclear War*, New York: Norton, 1985.

Allison, Graham T., and Philip Zelikow, *Essence of Decision: Explaining the Cuban Missile Crisis*, 2nd ed., New York: Longman, 1999.

Alsop, Joseph, and Stewart Alsop, "If Russia Grabs Europe," *The Saturday Evening Post*, Vol. 220, No. 25, 1947, pp. 15–17 and 62.

American Law Institute, *Restatement of the Law, the Foreign Relations Law of the United States*, St. Paul, Minn.: American Law Institute Publishers, 1987.

Andoni, Lamis, "Consequences of an Expulsion," *Al-Ahram Weekly Online*, No. 457, November 25, 1999. Online at http://weekly.ahram.org.eg/1999/457/re2.htm as of November 28, 2005.

Arnold, Henry H., *Second Annual Report of the Commanding General of the Army Air Force to the War Department*, Washington, D.C.: U.S. Air Force, 1945, quoted in Russell D. Buhite and W. Christopher Hamel, "War for Peace: The Question of an American Preventive War Against the Soviet Union, 1945–1955," *Diplomatic History*, Vol. 14, No. 3, 1990, pp. 367–384.

Associated Press, "Yemen Urges Terrorists to 'Repent' After Strikes," November 5, 2002.

Australia, New Zealand, and the United States of America, *Security Treaty Between Australia, New Zealand, and the United States of America*, San Francisco, Calif., September 1, 1951. Online at http://Canberra.usembassy.gov/anzus/anzus.pdf as of October 17, 2005.

Avigad, Doron, "An Amateur, Not Up to the Job," *Globes*, October 6, 1997.

Baldwin, David A., "The Power of Positive Sanctions," *World Politics*, Vol. 24, No. 1, 1971, pp. 19–38.

Baldwin, Hanson, *The New York Times*, September 1, 1950, p. 4:2.

Barbar, Arthur, "Briefing Book on US-Soviet Non-Diffusion Agreement for Discussion at the Moscow Meeting," June 12, 1963, Kennedy Papers, NSF, Box 265, U.S. Arms Control and Disarmament Agency, *Disarmament*, Vol. 1, pp. 1–7.

Bar-Joseph, Uri, "Variations on a Theme: The Conceptualization of Deterrence in Israeli Strategic Thinking," *Security Studies*, Vol. 7, No. 3, 1998, pp. 145–181.

Beck, Robert J., *The Grenada Invasion: Politics, Law, and Foreign Policy Decisionmaking*, Boulder, Colo.: Westview Press, 1993.

Belk, Samuel E., "Memorandum for the Record: Meeting with the President on United Nations Matters," November 18, 1964, 1:00 p.m., Washington, D.C., in U.S. Department of State, *Foreign Relations of the United States, 1964–1968, Volume XXX: China*, Washington, D.C.: U.S. Department of State, Doc. 66, 1998. Online at http://www.state.gov/www/about_state/history/vol_xxx/60_69.html as of December 22, 2005.

Ben-Horin, Yoav, and Barry Posen, *Israel's Strategic Doctrine*, Santa Monica, Calif.: RAND Corporation, R-2845-NA, 1981.

Benjamin, Daniel, and Steven Simon, *The Age of Sacred Terror*, New York: Random House, 2002.

Bensahel, Nora, *The Counterterror Coalitions: Cooperation with Europe, NATO, and the European Union*, Santa Monica, Calif.: RAND Corporation, MR-1746-AF, 2003. Online at http://www.rand.org/publications/MR/MR1746 as of October 17, 2005.

Beschloss, Michael R., *The Crisis Years: Kennedy and Khrushchev, 1960–1963*, New York: Edward Burlingame Books, 1991.

Betts, Richard K., "Nuclear Proliferation After Osirak," *Arms Control Today*, Vol. 11, 1981, pp. 1–7.

———, *Surprise Attack: Lessons for Defense Planning*, Washington, D.C.: Brookings Institution, 1982.

———, "Surprise Attack and Preemption," in Graham T. Allison, Albert Carnesale, and Joseph S. Nye, eds., *Hawks, Doves, and Owls: An Agenda for Avoiding Nuclear War*, New York: Norton, 1985, pp. 54–79.

———, "Systems for Peace or Causes of War? Collective Security, Arms Control, and the New Europe," *International Security*, Vol. 17, No. 1, 1992, pp. 5–43.

———, "Must War Find a Way? A Review Essay," *International Security*, Vol. 24, No. 2, 1999, pp. 166–198.

———, "The Soft Underbelly of American Primacy: Tactical Advantages of Terror," *Political Science Quarterly*, Vol. 117, No. 1, 2002, pp. 19–36.

Bhatia, Shyam, "Israel Accused of Jihad 'Execution,'" *The Observer*, October 29, 1995, p. 22.

Black, Ian, and Benny Morris, *Israel's Secret Wars: A History of Israel's Intelligence Services*, New York: Grove Weidenfeld, 1991.

Blanche, Ed, "Israeli Intelligence Agencies Under Fire," *Jane's Intelligence Review*, Vol. 10, No. 1, 1998, p. 18.

Blight, James G., and David A. Welch, *On the Brink: Americans and Soviets Reexamine the Cuban Missile Crisis*, New York: Hill and Wang, 1989.

Bostock, Ian, "Canberra Would Order Pre-Emptive Strikes," *Jane's Defence Weekly*, December 11, 2002, p. 18.

Bothe, Michael, "War Crimes," in Antonio Cassese, Paola Gaeta, and John R. W. D. Jones, eds., *The Rome Statute of the International Criminal Court: A Commentary*, Oxford and New York: Oxford University Press, 2002, pp. 379–426.

"Both Parties Back Truman's Arms Call: All-Out Support for Proposal of 3,000,000-Man Force Generally Approved," *The New York Times*, September 3, 1950, p. 11.

Bowers, Faye, and Philip Smucker, "Antiterror Allies: US and Yemen Test the Limits," *Christian Science Monitor*, November 29, 2002. Online at http://www.christiansciencemonitor.com/2002/1129/p01s03-wogi.html as of October 25, 2005.

Brecher, Michael, *Decisions in Israel's Foreign Policy*, New Haven, Conn.: Yale University Press, 1975.

Bregman, Ahron, *Israel's Wars, 1947–93*, London and New York: Routledge, 2000.

Brodie, Bernard, ed., *The Absolute Weapon: Atomic Power and World Order*, New York: Harcourt, Brace and Company, 1946.

Brzezinski, Zbigniew, *The Choice: Global Dominance or Global Leadership*, New York: Basic Books, 2004.

Buchan, Glenn C., David Matonick, Calvin Shipbaugh, and Richard Mesic, *Future Roles of U.S. Nuclear Forces: Implications for U.S. Strategy*, Santa Monica, Calif.: RAND Corporation, MR-1231-AF, 2003. Online at http://www.rand.org/publications/MR/MR1231 as of October 18, 2005.

Buhite, Russell D., and W. Christopher Hamel, "War for Peace: The Question of an American Preventive War Against the Soviet Union, 1945–1955," *Diplomatic History*, Vol. 14, No. 3, 1990, pp. 367–384.

Bullitt, William C., *The Great Globe Itself: A Preface to World Affairs*, New York: C. Scribner's Sons, 1946.

Bundy, McGeorge, "Notes on Discussion of the Thinking of the Soviet Leadership," Cabinet Room, February 11, 1961.

———, "Memorandum of Conversation Between the President's Special Assistant for National Security Affairs (Bundy) and the Soviet Ambassador (Dobrynin)," May 17, 1963, Washington, D.C., in U.S. Department of State, *Foreign Relations of the United States, 1961–1963*, Vol. V: *Soviet Union*, Washington, D.C.: U.S. Department of State, Doc. 322, 1998. Online at http://www.state.gov/www/about_state/history/vol_v/320_324.html as of December 22, 2005.

———, "Memorandum for the Record," September 15, 1964a, Washington, D.C., in U.S. Department of State, *Foreign Relations of the United States, 1964–1968*, Vol. XXX: *China*, Washington, D.C.: U.S. Department of State, Doc. 49, 1998. Online at http://www.state.gov/www/about_state/history/vol_xxx/41_49.html as of January 25, 2006.

———, "Memorandum of Conversation: Memorandum of Conversation with Ambassador Dobrynin," September 25, 1964b, 1–3:30 p.m., in U.S. Department of State, *Foreign Relations of the United States, 1964–1968*, Vol. XXX: *China*, Washington, D.C.: U.S. Department of State, Doc.

54, 1998. Online at http://www.state.gov/www/about_state/history/vol_xxx/50_59.html as of December 22, 2005.

———, "Memos to the President," Vol. 63, Lyndon B. Johnson Library, National Security File, September 25, 1964c.

———, "Memorandum for Record: Meeting of an Executive Group of the National Security Council," October 16, 1964d, in U.S. Department of State, *Foreign Relations of the United States, 1964–1968*, Vol. XXX: *China*, Washington, D.C.: U.S. Department of State, Doc. 57, 1998. Online at http://www.state.gov/www/about_state/history/vol_xxx/50_59.html as of December 22, 2005.

Bundy, William, memorandum, July 31, 1963, Washington National Records Center, RG 330, OSD Files: FRC 91-0017, 471.61 China Reds.

Burnham, James, *The Struggle for the World*, New York: The John Day Company, Inc., 1947.

Burr, William, and Jeffrey Richelson, "Whether to 'Strangle the Baby in the Cradle': The United States and the Chinese Nuclear Program, 1960–64," *International Security*, Vol. 25, No. 3, 2000, pp. 54–99.

Burrowes, Reynold A., *Revolution and Rescue in Grenada: An Account of the U.S.-Caribbean Invasion*, New York: Greenwood Press, 1988.

Bush, George H. W., "Remarks at the United States Military Academy at West Point, New York," West Point, N.Y.: January 5, 1993. Online at http://bushlibrary.tamu.edu/papers/1993/93010500.html as of October 13, 2005.

Bush, George W., *The National Security Strategy of the United States of America*, Washington, D.C.: Executive Office of the President, 2002a. Online at http://library.nps.navy.mil/uhtbin/hyperion-image/nss.pdf as of October 13, 2005.

———, *National Strategy to Combat Weapons of Mass Destruction*, Washington, D.C.: The White House, 2002b. Online at http://purl.access.gpo.gov/GPO/LPS24899 as of October 13, 2005.

———, *The National Security Strategy of the United States of America*, Washington, D.C.: The White House, 2006. Online at http://purl.access.gpo.gov/GPO/LPS6777 as of May 4, 2006.

Byers, Michael, "The Shifting Foundations of International Law: A Decade of Forceful Measures Against Iraq," *European Journal of International Law*, Vol. 13, 2002, pp. 21–41.

Byman, Daniel, "Should Hezbollah Be Next?" *Foreign Affairs*, Vol. 82, No. 6, 2003, pp. 54–66.

Calahan, Alexander B., *Countering Terrorism: The Israeli Response to the 1972 Munich Olympic Massacre and the Development of Independent Covert Action Teams*, M.M.S. thesis, Marine Corps Command and Staff College, 1995.

Cameron, Rebecca Hancock, and Barbara Wittig, eds., *Golden Legacy, Boundless Future: Essays on the United States Air Force and the Rise of Aerospace Power: Proceedings of the Aim High Symposium Held on May 28–29, 1997 at the Double Tree Hotel, Crystal City, Virginia*, Washington, D.C.: Air Force History and Museums Program, 2000. Online at http://purl. access.gpo.gov/GPO/LPS48567 as of October 18, 2005.

Carapico, Sheila, "Yemen and the Aden-Abyan Islamic Army," *Middle East Report Online*, October 18, 2000. Online at http://www.merip.org/mero/ mero101800.html as of October 25, 2005.

Carter, John R., Jr., *Airpower and the Cult of the Offensive*, Maxwell Air Force Base, Ala.: Air University Press, 1998. Online at http://purl.access.gpo. gov/GPO/LPS37334 as of October 14, 2005.

Cassese, Antonio, Paola Gaeta, and John R. W. D. Jones, eds., *The Rome Statute of the International Criminal Court: A Commentary*, Oxford and New York: Oxford University Press, 2002.

Castillo, Jasen J., "Nuclear Terrorism: Why Deterrence Still Matters," *Current History*, Vol. 102, No. 668, 2003, pp. 426–431.

Central Intelligence Agency, *The World Factbook*, undated Web page. Online at http://www.cia.gov/cia/publications/factbook/index.html as of October 22, 2005.

———, "Current Intelligence Weekly Review," October 12, 1962, Washington, D.C., in U.S. Department of State, *Foreign Relations of the United States, 1961–1963, Volume V: Soviet Union*, Washington, D.C.: U.S. Department of State, Doc. 244, 1998, pp. 3–4. Online at http://www. state.gov/www/about_state/history/vol_v/240_249.html as of December 22, 2005.

————, "Current Intelligence Weekly Review," January 18, 1963a, Washington, D.C., in U.S. Department of State, *Foreign Relations of the United States, 1961–1963, Volume V: Soviet Union*, Washington, D.C.: U.S. Department of State, Doc. 280, 1998, pp. 1–3. Online at http://www.state.gov/www/about_state/history/vol_v/280_289.html as of December 22, 2005.

————, "Current Intelligence Weekly Review," June 21, 1963b, Washington, D.C., in U.S. Department of State, *Foreign Relations of the United States, 1961–1963, Volume V: Soviet Union*, Washington, D.C.: U.S. Department of State, Doc. 334, 1998, pp. 2–4. Online at http://www.state.gov/www/about_state/history/vol_v/330_339.html as of December 22, 2005.

Chang, Gordon H., *Friends and Enemies: The United States, China, and the Soviet Union, 1948–1972*, Stanford, Calif.: Stanford University Press, 1990.

Chief of Staff, U.S. Air Force, "The Coming National Crisis," memorandum to the Joint Chiefs of Staff, August 21, 1953, Twining Papers, Series 2, Topical Series, Nuclear Weapons 1952–1961 folder, Colorado Springs, Colo.: U.S. Air Force, 1953.

"CIA Yemen Operation: Many See 'Assassination Without Jury, Judge,'" *GlobalSecurity.org*, November 18, 2002. Online at http://www.globalsecurity.org/intell/library/news/2002/intell-021118-wwwh21118.htm as of October 26, 2005.

Cleveland, J. Harlan, "Memorandum from the Assistant Secretary of State for International Organization Affairs (Cleveland) to Secretary of State Rusk: China and the UN," November 5, 1964, in U.S. Department of State, *Foreign Relations of the United States, 1964–1968*, Vol. XXX: *China*, Washington, D.C.: U.S. Department of State, Doc. 64, 1998. Online at http://www.state.gov/www/about_state/history/vol_xxx/60_69.html as of December 22, 2005.

Coalition for the International Criminal Court, "Status of U.S. Bilateral Immunity Agreements (BIAs)," 2005. Online at http://www.iccnow.org/documents/USandICC/BIAsByRegion_current.pdf as of October 17, 2005.

Cockburn, Patrick, "Killing of Hamas Bomber Delights Israel," *The Independent*, January 6, 1996, p. 9.

———, "Netanyahu 'Over-Ruled' Mossad Chief," *The Independent*, October 6, 1997, p. 10.

———, "Jordan Closes HQ of Hamas Militants," *The Independent*, August 31, 1999, p. 11.

Commission of the European Communities, *Commission Staff Working Paper: Albania: Stabilisation and Association Report 2003*, Brussels: Commission of the European Communities, 2003. Online at http://unpan1. un.org/intradoc/groups/public/documents/UNTC/UNPAN012931.pdf as of October 25, 2005.

Copeland, Dale C., *The Origins of Major War*, Ithaca: Cornell University Press, 2000.

"The Covenant of the Islamic Resistance Movement (Hamas)," *MidEast Web*, August 18, 1988. Online at http://www.mideastweb.org/hamas.htm as of October 26, 2005.

Crenshaw, Martha, "Why America: The Globalization of Civil War," *Current History*, Vol. 100, No. 650, 2001, pp. 425–432.

D'Amato, Anthony, "Trashing Customary International Law," *The American Journal of International Law*, Vol. 81, No. 1, 1987, pp. 101–105.

———, "Israel's Air Strike Against the Osiraq Reactor: A Retrospective," *Temple International and Comparative Law Journal*, Vol. 10, 1996, pp. 259–264.

David, Steven R., *Fatal Choices: Israel's Policy of Targeted Killing*, Israel: Bar-Ilan University, Mideast Security and Policy Studies No. 51, 2002.

Davis, Vincent, *Postwar Defense Policy and the United States Navy, 1943–1946*, Chapel Hill, N.C.: University of North Carolina Press, 1966.

"Deadly Jordan Crackdown Seen as Stark Warning for Pro-Iraq Uprising," *IslamOnline*, November 11, 2002. Online at http://www.islamonline.net/ english/news/2002-11/11/article73.shtml as of October 26, 2005.

"Detained Islamists Aimed at Giving Religious Character to War in Kosova, Daily Said," *Albanian Telegraphic Agency*, July 14, 1998. Online at http:// www.telpress.it/ata/1998%5Cjul_98%5Chdarch14.htm#08 as of October 25, 2005.

Duelfer, Charles, *Comprehensive Report of the Special Advisor to the DCI on Iraq's WMD, 30 September 2004*, Baghdad, Iraq: Central Intelligence

Agency, 2004. Online at http://www.cia.gov/cia/reports/iraq_wmd_2004 as of October 17, 2005.

Dulles, John Foster, memorandum to Dwight D. Eisenhower, September 6, 1953, in U.S. Department of State, *Foreign Relations of the United States, 1952–1954*, Vol. II: *National Security Affairs*, Washington, D.C.: U.S. Department of State, 1967, pp. 457–460.

Eckert, Amy, "The Non-Intervention Principle and International Humanitarian Interventions," *International Legal Theory*, Vol. 7, 2001, pp. 49–58.

"Editorial Note," in U.S. Department of State, *Foreign Relations of the United States, 1961–1963*, Vol. XXII: *China, Korea, Japan*, Washington, D.C.: U.S. Department of State, Doc. 164, 1996. Online at http://www.state.gov/www/about_state/history/frusXXII/151to197.html as of December 22, 2005.

Eisenhower, Dwight D., "Memorandum to Dulles," September 8, 1953, in U.S. Department of State, *Foreign Relations of the United States 1952–1954*, Vol. II: *National Security Affairs*, Washington, D.C.: U.S. Department of State, 1984, p. 461.

———, *The Eisenhower Diaries*, New York: Norton, 1981.

Eisenstadt, Michael, "'Preemptive Targeted Killings' as a Counterterror Tool: An Assessment of Israel's Approach," *PeaceWatch*, No. 342, 2001. Online at http://www.washingtoninstitute.org/templateC05.php?CID=2033 as of October 24, 2005.

Eldridge, William G., "Why Preemptive Counterproliferation Attack Works: Investigating Third Party Outcomes," paper presented at the International Studies Association, Montreal, Que., 2004. Online at http://convention2.allacademic.com/getfile.php?file=isa04_proceeding/2005-09-30/73792/isa04_proceeding_73792.PDF as of October 18, 2005.

Eliot, George Fielding, *If Russia Strikes*, Indianapolis: Bobbs-Merrill Co., 1949.

Engel, Richard, "Yemen Cautious on Battle Against al-Qaeda," *BBC News*, January 23, 2002. Online at http://news.bbc.co.uk/1/hi/world/americas/1777520.stm as of October 25, 2005.

Eshel, David, "Israel Refines Its Pre-Emptive Approach to Counterterrorism," *Jane's Terrorism and Security Monitor*, September 1, 2002.

Etzold, Thomas H., and John Lewis Gaddis, eds., *Containment: Documents on American Policy and Strategy, 1945–1950*, New York: Columbia University Press, 1978.

European Parliament, Directorate General for Research, Division for Agriculture, Regional Policy, Transport, Development, *Note on the Political and Economic Situation in Yemen*, 2002. Online at http://www2.europarl.eu.int/registre/etudes/note_information/deve/2002/030120/04A-DEVE_INF(2002)030120_EN.doc as of October 25, 2005.

"External Affairs, Yemen," *Jane's Online*, September 4, 2003.

Fahim, Kareem, "Jordan's South Rises, Again," *Village Voice*, March 18, 2003, p. 49.

Fearon, James D., "Rationalist Explanations for War," *International Organization*, Vol. 49, No. 3, 1995, pp. 379–414.

Feldman, Shai, *Israeli Nuclear Deterrence: A Strategy for the 1980s*, New York: Columbia University Press, 1982.

Fernandez de Gurmendi, Silvia A., "The Working Group on Aggression at the Preparatory Commission for the International Criminal Court," *Fordham International Law Journal*, Vol. 25, No. 3, 2002, pp. 589–605.

Finer, Herman, *America's Destiny*, New York: Macmillan Co., 1947.

Fischer, Fritz, *War of Illusions: German Policies from 1911 to 1914*, Marian Jackson, trans., New York: Norton, 1975.

Franck, Thomas M., "When, If Ever, May States Deploy Military Force Without Prior Security Council Authorization?" *Washington University Journal of Law and Policy*, Vol. 5, 2001, pp. 51–68.

Freedman, Lawrence, *The Evolution of Nuclear Strategy*, 3rd ed., New York: Palgrave Macmillan, 2003a.

———, "Prevention, Not Preemption," *The Washington Quarterly*, Vol. 26, No. 2, 2003b, pp. 105–114.

Fursenko, A. A., and Timothy J. Naftali, *One Hell of A Gamble: Khrushchev, Castro and Kennedy, 1958–1964*, New York: Norton, 1997.

Futrell, Robert Frank, *Ideas, Concepts, Doctrine: Basic Thinking in the United States Air Force*, Maxwell Air Force Base, Ala.: Air University Press, 1989. Online at http://purl.access.gpo.gov/GPO/LPS46806 as of October 18, 2005.

Gaddis, John Lewis, *We Now Know: Rethinking Cold War History*, New York: Oxford University Press, 1997.

———, "A Grand Strategy of Transformation," *Foreign Policy*, Vol. 133, 2002, pp. 50–57.

———, *Surprise, Security, and the American Experience*, Cambridge, Mass.: Harvard University Press, 2004.

Gallup Poll News Service, *The Gallup Poll No. 458*, July 7, 1950.

———, *The Gallup Poll No. 536*, August 24, 1954.

Ganor, Boaz, "Israeli Counter-Terrorist Policy," January 1, 1997, The Institute for Counter-Terrorism Web site (at http://www.ict.org.il under Articles by ICT Staff Members in descending chronological order as of October 24, 2005).

———, "Targeting Terrorists: A Cost-Benefit Analysis," August 1, 2001, The Institute for Counter-Terrorism Web site (at http://www.ict.org.il under Articles by ICT Staff Members in descending chronological order as of October 24, 2005).

Gardam, Judith Gail, "Proportionality and Force in International Law," *American Journal of International Law*, Vol. 87, No. 3, 1993, pp. 391–413.

Gavin, Francis J., "The Myth of Flexible Response: United States Strategy in Europe During the 1960s," *International History Review*, Vol. 23, No. 4, 2001, pp. 847–875.

"General Removed Over War Speech," *The New York Times*, September 2, 1950.

Gentile, Gian, "Planning for Preventive War, 1945–1950," *Joint Forces Quarterly*, No. 24, 2000, pp. 72–73.

George, Alexander L. and William E. Simons, eds., *The Limits of Coercive Diplomacy*, 2nd ed., Boulder: Westview, 1994.

Gilpin, Robert, *War and Change in World Politics*, Cambridge and New York: Cambridge University Press, 1981.

Glaser, Charles L., *Analyzing Strategic Nuclear Policy*, Princeton, N.J.: Princeton University Press, 1990.

Glaser, Charles L., and Chaim Kaufmann, "What Is the Offense-Defense Balance and Can We Measure It?" *International Security*, Vol. 22, No. 4, 1998, pp. 44–82.

Glennon, Michael J., "The Fog of Law: Self-Defense, Inherence, and Incoherence in Article 51 of the United Nations Charter," *Harvard Journal of Law and Public Policy*, Vol. 25, No. 2, 2002, pp. 539–558.

Goodpaster, Andrew J., March 30, 1956, dated April 2, 1956, April 1956-Goodpaster Folder, Dwight D. Eisenhower Diaries, Box 15, Ann C. Whitman File, Dwight D. Eisenhower Papers as President (ACWF-EPP).

Gray, Christine D., *International Law and the Use of Force*, Oxford and New York: Oxford University Press, 2000.

Gray, Colin S., "Nuclear Strategy: The Case for a Theory of Victory," *International Security*, Vol. 4, No. 1, 1979, pp. 54–87.

Gray, Colin S., and Keith Payne, "Under the Nuclear Gun: Victory Is Possible," *Foreign Policy*, No. 39, 1980, pp. 14–27.

Groupe d'Etats Contre la Corruption, Directorate General I, Legal Affairs, Department of Crime Problems, *First Evaluation Round, Evaluation Report on Albania, Adopted by GRECO at Its 12th Plenary Meeting (Strasbourg, 9–13 December 2002)*, Strasbourg: Groupe d'Etats Contre la Corruption, 2002. Online at http://www.greco.coe.int/evaluations/Default.htm as of October 25, 2005.

Groves, Leslie R., "Our Army of the Future—As Influenced by Atomic Weapons," January 2, 1946, in U.S. Department of State, *Foreign Relations of the United States*, Vol. I: *General: The United Nations*, Washington, D.C.: U.S. Department of State, 1972, pp. 1197–1203.

Haass, Richard N., "Sovereignty: Existing Rights, Evolving Responsibilities: Remarks to the School of Foreign Service and the Mortara Center for International Studies, Georgetown University, Washington, D.C., January 14, 2003," Washington, D.C.: U.S. Department of State, 2003. Online at http://www.state.gov/s/p/rem/2003/16648.htm as of October 14, 2005.

Haass, Richard, and Meghan L. O'Sullivan, *Honey and Vinegar: Incentives, Sanctions, and Foreign Policy*, Washington, D.C.: Brookings Institution Press, 2000.

Hagan, Kenneth J., *This People's Navy: The Making of American Sea Power*, New York: Free Press, 1991.

Hamzah, Khidhr 'Abd al-'Abbas, and Jeff Stein, *Saddam's Bombmaker: The Terrifying Inside Story of the Iraqi Nuclear and Biological Weapons Agenda*, New York: Scribner, 2000.

Hansen, James H., "Soviet Deception in the Cuban Missile Crisis," *Studies in Intelligence: Journal of the American Intelligence Professional*, Vol. 46, No. 1, 2002, Unclassified Edition. Online at http://www.cia.gov/csi/studies/vol46no1/article06.html as of October 21, 2005.

Harriman, W. Averill, "Telegram from the Embassy in the Soviet Union to the Department of State," Moscow, July 15, 1963a, 10:00 p.m., in U.S. Department of State, *Foreign Relations of the United States, 1961–1963*, Vol. VII: *Arms Control and Disarmament*, Washington, D.C.: U.S. Department of State, Doc. 325, 1995. Online at http://www.state.gov/r/pa/ho/frus/kennedyjf/vii/50956.htm as of December 22, 2005.

———, "Telegram from the Embassy in the Soviet Union to the Department of State," Moscow, July 18, 1963b, 5:00 p.m., in U.S. Department of State, *Foreign Relations of the United States, 1961–1963*, Vol. VII: *Arms Control and Disarmament*, Washington, D.C.: U.S. Department of State, Doc. 331, 1995. Online at http://www.state.gov/r/pa/ho/frus/kennedyjf/vii/50956.htm as of December 22, 2005.

———, "Telegram from the Embassy in the Soviet Union to the Department of State," Moscow, July 19, 1963c, 8:00 p.m., in U.S. Department of State, *Foreign Relations of the United States, 1961–1963*, Vol. VII: *Arms Control and Disarmament*, Washington, D.C.: U.S. Department of State, Doc. 333, 1995. Online at http://www.state.gov/r/pa/ho/frus/kennedyjf/vii/50956.htm as of December 22, 2005.

Harub, Khalid, *Hamas: Political Thought and Practice*, Washington, D.C.: Institute for Palestine Studies, 2000.

Hawthorne, Amy W., "Yemen and the Fight Against Terror," *Policywatch*, No. 572, 2001. Online at http://www.washingtoninstitute.org/templateC05.php?CID=1450 as of October 25, 2005.

Heisbourg, François, "A Work in Progress: The Bush Doctrine and Its Consequences," *Washington Quarterly*, Vol. 26, No. 2, 2003, pp. 75–88.

Henkin, Louis, "Kosovo and the Law of 'Humanitarian Intervention,'" *The American Journal of International Law*, Vol. 93, No. 4, 1999, pp. 824–828.

Henkin, Louis, Oscar Schachter, Richard C. Pugh, and Hans Smit, eds., *International Law: Cases and Materials*, 3rd ed., St. Paul, Minn.: West Pub. Co., 1993.

Herr, W. Eric, *Operation Vigilant Warrior: Conventional Deterrence Theory, Doctrine, and Practice*, Maxwell Air Force Base, Ala.: Air University Press, 1996.

Herzog, Chaim, *The Arab-Israeli Wars: War and Peace in the Middle East*, New York: Random House, 1982.

Hess, Pamela, "Experts: Yemen Strike Not Assassination," *United Press International*, November 8, 2002.

"Highlights of Secretary Rusk's Policy Planning Meeting," October 15, 1963, *Foreign Relations of the United States, 1961–1963*, Vol. XXII: *Northeast Asia*, Washington, D.C.: U.S. Department of State, Doc. 191, 1996. Online at http://www.state.gov/www/about_state/history/frusXXII/151to197.html as of December 22, 2005.

Hosmer, Stephen T., *Operations Against Enemy Leaders*, Santa Monica, Calif.: RAND Corporation, MR-1385-AF, 2001. Online at http://www.rand.org/publications/MR/MR1385 as of October 18, 2005.

House of Commons, *Parliamentary Debates: House of Commons Official Report*, January 23, 1948.

Howard, Michael Eliot, *The Causes of Wars and Other Essays*, Cambridge, Mass.: Harvard University Press, 1983.

Hoyle, Craig, and Andrew Koch, "Yemen Drone Strike: Just the Start?" *Jane's Defence Weekly*, November 8, 2002.

Ikenberry, G. John, ed., *America Unrivaled: The Future of the Balance of Power*, Ithaca, N.Y.: Cornell University Press, 2002.

Inbar, Efraim, and Shmuel Sandler, "Israel's Deterrence Strategy Revisited," *Security Studies*, Vol. 3, No. 2, 1993, pp. 330–358.

Indyk, Martin S., "The Iraq War Did Not Force Gadaffi's Hand," *Financial Times*, March 9, 2004.

Institute for Strategic Studies, *The Military Balance, 2003–2004*, London, 2003.

International Court of Justice, *Military and Paramilitary Activities in and Against Nicaragua (Nicaragua v. United States)*, International Court of Justice, 1986.

International Crisis Group, *Bin Laden and the Balkans: The Politics of Anti-Terrorism*, Belgrade and Brussels: International Crisis Group, 2001.

————, *Red Alert in Jordan: Recurrent Unred in Maan*, Amman and Brussels: International Crisis Group, 2003a.

————, *Yemen: Coping with Terrorism and Violence in a Fragile State*, Amman and Brussels: International Crisis Group, Middle East Report No. 8, 2003b. Online at http://www.crisisgroup.org/home/index.cfm?id= 1675&CFID=9346951&CFTOKEN=52621559 as of October 25, 2005.

"Islamist Murder Suspect Sentenced in Albania," *Radio Free Europe/Radio Liberty Newsline: Southeastern Europe*, November 16, 1998. Online at http://www.rferl.org/newsline/1998/11/4-see/see-161198.asp as of February 25, 2006.

"Israeli Mossad Report on Amman Fiasco: Background," *ArabicNews. com*, February 16, 1998. Online at www.arabicnews.com/ansub/Daily/ Day/980216/1998021601.html as of October 24, 2005.

Jane's Sentinel Security Assessment, Eastern Mediterranean, "Internal Affairs, Jordan," June 27, 2003a.

Jane's Sentinel Security Assessment, The Gulf States, "Internal Affairs, Yemen," September 4, 2003b.

"Japan Threatens Force Against N Korea," *BBC News*, February 14, 2003. Online at http://news.bbc.co.uk/2/hi/asia-pacific/2757923.stm as of October 13, 2005.

"JCS to Wilson, 23 June 1954," in U.S. Department of State, *Foreign Relations of the United States 1952–1954*, Vol. II: *National Security Affairs*, Washington, D.C.: U.S. Department of State, 1984, pp. 680–686.

Jervis, Robert, "Cooperation Under the Security Dilemma," *World Politics*, Vol. 30, No. 2, 1978, pp. 167–214.

————, *The Illogic of American Nuclear Strategy*, Ithaca, N.Y.: Cornell University Press, 1984.

————, *The Meaning of the Nuclear Revolution: Statecraft and the Prospect of Armageddon*, Ithaca, N.Y.: Cornell University Press, 1989.

————, "Understanding the Bush Doctrine," *Political Science Quarterly*, Vol. 118, No. 3, 2003, pp. 365–388.

Joffé, George, "Libya: Who Blinked, and Why," *Current History*, Vol. 103, No. 673, 2004, pp. 221–225.

Johnson, David E., Karl P. Mueller, and William H. Taft V, *Conventional Coercion Across the Spectrum of Operations: The Utility of U.S. Mili-*

tary Forces in the Emerging Security Environment, Santa Monica, Calif.: RAND Corporation, MR-1494-A, 2002. Online at http://www.rand.org/publications/MR/MR1494 as of October 14, 2005.

Johnson, Robert, "Paper Prepared in the Policy Planning Council: The Implications of a Chinese Communist Nuclear Capability," undated, Washington, D.C., in U.S. Department of State, *Foreign Relations of the United States, 1964–1968*, Vol. XXX: *China*, Washington, D.C.: U.S. Department of State, Doc. 30, 1998. Online at http://www.state.gov/www/about_state/history/vol_xxx/27_34.html as of December 22, 2005.

————, "Paper Prepared in the Policy Planning Council: An Exploration of the Possible Bases for Action Against the Chinese Communist Nuclear Facilities," April 14, 1964, in U.S. Department of State, *Foreign Relations of the United States, 1964–1968*, Vol. XXX: *China*, Washington, D.C.: U.S. Department of State, Doc. 25, 1998. Online at http://www.state.gov/www/about_state/history/vol_xxx/21_26.html as of December 22, 2005.

Johnston, David, and David E. Sanger, "Fatal Strike in Yemen Was Based on Rules Set Out by Bush," *The New York Times*, Late Edition East Coast, November 6, 2002, p. A16.

Joint Chiefs of Staff, "Evaluation of Effect on Soviet War Effort Resulting from the Strategic Air Offensive," May 12, 1949, JCS 1953/1, in Steven T. Ross and David Alan Rosenberg, eds., *America's Plans for War Against the Soviet Union, 1945–1950: A 15-Volume Set, Reproducing in Facsimile 98 Plans and Studies Created by the Joint Chiefs of Staff*, New York: Garland, 1989a, Vol. 11.

————, "p. 152–96, Plus Letter from Lieutenant General Hull to Joint Chiefs of Staff: Evaluation of Effectiveness of Strategic Air Operations, 13 January 1950, and Enclosures C, D, E, F, G, H, and K," February 10, 1950, JCS 1952/11, in Steven T. Ross and David Alan Rosenberg, eds., *America's Plans for War Against the Soviet Union, 1945–1950: A 15-Volume Set, Reproducing in Facsimile 98 Plans and Studies Created by the Joint Chiefs of Staff*, New York: Garland, 1989a, Vol. 13.

————, memorandum, May 19, 1953, in U.S. Department of State, *Foreign Relations of the United States, 1952–1954*, Vol. XV: *Korea*, Washington, D.C.: U.S. Department of State, 1984, p. 1061.

————, memorandum, JCSM-986-63, December 14, 1963, Washington National Records Center, RG 330, OSD Files: FRC 91-0017, 471.61 China Reds.

————, *Department of Defense Dictionary of Military and Associated Terms*, Washington, D.C.: Joint Chiefs of Staff, JP 1-02, 2004. Online at http://purl.access.gpo.gov/GPO/LPS14106 as of October 14, 2005.

Joll, James, *The Origins of the First World War*, 2nd ed., New York: Longman, 1992.

Jones, Rodney W., Mark G. McDonough, and Leonard S. Spector, *Tracking Nuclear Proliferation: A Guide in Maps and Charts, 1998*, Washington, D.C.: Carnegie Endowment for International Peace, 1998.

"Jordan Security Sweep Nets Militants," *BBC News*, November 13, 2002. Online at http://news.bbc.co.uk/2/hi/middle_east/2468211.stm as of October 26, 2005.

Kaplan, Fred M., *The Wizards of Armageddon*, New York: Simon and Schuster, 1983.

Karon, Tony, "Yemen Strike Opens New Chapter in War on Terror," *Time*, November 5, 2002.

Kearley, Timothy, "Raising the Caroline," *Wisconsin International Law Journal*, Vol. 17, No. 2, 1999, pp. 325–346.

Keegan, John, *The First World War*, New York: A. Knopf, 1999.

"Keep Atomic Bomb Secret, Gen. Groves Urges: Atomic Bomb Project Director Honored," *The New York Times*, September 22, 1945, p. 3.

Kennedy, John F., "Telegram from the Department of State to the Embassy in the Soviet Union," Washington, July 15, 1963a, in U.S. Department of State, *Foreign Relations of the United States, 1961–1963*, Vol. VII: *Arms Control and Disarmament*, Washington, D.C.: U.S. Department of State, Doc. 326, 1995, p. 801.

————, "Telegram from the Department of State to the Embassy in the Soviet Union," Washington, July 18, 1963b, in U.S. Department of State, *Foreign Relations of the United States, 1961–1963*, Vol. VII: *Arms Control and Disarmament*, Washington, D.C.: U.S. Department of State, Doc. 332, 1995, p. 813.

Kennedy, Paul M., "The First World War and the International Power System," *International Security*, Vol. 9, No. 1, 1984, pp. 7–40.

Kennedy, Robert F., *Thirteen Days: A Memoir of the Cuban Missile Crisis*, New York: W. W. Norton, 1969.

Kent, Glenn A., and David E. Thaler, *First-Strike Stability: A Methodology for Evaluating Strategic Forces*, Santa Monica, Calif.: RAND Corporation, R-3765-AF, 1989.

Kent, Sherman, *Sherman Kent and the Board of National Estimates: Collected Essays*, Washington, D.C.: History Staff, Center for the Study of Intelligence, Central Intelligence Agency, 1994. Online at http://purl.access.gpo.gov/GPO/LPS61102 as of October 21, 2005.

Khong, Yuen Foong, *Analogies at War: Korea, Munich, Dien Bien Phu, and the Vietnam Decisions of 1965*, Princeton, N.J.: Princeton University Press, 1992.

Khrushchev, Nikita Sergeevich, *Khrushchev Remembers: The Last Testament*, Strobe Talbott, trans., Boston: Little, Brown, 1974.

Kirshner, Jonathan, *Currency and Coercion: The Political Economy of International Monetary Power*, Princeton, N.J.: Princeton University Press, 1995.

———, "Rationalist Explanations for War?" *Security Studies*, Vol. 10, No. 1, 2000, pp. 143–150.

Kissinger, Henry, "Preemption and the End of Westphalia," *New Perspectives Quarterly*, Vol. 19, No. 3, 2002, pp. 31–36.

Kohler, Foy D., "Telegram from the Embassy in the Soviet Union to the Department of State," November 11, 1964, 10:00 p.m., Moscow, in U.S. Department of State, *Foreign Relations of the United States, 1964–1968*, Vol. XIV: *Soviet Union*, Washington, D.C.: U.S. Department of State, Doc. 70, 2001. Online at http://www.state.gov/r/pa/ho/frus/johnsonlb/xiv/1309.htm as of December 22, 2005.

Komer, Robert W., "Memorandum from Robert W. Komer of the National Security Council Staff to the President's Special Assistant for National Security Affairs (Bundy)," November 5, 1963, Washington, D.C., in U.S. Department of State, *Foreign Relations of the United States, 1961–1963*, Vol. XXII: *China, Korea, Japan*, Washington, D.C.: U.S. Department of State, Doc. 193, 1996. Online at http://www.state.gov/www/about_state/history/frusXXII/151to197.html as of December 22, 2005.

———, "Memorandum from Robert W. Komer of the National Security Council Staff to the President's Special Assistant for National Security Affairs (Bundy)," Washington, D.C., February 26, 1964a, Johnson Library,

National Security File, Komer Files, China (CPR), Nuclear Explosion/ Capability. Online at http://www.globalsecurity.org/wmd/library/report/ other/frus_30_014.htm as of October 20, 2005.

————, "Memorandum from Robert W. Komer of the National Security Council Staff to the President's Special Assistant for National Security Affairs (Bundy)," September 18, 1964b, Washington, D.C., in U.S. Department of State, *Foreign Relations of the United States, 1964–1968*, Vol. XXX: *China*, Washington, D.C.: U.S. Department of State, Doc. 51, 1998. Online at http://www.state.gov/www/about_state/history/vol_ xxx/50_59.html as of December 22, 2005.

Kramer, Mark, "Tactical Nuclear Weapons, Soviet Command Authority, and the Cuban Missile Crisis," *Cold War International History Project Bulletin 3*, Washington, D.C.: Woodrow Wilson Center, 1993. Online at http://www.wilsoncenter.org/index.cfm?topic_id=1409&fuseaction= library.document&id=315 as of October 21, 2005.

Kugler, Jacek, and A. F. K. Organski, "The Power Transition: A Retrospective and Prospective Evaluation," in Manus I. Midlarsky, ed., *Handbook of War Studies*, Boston, Mass.: Unwin Hyman, 1989, pp. 171–194.

Kupchan, Charles, *The End of the American Era: U.S. Foreign Policy and the Geopolitics of the Twenty-First Century*, New York: Vintage Books, 2003.

Lay, James S., Jr., "Note by the Executive Secretary to the National Security Council on the Position and Actions of the United States with Respect to Possible Further Soviet Moves in the Light of the Korean Situation," August 24, 1951, NSC 73/4, in U.S. Department of State, *Foreign Relations of the United States, 1950*, Vol. I: *National Security Affairs; Foreign Economic Policy*, Washington, D.C.: U.S. Department of State, 1977, pp. 375–389.

————, "NSC Staff Study on Reappraisal of United States Objectives and Strategy for National Security: Annex to a Report to the National Security Council by the Executive Secretary," August 22, 1952, NSC 135/1 Annex, in U.S. Department of State, *Foreign Relations of the United States, 1952–1954*: Vol. II, *National Security Affairs*, Washington, D.C.: U.S. Department of State, 1984, p. 89.

Lebow, Richard Ned, "Windows of Opportunity: Do States Jump Through Them?" *International Security*, Vol. 9, No. 1, 1984, pp. 147–186.

Lederer, Gyorgy, *Contemporary Islam in East Europe*, Individual Democratic Institutions Research Fellowship (IDIR), 1999. Online at http://www. nato.int/acad/fellow/97-99/lederer.pdf as of October 25, 2005.

Lee, Robert M., "The Coming National Crisis," memorandum for the Chief of Staff, U.S. Air Force, August 21, 1953, 1952–1957, Subject File, Box 121, Nathan F. Twining Papers, Library of Congress.

Leffler, Melvyn, *A Preponderance of Power: National Security, the Truman Administration, and the Cold War*, Stanford, Calif.: Stanford University Press, 1992.

Lesser, Ian O., Bruce Hoffman, John Arquilla, David F. Ronfeldt, Michele Zanini, and Brian Michael Jenkins, *Countering the New Terrorism*, Santa Monica, Calif.: RAND Corporation, MR-989-AF, 1999. Online at http:// www.rand.org/publications/MR/MR989 as of October 14, 2005.

"Letter from Mr. Webster to Mr. Fox, April 24, 1841," *British and Foreign State Papers*, Vol. 29, 1857, pp. 1129–1139.

Levey, Zach, *Israel and the Western Powers, 1952–1960*, Chapel Hill, N.C.: University of North Carolina Press, 1997.

———, "Israeli Foreign Policy and the Arms Race in the Middle East, 1950–1960," *Journal of Strategic Studies*, Vol. 24, No. 1, 2001, pp. 29–48.

Levy, Jack S., "Declining Power and the Preventive Motivation for War," *World Politics*, Vol. 40, No. 1, 1987, pp. 82–107.

———, "The Causes of War and the Conditions of Peace," *Annual Review of Political Science*, Vol. 1, 1998, pp. 139–165.

———, "Preferences, Constraints, and Choices in July 1914," *International Security*, Vol. 15, No. 3, 1990, pp. 151–186.

Levy, Jack S., and Joseph R. Gochal, "Democracy and Preventive War: Israel and the 1956 Sinai War," *Security Studies*, Vol. 11, No. 2, 2001, pp. 1–49.

Liddell Hart, Basil Henry, *The Real War, 1914–1918*, Boston: Little, Brown, 1964.

Lieber, Keir A., "Grasping the Technological Peace: The Offense-Defense Balance and International Security," *International Security*, Vol. 25, No. 1, 2000, pp. 71–104.

Lobe, Jim, "Sovereignty Takes Major Hits in Yemen, Mauritius," *Inter Press Service*, November 8, 2002.

Lobel, Jules, and Michael Ratner, "Bypassing the Security Council: Ambiguous Authorizations to Use Force, Cease-Fires, and the Iraqi Inspection Regime," *American Journal of International Law*, Vol. 93, No. 1, 1999, pp. 124–154.

Luttwak, Edward, and Dan Horowitz, *The Israeli Army*, Cambridge, Mass.: Abt Books, 1983.

Lynch, Marc, *State Interests and Public Spheres: The International Politics of Jordan's Identity*, New York: Columbia University Press, 1999.

Lynn-Jones, Sean M., "Offense-Defense Theory and Its Critics," *Security Studies*, Vol. 4, No. 4, 1995, pp. 660–691.

Mabrey, Vicki, "Culture Clash in Yemen," *60 Minutes II*, April 10, 2002.

McCormack, Timothy L. H., *Self-Defense in International Law: The Israeli Raid on the Iraqi Nuclear Reactor*, New York: St. Martin's Press, 1996.

McFall, Jack K., "Memorandum by the Assistant Secretary of State for Congressional Relations (McFall) to the Under Secretary of State (Webb)," January 26, 1950, in U.S. Department of State, *Foreign Relations of the United States, 1950*, Vol. I: *National Security Affairs; Foreign Economic Policy*, Washington, D.C.: U.S. Department of State, 1977.

MacFarquhar, Neil, "Threats and Responses: Terror; Three U.S. Citizens Slain in Yemen in Rifle Attack," *The New York Times*, December 31, 2002, p. A1.

McKinnon, Dan, *Bullseye One Reactor*, San Diego, Calif.: House of Hits, 1987.

Mearsheimer, John J., *Conventional Deterrence*, Ithaca: Cornell University Press, 1983.

———, *The Tragedy of Great Power Politics*, New York: Norton, 2001.

"Memorandum of a Conversation: Chinese Communist Nuclear Detonation," October 20, 1964, 6:10 p.m., Washington, D.C., in U.S. Department of State, *Foreign Relations of the United States, 1964–1968*, Vol. XXX: *China*, Washington, D.C.: U.S. Department of State, Doc. 61, 1998. Online at http://www.state.gov/www/about_state/history/vol_xxx/60_69.html as of December 22, 2005.

Menges, Constantine Christopher, *Inside the National Security Council: The True Story of the Making and Unmaking of Reagan's Foreign Policy*, New York: Simon and Schuster, 1988.

Mets, David R., "Technology, Thought, Troops: Gen. Carl A. Spaatz and the Dawn of the Nuclear Age," in Rebecca Hancock Cameron and Barbara Wittig, eds., *Golden Legacy, Boundless Future: Essays on the United States Air Force and the Rise of Aerospace Power: Proceedings of the Aim High Symposium*, Washington, D.C.: Air Force History and Museums Program, 2000, pp. 179–240.

"Militants Killed by Yemeni Forces," *BBC News*, June 25, 2003.

Minnich, L. A., "Minutes, BiPartisan Legislative Meeting, 5 January 1954," Staff Notes, January–December 1954 Folder, Box 54, Dwight D. Eisenhower Diary, Dwight David Eisenhower Library.

"Minutes of NSC Meeting, 3 September 1952," 1952, in U.S. Department of State, *Foreign Relations of the United States, 1952–1954*, Vol. II: *National Security Affairs*, Washington, D.C.: U.S. Department of State, 1984, p. 121.

"Minutes of NSC Meeting, May 13, 1953," 1953, in U.S. Department of State, *Foreign Relations of the United States, 1952–1954*, Vol. XV: *Korea*, Washington, D.C.: U.S. Department of State, 1984, p. 1016.

Misha, Teodor, "Albania Denies Terrorist Links," Institute for War and Peace Reporting, Balkans Crisis Report No. 283, September 26, 2001. Online at http://www.iwpr.net/index.pl?archive/bcr/bcr_20010927_3_eng.txt as of October 24, 2005.

Mishal, Shaul, and Avraham Sela, *The Palestinian Hamas: Vision, Violence, and Coexistence*, New York: Columbia University Press, 2000.

Moaveni, Azadeh, "They Didn't Know What Hit Them," *Time*, Vol. 160, No. 21, November 18, 2002, p. 58.

Moody, Walter S., *Building a Strategic Air Force*, Washington, D.C.: Air Force History and Museums Program, 1996.

Moore, William B., "Memorandum Op-36C/jm," memorandum from Executive Assistant to the Director of Op-36, the Atomic Energy Division, Office of the Chief of Naval Operations, to Rear Admiral George C. Wright USN, Director of Op-36C, March 18, 1954, in David Alan Rosenberg and W. B. Moore, "'Smoking Radiating Ruin at the End of Two Hours': Documents on American Plans for Nuclear War with the Soviet Union, 1954–55," *International Security*, Vol. 6, No. 3, 1981, pp. 3–38, p. 18.

Moran, Charles McMoran Wilson, *Winston Churchill: The Struggle for Survival, 1940–1965*, London: Constable, 1966.

Morgenthau, Hans Joachim, *Politics Among Nations: The Struggle for Power and Peace*, 4th ed., New York: Knopf, 1967.

Morris, Benny, *Righteous Victims: A History of the Zionist-Arab Conflict, 1881–2001*, New York: Vintage Books, 2001.

Mueller, John E., *Retreat from Doomsday: The Obsolescence of Major War*, New York: Basic Books, 1989.

―――, "Six Rather Unusual Propositions About Terrorism," *Terrorism and Political Violence*, Vol. 17, No. 4, 2005, pp. 487–507.

Mueller, John E. and Karl P. Mueller, "The Methodology of Mass Destruction: Assessing Threats in the New World Order," *Journal of Strategic Studies*, Vol. 23, No. 1, 2000, pp. 163–187.

Mueller, Karl P., *Strategy, Asymmetric Deterrence, and Accommodation: Middle Powers and Security in Modern Europe*, dissertation, Princeton, N.J.: Princeton University, 1991.

―――, "Strategic Airpower and Nuclear Strategy: New Theory for a Not-Quite-So-New Apocalypse," in Phillip S. Meilinger, ed., *The Paths of Heaven: The Evolution of Airpower Theory*, Maxwell Air Force Base, Ala.: Air University Press, 1997, pp. 279–320. Online at http://permanent. access.gpo.gov/websites/dodandmilitaryejournals/www.maxwell.af.mil/ au/aul/aupress/books/Meil-Paths/paths.pdf as of October 14, 2005.

Mundis, Daryl A., "The Assembly of States Parties and the Institutional Framework of the International Criminal Court," *American Journal of International Law*, Vol. 97, No. 1, 2003, pp. 132–146.

Naegele, Jolyon, "Albania: Country Free of Terrorists, Officials Say," *Radio Free Europe/Radio Liberty*, September 23, 2001. Online at http://www. rferl.org/features/2001/09/23092001101212.asp as of October 25, 2005.

Nakdimon, Shelomoh, *First Strike: The Exclusive Story of How Israel Foiled Iraq's Attempt to Get the Bomb*, New York: Summit Books, 1987.

Nalty, Bernard C., ed., *Winged Shield, Winged Sword: A History of the United States Air Force*, Washington, D.C.: Air Force History and Museums Program, 1997.

National Commission on Terrorist Attacks upon the United States, *The 9/11 Commission Report: Final Report of the National Commission on Terrorist*

Attacks upon the United States, New York: Norton, 2004. Online at http://www.gpoaccess.gov/911 as of October 17, 2005.

"National Intelligence Estimate: Estimate of the World Situation," NIE 1-61, January 17, 1961, in U.S. Department of State, *Foreign Relations of the United States 1961–1963*, Vol. V: *Soviet Union*, Washington, D.C.: U.S. Department of State, Doc. 6, 1998. Online at http://www.state.gov/www/about_state/history/vol_v/01_09.html as of December 22, 2005.

National Security Council, "United States Policy on Atomic Warfare," 1948, in U.S. Department of State, *Foreign Relations of the United States, 1948*, Vol. I: *General: United Nations*, Washington, D.C.: U.S. Department of State, 1975, pp. 624–628.

———, "Objectives and Programs for National Security," 1950a, in U.S. Department of State, *Foreign Relations of the United States, 1950*, Vol. I: *National Security Affairs; Foreign Economic Policy*, Washington, D.C.: U.S. Department of State, 1977, pp. 234–292.

———, "United States Objectives and Programs for National Security (April 14, 1950): A Report to the President Pursuant to the President's Directive of January 31, 1950," NSC 68, Washington, D.C., 1950b. Online at http://www.fas.org/irp/offdocs/nsc-hst/nsc-68.htm as of October 19, 2005.

———, "Basic National Security Policy," NSC 5501, January 6, 1955.

———, "Basic National Security Policy," NSC 5602/1, March 15, 1956, Basic National Security Policy Folder, NSC Series, Public Policy Subseries, Box 17, WHO-SANSA, Dwight D. Eisenhower Library, pp. 1–11.

Neustadt, Richard E., and Ernest R. May, *Thinking in Time: The Uses of History for Decision-Makers*, New York: Free Press, 1986.

New York Times, The, November 15, 1945, quoted in Alfred Vagts, *Defense and Diplomacy*, New York: Kings Crown Press, 1956, p. 330.

———, January 14, 1946, quoted in Alfred Vagts, *Defense and Diplomacy*, New York: Kings Crown Press, 1956, p. 330.

———, February 14, 1946, quoted in Alfred Vagts, *Defense and Diplomacy*, New York: Kings Crown Press, 1956, p. 330.

———, November 21, 1946, quoted in Alfred Vagts, *Defense and Diplomacy*, New York: Kings Crown Press, 1956, p. 330.

————, January 18, 1948, quoted in Alfred Vagts, *Defense and Diplomacy*, New York: Kings Crown Press, 1956, p. 332.

Newsweek, February 13, 1950, p. 20.

"No Hiding Place: How Unmanned U.S. Spy Plane Homed in on Satellite Phone Call to Wipe Out Al Qaeda Gang with Missile," *London Daily Mail*, November 6, 2002, p. 21.

Nolan, Janne E., *Guardians of the Arsenal: The Politics of Nuclear Strategy*, New York: Basic Books, 1989.

"Notes of NSC Meeting," March 4, 1954a, in U.S. Department of State, *Foreign Relations of the United States 1952–1954*, Vol. II: *National Security Affairs*, Washington, D.C.: U.S. Department of State, 1984, p. 636.

————, June 24, 1954b, in U.S. Department of State, *Foreign Relations of the United States 1952–1954*, Vol. II: *National Security Affairs*, Washington, D.C.: U.S. Department of State, 1984, p. 696.

"NSC 68: United States Objectives and Programs for National Security (April 14, 1950): A Report to the President Pursuant to the President's Directive of January 31, 1950," April 7, 1950, in U.S. Department of State, *Foreign Relations of the United States, 1950*, Vol. I: *National Security Affairs; Foreign Economic Policy*, Washington, D.C.: U.S. Department of State, 1977. Online at http://www.fas.org/irp/offdocs/nsc-hst/nsc-68.htm as of January 25, 2006.

Ochmanek, David A., *Military Operations Against Terrorist Groups Abroad: Implications for the United States Air Force*, Santa Monica, Calif.: RAND Corporation, MR-1738-AF, 2003. Online at http://www.rand.org/publications/MR/MR1738 as of October 18, 2005.

Oppenheim, L., Robert Y. Jennings, and Arthur Watts, eds., *Oppenheim's International Law*, 9th ed., London: Longmans, 1992.

Oren, Michael B., *Six Days of War: June 1967 and the Making of the Modern Middle East*, New York: Ballantine Books, 2003.

Organski, A. F. K., and Jacek Kugler, *The War Ledger*, Chicago: University of Chicago Press, 1980.

"Panel Discussion: Association of American Law Schools Panel on the International Criminal Court," *American Criminal Law Review*, Vol. 36, No. 2, 1999, pp. 223–264.

Pappé, Ilan, *A History of Modern Palestine: One Land, Two Peoples*, Cambridge, UK, and New York: Cambridge University Press, 2004.

Parachini, John, "Putting WMD Terrorism into Perspective," *The Washington Quarterly*, Vol. 26, No. 4, 2003, pp. 37–50.

Parks, W. Hays, "Air War and the Law of War," *Air Force Law Review*, Vol. 32, No. 1, 1990, pp. 1–226.

Parry, Clive, and John P. Grant, eds., *Parry and Grant Encyclopaedic Dictionary of International Law*, New York: Oceana Publications, 1986.

Pelham, Nick, "Yemen: Centre Stage of War on al-Qaeda," *BBC News*, March 14, 2002a. Online at http://news.bbc.co.uk/2/hi/middle_east/1860413. stm as of October 25, 2005.

———, "Jordanian Attack on Militants Reveals a National Rift," *Christian Science Monitor*, November 15, 2002b, p. 7.

Perkins, Ray, "Bertrand Russell and Preventive War," in Alan Schwerin, ed., *Bertrand Russell on Nuclear War, Peace, and Language: Critical and Historical Essays*, Westport, Conn.: Praeger, 2002, pp. 3–14.

Peterson, Scott, "Yemen Quakes in Cole's Shadow," *Christian Science Monitor*, September 21, 2001, p. 6.

Pious, Richard M., "The Cuban Missile Crisis and the Limits of Crisis Management," *Political Science Quarterly*, Vol. 116, No. 1, 2001, pp. 81–105.

Politi, Mauro, "Elements of Crimes," in Antonio Cassese, Paola Gaeta, and John R. W. D. Jones, eds., *The Rome Statute of the International Criminal Court: A Commentary*, Oxford and New York: Oxford University Press, 2002, pp. 446–447.

Prados, Alfred B., *Jordan: U.S. Relations and Bilateral Issues*, Washington, D.C.: Congressional Research Service, June 2, 2003.

"Predator Drone Kills Six Al Qaeda Suspects," *ABCNews.com*, November 5, 2002.

Priest, Dana, "CIA Killed U.S. Citizen in Yemen Missile Strike: Action's Legality, Effectiveness Questioned," *The Washington Post*, November 8, 2002, p. A1.

Quandt, William B., "Lyndon Johnson and the June 1967 War: What Color Was the Light?" *Middle East Journal*, Vol. 46, No. 2, 1992, pp. 198–228.

Quester, George H., *Offense and Defense in the International System*, New York: Wiley, 1977.

Rabinovich, Abraham, *The Yom Kippur War: The Epic Encounter That Transformed the Middle East*, New York: Schocken Books, 2004.

Ravenal, Earl C., "Counterforce and Alliance: The Ultimate Connection," *International Security*, Vol. 6, No. 4, 1982, pp. 26–43.

Raviv, Dan, and Yossi Melman, *Every Spy a Prince: The Complete History of Israel's Intelligence Community*, Boston: Houghton Mifflin, 1990.

Reagan, Ronald, "Address to the Nation on Defense and National Security," March 23, 1983. Online at http://www.reagan.utexas.edu/archives/speeches/1983/32383d.htm as of October 22, 2005.

Reiss, Mitchell, *Without the Bomb: The Politics of Nuclear Nonproliferation*, New York: Columbia University Press, 1988.

———, *Bridled Ambition: Why Countries Constrain Their Nuclear Capabilities*, Washington, D.C.: Woodrow Wilson Center Press, 1995.

Reiter, Dan, "Exploding the Powder Keg Myth: Preemptive Wars Almost Never Happen," *International Security*, Vol. 20, No. 2, 1995, pp. 5–34.

———, "Preventive Attacks Against Nuclear Programs and the 'Success' at Osiraq," *The Nonproliferation Review*, Vol. 12, No. 2, 2005, pp. 355–371.

Richelson, Jeffrey T., "When Kindness Fails: Assassination as a National Security Option," *International Journal of Intelligence and Counterintelligence*, Vol. 15, No. 2, 2002, pp. 243–274.

Ricks, Thomas E., "NATO Allies Trade Barbs Over Iraq," *The Washington Post*, February 9, 2003, p. A1.

Ridgway, Matthew, "Memorandum for the Record," May 17, 1954, Historical Record, January 15 to June 30, 1954, Box 30, Ridgway Papers, U.S. Army Military History Institute.

Risen, James, and Marc Santora, "Threats and Responses: The Terror Network; Man Believed Slain in Yemen Tied by U.S. to Buffalo Cell," *The New York Times*, November 10, 2002, p. A17.

Rosen, Stephen Peter, "Nuclear Arms and Strategic Defense," *Washington Quarterly*, 1981, pp. 82–99.

Rosenberg, David Alan, "American Atomic Strategy and the Hydrogen Bomb Decision," *The Journal of American History*, Vol. 66, No. 1, 1979, pp. 62–87.

———, "The Origins of Overkill: Nuclear Weapons and American Strategy, 1945–1960," *International Security*, Vol. 7, No. 4, 1983, pp. 3–71.

Rosenberg, David Alan, and W. B. Moore, "'Smoking Radiating Ruin at the End of Two Hours': Documents on American Plans for Nuclear War with the Soviet Union, 1954–55," *International Security*, Vol. 6, No. 3, 1981, pp. 3–38.

Ross, Steven T., and David Alan Rosenberg, eds., *America's Plans for War Against the Soviet Union, 1945–1950: A 15-Volume Set, Reproducing in Facsimile 98 Plans and Studies Created by the Joint Chiefs of Staff*, New York: Garland, 1989a.

———, eds., *The Atomic Bomb and War Planning: Concepts and Capabilities*, New York: Garland, 1989b.

Royce, Knut, and Craig Gordon, "A Blow to Al-Qaida: CIA Missile Kills a Leading Target of the U.S. War on Terror," *Newsday*, November 5, 2002.

Sagan, Scott Douglas, "Nuclear Alerts and Crisis Management," *International Security*, Vol. 9, No. 4, 1985, pp. 99–139.

———, "1914 Revisited: Allies, Offense, and Instability," *International Security*, Vol. 11, No. 2, 1986, pp. 151–175.

———, "SIOP-62: The Nuclear War Plan Briefing to President Kennedy," *International Security*, Vol. 12, No. 1, 1987, pp. 22–51.

———, "The Origins of the Pacific War," *Journal of Interdisciplinary History*, Vol. 18, No. 4, 1988, pp. 893–922.

———, *Moving Targets: Nuclear Strategy and National Security*, Princeton, N.J.: Princeton University Press, 1989.

———, "From Deterrence to Coercion to War: The Road to Pearl Harbor," in Alexander L. George, William E. Simons, and David Kent Hall, eds., *The Limits of Coercive Diplomacy*, 2nd ed., Boulder, Colo.: Westview Press, 1994a, pp. 57–90.

———, "The Perils of Proliferation: Organization Theory, Deterrence Theory, and the Spread of Nuclear Weapons," *International Security*, Vol. 18, No. 4, 1994b, pp. 66–107.

————, "Why Do States Build Nuclear Weapons? Three Models in Search of a Bomb," *International Security*, Vol. 21, No. 3, 1996, pp. 54–86.

Sanger, David E., "Pakistani Says He Saw North Korean Nuclear Devices," *The New York Times*, April 13, 2004, p. A12.

Schachter, Oscar, "The Rights of States to Use Armed Force," *Michigan Law Review*, Vol. 82, 1984, pp. 1620–1646.

————, "In Defense of International Rules on the Use of Force," *University of Chicago Law Review*, Vol. 53, 1986, pp. 113–146.

Schanzer, Jonathan, "Jordan's War Worries: Saddamistan, Palestinians, and Islamism in the Hashemite Kingdom," *PolicyWatch*, No. 680, November 22, 2002. Online at http://www.washingtoninstitute.org/templateC05.php?CID=1558 as of October 26, 2005.

Schelling, Thomas C., *Arms and Influence*, New Haven: Yale University Press, 1966.

Schiff, Zeev, *A History of the Israeli Army (1870–1974)*, San Francisco: Straight Arrow Books, 1974.

Schlesinger, Arthur Meier, *A Thousand Days: John F. Kennedy in the White House*, Boston: Houghton Mifflin, 1965.

Schlesinger, Robert, "In Djibouti, US Special Forces Develop Base Amid Secrecy," *The Boston Globe*, December 12, 2002, p. A45.

Schmemann, Serge, "Palestinian Believed to Be Bombing Mastermind Is Killed," *The New York Times*, January 6, 1996, p. A3.

Schmidt, Fabian, "No Welcome Mat Here," *Transitions*, Vol. 4, No. 10, 1998. Online at http://www.tol.cz/look/Transitions/article.tpl?IdLanguage=1&IdPublication=7&NrIssue=17&NrSection=7&NrArticle=5429 as of November 28, 2005.

Schmitt, Eric, and Thom Shanker, "Threats and Responses: The Military; War Plan Calls for Precision Bombing Wave to Break Iraqi Army Early in Attack," *The New York Times*, February 2, 2003, p. A12.

Schmitt, Michael N., "Preemptive Strategies in International Law," *Michigan Journal of International Law*, Vol. 24, 2003, pp. 513–548.

Schneider, Howard, "Canada Pulls Ambassador from Israel; Reputed Murder Plot Stirs Diplomatic Protest," *The Washington Post*, October 3, 1997a, p. A29.

————, "Israelis Apologize to Canada; Forged Passports Case Had Strained Relations," *The Washington Post*, October 11, 1997b, p. A17.

Schwarzkopf, H. Norman, and Peter Petre, *It Doesn't Take a Hero: General H. Norman Schwarzkopf, The Autobiography*, New York: Bantam Books, 1992.

Schwedler, Jillian, "Occupied Maan: Jordan's Closed Military Zone," *Middle East Report Online*, December 3, 2002. Online at http://www.merip.org/mero/mero120302.html as of October 26, 2005.

Schweller, Randall L., "Domestic Structure and Preventive War: Are Democracies More Pacific?" *World Politics*, Vol. 44, No. 2, 1992, pp. 235–269.

Schwerin, Alan, ed., *Bertrand Russell on Nuclear War, Peace, and Language: Critical and Historical Essays*, Westport, Conn.: Praeger, 2002.

"Secretary Dulles' Address, 12 January 1954," *Current History*, Vol. 26, 1954, pp. 308–309.

Sedan, Gil, "Jordan's King Puts His Foot Down on Hamas Activity," *Jewish Telegraphic Agency*, October 1, 1999. Online at http://www.jewishsf.com/content/2-0-/module/displaystory/story_id/12160/edition_id/234/format/html/displaystory.html as of October 26, 2005.

Shanker, Thom, and Eric Schmitt, "Threats and Responses: The Hunt; U.S. Moves Commandos to Base in East Africa," *The New York Times*, September 18, 2002, p. A20.

Shen, Jianming, "The Non-Intervention Principle and Humanitarian Interventions Under International Law," *International Legal Theory*, Vol. 7, 2001, pp. 1–32.

Sherry, Michael S., *Preparing for the Next War: American Plans for Postwar Defense, 1941–45*, New Haven: Yale University Press, 1977.

Shlaim, Avi, "The Protocol of Sevres, 1956: Anatomy of a War Plot," *International Affairs*, Vol. 73, No. 3, 1997, pp. 509–530.

————, *The Iron Wall: Israel and the Arab World*, New York: W. W. Norton, 2000.

Shultz, George Pratt, *Turmoil and Triumph: My Years as Secretary of State*, New York: Scribner's, 1993.

Slocombe, Walter B., "Force, Pre-Emption, and Legitimacy," *Survival*, Vol. 45, No. 1, 2003, pp. 117–130.

Smith, R. Jeffrey, "U.S. Probes Blasts' Possible Mideast Ties; Alleged Terrorists Investigated in Albania," *The Washington Post*, August 12, 1998a, p. A19.

————, "U.S. Embassy Threatened in Albania: Warning Against Americans Follows Crackdown on Extremists," *The Washington Post*, August 15, 1998b, p. A11.

————, "Albania Expands Crackdown on Arabs: Officials Say Islamic Groups Used the Nation as Haven, Gateway for Terrorism," *The Washington Post*, August 29, 1998c, p. A10.

Smucker, Philip, "The Intrigue Behind the Drone Strike," *Christian Science Monitor*, November 12, 2002, p. 1.

Snyder, Glenn Herald, *Deterrence and Defense: Toward a Theory of National Security*, Princeton, N.J.: Princeton University Press, 1961.

Snyder, Jack, "Civil-Military Relations and the Cult of the Offensive, 1914 and 1984," *International Security*, Vol. 9, No. 1, 1984a, pp. 108–146.

————, *The Ideology of the Offensive: Military Decision Making and the Disasters of 1914*, Ithaca: Cornell University Press, 1984b.

"Special Report Part 1: The Release of Sheikh Yassin," *ArabicNews.com*, October 1, 1997. Online at http://www.arabicnews.com/ansub/Daily/Day/971001/1997100118.html as of October 24, 2005.

"Special Report Part 2: The Release of Hamas's Spiritual Leader, Sheikh Yassin," *ArabicNews.com*, October 1, 1997. Online at http://www.arabicnews.com/ansub/Daily/Day/971001/1997100119.html as of October 24, 2005.

"Special Report Part 3: The Downfall of Netanyahu: Mossad's Assassination Fiasco in Jordan," *ArabicNews.com*, October 3, 1997. Online at http://www.arabicnews.com/ansub/Daily/Day/971003/FP.html as of October 24, 2005.

"The State of Albania," Tirana: International Crisis Group, ICG Balkans Report No. 54, 1999. Online at http://www.crisisgroup.org/home/index.cfm?id=1470&l=1 as of October 25, 2005.

State-War-Navy Coordinating Committee, "Basis for the Formulation of a U.S. Military Policy," SWNCC 282, 1945, in Thomas H. Etzold and John Lewis Gaddis, eds., *Containment: Documents on American Policy and Strategy, 1945–1950*, New York: Columbia University Press, 1978, pp. 39–44.

Stephen, Chris, "Bin Laden Opens European Terror Base in Albania," *The Sunday Times*, November 29, 1998, p. 23.

Stevens, Austin, "General Removed Over War Speech," *The New York Times*, September 2, 1950, p. 1.

Stoelting, David, "Status Report on the International Criminal Court," *Hofstra Law and Policy Symposium*, Vol. 3, 1999, pp. 233–285.

Student Composite Solution, Problem Nos. 9 and 12, U.S. Air War College, Air University, undated.

"Suicide and Other Bombing Attacks in Israel Since the Declaration of Principles (Sept 1993)," April 6, 1994 [sic], Israel Ministry of Foreign Affairs Web site. Online at http://www.mfa.gov.il/mfa/go.asp?MFAH0i5d0 as of October 24, 2005.

"Summary of Points Made in Discussion Following Presentation by Task Forces," July 16, 1953, in U.S. Department of State, *Foreign Relations of the United States, 1952–1954*, Vol. II: *The United Nations; The Western Hemisphere*, Washington, D.C.: U.S. Department of State, 1976, p. 434.

"Summary of United States–United Kingdom Discussions," July 20–24, 1950, in U.S. Department of State, *Foreign Relations of the United States, 1950*, Vol. *VII: Korea*, Washington, D.C.: U.S. Department of State, 1976, p. 463.

Symington, W. Stuart, "Current History of National Planning Policy— Diplomatic, Economic and Military; and Reasons Why It Is Essential That These Three Segments of National Security Be Further Integrated: Memorandum by the Chairman of the National Security Resources Board (Symington) to the President," undated, in *Foreign Relations of the United States, 1951*, Vol. I, *National Security Affairs; Foreign Economic Policy*, Washington, D.C.: U.S. Government Printing Office, 1980, pp. 21–33. Facsimile images online at http://images.library.wisc.edu/FRUS/EFacs/1951v01/M/0037.jpg through ../0049.jpg as of January 25, 2006.

———, "Recommended Policies and Actions in Light of the Grave World Situation," January 11, 1951, NSC 100, in U.S. Department of State, *Foreign Relations of the United States, 1951*, Vol. I, *National Security Affairs; Foreign Economic Policy*, Washington, D.C.: U.S. Department of State, 1980, pp. 7–18.

Taylor, A. J. P., *The Struggle for Mastery in Europe, 1848–1918*, Oxford: Clarendon Press, 1954.

Taylor, Scott, "Bin Laden's Balkan Connections: Al-Qaeda Fighters Have Been Quietly Infiltrating the Ranks of Ethnic Albanian Guerrilla Forces in Macedonia Croatia, Bosnia and Kosovo for Years," *The Ottawa Citizen*, December 15, 2001, p. B3.

"Third Egyptian Accused of Terrorism Arrested in Tirana—Paper," *Albanian Telegraphic Agency*, July 21, 1998. Online at http://www.telpress.it/ata/1998/jul_98/hdarch21.htm#05 as of October 25, 2005.

Thomas, Gordon, *Gideon's Spies: The Secret History of the Mossad*, New York: St. Martin's Press, 1999.

Thompson, William R., *The Emergence of the Global Political Economy*, London and New York: Routledge, 2000.

Thomson, James C., Jr., "Memorandum from James C. Thomson, Jr., of the National Security Council Staff to the President's Special Assistant for National Security Affairs (Bundy): The U.S. and Communist China in the Months Ahead," October 28, 1964, Washington, D.C., in U.S. Department of State, *Foreign Relations of the United States, 1964–1968*, Vol. XXX: *China*, Washington, D.C.: U.S. Department of State, Doc. 63, 1998. Online at http://www.state.gov/www/about_state/history/vol_xxx/60_69.html as of December 22, 2005.

"Thousands of Jordanian Troops Control Town," *Reuters*, November 11, 2002.

Thucydides, *History of the Peloponnesian War*, Rex Warner, trans., Baltimore, Md.: Penguin, 1954.

Time, April 4, 1948, quoted in Alfred Vagts, *Defense and Diplomacy*, New York: Kings Crown Press, 1956, p. 332.

———, December 18, 1950, pp. 20–21.

Trachtenberg, Marc, "A 'Wasting Asset': American Strategy and the Shifting Nuclear Balance, 1949–1954," *International Security*, Vol. 13, No. 3, 1988, pp. 5–49.

———, "The Meaning of Mobilization in 1914," *International Security*, Vol. 15, No. 3, 1990, pp. 120–150.

———, *History and Strategy*, Princeton, N.J.: Princeton University Press, 1991.

————, *A Constructed Peace: The Making of the European Settlement, 1945–1963*, Princeton, N.J.: Princeton University Press, 1999.

Travalio, Greg, and John Altenburg, "Terrorism, State Responsibility, and the Use of Military Force," *Chicago Journal of International Law*, Vol. 4, No. 1, 2003, pp. 97–120.

Truman, Harry S, "Special Message to the Congress Reporting on the Situation in Korea," 1950, in U.S. Department of State, *Foreign Relations of the United States, 1951*, Vol. I: *National Security Affairs; Foreign Economic Policy*, Washington, D.C.: U.S. Department of State, 1980, pp. 527–537.

————, *Memoirs by Harry S Truman: Years of Trial and Hope* (Vol. 2), New York: Doubleday, 1956.

"Truman Speaking to the World Last Night," *The New York Times*, 1950, p. 4.

Tuchman, Barbara Wertheim, *The Guns of August*, New York: Macmillan, 1962.

Tucker, David, "Hellfire," Ashbrook Center for Public Affairs at Ashland University Web site, November 2002. Online at http://www.ashbrook. org/Publicat/Oped/Tucker/02/Hellfire.Html as of October 26, 2005.

Tyler, Patrick E., and David E. Sanger, "Pakistan Called the Libyans' Source of Atom Design," *The New York Times*, January 6, 2004, p. A1.

Tyler, William R., oral history, March 7, 1964.

United Nations, *Charter of the United Nations*, San Francisco: United Nations, 1945. Online at http://www.un.org/aboutun/charter/index.html as of October 15, 2005.

————, *Declaration on Principles of International Law Concerning Friendly Relations and Cooperation Among States in Accordance with the Charter of the United Nations*, G.A. Res. 2625, U.N. GAOR, 25th Sess., Su No. 28, U.N. Doc. A/8018, 1970. Online at http://daccessdds.un.org/doc/ RESOLUTION/GEN/NR0/348/90/IMG/NR034890.pdf as of October 15, 2005.

————, *Resolution 487 (1981) of 19 June 1981*, S.C. Res. 487, U.N. SCOR, 36th Sess., 228th Mtg., U.N. Doc. S/Res/487, 1981. Online at http:// daccessdds.un.org/doc/RESOLUTION/GEN/NR0/418/74/IMG/ NR041874.pdf as of October 15, 2005.

————, *Measures to Prevent International Terrorism Which Endangers or Takes Innocent Human Lives or Jeopardizes Fundamental Freedoms and Study of the Underlying Causes of Those Forms of Terrorism and Acts of Violence Which Lie in Misery, Frustration, Grievance and Despair and Which Cause Some People to Sacrifice Human Lives, Including Their Own, in an Attempt to Effect Radical Changes*, G.A. Res. 40/61, U.N. GAOR, 40th Sess., Su No. 53, U.N. Doc. A/40/53, 1985. Online at http://www.un.org/documents/ga/res/40/a40r061.htm as of October 15, 2005.

————, *Resolution 687 (1991) of 3 April 1991*, S.C. Res. 687, 46th Sess., 1991. Online at http://daccessdds.un.org/doc/RESOLUTION/GEN/NR0/596/23/IMG/NR059623.pdf as of October 15, 2005.

————, *Resolution 748 (1992) of 31 March 1992*, S.C. Res. 748, U.N. SCOR, 47th Sess., 3063d mtg., U.N. Doc. S/RES/748, 1992. Online at http://daccessdds.un.org/doc/RESOLUTION/GEN/NR0/011/07/IMG/NR001107.pdf as of October 15, 2005.

————, *Report of the International Law Commission on the Work of Its Forty-Sixth Session*, Draft Statute for an International Criminal Court, U.N. GAOR, 49th Sess., U.N. Doc. A/49/10, 1994.

————, *Resolution 1189 (1998)*, S.C. Res. 1189, U.N. SCOR, 52d Sess., 3915th Mtg. at 110, U.N. Doc. S/RES/1189, 1998a. Online at http://daccessdds.un.org/doc/UNDOC/GEN/N98/237/77/PDF/N9823777.pdf as of October 15, 2005.

————, *United Nations Diplomatic Conference of Plenipotentiaries on the Establishment of an International Criminal Court, Rome, Italy, 15 June–17 July 1998*, A/CONF.183/9, July 17, 1998b. Online at http://documents-dds-ny.un.org/doc/UNDOC/GEN/N98/281/44/img/N9828144.pdf as of October 17, 2005.

————, *Resolution 1368 (2001) Adopted by the Security Council at Its 4370th Meeting, on 12 September 2001*, S.C. Res. 1368, U.N. SCOR, 56th Sess., 4370th Mtg., U.N. Doc. S/RES/1368, 2001a. Online at http://daccessdds.un.org/doc/UNDOC/GEN/N01/533/82/PDF/N0153382.pdf as of October 15, 2005.

————, *Resolution 1373 (2001) Adopted by the Security Council at Its 4385th Meeting, on 28 September 2001*, S.C. Res. 1373, U.N. SCOR, 56th Sess., 4385th Mtg. at 1, U.N. Doc. S/RES/1373, 2001b. Online at http://daccessdds.un.org/doc/UNDOC/GEN/N01/557/43/PDF/N0155743.pdf as of October 15, 2005.

————, *Resolution 1378 (2001) Adopted by the Security Council at Its 4415th Meeting, on 14 November 2001*, S.C. Res. 1378, U.N. SCOR, 56th Sess., 4415th Mtg., U.N. Doc. S/RES/1378, 2001c. Online at http://daccessdds.un.org/doc/UNDOC/GEN/N01/638/57/PDF/N0163857.pdf as of October 15, 2005.

————, *Assembly of States Parties to the Rome Statute of the International Criminal Court, First Session, New York, 3–10 September 2002 Official Records*, ICC-ASP/1/3, 2002. Online at http://documents-dds-ny.un.org/doc/UNDOC/GEN/N02/603/35/pdf/N0260335.pdf as of October 17, 2005.

————, *Security Council, Fifty-Eighth Year, 4772nd Meeting, Thursday, 12 June 2003, 10 a.m., New York*, U.N. Doc. S/PV.4772, 2003. Online at http://daccessdds.un.org/doc/UNDOC/PRO/N03/393/24/PDF/N0339324.pdf as of October 15, 2005.

U.S. Department of Defense, "Secretary Rumsfeld Speaks on '21st Century Transformation' of U.S. Armed Forces (Transcript of Remarks and Question and Answer Period): Remarks as Delivered by Secretary of State Donald Rumsfeld, National Defense University, Fort McNair, Washington, D.C., Thursday, January 31, 2002," Washington, D.C.: Fort McNair, 2002. Online at http://www.defenselink.mil/speeches/2002/s20020131-secdef.html as of October 13, 2005.

U.S. Department of Justice, "FBI Executive Summary: Bombings of the Embassies of the United States of America at Nairobi, Kenya, and Dar es Salaam, Tanzania, August 7, 1998, US Dept. of Justice, Federal Bureau of Investigation, Washington, D.C. 20535, November 18, 1998, Orcon/Law Enforcement Sensitive," *Frontline: Hunting bin Laden*. Online at http://www.pbs.org/wgbh/pages/frontline/shows/binladen/bombings/summary.html as of October 25, 2005.

U.S. Department of State, *Digest of International Law*, Washington, D.C.: U.S. Department of State, 1906.

————, *Foreign Relations of the United States, 1946*, Vol. I: *General: The United Nations*, Washington, D.C.: U.S. Department of State, 1972.

————, *Foreign Relations of the United States, 1948*, Vol. I: *General: United Nations, Part 1*, Washington, D.C.: U.S. Department of State, 1975.

————, *Foreign Relations of the United States, 1948*, Vol. I: *General: United Nations, Part 2*, Washington, D.C.: U.S. Department of State, 1976.

————, *Foreign Relations of the United States, 1950*, Vol. I: *National Security Affairs; Foreign Economic Policy*, Washington, D.C.: U.S. Department of State, 1977.

————, *Foreign Relations of the United States, 1951*, Vol. I: *National Security Affairs; Foreign Economic Policy*, Washington, D.C.: U.S. Department of State, 1980.

————, *Foreign Relations of the United States, 1952–1954*: Vol. II, *National Security Affairs*, Washington, D.C.: U.S. Department of State, 1984.

————, *Foreign Relations of the United States, 1952–1954*, Vol. XV, *Korea*, Washington, D.C.: U.S. Department of State, 1984.

————, *Foreign Relations of the United States, 1961–1963*, Vol. VII, *Arms Control and Disarmament*, Washington, D.C.: U.S. Department of State, 1995.

————, *Foreign Relations of the United States, 1961–1963*, Vol. VIII: *National Security Policy*, Washington, D.C.: U.S. Department of State, 1996a.

————, *Foreign Relations of the United States, 1961–1963*, Vol. XXII: *China, Korea, Japan*, Washington, D.C.: U.S. Department of State, 1996b. Online at http://www.state.gov/www/about_state/history/frusXXII/index.html as of December 22, 2005.

————, *Foreign Relations of the United States, 1961–1963*, Vol. V, *Soviet Union*, Washington, D.C.: U.S. Department of State, 1998a. Online at http://www.state.gov/www/about_state/history/vol_v/index.html as of December 22, 2005.

————, *Foreign Relations of the United States, 1964–1968*, Vol. XXX, *China*, Washington, D.C.: U.S. Department of State, 1998b. Online at http://www.state.gov/www/about_state/history/vol_xxx/index.html as of December 22, 2005.

————, *Foreign Relations of the United States, 1964–1968*, Vol. XIV, *Soviet Union*, Washington, D.C.: U.S. Department of State, 2001. Online at http://www.state.gov/r/pa/ho/frus/johnsonlb/xiv/ as of December 22, 2005.

————, "International Criminal Court: Letter to UN Secretary General Kofi Annan, Press Statement, Richard Boucher, Spokesman, Washington, D.C., May 6, 2002," Washington, D.C.: U.S. Department of State, 2002a. Online at http://www.state.gov/r/pa/prs/ps/2002/9968.htm as of October 15, 2005.

————, *Patterns in Global Terrorism*, Washington, D.C.: Government Printing Office, 2002b. Online at http://www.state.gov/s/ct/rls/pgtrpt/2002 as of October 17, 2005.

————, "Background Note: Albania," 2005a. Online at http://www.state.gov/r/pa/ei/bgn/3235.htm as of October 17, 2005.

————, "Background Note: Jordan," 2005b. Online at http://www.state.gov/r/pa/ei/bgn/3464.htm as of October 17, 2005.

————, "U.S. Signs 100th Article 98 Agreement, Press Statement, Richard Boucher, Spokesman, Washington, D.C., May 3, 2005," Washington, D.C.: U.S. Department of State, 2005c. Online at http://www.state.gov/r/pa/prs/ps/2005/45573.htm as of October 17, 2005.

"US Military 'Missed' Taleban Leader," *BBC News*, October 15, 2001. Online at http://news.bbc.co.uk/1/hi/world/south_asia/1600131.stm as of October 26, 2005.

"U.S. Missile Strike Kills Al Qaeda Chief: CIA Drone Launched Missile," *CNN*, November 5, 2002. Online at http://archives.cnn.com/2002/WORLD/meast/11/05/yemen.blast/index.html as of October 25, 2005.

U.S. Senate, *Hearings on Universal Military Training*, Washington, D.C., 79th Congress, 2nd Session, 1946.

"U.S. Takes Anti-Terror Fight in Yemen into Its Own Hands," *IslamOnline.net*, November 5, 2002. Online at http://www.islamonline.net/English/News/2002-11/05/article51.shtml as of October 25, 2005.

Utgoff, Victor, "In Defense of Counterforce," *International Security*, Vol. 6, No. 4, 1982, pp. 44–60.

Vagts, Alfred, *Defense and Diplomacy*, New York: Kings Crown Press, 1956.

Vagts, Detlev F., "Review: Going to Court, Internationally," *Michigan Law Review*, Vol. 87, No. 6, 1989, pp. 1712–1717.

Van Creveld, Martin L., *The Sword and the Olive: A Critical History of the Israeli Defense Force*, New York: Public Affairs, 1998.

Van Evera, Stephen, "The Cult of the Offensive and the Origins of the First World War," *International Security*, Vol. 9, No. 1, 1984, pp. 58–107.

————, *Causes of War: Power and the Roots of Conflict*, Ithaca: Cornell University Press, 1999.

Wallace, Rebecca M. M., *International Law: A Student Introduction*, 3rd ed., London: Sweet and Maxwell, 1997.

Walt, Stephen M., "Beyond bin Laden: Reshaping U.S. Foreign Policy," *International Security*, Vol. 26, No. 3, 2001/2002, pp. 56–78.

Walzer, Michael, *Just and Unjust Wars: A Moral Argument with Historical Illustrations*, 3rd ed., New York: Basic Books, 2000.

Webster, Daniel, letter to British Foreign Minister Lord Ashburton, August 6, 1842, in U.S. Department of State, *Digest of International Law*, Washington, D.C.: U.S. Department of State, 1906, p. 412, in Louis Henkin, Oscar Schachter, Richard C. Pugh, and Hans Smit, eds., *International Law: Cases and Materials*, 3rd ed., St. Paul, Minn.: West Pub. Co., 1993, p. 872.

Wehr, Hans, and J. Milton Cowan, *A Dictionary of Modern Written Arabic: Arabic-English*, 4th ed., Ithaca, N.Y.: Spoken Language Services, 1994.

Weiser, Benjamin, "U.S. to Offer Detailed Trail of bin Laden in Bomb Trial," *The New York Times*, January 13, 2001, p. A1.

White, Mark J., *Missiles in Cuba: Kennedy, Khrushchev, Castro, and the 1962 Crisis*, Chicago: Ivan R. Dee, 1997.

White House, "President Bush Delivers Graduation Speech at West Point, United States Military Academy, West Point, New York," West Point, N.Y.: The White House, 2002a. Online at http://www.whitehouse.gov/news/releases/2002/06/20020601-3.html as of October 13, 2005.

———, "President Bush Outlines Iraqi Threat: Remarks by the President on Iraq, Cincinnati Museum Center, Cincinnati Union Terminal, Cincinnati, Ohio," Cincinnati, Ohio: The White House, 2002b. Online at http://www.whitehouse.gov/news/releases/2002/10/20021007-8.html as of October 13, 2005.

———, "President Delivers State of the Union Address: The President's State of the Union Address, The United States Capitol, Washington, D.C.," Washington, D.C.: The White House, 2002c. Online at http://www.whitehouse.gov/news/releases/2002/01/20020129-11.html as of October 13, 2005.

Wohlforth, William C., "The Perception of Power: Russia in the Pre-1914 Balance," *World Politics*, Vol. 39, No. 3, 1987, pp. 353–381.